# The Hidden Children of France, 1940–1945

# The Hidden Children of France, 1940–1945

## Stories of Survival

EDITED BY Danielle Bailly

TRANSLATED BY Betty Becker-Theye

FOREWORD BY Pierre Vidal-Naquet

excelsior editions

State University of New York Press
Albany, New York

Originally published as *Traqués, Cachés, Vivants: Des Enfants juifs en France, 1940–1945.*

Édith Moskovic's testimony, published in *Tsafon, revue d'études juives du Nord* 41 (2001), is published in translation here with permission of the editor, Madame Danielle Delmaire.

Published by State University of New York Press, Albany

Excelsior Editions is an imprint of State University of New York Press

For information, contact State University of New York Press, Albany, NY
www.sunypress.edu

Production by Kelli W. LeRoux
Marketing by Fran Keneston

**Library of Congress Cataloging-in-Publication Data**

Traqués, cachés, vivants. English
    The hidden children of France, 1940–1945 : stories of survival / [collected and edited by] Danielle Bailly ; translated by Betty Becker-Theye.
        p. cm.
    Translation of: Traqués, cachés, vivants. Paris : L'Harmattan, 2004.
    Includes bibliographical references and index.
    ISBN 978-1-4384-3196-3 (pbk. : alk. paper)  1. Jewish children—France—Biography.  2. Jewish children in the Holocaust—France—Biography.
3. Holocaust survivors—France—Biography.  4. Holocaust, Jewish (1939–1945)—France.  I. Bailly, Danielle.  II. Title.
    DS135.F89T7313 2010
    940.53'18092244—dc22

                                                                          2009051692

10  9  8  7  6  5  4  3  2  1

To those who saved us

Our heartfelt thanks go to all those—known and unknown—who put themselves in danger that we might survive: individuals or institutions, rural residents or city dwellers. Those who falsified papers, those who took us in, those who organized networks to help and place the children. All those who resisted the murderous ideology of the Nazi and Pétain regimes. Those who allowed France, of all the occupied countries, proportionately to deport the fewest children and adults. The testimonies given in this book clearly show that some of our families were denounced, arrested, sent to death—not only by the Nazi occupiers but by French—that some of us were not well treated by those who hid us; that many people, more or less Vichy supporters, remained indifferent. These historic facts only magnify the courage of those who took risks to save us. They forever have our gratitude for their magnificent expression of humanity.

# Contents

# Illustrations

# Foreword

To the memory of Gérard Brunschwig, my cousin and my friend, 1924–2003

There are few circumstances in history or in my own personal memory of the years 1940–1945 that touch me as deeply as that of the hidden child, or rather "the hidden children," simply because my brothers, my sister, and I were, during a brief but critical period of time, "hidden children." Our situation was extremely serious because it immediately followed the arrest of our parents in Marseille on May 15, 1944, but infinitely more comfortable than those recounted in this book. And as there was no "return" of our parents, there was also no opportunity to grieve, no rites of passage, no condolences. Little by little, our hope faded into an endless wait.

And yet, as we know, despite the Vichy government and its Marshal Pétain, and contrary to what was drummed into us after 1943, three out of four Jews and six out of every seven of their children living in France escaped deportation. As Asher Cohen pointed out in his seminal book, *Persécutions et sauvetages*,[1] while French society—still stunned by defeat—did not collectively resist the law that created a Jewish apartheid, it did refuse, as best it could, the massive deportation begun in 1942, which spread to the Unoccupied Zone with Laval's and Bousquet's delivery of thousands of families of Jewish "foreigners" considered by the Vichy government to be the "dregs of society." Statements made then by numerous bishops—even if they did not all use the strong tone of His Excellency Monsignor Saliège, Archbishop of Toulouse—marked a change in the attitude of the Catholic Church. The small avant-garde, which in Lyon circulated the *Cahiers du témoinage chrétien*,[2] was then joined by huge numbers of supporters at the end of 1942. My literature teacher, Léon Auger, an anarchist and extreme anti-Nazi, asked me to help widely disseminate this publication beyond Catholic circles. The solidarity of Protestants—more than one example can be found in this book—was very determined. This explains why, like my childhood friend Philippe Fouquey, I was enrolled, as were most of the boys of my family who were given refuge in Marseille, with the Cub Scouts and later the Boy Scouts of the Protestant movement. For some Protestants this was a matter of solidarity among minorities; for others it was a shared reference to the Old Testament. I found proof of this in two villages where there were numerous Protestants: Saint-Agrève in the Ardèche region and Dieulefit in the Drôme region. For a time, my sister attended junior high at Collège Cévenol in Chambon-sur-Lignon, ten kilometers from Saint-Agrève.

Taking into consideration just the grandchildren of my own grandparents, eighteen in all—ten grandsons, eight granddaughters—only one, my brother Yves, died during the war in the June exodus of 1940, and he not directly at the hands of the Nazis. The other seventeen survived the Occupation as did my two grandmothers. In my parents' generation—besides my mother and father—my uncle Germain Lang-Verte, husband of my mother's oldest sister, disappeared at Auschwitz. He had been arrested and turned over to the Germans at the border in the Pyrenees.

My uncle Georges Vidal-Naquet, my father's brother and husband of my mother's twin sister Martha, managed to cross the border and get to North Africa, where he reappeared as a captain and medic in the army. His wife and children, along with my maternal grandmother, found refuge in Saint-Agrève, while my father's sister Isabelle with her mother and three sons settled after the Occupation in the Southern Zone at Dieulefit. The oldest of these boys, Gérard (1924–2003)—the only one of my cousins to be of military age—joined the Resistance at Marseille and by June 1944, had made it to the Resistance fighter group at Belledone, not far from Grenoble. He participated in the liberation of the town of Vizille (one of the Gestapo headquarters) before returning to Paris and, following in the footsteps of his father, Robert (1893–1939), was admitted to the prestigious École Polytechnique. My mother's older sister, Hermine, who with her two daughters had accompanied General Bloch (called Dassault)—a military adviser to the National Front (i.e., the Communist Party)[3]—also participated in the Resistance in Paris. Félix Valabrègue, my mother's older brother, got away to Morocco with his wife and two sons while his younger brother Georges and his Russian wife, Véra de Gunzburg, went to America in 1940, where they settled near San Francisco.

All in all, only my parents did not get to Algiers or London or New York or Paris, although my father had several opportunities to do so after being demobilized in 1940. He first joined the Resistance at the end of 1940 with the Musée de l'Homme group, and then the National Front when he was able to join my mother at my maternal grandmother's home in Marseille. Everyone urged him to leave, but with my mother supporting his decision, he refused to do so out of dignity, even though his sister had a house waiting for us in Dieulefit. It was clearly an irrational, if courageous, decision. My mother showed perhaps even greater courage by giving birth on January 23, 1944, to a fourth son, Claude, who only lived to age twenty. At least my parents had instructed us, in case of emergency, not to rejoin them under any circumstances. My mother encouraged my brother François (born in 1932) to flee. He was not caught. My sister Aline and I were warned by our teachers and classmates, thanks to the cook, Joséphine Marchais. Even the Gestapo agents acted in a contradictory manner by searching for us while letting my baby brother be taken by the neighbors.

My sister Aline (born in 1933), now a retired medical doctor, took refuge with her history teacher, Madame Passelaigue. She never left our baby brother whom she refers to in her diary as her son. They both quickly made it to Saint-Agrève. François spent two nights on rue Saintes with people he never could find again. As for me, I went to the home of my former English teacher, André Bouttes, who recently died at age one hundred and who, after the war, taught in an American military academy. I don't know if André Bouttes was part of a Resistance organization as many of my teachers were—one of whom at least, Pierre-Jean Miniconi, was recruited by my father. My brother François and I, after May 17, were taken by car to Cucuron in the Vaucluse region to the farmhouse of Baptistine and Maurice Lanchier. Maurice had been my grandfather's chauffeur before the war. I give this detail to show just how much a part of the bourgeoisie my family had been. However French my paternal grandmother was, she had been born in Odessa and retained a slight Russian accent. She was the daughter of a rich manufacturer of glass who went to Belgium when the pogroms began. His house on rue de la Loi in Brussels even had a ballroom. My other grandmother was Alsatian, which in our family balanced the Ashkenazi tradition with that of the Sephardic lineage who left Spain for the south of France in the fourteenth century.

Cucuron was a rich village in Provence of diversified farming on countless small plots of land. The twenty-nine days François and I spent there was our only experience as hidden children. Nothing identified us as Jewish. We were refugees from Marseille. I don't recall having heard a single anti-Semitic remark.

Events nevertheless took a dramatic turn when shortly after the Normandy Landings on June 6, 1944, the village's young men were armed with machine guns. On June 14, a busload of German soldiers arrived to disarm the residents and arrest a few of them, including the oldest son of our host family. There was talk of burning the village, and our hosts gave us their bicycles in case we needed to flee. Finally the Germans left, taking all the weapons with them. No one remained under arrest. I tried unsuccessfully to get information about this episode that seems to have been erased from memory. Research in the archives of the *département* gave the only proof that François and I had not just dreamed this tragicomedy: a brochure about Cucuron states that the mayor and parish priest offered themselves as hostages and saved the village when the German occupiers wanted to burn it. This was not glorious but it was not bloody. The Germans were still there when on Friday, June 16, a car sent by friends of our uncle Félix Valabrègue came to take us to Saint-Agrève in Ardèche to stay with my maternal grandmother and her daughter, my mother's twin. My sister Aline and the baby Claude were already there. Saint-Agrève was in the zone liberated by the Free French after June 6, and we had to cross a true boundary at Lamastre. We stayed in Saint-Agrève until September 13 when, by various means, we reached Dieulefit where my paternal grandmother and her daughter Isabelle lived. Isabelle was to guide my education until 1948. She had as great an influence on my childhood and adolescence as my parents. The return to Paris took two and one-half days, in a tarp-covered truck in October 1944. Until late in 1945, I waited in vain for my parents to return. No one around me, except perhaps my second cousin Jacques, who was like a brother to me, imagined the unimaginable—their anonymous slaughter.

By giving a brief account of these events, I intend to add my own brief testimony to the eighteen others the readers of this book have at hand. As Danielle Bailly, the coordinator of this collection says, this story, "less tragic than that of deportation" to which many of the parents of these narrators were subjected, is no less "an integral part of the Holocaust" even if it ends with survival. No one who lived this experience came out unscarred. This history, which took place in France—and to a lesser extent in Belgium while the Belgian government was in London—has often been told. But other studies have focused either on the Vichy government's involvement or on rescue organizations such as the General Union of Israelites in France (UGIF), the Commission on Jewish Issues, the Children's Aid Society (OSE), the churches—Catholic or Protestant—or the villages of refuge like Chambon-sur-Lignon and Dieulefit. History teaches us that man lives in society but we must never forget the individuals, the "unique souls" Valéry refers to in his poem "Le Cimetière marin."

I am not acquainted with all the individuals who testify in this book. One of them, Philippe Fouquey, was a childhood friend of mine, even if our memories vary on certain points—for example, while I know that I and one other schoolmate refused to turn in an assignment about the visit of Pétain to Marseille in 1940, I don't remember, as he does, having participated in an honor guard with the Cub Scouts on the Canebière, an avenue leading to the harbor in Marseille. Nicole Eizner and I were activists together during and after the Algerian War. I am also somewhat acquainted with Gaby and Serge Netchine, but I only met Danielle Bailly when I was given the book. Some of these texts take the form of dialogues or were interviews before being rewritten by their authors. That said, it would be incorrect to speak of them as "oral histories" because many of these accounts have written sources. Their authors, born between 1929 and 1941, belong to the last generation of those who have something personal to say, even if it is sometimes secondhand, about these tragic events. If there are now only thirty-six soldiers left from World War I to tell about it, the number of survivors of the Holocaust is likewise doomed to extinction. I lived intensely the time during the return and the non-return of the deportees; but what about those born ten years after me?

What then do these eighteen people have in common? All but one, Odette Kozuch who chose Israel, are French—by birth or by naturalization (of their parents usually); the majority are of Polish or Belarusian origin. As a general rule, they refuse cultural separatism. Nicole Eizner has a way of saying it: "I have always tried to place myself in the junction between bœuf bourguignon and gefilte fish. It is extremely satisfying to have several identities at the same time." A funny detail: the first time I ate with Philippe Fouquey and his parents, his mother, an extremely charming woman, served something she described as an example of Jewish cooking. In my family "Jewish cooking" was unknown except for matzo at Passover. We didn't even use that vocabulary. We called it "unleavened Passover bread."

All, or almost all, have taken from their experience a passionate will to fight against injustice, and some among them have credited the Soviet Union for having liberated Auschwitz and defeated Hitler. Only one, Daniel Krakowski, is still Communist. The great majority—here again Philippe Fouquey is the exception—have parents who were modest craftsmen, furriers, shoemakers, leather workers or tanners. All, or almost all, are passionate readers, and as they say, "did well" in school. It is difficult to say whether that comes from tradition or their situation as members of a minority or from a feeling that scholastic excellence is a means of upward mobility. This brings to mind Péguy's comment that Jews have been reading for two thousand years, the Protestants since Calvin, and the Catholics since Jules Ferry. Yet I note that tradition won't work for the women; the Hebrew word *bocher*, "yeshiva student," as far as I know has no feminine form. All wanted to live passionately. All have lived, consciously or not, against a background of tragedy.

When Nelly Scharapan, author of the testimony that most struck me, wrote: "One evening in 1943 my mother didn't come home. The Gestapo had hunted her down at her workplace. I didn't get to tell her goodbye." And yet she had the rare privilege of seeing both her parents again. She recounts a scene rarely described: at a camp located near the Gare d'Austerlitz that Michel Lafitte describes (in *Un Engrenage fatal*)[4] the detainees were breaking up the valuables taken from Jews in order to deprive the Nazis of them.

But there is also contrast. These children, like those in the majority of Jewish families, were city children. Granted, Nelly Scharapan appreciated certain things: the grass, the air, the berries. But poorly cared for by a farmwoman who was the mistress of a German, she felt a loss of her "sense of self." At a second farm in the Sarthe region, she was lower than a domestic servant: a slave. When she asked about going to school, the farmers laughed in her face. Safety came for her only after the Liberation—in a children's home operated by the OSE. But on the other hand, look at Nicole Eizner, daughter of an officiant rabbi and who is now a sociologist, specializing in rural life. She knew joyful times in the Figeac region: "the freedom of myself in my own body—free to run around, to ride bicycles, to swim in the river." As a sociologist she made professional use later of the observations of rural life that she made then. As a child, she was devoid of tenderness for these farmers: "I remember we spent a lot of time making fun of the country folk: their actions, their way of life and especially the fact that there were light-years between us; I mean we were totally in modern times and they had an unbelievable life style." When she told her students about the chickens that would get on the table and the foul-smelling grandmother whom the family left in a corner, "they couldn't believe it." I must say, the country people I lived with in Cucuron led a completely different life, even though they, too, had an elderly grandmother whom they called "La Martine."

In this group of accounts one also finds, albeit rarely, stories of conversion. Even without being baptized, it was necessary to mimic Catholicism. After the war there was the notorious Finaly affair: two children who became Catholic and their guardian who refused to send them to their aunt in Israel. There were conversions, either sincere or insincere, often at the initiative of the parents. I saw it in my own family. But as for the nuns of the Notre-Dame de Sion, committed since the nineteenth century to the conversion of Israelites, Madeleine Comte, who studied this problem very carefully in *Sauvetages et baptêmes*,[5] concluded there to have been no case of a child hidden by Sion in Paris being baptized while lodged in that convent. Conversely, among certain of our witnesses, there was, after the war, a return to Judaism. Thus, Danièle Menès, who although she passed "nothing" on to her son, nevertheless learned Yiddish late in life: "But it evoked nothing. I had never heard my parents speak it; it was a foreign language."

There are times in these accounts of "inner films" when reality surpasses fantasy as in the testimony of Édith Moskovic's brother Ernest who in 1944 sees his sister, who was hidden in a Belgian children's home, dancing the classical ballet repertoire piece *The Dying Swan*, to music by Saint-Saens. There is an unbelievable diversity of testimony—diversity of rescuers who weren't always volunteers; diversity of behavior. There were headmasters who did whatever it took to save the Jewish children and at least one of them who didn't hide her intention of obeying orders if the situation arose. The same could be said of the concierges.

The commitment some of our witnesses have to the extreme Left is not surprising in that one of the major tenets of the Communist Party, even at its most "nationalistic," was socialization of the working/immigrant class. The account by Noël Kuperman on this subject is all the more striking in that even though he was born in Paris and is the son of two Polish Jews, his father made a failed attempt to settle in Palestine, and he himself later worked with theater companies that were performing in the "Red" suburbs. Indirectly, he was a disciple of Bertolt Brecht. Listen to him: "The Party was my family, my church, my school. I think there were several reasons for my fidelity, but among them there was the desire not to be singled out, but to be a member of a much larger totality, to be like everyone else, with a collective goal."

To be like everyone else or to be Jewish? There are often contradictions. There is contrast, for example, between the testimony of Nicole Eizner and that of Odette Kozuch. The latter decided one day to be Jewish and made her *alyah* to Israel. The Six Day War in 1967 caused her great anguish. I understand her all the more because I witnessed those hours of exaltation that I called the "Days of Madness" in an article I wrote for *Le Monde*, published June 10, 1967. But then look at the testimony of Serge Netchine, whose Bolshevik father was inspired by "a faith retained throughout the vicissitudes of his life, a faith which despite his convictions and his denials of Judaism, and perhaps paradoxically also because of them, portrays an indelible *Yiddishkeit*." Such was the faith of hawkers of the Third International. His older brother, Victor Leduc, summed up his own experiences in a book called *Les tribulations d'un idéologue*. Today Serge Netchine himself needs to create this "distancing" about which Brecht spoke. And finally, what about Francis Bailly, a physicist at the National Center for Scientific Research whose passionate Resister father was not Jewish? Today he is publishing a book entitled *Mosaïsme et société: De la tradition à la révolution*.

It is impossible, I believe, to read the Jewish condition other than through this image of a prism or, if one prefers, this rainbow that passes imperceptibly from violet to red. For all of these people what is at stake is to carry on the History, yet no one has the right to criticize those who leave the path of Jewish tradition so long as they do not join the ranks of the persecutors.[6]

—Pierre Vidal-Naquet
December 3, 2003

# Introduction

"Marshal Pétain, here we are!"[1]—but not because of you or your followers. We are here because of those who—spontaneously or after reflection, willingly or somewhat reluctantly, paid or unpaid—refused to accept Nazi barbarianism and the complicity of zealous collaboration. We are here because of those who—sometimes without even being fully aware—refused, either passively or actively, to collaborate with genocide and who helped save the Jewish children condemned by the Nazis to death solely because of their origin—as were their parents and families—and who were pursued and tracked as we were in the occupied countries during the war.

The situations endured by these "hidden children" are portrayed in the testimonies that follow, each with its major issues. Each began as a taped interview and emerges, rewritten or not, according to a style selected by the witnesses themselves.

These stories, less tragic than those of the death camps (although the children often felt the tragic loss, through extermination, of one or both of their parents or the entire family), are an integral part of the Holocaust and carry their personal share of misery. How could it be otherwise when a young person, especially a very young person, has to change identity and live in fear and incomprehension—usually separated from his or her own family? How could he or she emerge unscarred?

We do not intend to write an objective page of the history of that war and the attempts to exterminate, particularly the Jews, that it entailed. The work of historians is well known, and historical documentation has established a truth that denial can never erase. A number of other personal testimonies have also been published that bring a subjective vision of that historic period. But all has not been said. There is much more because it is only now, because of repression and suffering, that a number of witnesses, feeling the approach of age, are ready to give testimony and are finding the strength to tell about their war. It is not easy to establish a connection between the childhoods that were uniquely ours and the values that inform our lives as adults.

Each of the specific "inner films" portrayed in this volume has its own truth (even if on some minor points, reworked by memory over the years, a flaw or error may have slipped in). Furthermore, there is a dimension that escapes truth and historic rigor: a dimension that comes from the meaning the subjects give to the lives they have lived. Sense and meaning, as constructed by these actors from their own experiences and now reinterpreted by them after the events, hold lessons for everyone's future if we want to prevent repetition of the past in the same form or in any other. After all, as we know, while the Holocaust was characterized by its radical uniqueness, barbarianism and genocide have not disappeared from the earth.

My own motive for collecting these testimonies can be summed up in a single word: urgency. The members of our group are now in our mid-sixties and seventies. Before passing away, and often after a lifetime of silence, we now must speak. Our descendants as well as the whole society must know. Only we—the deported, the children of deportees, the hidden children, all the diverse victims—can tell what we experienced during those years. Aside from the historical studies, who will really know, with the heart as well as the mind, what it was like for the victims of the Nazi and collaborator genocide? Thousands of testimonies remain to be collected; it is urgent to collect these personal memories.

This collection of testimonies does not claim to be a scientific or exhaustive representation of all "hidden children," for it essentially came about through the connections of friendships, professional encounters, family ties, from person to person. For this reason, the work is characterized by a certain bias: completely Ashkenazi, mostly Parisian, often politically connected. This is unimportant; other groups of witnesses can be formed with different biases and they can then contribute balance to the overall group. Clearly the testimonies are diverse—each life unique; even the concept of a representative group remains of secondary importance. The juxtaposition of these intimate and very different accounts tempers any potential bias and contributes to an overall expression of truth.

Eighteen stories of hidden children (sixteen in France, two in Belgium) are told. For some, both parents were deported without returning; for others, it was a father or a mother; for others still, one or both parents returned from the camps weak and extremely traumatized. For all these witnesses, the family—whether closely or distantly related—was decimated. All were separated from their parents while hidden except two, and there is a visible contrast between those who were separated and these two for whom the security so vital to psychological development was maintained. The accounts are arranged according to the age of the witness: from youngest (born in 1941) to oldest (born in 1929). This grouping shows how experiences differed according to the child's age. The experiences of the very young children who lacked understanding first resulted in more or less fantasy effects—such as feeling that to be hidden was to be abandoned—and later on sometimes exhibited itself in persistent trauma and identity crises. The preadolescents perceived more lucidly the reality of the Occupation and the experience of being hunted through the ambience of what was left unsaid. Old before their time, yet too young to be a Resistance fighter—armed only with the confidence of youth—they relied on intelligence and self-control to save themselves and help others.

The testimonies of the contributors who chose to keep the original form of an oral interview—a simple transcript minimally edited—illustrate the information requested of each one of them: 1) description of the place of origin and the obstacles encountered by the emigrant family; 2) chronology and perception of the events lived by the child-witness, from before the war—depending on his or her age—and especially during the war (the hiding, the hunt, the protection, the environment); 3) reconstruction of life after the war; 4) personality and values of the witness as an adult, in connection with this childhood.

For the contributors who chose to give a straightforward autobiographic narrative, whether or not it began as an interview, the more distanced writing enables them to give a more self-controlled account. In all cases each contributor maintained complete control over the version of his or her testimony as it appears in the book.

With one exception, each testimony begins with a photo of the narrator as a child during the war. At the end of the book the reader will find a succinct history of that time period, an annotated listing of acronyms, a glossary, and a selected bibliography.

In reading these stories, one discerns each one's irreducible uniqueness, despite the common fate of the Jews. Everything played a role in the course of events for each individual: origin (Jews from Eastern Europe, French Jews), social class, family structure, geographic region of refuge, chance, small miracles or shameful betrayals. Equally varied are the "rebirths" after the war—the consequences and the life choices. Nevertheless, a common characteristic unites us: our will to rebound. Educated or not, each of us has emerged with similar vitality, with strong support for the families we have started and for society. All of our messages carry the imprint of this same vital force. And starting from our wounded Jewishness or from the attack perpetrated on our human condition, each of us turns to humanism or universalism.

I hope that these messages, coming out of a twentieth century that knew such absolute savagery in the very heart of our extremely civilized European continent, can speak to readers of the present century that has begun with so many uncertainties.

I take pleasure in thanking my friend Ariane Kalfa, editor of the Judaic Studies series at L'Harmattan Publishing, who put complete confidence in us and gave us wise counsel; the great historian Pierre Vidal-Naquet, who did us the honor and friendship of writing a foreword for our book; Marie-France Dupuy, who transcribed our audio cassettes with patience and competence; Danièle Menès and Éliane Séravalle, who backed me throughout the work; Gaby and Serge Netchine, who helped put together the bibliography and the chronology; Nicole Eizner, who first put us in contact with Pierre Vidal-Naquet. And I emphasize that this collective effort was made in the warmest of friendships and by listening attentively to one another.

This book, originally written in French, mainly addressed a French reading public. For this reason we ask our American readers to forgive us for referring to a historical context so far from them in time and space, and for occasionally simply alluding to events, people, and places familiar to us and foreign to you.

Despite our awareness of these special characteristics of the book, our group wanted to see it translated into English as soon as possible—not only to transmit facts about the tragedies of the Second World War long after others had done so, but because we believe the individual experiences recounted here have importance across borders. We especially want to communicate with you—citizens of a country particularly dedicated to democracy and liberty and fortunate not to have experienced this war directly on your soil nor to have been occupied by or subjected to dictators. Motivated by these same values of democracy and liberty, Americans contributed greatly to our liberation from oppression. We believe, as you do, that resistance to the forces of destruction and collective misery is one of the universal ethical values. Unfortunately, vigilance in protecting these values is just as urgent today.

When our group had the good fortune to meet Betty Becker-Theye, through contacts at Mount Holyoke College where I was a Fulbright scholar in 1955–1956, she offered to translate our book into English in a spirit of solidarity with our fractured childhoods. For this we express our appreciation and gratitude.

—Danielle Bailly
August 2008

FIGURE 1.1. Simon at age four in 1945 at
Houppe-Flobecq, Belgium, with the man
who hid him from 1942 until the Liberation.

# 1

# Simon Marjenberg

· **March 3, 2003**

*Simon Marjenberg is retired after a professional career as a specialist in the metals business. Born in Belgium, orphaned by the Holocaust (his parents, Polish Jews, were leather crafters), he settled in Metz and started a family. He is very involved in the Jewish community in Metz and participates with his friends in the community's cultural activities.*

MARJENBERG: My name is Simon Marjenberg. I was born September 1, 1941, so I am sixty-one and one-half years old. I was born in Belgium. I came to France in 1945. I'm going to start by talking about my grandparents, then my parents, to give a family history.

My paternal grandparents came from Warsaw. My grandfather was a very Orthodox rabbi. He came to Brussels, probably about 1930–1931, and was the rabbi of the Orthodox synagogue on rue de la Clinique in that city.

BAILLY: Did he leave because of the pogroms or for a rabbinical mission?

1

MARJENBERG: No. I think he wanted to live somewhere other than Warsaw where things were just so-so but I don't know. .

BAILLY: Was this a family of rabbis?

MARJENBERG: On my grandfather's side, I don't know much. My grandmother's family had a hotel or an inn and kosher restaurant in Warsaw. My grandparents were married very young; my grandfather was fourteen and my grandmother thirteen years old! They were married as children and were permitted to live together one or two years later. When they celebrated their Golden Wedding anniversary, they were sixty-four and sixty-three years old, almost my age now. They came to live in Belgium after one of their daughters left Warsaw with her husband and one or two children to set themselves up as leather crafters in Brussels.

BAILLY: And on your mother's side?

MARJENBERG: No one on my mother's side left Poland. Everyone died there except my mother's youngest sister and brother, who escaped to Russia at the time of the invasion of Poland and who then retreated as far as Siberia as the Germans advanced. They are the only two survivors on my mother's side.

(In memory of the Holocaust, I will make a more precise accounting: on my mother's side [she herself was deported to Auschwitz, never returning], a total of forty-nine persons were deported [including my grandparents], mostly to Treblinka, and never returned. On my father's side, a total of forty persons, including infants, were deported. Of these forty people, only one returned from the camps. This one was my cousin, Maurice Nagel, who had just finished his medical studies when he was arrested and deported first to Auschwitz where he remained one year. In all, he was in five camps, including the infamous Dora camp. He returned very ill, weighing only thirty kilos. At Auschwitz he was forced to keep people alive after the monstrous experiments of the evil Dr. Mengele. Then he was in two death marches. After the war, he was a witness in several important trials of Nazis. In total, on the two sides of just my family, ninety individuals disappeared.)

My father arrived alone in Brussels; he didn't know my mother.

BAILLY: Your parents met in Brussels?

MARJENBERG: No! It's really funny. I learned only recently how my parents met from a book about the family that my mother's youngest sister—the one who survived in Siberia—published last year. As I said, my father came to Brussels in 1931 or 1932. My grandfather made a simple round trip between Brussels and Warsaw—accompanied by one of my father's sisters and a brother—to attend some kind of Jewish ceremony. While they were there my aunt (my father's sister) saw a young woman she thought was very beautiful and whom she liked. She went up to her and said, "I think you are wonderful. I have an unmarried brother in Brussels about your age and I am sure you are just who he needs!" The two women exchanged addresses and my aunt returned to Brussels and got my father to go to Warsaw a few weeks later. He then fell madly in love with my mother. But she didn't have an entry visa for Belgium, and not being married, she could not follow my father when he returned. So they managed to get a fake marriage certificate, but she was still unable to join my father when he returned. The real wedding didn't take place until 1933 or 1934, once they were together again in Belgium. They were both from very religious families; my maternal grandfather was very religious and my paternal grandfather was an Orthodox rabbi with the long, curled sidelocks called *payot.*

BAILLY: Before going on to your parents, have you any memories, from what you've been told or otherwise, of how people lived in Poland during your grandparents' time?

MARJENBERG: No, absolutely not. I know nothing about their life in Poland except that all my father's brothers and sisters, except those who were already leather crafters (as my father was later until he died), worked with their own maternal grandparents in the inn-restaurant they owned in Warsaw. My father worked there, too, at that time.

That's all I know about my grandparents.

My parents were married in Brussels and established themselves as leather crafters, not far from where my father's brothers and sisters and my grandfather lived. They lived the peaceful life of all Jews in Belgium, and it was probably not a bad life.

BAILLY: Did they belong to a Jewish community?

MARJENBERG: Yes, there was a large Jewish community. There were people from Warsaw, beginning with my father's brothers and sisters (with the exception, as I mentioned earlier, of his oldest brother who stayed in Poland and died in the Holocaust). Remember there were very few of us in the family who survived; only some first cousins and two uncles and aunts.

BAILLY: No one escaped to the United States or Israel?

MARJENBERG: No. In Israel, I have some first cousins, my aunts' and uncles' children, who lost their parents in the Holocaust as I did, including a brother and sister whose parents were picked up with mine because they were visiting them when the Gestapo arrived. I will talk about them again later.

Until war was declared, my parents stayed in Belgium and worked at their trade. They had a leather workshop. After the declaration of war, during the 1940 exodus, they left for Toulouse, then Pau. But there was no work there in my father's craft. Who was going to buy luxury handbags at a time like that?

BAILLY: Do you know the exact circumstances that made them leave Brussels and go to the south of France?

MARJENBERG: No, I don't know. They left like everyone else, because it was dangerous to stay in Brussels.

BAILLY: In 1940?

MARJENBERG: They left in 1940 with almost everybody, except one uncle and aunt who remained hidden with their children in Brussels during the entire war. This aunt and uncle were in the Belgian Resistance and they and their children survived, but I don't know how.

BAILLY: In 1940, in Belgium, were the same anti-Jewish laws in place as those in France?

MARJENBERG: Yes, that was exactly the same.

BAILLY: So your parents left Belgium, not simply because of the May 1940 exodus of the population leaving the cities, but rather to flee the anti-Jewish persecutions that started shortly thereafter?

MARJENBERG: It was to flee the anti-Jewish persecutions. Then near the end of 1940 or the beginning of 1941, my father, in contact with his older sister still in Brussels, learned that if he were to live well hidden, shutters closed all day, house closed, he could stay in his home and work in the leather shop. As long as there were people who provided you with raw materials and took the finished handbags around to the stores to be sold, you could live shut up in a house or an apartment, you could make a living and feed your children. So they returned to Belgium with my grandfather, but he died of diabetes on the way and is buried here in Paris. My parents then left again for Belgium where they moved back into their house and lived with the windows and doors locked and the shutters closed.

BAILLY: Without false papers?

MARJENBERG: Without false papers. They were told it was dangerous to live like that after 1941, in 1942. Before the end of 1942, the Resistance sent someone to explain to them that at least their children must not stay with them, and they arranged to hide us with different families outside the city.

BAILLY: Your parents' reason for living like shut-ins was that it was the only way they could support the family? That was what was most important?

MARJENBERG: Absolutely, to be able to make a living and feed the children. They held on like that for a year, fifteen months.

BAILLY: The non-Jewish neighbors must have known; did they close their eyes?

MARJENBERG: Yes, but unfortunately next door to them was a Belgian policeman to whom they confided one day—as I learned later from my brothers and a cousin—that if something happened to them, there was a certain double-bottomed machine where money was hidden that would provide for their children. So in the next day or two the Gestapo arrived. That's how the tragedy began. They had already hidden me. I was about fifteen months old when I was separated from my parents. The Resistance had come for me and placed me with a forest warden's family some forty kilometers from Brussels.

BAILLY: Before your parents were arrested?

MARJENBERG: Yes, my parents were still alive and the Resistance had placed each of their three children with families. I, the youngest, was all alone with the forest warden's family in a place called Houppe-Flobecq. It was an isolated house in a big clearing on the edge of a large forest. It wasn't even a house; it was a big chalet with a forest behind it where there was a sand pit, because the land under the trees was sand. Every time trees were cut, you could scratch and there was sand underneath. The warden operated the sand pit manually. It is still a commercial sand operation today.

BAILLY: It was specifically the Belgian Jewish Resistance that placed you there?

MARJENBERG: Yes. My two brothers spent the entire war in two other places. My oldest brother came two or three times to spend three or four days or a week with me, but he didn't get along at all with the people who were hiding me. They couldn't keep him with me. They had to use a switch on him because he wouldn't obey.

BAILLY: This kid was destabilized by the uprooting of the family?

MARJENBERG: Completely. My other brother, who was only a little older than I, probably didn't know much about what was happening either.

BAILLY: You yourself have no precise memory?

MARJENBERG: I, no. Of the beginning of that period when I was hidden there, I remember nothing.

As for my parents, on April 5, 1943, the Gestapo, because of that denunciation I told you about before, came to where we lived to get them. That day, my father's brother and his wife (who was also my father's first cousin) were visiting my parents. So the Gestapo took my parents and my aunt and uncle, too. We children were no longer at home.

The Gestapo almost got another cousin of mine, who is now seventy-nine years old and lives in Brussels. (In the course of my life my fate always stays connected to this cousin. I'll explain later.) On the day I'm speaking of, this is what happened. Since my parents did not want to and really could not go out, this cousin, Jacques—then fifteen years old and already in the Resistance with his brothers, one of whom was a doctor—used to run errands two or three times a week for my parents. When he got to their house, he would go first to the grocery store across the street to get what they needed. The grocer—also a member of the Resistance—would have my cousin wait before going to his uncle and aunt's place so he could inspect the street to see that the coast was clear. So on this fifth day of April 1943, after serving my cousin, the grocer told him to wait until he could look up and down the street. When the grocer went out to look he told him, "Don't move! They're taking your aunt and uncle!" And then the Gestapo took my mother out on a stretcher because she had lost consciousness. She realized while being arrested that she would never see her children again.

BAILLY: Your cousin told you about this later?

MARJENBERG: Only five or six years ago. That day this cousin left and that's it. My parents were put in what was the Belgian equivalent of Drancy[1]—the Dossin barracks in the Brussels suburbs.

BAILLY: Guarded by Belgian police?

MARJENBERG: No, by Germans. Unlike in France, it wasn't the guard members and police who arrested the Jews, it was the Germans. There was no "Vichy-type" government in Belgium.

BAILLY: So there was no official collaboration?

MARJENBERG: Openly, no. My parents were taken to the Dossin barracks in Liège on April 5, 1943, and were there until April 19 when they were sent with what is now the well-known, unfortunately too well-known, Convoy Number Twenty to Auschwitz. It was not entirely unfortunate because two hundred thirty people managed to escape this convoy.

It is the only convoy in all of Europe during the entire war that was attacked by a national Resistance, in this case Belgian, on the way to a concentration camp. It left the Dossin barracks for Auschwitz at 8 p.m. It had been moving for about forty minutes and then was attacked by three armed young men who boarded the train and subdued the operator, who then very docilely stopped the train. One of the three kept him in his line of fire while the other two opened the doors of the cars so that the people could run away. There were two thousand three hundred deportees leaving for Auschwitz on that train. The two young men opened a few doors. There were some who ran to the back of the cars. An eleven-year-old boy was saved; he has become a Belgian celebrity today. He is an important lawyer and he recently received recognition during official events in his honor in Belgium for being the youngest deportee to have escaped. He has worked in Jewish organizations in Belgium all his life.

My father was the first one out of the car; he opened one or two doors and got out all the people he could during a short time.

BAILLY: Your parents were together?

MARJENBERG: Yes. Unfortunately for my father, after one or two minutes of initial surprise, the German guards began firing into the crowd and my father, who was outside the railway car, was hit. He died there and my mother was severely wounded. The German guard closed the cars and the train left a few minutes later. Twenty-three detainees died alongside the railway cars, including my father, and my mother and five others were seriously wounded. Then Convoy Number Twenty left for Auschwitz, leaving the dead and wounded. The wounded were picked up by the Germans and taken to Tirlemont, the nearest hospital under the Occupation, some twenty kilometers from Brussels. My mother was kept there for two weeks, from April 19 to May 4. I underline this: April 19, 1943. It's the same date as the beginning of the uprising in the ghetto at Warsaw. Every time this event is observed in the world (like Holocaust Remembrance Day in the United States, for example), it is also the anniversary of my father's death.

BAILLY: You reconstructed all these events later?

MARJENBERG: I learned about them from a book called *L'Étoile et le fusil* by the Belgian historian Maxime Steinberg,[2] who worked with Klarsfeld (he is Klarsfeld's Belgian counterpart). My mother was kept in the hospital for treatment. On May 4, 1943, a team of Belgian Resistance fighters came to this German-occupied hospital to free the six Jews being deported, including my mother, taking them away in two cars. Unfortunately, the driver and owner of one of the cars involved was a Polish count, Count Romanovski (who later, at the end of the war, was put on trial for collaboration). This man actually worked with the Resistance and the Gestapo at the same time. So on May 5 the Gestapo came to the place where the Resistance fighters had taken the six people and recaptured them. My mother was returned to Dossin barracks. She was there until July 31, 1943, the day she left for Auschwitz with the next convoy: the Twenty-First. Immediately after her arrival at Auschwitz, she was taken to the gas chamber.

But what is incredible is that she left the Dossin barracks on July 31 at eight o'clock in the evening and on another July 31 at eight o'clock in the evening, twenty-one years later, her first grandchild, my oldest son, was born, the same day, at the same time. My whole life has been marked by anniversaries like that . . .

That's how my mother left for Auschwitz and never returned. I remained hidden with the forest warden until the end of the war.

BAILLY: Do you remember anything about it?

MARJENBERG: Yes, I remember it very well.

BAILLY: This forest warden had a wife?

MARJENBERG: Yes, his name was Marcel Fort and his wife's name was Zoé.

BAILLY: Did you see your brothers who were hidden elsewhere?

MARJENBERG: I hardly even knew them during that time, except for my oldest brother, Maurice, who came to see me two or three times, off and on. I stayed with these people until the end of the war without really having any problems, except one day: Brussels was liberated at the beginning of September 1944, and during that week the Germans arrived in my village. There was a column of trucks. I still remember Sylvain, Marcel Fort's son, coming up on his bicycle, pedaling like crazy. He said to his father, speaking of me, "He has to be hidden!" because this column of trucks was probably going to set up camp on the square in front of the house. And a lone child living with older people really wasn't normal.

BAILLY: You didn't have any individual papers?

MARJENBERG: No papers, nothing. "How can you justify the presence of this child?" Just imagine! So the people hiding me told me to hide myself in the woods. They told me—I remember as if it were yesterday—"Don't come back until you no longer see the trucks."

BAILLY: You were still very young!

MARJENBERG: Four or five days earlier, I had just turned three. I hid myself in the woods until the following evening. I spent the whole day, all night and all day the next day there. The next evening, the column of trucks left. I stayed alone; I slept; I lay down on a bed of branches. I see it as if it were only yesterday.

BAILLY: You weren't hungry? You don't remember?

MARJENBERG: I was probably hungry but I knew I mustn't show myself. They told me that I must not be seen, that I must not return, and I obeyed, that's all. I slept on a bed of branches in the forest. I must say that this was not particularly courageous because, although I was little, I knew this forest very well. It was my natural playground, I knew the little trails. I stayed there until the column left; then I returned.

A little after this happened, I left these people. My cousin, the same one who as an adolescent had been present when my parents had been arrested two or three years earlier—April 5, 1943—came to get me to take me to France to an uncle who had also survived.

BAILLY: So your memories of these forest wardens are good? They treated you well?

MARJENBERG: They were very kind. He was a man who had been in the Resistance. Two years ago, I went to visit their grandson who took over the sand excavation business.

BAILLY: So you kept contact with this family?

MARJENBERG: I didn't keep contact with the son because for a long time I couldn't go back there for many reasons. During my entire childhood and adolescence there were things that didn't go as they should have. I made contact with the grandson only a few years ago. I took him photos of his grandparents. They were photos that I had taken with me when leaving Belgium. When he saw these photos, he knew immediately who I was and he broke into tears. A few days before the day we saw each other again, he had said to his own son, "I would like to know what happened to little Simon, who was at my grandparents' place." And then, three or four days later, I showed up! That, too, was very strange!

So I left their place at the end of 1945, after the Liberation, and I came to France.

BAILLY: You have no memory of the Liberation of the Houppe-Flobecq region?

MARJENBERG: No, because it took place while I was hiding in the woods, when this column of trucks fleeing Brussels arrived in the village. And I wasn't old enough to know what was really happening.

BAILLY: In general, that is what the Liberation fighting was like.

MARJENBERG: Yes, this column of German trucks left Brussels and camped in our village for twenty-four to thirty-six hours. It was when Brussels and the area around it were being liberated. One day, as I said, my young cousin—he was then nineteen years old—came to get me to take me to my paternal uncle (a leather worker like the rest of the family) who had survived in Paris. Remember that no one in my mother's family survived, other than her brother and sister who took refuge in Siberia and who later, in 1948, made their way to Australia where they still live in Melbourne. I will tell their story later.

Here are the details of our departure from Belgium for France: At that time, my cousin was a soldier in the Belgian army and as such didn't have the right to leave Belgium. Furthermore, how would he explain that he had this child with him, with no papers, no passport, nothing? It was a morning at the end of 1945. We had taken the train up to the last Belgian town before the border where we both got off. He told me, "We are going to go on foot together and at a certain point we are going to separate. You are going to let me go ahead of you and when I turn around, I will give you the signal to start walking again."

BAILLY: It was after the Liberation and you still had to take all these precautions?

MARJENBERG: Yes, simply because, being in the army, he didn't have the right to leave Belgium and I couldn't cross a border because I no longer had parents or identity papers. He moved away and began to walk ahead. He was just a little young guy of nineteen. I can still see him; he was wearing navy blue pants and a white shirt. At a certain moment, he turned and signaled that I could begin to walk. And we walked for, I don't know, an hour or two maybe. I followed him at a distance of maybe a hundred, hundred fifty meters. We walked and walked and walked.

BAILLY: How old were you then?

MARJENBERG: I wasn't yet five, four and one-half. So I followed him like that for an hour or two until he stopped, turned and gave me the sign to join him. Then he said, "Here we are; we're in France. Now we'll walk to a town where there is a railway station and take the train and go to Paris." That's how I crossed the border clandestinely, without a single document.

BAILLY: As you had no papers, you had no photos of your parents either?

MARJENBERG: In fact, I didn't get copies of them until much later. I have very few photos but I do have one or two of my mother and one or two of my father that were sent to me from Australia by my mother's brother and sister long after these events.

So I had entered France clandestinely, without a single paper to document my identity. No one had been able to get papers in my name because my parents had been taken when I was a baby, and how does one cross a border in these circumstances? At the time, you needed both a passport and a visa to cross.

BAILLY: How did things turn out in Paris?

MARJENBERG: When I arrived in Paris, I stayed at my uncle's, then in an OSE orphanage, still without papers. It wasn't until later, much later, that I was able to get papers: an identity card, a refugee passport from the Office for Protection of Refugees and Stateless Persons—a non-national passport that I used until I became a French citizen in 1973.[3] This passport required that I go to the commission every six months to have my resident card reissued in order to stay in France. And there, like all foreigners who have to go to a police precinct to have their refugee card stamped, I heard all the derogatory comments from the police employees.

So in 1973 when I had been married for eleven years and already fathered two children I took steps to become French. I tell you in all honesty, I didn't take these steps until I was completely free of potential military service because I wouldn't have been entitled to an exemption. My parents hadn't died for France because we lived in Belgium. Those whose parents were deported from France were exempt from military service but I would not have been.

BAILLY: Belgium couldn't do anything for you in this regard?

MARJENBERG: No, I had been in France since 1945. That was over.

BAILLY: It's worthwhile mentioning this additional aspect of vulnerability from administrative complications. As I think about it, given the circumstances and your being a young child, the authorities should have been able to understand that you were deprived of identity papers!

MARJENBERG: It's true. It is never the child's fault if he goes around without papers. Children are always by nature innocent.

So I'll continue the story. My uncle couldn't keep me because he had a son and lived in one room—the kitchen was a small corner and there was no bathroom. He couldn't keep me with him so almost immediately he put me in an OSE orphanage. I was there for three years, first at Brunoy, then at Draveil.

BAILLY: The OSE had institutions at these locations?

MARJENBERG: Yes, Brunoy was fine but Draveil was a horror of horrors. My impressions generally concern the educational methods, from some other age, of the director, a certain Monsieur K—— and not my overall impression of the Draveil institution. This director made a small fortune, enough to later open an upscale camp for children at Neuilly, but this was done at our expense because he did it by skimming money intended for the children of Draveil.

BAILLY: How awful!

MARJENBERG: The children who still had a mother or a father—who had put them there while they reorganized their lives—were watched over and properly cared for. But for me there really was no one and I was a black sheep to this guy. I was always hungry when I was little.

BAILLY: And you attribute this to the fact that no one was paying for you?

MARJENBERG: No one was paying for me so Monsieur K—— behaved badly. Since I was stealing from the kitchen—I'll be frank with you—to add to the regular meals because there was never enough to eat, I was always being punished and put in isolation. The punishments which started when I was five years old consisted of depriving me of the evening meal because I had stolen food. I wasn't put to bed in the dormitory, I was put down in the coal cellar of the chateau and I had to sleep on the pile of coal. During a good part of the night, until two or three o'clock in the morning, I tossed pieces of coal at the rats who were all around me. (During a recent visit to Draveil with my wife, the person who took us around told us that visitors on pilgrimage almost all wanted to see this cellar, which indicates that I was not the only one submitted to this treatment.)

Lots of people have heard about Monsieur K—— because he opened this upscale camp for children (some of my friends today still talk about it because about forty years ago they used to send their children there for vacations). I spent my nights on this pile of coal fighting off the rats and tossing pieces of coal at them. At two or three o'clock in the morning, an aide would come to get me and I could end the night in my bed. I was five years old. That went on until I was eight.

BAILLY: Were you being educated at that time?

MARJENBERG: No, not at all. When I went to Metz, the town where I grew up after that and where I still live, I was going on eight years old and hadn't been to school yet. No one cared whether I went to school or not. I remember having gone to pre-school and then long afterward, I began school a year behind the other children my age.

BAILLY: You had been left to yourself.

MARJENBERG: Yes, but in 1948 the Jewish community at Metz was asked if anyone wanted to take a child, an orphan, for vacation time. A couple accepted; a couple who weren't married. He was Jewish and had lost his wife and one daughter in the deportation. His partner was not Jewish, she was someone who had hidden him during the war and with whom he then lived for thirty-eight years—the rest of his life. As she had no children—she had suffered a miscarriage the year before—she felt something was lacking. It was she who wanted to have a child in the house. So I arrived at Metz to stay during vacation and when vacation was over and I was supposed to go back to Draveil, she didn't want me to go. This couple asked the orphanage if they could contact my guardian—that is my uncle in Paris who was legally responsible for me. He was only too happy to let me stay there rather than in an orphanage, especially since it didn't cost him anything. And it is true that I was probably better off there than at an orphanage. That's what happened. And I stayed in Metz.

BAILLY: This couple sort of adopted you?

MARJENBERG: No, because things hadn't gone so well for them. The man had lost his wife and one daughter, but still had another daughter who was completely opposed to his taking in a child after the war. She was afraid the couple would adopt me and that I would eventually take her place in her father's heart. I think also that officially adopting me would have given me inheritance rights, which they didn't want to do. The rest of my experience with them made this very clear.

BAILLY: You don't want to give this family's name?

MARJENBERG: No, it's not essential to this story.

BAILLY: Let's talk a little now about what happened to your brothers.

MARJENBERG: My brothers had been placed in an orphanage in Belgium at Antwerp. I saw them during a visit to Brussels, one Sunday in 1949. They then left in December of 1950 for Australia. I didn't see them again until 1978, at a family event in Paris. That was very moving.

But to elaborate on my brothers' fate, I have to go back in time. This is what happened: My mother had an aunt in Krakow whose husband in the 1930s had made some mistakes which made it urgent for them to leave Poland, and probably even Europe. So in about 1935–1936, my parents sent money to this aunt and her husband so they could immigrate to Australia. They then left around 1936 and thanks to what my father had done for them, they escaped the Holocaust. They never had children.

By 1947–1948, my great-aunt had a search carried out for missing relatives and she learned who had survived: my mother's sister (one of her nieces) and my mother's brother (her nephew). They had both married and had children. The other survivors were the three children of one of her other nieces (my mother)—that is to say, my two brothers and I. She knew that my two brothers were then in an orphanage in Belgium and it was not difficult for her to get them to come to Australia, except that my oldest brother had promised my parents that whatever happened he would never leave without taking the littlest one, that is to say, me.

My brothers left for Australia in 1950. But the year before they left, in 1949, I was allowed to visit them in Belgium.

BAILLY: At that time you knew where they were?

MARJENBERG: Yes. Then I saw them again in December 1950 in Paris where they were making a stop before going to Marseille to take the boat headed for Australia. After that, I didn't see them again until twenty-eight years later, in 1978.

BAILLY: Did you stay in touch with them?

MARJENBERG: Yes. We wrote but not often, and we didn't really know each other because my brothers were twelve and fifteen years old when they left for Australia on the boat. They traveled for a month, then once arrived in Australia they were separated. My older brother, Maurice, went to live with my mother's old aunt. My second brother, Boris—the one who was three and one-half years ahead of me—went to live with my mother's brother. Boris didn't get along with our uncle's wife who was mentally ill. She ended her life in an insane asylum. But this uncle didn't get along with my brothers either. So my two brothers, at fourteen and sixteen years old—the year after their arrival—ended up taking an apartment together in Melbourne and starting to work, living alone on their own resources.

BAILLY: What work did they do down there?

MARJENBERG: Like many Jews, *peckle'h-ma'hers* (literally, "package makers"), that is to say they would buy merchandise wholesale on credit and they would sell it during the day to pay their provider in the evening, either returning what they hadn't sold or keeping it for the next day when they would take new merchandise. They lived like that for years, working this way at an age when one usually goes to school.

BAILLY: Are your brothers still living?

MARJENBERG: My oldest brother died last year, fourteen months ago, in January 2002.

BAILLY: And do you see your other brother from time to time?

MARJENBERG: No, he doesn't come to Europe and I don't go to Australia because it is a long way to travel now that we are no longer young. Australia takes twenty-seven hours in a plane. That's how our lives evolved. My brother Boris had a very difficult existence. Throughout his life he needed help. His health hasn't been good and poverty followed him everywhere.

Both of my brothers had chaotic lives, with a lot more downs than ups, and finally they cut off all relations with the whole family except with Mom's sister who lived in Melbourne.

BAILLY: So, from what you say, there is an absolute direct and automatic connection between the loss of your parents and the chaotic lives of your brothers?

MARJENBERG: Yes, absolutely, because they had no point of reference. They had had no example of making a living for a family, putting money aside for the children's future. I've had a more normal life, and when they needed help I gave it to them because they were my brothers. Even though I hadn't lived with them, although my life had been quite different, I helped them because I wanted to be able to think about my parents while telling myself that I was doing what had to be done. That's why I always did it.

BAILLY: Now let's come back to you in the present.

MARJENBERG: I was married in 1962 at the age of twenty-two, first because I was in love (and I still am) and secondly because it was urgent that I leave the family who had taken me in.

BAILLY: The early years of your marriage were somewhat difficult financially?

MARJENBERG: Very difficult.

BAILLY: Then you had your children?

MARJENBERG: Almost in poverty; I was earning only minimum wage.

BAILLY: What did your wife do?

MARJENBERG: She did accounting for friends of ours who were in wholesale clothing.

So to briefly recapitulate the course of our lives, I will say this: I worked as a foundry worker in my foster family's factory for twenty-four years, then as director of this factory after the death of the man who had taken me in. This I did for six years until my licensing in 1986. Then my wife and I started a metals company, trading exclusively in zinc.

Now I am retired and our family trade business since then has been managed by my youngest son Dan, who returned from the United States after a five-year professional stint there. He has a degree from the School of Advanced Studies in Economics and the Social Sciences and lives in Louveciennes. He is married and has two children. My oldest son Boris is an orthodontist in Metz, having completed his studies in dentistry in Nancy and his specialization in Reims. He is married and has three children.

My two sons married Jewish girls, which is what I had hoped for out of regard for the memory of my parents. I refused to accept the idea that they died because they were Jews and that their grandchildren would not be Jews. I would have felt that to be an outrage against them. That said, I am not religious. I have a problem with God. I don't know where He was during the Holocaust, during the massacre of our people and my own family. Nevertheless, I am much attached to the philosophic and cultural aspects of Judaism, as I am to Israel where my wife's family lives and where the few cousins of my family who escaped also live.

This then is the general story of my parents, of my childhood and, without too many details, the course of my life.

Well into my adult life, I felt an enormous need to know who my parents had been, what their personalities were like, what I had inherited of their character, and that is why I questioned everyone who had known them. I have also learned Yiddish from my mother-in-law and I sing in a choral group in Yiddish, basically because that was my parents' language. I have certainly idealized them as I have aged. I have often behaved according to what they would have wanted me to do regarding my family abroad. This is surely a little childish, but their memory has often guided my acts. Nowadays it has become somewhat difficult to speak on the telephone with my mother's younger sister in Australia because the emotion is overpowering for both of us and we end in tears.

In conclusion, I will say that life without the memory of my parents was terrifying, especially after the birth of my children. I didn't know to whom to confide my fears, my doubts facing the uncertain future that prevailed during that time that was so difficult for my wife and me. Despite everything, today we live happily surrounded by our children and our five grandchildren, who keep us very busy.

FIGURE 2.1. "Charlie" age twenty-two months in 1942 at
the home of the nanny in the Val d'Oise. Anxious look.
Photo taken at the request of his parents for
identification if they were arrested.

# 2

# Charles Zelwer

**March 2000**

*Charles Zelwer is a researcher in structural biology at the National Center for Scientific Research (CNRS). He was born in 1940 into a family of Polish immigrant workers. He was separated from his parents from 1942 to 1944, hidden at the home of a Catholic nanny outside of Paris. His parents were activists and extreme Leftists, not Zionists.*

Unlike the other testimonials rich in dramatic episodes, the few memories I have of the time I was hidden could be considered mild compared to what others experienced. But the physically secure situation I had after being separated from my parents at the age of eighteen months was so destructive it took sixty years to free myself from its weight. Affected by a psychological handicap, the cause of which eluded me at every manifestation, I adapted myself, I compensated. I managed to complete my studies, lead a normal-appearing life, with a family, children, then a divorce and remarriage. I became a researcher at CNRS and undertook a scientific career that has brought me intellectual satisfaction, especially near its end. For more than thirty years, I was a trade union activist, which was, I hope, useful to the organization and which also benefited me.

My first memories, necessarily fragmented and limited to the means of representation of early infancy, have taken their current significance from contact with the stories of others, like those of my parents, and from therapy that brought up other memories to fill in certain blanks. My testimony is necessarily the result of these three sources. The testimonies of children hidden at my age are rare and especially subjective. Is there nothing then to be said about the traumas they suffered and their consequences? "Infant" etymologically signifies "not speaking." That's the risk I take with this testimony, in giving words to the child I was. The younger a child is, the more the trauma to which he is subjected weighs on him in a subconscious, insidious manner. The trauma therefore becomes even more difficult to identify and overcome.

I have had both good and bad fortune. I have fought against my handicap all my life. If I had understood its cause earlier, my life could have been different. But my handicap also gave me purpose. Now I must communicate this experience to help others—first of all my own children—but also those who fight in this impossible world against all the mass tragedies and their consequences that most severely affect the children.

My name is Charles Zelwer. I am an only child, born December 9, 1940, in Paris. My father's name was David. He was born in 1897 in Czestochowa, a stronghold of Polish Catholicism, at that time part of the Czarist empire. My mother, Fayga Berliner, was born in 1899 near Czestochowa. Therefore my parents were originally Russian. My father was third in a family of six children. He had two older sisters, one younger brother, and two younger sisters. His father was a very pious Hasidic Jew who managed a forest belonging to his brother-in-law. This uncle of my father owned a factory that manufactured metal chains. My mother also came from a very religious family. Her father dealt in fabrics in Czestochowa.

Perhaps with the assistance of this industrialist uncle, my father's older sisters studied and my father was trained to be an electrician at a technical school. Soon influenced by revolutionary ideas, my father rejected religion, which he considered to be a web of superstitions and absurd rites. He joined the Bund at age fifteen, showing an attachment to Yiddish culture and to progressive, secular Judaism. When the

Germans replaced the Russians in Poland during the war of 1914, my father went more or less voluntarily to work as an electrician in a coal mine in Upper Silesia (then part of Germany). There he joined the Democratic Socialist Party of Germany. The debut of Polish independence was marked by a period of instability, and my father barely escaped being lynched during a pogrom in Warsaw. Since his sister Pola was studying history in Paris, he left for France. Working illegally at first, he succeeded in getting a work permit. He joined the French Communist Party shortly after the Congrès de Tours in 1920. A younger sister (Saula) later moved to France and married first a Jewish shoe wholesaler; then after a divorce, a Georgian and former White Army officer who was an Orthodox Christian. My father's parents left Poland with another sister and my father's younger brother in 1928 to immigrate to Palestine, following their daughter Hela who was a dentist and had been established there since 1921. My father's younger brother, Wilek, became a Communist in Palestine, broke with Zionism after a time in a kibbutz, and came back to France with his wife Clara in 1930.

My mother lost her older brother during World War I, taken by an epidemic that she herself escaped. She had two sisters and a younger brother, Lipmann, who had to leave Poland in the 1920s because he was a Communist and was threatened with arrest. He moved to Brussels and worked in a tannery. My mother became a teacher in a kindergarten organized according to the pedagogical philosophy of Janusz Korczak and was more or less trained on the job because she hadn't studied. Schools like this envisioned maintaining Yiddish culture in Poland while promoting progressive education. My mother's group fought for the creation of a Jewish State in Uganda because with another people already living in Palestine, the Jews could not avoid conflict with them. The Polish government, opposed to the reinstatement of cultural autonomy for the Jews, closed these schools and my mother, unemployed, joined her brothers in Brussels. In 1933 my mother and her sister-in-law were arrested at a meeting honoring Lenin, Liebknecht, and Rosa Luxemburg. This celebration worked like a trap to allow numerous Jewish Communists and sympathizers to be expelled from Brussels. These are the circumstances under which my mother arrived in Paris "without papers" and found my father whom she had already met in Czestochowa. Marriage gave her legal status and she was employed as a worker in the Jewish knitting factories. All the members of my mother's immediate family who stayed in Poland (that would be over one hundred people) disappeared during the Holocaust. Her brother in Brussels and her cousins living in France all survived.

During the 1920s my father became a taxi driver and went on his own in 1936, having bought a used Peugeot. My parent's situation was very precarious. They lived in a hotel until 1939 and didn't want to have children. In 1939 they moved to a room with a kitchen in an apartment building at 209 rue Saint-Maur in the Tenth Arrondissement where many Jewish immigrant families lived. My father was fairly well assimilated into French culture, reading *L'Humanité* every week, working outside the Jewish milieu, active in the Communist Party and his union. He expressed himself well in French. My mother was employed in a Jewish workshop; she had come to France later and for this reason was not well assimilated. Her French was minimal.

When the war broke out, my father was convinced that the Soviet–German pact was nothing but a shrewd tactic of Stalin and that the USSR would one day end up at war with Hitler. He tried to join the Foreign Legion but was not mobilized until early 1940. After he was home on leave, my mother became pregnant. She was almost forty-one years old and thought herself no longer able to bear a child because of an earlier miscarriage. When the Front was penetrated by the German army in May of 1940, my father's company—made up of hastily trained and somewhat older soldiers fighting along Châlon-sur-Marne—didn't march fast enough. Stopping on a farm for the night, they awoke the next morning behind the enemy lines. The captain then had to disband the company. Their uniforms were buried and my father decided to get to Paris on foot rather than try to go back to the regiment's base at Septfonds in Ariège. He arrived in Occupied Paris and was decommissioned after the Armistice was signed.

The fact that my mother was pregnant weighed heavily on his decision. She was probably desperate and, as she told me herself when I was old enough to understand, there was no one in Paris doing abortions. I think my father was happy with the idea of having a child. My mother was extremely anguished given her age and the circumstances. At my birth, she gave as a first name "Karl" at City Hall. What did she intend? To give me the first name of her recently deceased father "Kopel"? My aunt Pola created a scene, saying she couldn't give me a

German first name. The first name was changed to "Charles"—the altered letters still visible on my birth certificate. My parents were foreigners, but I was declared "French," which was possible because I had been born in France. I still have the idea that my status has been uncertain ever since coming into the world. I have the same uncertainty about my having roots in the world of the living.

From what friends of the family have told me, the first weeks of my existence were chaotic. December of 1940 was exceptionally cold and the heat insufficient in the room where we lived. A friend of my mother's named Réga saw that I was in a critical state and warmed me, holding me against her own body. As a last resort, shots of salt water were administered, which saved me. I then had an intestinal infection. After this difficult crisis, my mother took me to the country for a few weeks to regain my strength. I think this stay enabled her to situate herself in relation to me. She often refers to it. I am obviously unable to evaluate the impact this difficult beginning had on my future.

Up until July of 1942, I led a normal existence, despite the restrictions and anti-Jewish measures of which I was unaware. My parents refused to speak Yiddish as a precaution even though it was the language of communication between them. My "native" language was therefore French, the idea being to speak to me in public in this language. My father, unable to work as a taxi driver (there was no gasoline, his car was hidden in a cooperative owned by a White Russian), again took up his trade as an electrician. He worked in a firm at Courbevoie that had belonged to a Jew but had been subjected to Aryanization under the name of a French firm. This business manufactured electric heaters, which allowed my father to rig up radiators for himself and for one of my mother's cousins living in Paris. My father's brother Wilek worked at the same firm. He lived with his wife and child not far from rue St. Maur on rue Corbeau (which is now called rue Jacques Louvel-Tessier).

My mother cared for me at home and I must have developed normally, that is to say, by giving my parents more and more problems just like any growing child. They tell me that when I was just starting to walk (February 1942), there was a family get-together at my uncle Wilek's one Sunday afternoon. There was cheese and a knife on the table. I got hold of the cheese and the knife and threw them out the open window of the third or fourth floor. This illustrated an unruly child's inclination to assert himself and an obvious lack of attention on the part of the parents. My father had to go down to pick up the knife, but a passerby wanted to go to the police with it because it fell just in front of him, so I was already the source of a drama that could potentially have led to my parents' arrest. Another time I left my uncle's apartment carrying a padlock. This padlock was used to make it appear that no one was home because it could be removed from the inside while remaining in place on the outside. That night after the curfew specifically imposed on Jews, my aunt noticed that the padlock was missing, and my uncle had to go out to retrieve it at my parents' place.

The first memory of my own has to do with the Vel' d'Hiv' Roundup of Jews on July 16, 1942.[1] Not being aware of what was happening, I was only able to memorize details that struck me by their unusual and isolated character, without attaching any particular sense to them. Well after the war when I was around ten years old, I questioned my parents about the day (without being able to situate it in time) when I was still in my bed and someone was knocking at the door of our one-room apartment and, contrary to their habit, my parents hadn't opened the door. My mother, in her nightgown, took me in her arms and into their bed for the first time—which was a moment of supreme happiness! My parents, overwhelmed and surprised, understood from certain details what this memory pertained to, but they themselves were unable to talk to me directly about it. They gave this task over to Réga, my mother's friend I've already mentioned and who taught at the same school as my mother in Czestochowa. At the beginning of the school vacation, she took me to her place near Châtelet. She told me what happened the night of July 16, 1942, but without evoking the flashback I had. Nor did she tell me that it was French police who had knocked at the door. I thought they were Germans. After the Liberation, there was self-censorship on this subject by Jews and Jewish organizations. In fact, I didn't really make the connection between my memory and Réga's account, which didn't directly answer the questions I had asked my parents. She tried to explain it to me, but it was impossible for me to understand—I missed a lot by having been cut off from my parents for more than two years at an age of rapid and critical development. Perhaps she wanted me to respond, but I said nothing because no one had enlightened me about the events underway during the time I stayed with the nanny. Under the circumstances, direct dialog with my parents was cruelly missing. This attempt at amateur therapy nevertheless permitted my parents to more freely bring up these events factually, which is to say without reference to my own experiences.

My father had been warned the night of July 16, 1942, by friends in the Union of Jews for Resistance and Mutual Aid (UJRE)—which was still called "Solidarity" at the time—and in the Communist Party that something serious was about to take place. He had gone down to the courtyard of the apartment building at four or five in the morning and noticed that the conciergerie, which opened onto the passageway from the courtyard to the street, was full of police. It was too late to run. The police had a list of all the Jews who were registered and had located each apartment using the residential register. My father understood this and went back up. So my parents were alerted and when the police knocked on the door, my mother, after putting a candy in my mouth, took me from my bed and into hers—which she had never before done. Réga told me (on this subject), "You saved the lives of your family because you didn't cry!" In fact, I believe it was more from my lack of awareness than my silence that I didn't betray our presence in the apartment. There were several violent knocks on the door. I remember also having heard loud shouting. The roundup was planned in such a way that people couldn't escape. The police began by combing the ground floor, then the first, then the second floor. Since my parents lived on the fourth floor, they could hear them on the other floors and the cries of families being forced from their homes. My parents were not taken then. The first day, the sixteenth, perhaps in this neighborhood and maybe in others, the police were not breaking down doors. They must have believed we were gone, that we had gotten away or had already been arrested. But on the second day, the seventeenth, they did break down doors. My father, on the other side of the door, played dead. Later he told me, "There I was facing my fate. I chose not to open and told myself, 'Let them break down the door.'" And they didn't. Then I remembered my mother saying, "They're gone," and my father saying, "Now, let's get the hell out of here." Later, when I told my parents about the flashback I had, I repeated these two sentences to them and I even described the color of the jacket my father was wearing as a bathrobe, they were astonished. I then said, "And then you cut your clothes." My father remembered they had spread their clothing on the bed where I still lay and used scissors to cut off all the yellow stars. It was this detail that convinced my parents of the authenticity of my memory. As for the concierge at 209 rue Saint-Maur, it can be said that this woman was a Resister, one of the "Righteous," without belonging to any organization. Her name was Madame Massacré. This concierge had several Jewish families in the building who, thanks to her, got through the war without having to go out to run errands. She falsified the register to hide Jews. And this concierge died of a heart attack during the Liberation of Paris. It seems she was relieved to see us escape the Roundup and she offered to take care of our apartment for us. In fact my parents went back there shortly after the Liberation.

Upon leaving the apartment on July 16, my parents went in different directions. My mother and I went to rue Corbeau. She shut me up in my uncle's empty apartment to which she had the key. She must have left me there for several hours. My mother told me in a no-nonsense tone of voice, "I am leaving you here and you are not to move or to make any noise." I was eighteen months old and she went off and left me alone in the apartment. I don't know how long she was gone, but I must not have moved much. After a certain length of time she came to get me. We went down; she met my father in the street and said to me, "Here's Papa!" I was taken right away to a nanny who lived in a private house in an area near Argenteuil. My mother's absence must have given my parents a chance to find a place for me, and then they left me with this unknown nanny in this dramatic context. I understood then that this was a real separation. My parents lit a candle, perhaps to fix a moment in my memory. Then they said, "We'll come back to see you." I started to cry and they left. My parents were unable to face the situation created by July 16, 1942, assure their survival in hiding, and earn their living while caring for an eighteen-month-old child all at the same time. It was virtually impossible. They had to find a way to survive and they couldn't entrust me to family members, all of whom were being pursued as they were.

"Nana" was a gray-haired woman in her fifties, a practicing Catholic and mother of six. She had been deserted by her husband and did not have a profession. I don't know what she lived on. She lived in a single-family house at the edge of town with a little yard. Maybe she had a trust to draw on. My parents paid her; she had to make a living. My parents were going to have to work to be able to pay my board, and furthermore, they regularly brought food for me, which I never even got to taste! The nanny had a twelve-year-old son, Roger, the next to the last of the family. The youngest child, Yolande, was seven or eight years old and the other daughters still at home—Simone, Jeanne, and Céline—were adolescents. The nanny also had a married daughter, Françoise, who lived in the same township. Maybe there were other children whom I don't remember.

I have fragmented but precise recollections of my stay at Nana's. As an adult I started psychotherapy and went through several schools of it; I did neo-Reichian when I was about forty; then I divorced my first wife at age forty-six. I had three children in this first marriage. I had already met my current wife, who is not Jewish. My first wife was part-Jewish. She had a mother who was Jewish and a father who was not. It was during this therapy that I regained a memory—one of the first I had of my stay with this woman.

It was evening, almost night (in my mind it was that way) when we arrived at her house. The next day I met the children. They showed me the front yard and one of them told me, "You can play around the house but you aren't allowed to go up to the fence. No one must see you! You are hidden. You are a Jewish child and if they find you, you will be taken and we will all be taken with you." Another said, "There's no use telling him, he's too little, he won't understand." Actually, I hadn't understood, except that I wasn't to go to the street side, that something was threatening me and that I had to obey, to put myself completely in the hands of those who were keeping me. They were serious; this was not a game and for two years I didn't make a wrong move—either on the street side or anywhere else. (Even if this was an auto-suggestion produced by therapy, these words describe well the reality of the restrictions and guilt placed on me.) I spent most of my time there between the kitchen, which was in the basement, and my room. I had internalized the vague threat and the fact that in this family I was protected as long as I didn't attract attention.

At the age of eighteen months, I had to bear the consequences of my clandestine situation. This clandestine way of life could present itself to me in different forms: first, I didn't know I was "Jewish" or what the word implied. (It was therefore left unsaid.) And I didn't know my family name. I had a first name; my name was Charlie. I was therefore without a connection, even a semantic one, to my absent family. Then I had parents who had left me there, who had said to me, "We'll come back to see you." After the Liberation my parents told me they came to see me every week, but I only remember a few visits, even though this situation must have lasted more than two years. I stayed with this family from July 16, 1942, to September 1944, after the Liberation of Paris. In fact, for a year my parents came to see me (as my mother later told me) while I slept in order not to cause a scene.

I became attached to this nanny even though she had a strict manner and frightened me. I think she was attached to me, too, when affection overcame the sense of danger. I had confidence in her and she hugged me when I asked her to. The family practically lived in the basement kitchen, dominated by a wood or coal cook stove that also heated the house and warmed bricks for my bed in the winter. The first day, the baby bed wasn't yet set up and I slept in a big bed with the boy Roger. I would have liked to continue sleeping with him. The problem was I wet the bed and therefore couldn't continue to share his bed.

I was intrigued by an unusual object—a bronze crucifix over the bed. I had never seen one and it was something vaguely disturbing. I asked the boy, "What is that?" He answered, "You don't know Baby Jesus!" Something didn't mesh with what he said because "Baby Jesus" made me think of a child. But I was seeing the statue of a tortured man (and the crucifixes of that time were very realistic). In my subconscious, I didn't know why but "Baby Jesus" *could have something to do with me!* I don't know why I had this intuition. But the fact is, the next day when I went to bed the crucifix was gone, and in its place I could see the discolored outline of a cross on the wall. I tried to find out more about this curious object that had disappeared, but I came up against absolute silence. It was as if it had never existed.

This recollection was not recovered from what adults said. It is authentic. I can now understand that it represented the noncommunication and prohibitions resulting from the situation; everything that could be a reminder of Jewishness, Judaism, or Christianity must be hidden from me, dissimulated. Anything that had to do with my identity was taboo. The security of the family (and my own) was dependent on my being kept in the most complete ignorance of my origin and my situation. There had to be a complete erasure of anything that could betray us. If anyone, inadvertently, were to question me, I would be unable to reveal the identity of either my parents or my host family. I had to be naïve and completely passive so I would not ask questions about my family name. I could not know the name of the family with whom I was staying or even the idea of a "family name." I would not learn the name of my "Nana" until much later, after the war.

Erasing from my mind anything that could compromise my situation came about through deliberate will—a real "conspiracy." That did not keep me from emotionally attaching to the nanny and one of her daughters, Simone. Even so, there is something else important that must be said: I think the nanny took the risk of taking me in because I hadn't been circumcised. My parents, having refused religion, had refused circumcision, which was exceptional even among atheist Jews—even among Jewish Communists. They were asserting a Jewish and secular identity represented by the Yiddish culture. They were also, ideologically, very hostile to Zionism. They refused to circumcise me perhaps because they saw already in 1940 that it could become an additional problem. They didn't allow themselves, despite their cultural attachment, to speak Yiddish to me or to teach it to me from birth. On the other hand, after the war my parents wanted me to learn it under the sponsorship of the UJRE, as if to erase the "de-Jewification" imposed by the circumstances. The classes there were directed to children who had been forbidden to speak the language and were now learning to read and write it. But for me it was a foreign language that had to be learned, so I blocked it out. It reminded me that my not being a little French child like the other children was what put me in jeopardy, in danger, and it was an intimate wound, an irrational, inexplicable handicap. To endorse everything that had been hidden for two years—including things that were unforgivable—upon reuniting with my family obviously wasn't so easy.

I had internalized the restrictions under the Occupation at an age when I didn't have the means of interpretation. One thing I remember, which made me feel guilty and absolutely terrified me, was that this nanny had to take care of her daughters, already teenagers, and had to rule them with an iron hand. And she beat her daughters to a pulp if they were late coming home from school. No doubt she was trying to isolate them from the outside world so no one would know she was keeping a Jewish child in her home. Everything depended on secrecy. And I felt, rightly or wrongly, that these punishments I witnessed had to do with me because no one gave me an explanation. But nonverbal communication can't be controlled and it must have affected me. Nana was a woman alone, the only adult among all these

children. A man came sometimes. No one introduced me and the children were always away. I now think it must have been a special
"friend" of the nanny whom she saw secretly. I seem to remember
that whenever he came, she would tell me to wait for her in the
kitchen, which—other than my own room—was the only room in the
house that was familiar to me.

At the end of a year there were several Sunday visits from my parents. I remember the first one: my father arrived first and introduced
himself, "I'm Papa." Then my mother arrived and my father introduced
her to me because she dared not speak and stayed back—no doubt to
hide her accent and her broken French. (My father's French was quite
good.) I was happy about my parents' visit, even if I didn't recognize
them. They were strangers to me, but I believed my father when he introduced himself. This visit I remember probably took place in 1943.
On another visit, they came accompanied by someone named Henriette, who was not Jewish. She was a Communist, a Resister who also
took part in the solidarity network that helped Jews. (She came because
it was she who had given my parents the address of this nanny.) "Henriette" was a pseudonym. She was arrested and deported because she
was denounced. She did not return from the camps.

I now regret that my parents didn't understand how important it
was to me to have as many details as possible after the war to reconstruct memories. My mother, for example, never talked to me about her
underground activities during the war, and I believe she had some. The
fact that she did housekeeping, sometimes in the affluent neighborhoods, would have allowed her to carry messages. She worked for a
while for a doctor who kept guinea pigs. He used them for experiments
and fed them crusts of bread. But my mother took the bread crusts for
herself and gave the guinea pigs scraps instead. When the doctor found
out, he dismissed her! My parents lived in Alfortville, in a space they
had sublet from a neighbor at 209 rue Saint-Maur. This neighbor's name
was Monsieur Boury. He was in the same cell of the Communist Party
as my father, and his wife Louka was a Jewess from Bessarabia. He was
disabled and had one shoulder higher than the other. He also had tat-
toos everywhere. How did he happen to marry Louka? She was an
immigrant without documents. She then contracted a marriage of con-
venience with Monsieur Boury to become French and have the right to
remain in France. But once they left City Hall he told her in no uncer-

tain terms that she was his wife and that she would have to live with him! It was this Monsieur Boury who had sublet this apartment to my parents, and my father made the dangerous trip everyday between Alfortville and Courbevoie.

My father told me later that when they came to see me (they had to take the suburban train), he and my mother would travel separately and they had agreed that if one were taken, the other would not react. This was the climate! This did not prevent my parents from trying to connect with life by any means they could. Every week they took the risk of going to the movies. French film had a true revival during the Occupation because there was no foreign competition. My parents saw all the films even though Jews were especially hunted in the movie houses.

I remember a weekend spent with my parents. One day it was very nice weather (it was Pentecost 1944). My father arrived alone at the nanny's place and something absolutely extraordinary happened: I left the house with him. He took me with him. I believed the war was over and a page was about to be turned. We didn't walk far but since I wasn't used to walking, I tired quickly. On the way, I asked him, "Have you been a soldier?" "Yes." I was proud of his answer. It really was a completely extraordinary day for me with my father holding my hand (my father was short but to me he seemed tall). After a moment I dared to ask him the question that haunted me, "Tell me, Papa, what's your name?" I had to repeat my question twice, then he stopped. "What do you mean by that?" "Well, my name is Charlie and you, what's your name?" Then I had the impression the sky fell on him and he answered me, babbling—first making sure no one was around to hear. "My name is David. But you mustn't tell!" I felt the blue sky had changed color. I was ashamed to have put my father in a situation where he had to let me see his fear. And I understood "it" was not over. The joy of this information evaporated. It is one of the sharpest memories I have. Once I tried to talk to him about it again but he didn't remember it. I then arrived at the place where my parents lived in Alfortville. I slept in their bed. The next morning my mother called me a "bed-wetter" and then left to run errands. After a certain length of time, my father began to pace the floor and said to me, "Mama isn't back." Then he started to cry and said, "We won't see her again." At these words my mother arrived. She had gone I don't know where to find meat for me but without success. Then my father took me back to my nanny.

One day, little Yolande said to me: "You, you're an ol' Yid!" I didn't understand what that meant. When my father came to see me, I asked him, "Papa, what's an ol' Yid?" "Who said that to you?" he asked. "Yolande." The nanny was there, face to face with us. My father after a moment's hesitation, dismissing my question with a wave of his hand, "Oh, she called you a hoodlum? But that's nothing." This is something my father reminded me of one day and I was able to complete the recollection. The next day Simone (one of the girls who took care of me) scolded me severely and called me a tattletale. I also saw Yolande in tears, "Why did you tell this story of ol' Yid? It was between us, a joke!" Yolande must have been reprimanded by her mother. A rule had been broken.

All of this was part of the system of obfuscation around me. My recollections are always associated with events that broke the daily monotony. Simone took me, at her mother's request, to a place where cocoa was being distributed. This distribution was organized by the Sisters of a priory. The cocoa pleased me enormously. I saw on the wall a photo of a kindly looking grandfather in a kepi. And I asked Simone, "Who is that?" Simone gave me a vague answer. "But who is it?" "It's the Head of State," she told me. "But who's the Head of State?" She says, "It's Pétain." "But who is Pétain?" Then she really panicked; she rushed me back to the house. Obviously, I couldn't be taken anywhere.

They also told me the following episode: The nanny had errands to run and took me with her. A man in a beret came up to her and said, "That child with you has really curly hair. He's not by chance a Jewish child is he?" She said, "No, not at all!" She said to me then, "Go pee by that tree!" and to the man she said, "You see he's not Jewish!" The nanny did not try to convert me. She nevertheless had told my parents that if they were arrested, she would keep me and raise me as her son but in the Catholic religion. In any case, they were in no position to protest.

To finish with this problem of obfuscation, the ambiance changed after the Normandy Landings. I heard the word "Landings." And from that moment on, we began to see people again. I could go out. The climate had changed because people had stopped being afraid. I remember going to the neighbor's. A girl was painting a picture in the garden.

Then there were air raid alerts between June and August 1944; we went to safety in the baker's cellar. And there people played dominoes. So in a certain way from that time on, I was less hidden and my host family became less isolated. The nanny's special "friend" couldn't believe I was a little Jewish boy who hadn't been circumcised. Nana asked me to show her friend this weenie so he could judge for himself. It was like a passport; a strange piece of identification. What was special about it? It was worrisome.

I remember the arrival of the Americans. All at once, we heard shouting, a lot of noise, and the nanny was in an extraordinary state of excitement! She led me by the hand, shouting, "The Americans! The Americans!" There were military trucks and a jubilant crowd at a cross-roads. There Nana held me up to a soldier who helped me get up on the truck. She shouted something to the American soldier who evidently didn't understand her. I can't be sure what she said, but what could she have said about me other than "He's a Jewish child!" If that's the case, my brain censured the phrase.

A little later, my father came to take me away for good. For the first time I heard the nanny speak his name: "Monsieur Zelwer." I discovered a name that seemed strange to me and I still didn't know it was also my own. I was taken back to the apartment at 209 rue Saint-Maur, which I didn't remember at all—a new place, strange. I was again with my parents whom I really didn't even know. My father had me choose my place at the table and explained to me that I was also a Zelwer. In fact, I had difficulty making this name mine, even though I had no doubts about my parents. After a long time without an identity, one is like an amnesiac who is retaught his name and has difficulty internalizing what he is being taught. I was a little sad to leave Nana but my father said we would see her again. I remember that once settled with my parents in the kitchen, I wanted to find the garden I had lost—the peas I had planted, and my Nana. I was going to all the neighbors, to try to get away. Everyone but me seemed to know who I was. My parents made me feel they loved me, of course, but there had been a two-year break between us—a break in continuity of our relationship, experienced unevenly for them and for me. Mother was worried about my physical health, which no one had worried about for two years. As I had been undernourished, you could count my ribs on my chest above my protruding belly. A neighbor (Jewish) told me I was a

"French Jew." I didn't really understand. They introduced me to a family, Uncle Wilek, his wife, Clara, my cousin, Arlan, the aunt married to a Georgian, "Uncle Georges"; people who were perfect strangers to me. On my father's side, my aunt Pola and her husband had been deported, never to return.

It was only at the end of the Occupation that I was hungry! For example, I once bit into a piece of soap. The last weeks were the most difficult. I ate practically nothing but thin gruel and I lacked muscular development and strength from this period of undernourishment. When I was back with my parents, I wouldn't eat. I refused my mother's cooking, too. Throughout my childhood I had health problems that became my mother's obsession. She took me from doctor to doctor because I didn't eat; I was considered a "fragile" and "sickly" child.

Since there was nothing to eat in Paris in 1944, in order to build me up my parents immediately placed me with another nanny in Coulommiers! I think they also needed to reorganize themselves, to find work. Right after the war, the Jewish organizations had immediately opened hostels for Jewish orphans and let families place their children there for a while. My parents didn't want this solution. Maybe there was food at Coulommiers. In any case, they boarded me with Madame Planquet, whom my parents contacted through a Soviet, a Resistance commander who lived in the apartment building. (I saw him in a French army uniform.) His name was Commander Yarouj and he had probably worked in the Resistance in that area. I obviously wasn't happy about this new separation. After a few weeks, I think Madame Planquet must have said it wasn't working well with me and my father came to get me.

My father resumed his work as a taxi driver at the end of the year when gas was once again more available. He repaired his old Peugeot. My mother kept doing housekeeping, then started working again sewing in the little cottage industries, mainly in the Jewish quarter. It was seasonal work. She did finish work. I then went to preschool but I didn't fit in well. I had some problems with a teacher. My mother took me out of preschool at age five and one-half because I had slightly pushed a little girl during a school event. The headmistress had threatened to expel me. As the school year was ending and it was the slow time for sewing, my mother could take care of me at home. After that, she enrolled me in elementary school in the fall at the age of six. I was then confronted by the school system and its restrictions, which didn't bother me. But I was incapable of responding to the aggressiveness of the other children because during the time I was hidden, I hadn't seen children of my own age. I didn't know what a child was. I felt different without knowing exactly why.

I was too young to be told about the concentration camps and the "Final Solution." The Nazis were evil, but they had lost the war. My understanding stopped there. In my opinion, despite the efforts to protect me, my parents should have talked to me more, brought up memories, explained quickly to me the reason for this two-year separation. But their problem was to plan the future and turn a page on the past. I sometimes heard the word "deported," a rather innocuous term that revealed its sinister connotation in the context in which it was used without my understanding what the term hid. My father tried to give me some facts about the Jewish religion because I needed to know what I belonged to. For this reason, after age six, in addition to elementary school, they put me in a Jewish youth center organized by the UJRE, and there I learned, at about age eight, a certain number of historic facts about the Jews, about the Occupation, anti-Semitism. The UJRE organized children's homes for orphans and vacation camps where the children from these homes interacted with children who had found a recomposed or intact family. The youth center on rue Faubourg-du-Temple was overseen by a very nice, mature headmistress named Baschka. For the first time, I was among Jewish children and there, to them, I was the "weirdo." I felt totally out of place. I probably didn't act as they expected me to, which kept me in a situation of permanent unease. They, no doubt, didn't have the same identity problems, having perhaps been hidden under different circumstances. (I'll risk an explanation: all the Jewish children born into immigrant families—hidden with or without their parents—have had to reach a point of self-acceptance of their status as a Jewish child. I had not reached this point and for this reason I couldn't help but bring back concealed traumas for the others. Their rejection of me was probably a defense mechanism.) For me being Jewish had no positive value. I had friends in adolescence who were Jewish or Communist. We talked about everything; we shared everything, but we never spoke of our personal history during the war. It was not a subject to verbalize. With friends, even at summer camp, we never had even the least personal exchange about the Occupation.

We who had been hidden, we were the miracle children. When other children had been burned, had been killed, when so many people had died, how could we ponder our personal problems? We didn't have the right; in this context it would have seemed indecent. I was having problems and I think my mother felt guilty about that; she tried to feel less guilty by dragging me from doctor to doctor.

Only recently have I understood and dissected the workings of my identity crisis. I realized while watching an American miniseries B-movie that what I felt was like what an amnesiac waking from a coma feels: he doesn't remember his previous personality and finds friends he doesn't identify as his own, a wife who isn't *his* wife, children that aren't *his* children, a mistress not really *his* mistress, and so forth. In a word, those around him know things about him that he himself doesn't know and he is dependent on how others see him because he doesn't have a clear image of himself. I was separated from my parents for two years, not knowing my name (or theirs) and my only connection to them was through the nanny. This identification with the situation of the amnesiac only came about recently. It has given me a new view of myself and taken away all feeling of guilt. The disorientation I experienced as a personal characteristic did not come from me; it was the result of external circumstances imposed on me. I could at last put what I felt into a rational chain of events. I could for the first time feel rebellious and accept my own hostility as legitimate. In 1944, I found myself in a Jewish family and at age four I had to meld into a new identity that was foreign to me.

Not all my experience as a hidden child has been incorporated into language; into my language. The problems I encountered escape any verbal expression. I adapted to my handicap, I used "crutches" while waiting to find my legs and my roots. The paradox of the situation was that with my nanny, I wasn't afraid; I felt safe in this French family, and then suddenly in 1944 in this Jewish family I felt insecure. I sensed the difference between my parents and the French. They didn't speak the same; they spoke Yiddish—a language I didn't know. And I knew this sense of Jewishness to be connected to a sense of danger; so from that time on I felt I was in a state of insecurity, about to be persecuted. I was afraid of everything: airplanes, thunder, fireworks. I was incapable of facing life, of taking my place in it and growing up.

I actually did have "crutches"; the first was school because it gave me my only means of existence. I understood that with success in school I could get something tangible for myself. My mother told me that students who worked hard could go on to *lycée*, so I saw possibilities for advancement, for a future. And above all, I loved reading; I read a lot as a child. I wasn't a particularly gifted student but I succeeded according to school criteria. In elementary school I had friends who weren't Jewish and whose parents were Leftists (some of the French had compassion, even sympathy; there were also anti-Semites), but I had not had Jewish friends there even though a third of the class was from Jewish families. I managed to enter the first year at Collège Turgot (junior high) at the age of nine and one-half. It still was not a very healthy situation because I was too young, the youngest, in a protected situation—even more so because at the time some children had been seriously delayed in their schooling and could be twelve or thirteen years old. At Collège Turgot, I had Jewish friends and also non-Jewish friends from moderate Communist families like me. I showed great interest in school, but I asked questions all the time; I wanted a personal relationship with the teachers so I was seen as a little twit.

The subconscious manifests itself in attitudes, gestures, body language. Language does not serve to communicate the inner reality. I was someone with an identity problem, a "who am I?" and the others to me were other "who am I's?" or "black boxes" with whom I could communicate about rational, codified matters but not about emotional matters, which, it goes without saying, was the source of my failure to adapt. What I later discovered, very late in life, is that someone who is *aware* is someone who sees himself as visible, who is capable of incorporating how others see him into his behavior. My own reflection in a mirror wasn't familiar and in any case, I had been told it was bad to be aware of how others see us or to spend time looking at yourself. My mother understood when I got to be nine or ten years old that I perhaps needed some help. So there were attempts, first with primal therapy with Réga Federman. She had lost her only daughter to an appendicitis attack before the war and she was rearing her nephew Michou, whose parents had been deported. He was always taking potshots at me, making fun of me. I was unable to be objective about myself and I didn't understand the humor, the teasing. I didn't catch on that he no longer had his parents while I had mine. He had to compensate for a feeling of inferiority. There was a second attempt to help: when my mother said we were going to see a doctor whom my cousin had seen and who had really helped. I asked why. "You are constipated . . ."

My faint recollections make me now wonder if this doctor, who was a psychotherapist or psychiatrist—some kind of analyst—was Françoise Dolto from the description of a therapy session she gave in her book. There was a dialogue: the psychologist asks, "Does he know his name?" My mother repeated it to me later because I had missed what was said right in front of me. She had answered the question defensively. After this exchange in my presence, my mother asked to speak alone with the therapist. That was a mistake because I guessed what it was about. I had suffered some sexual abuse during my stay with the nanny by the girl I was closest to. I won't go any further into that. It was "very bad" and I must not be "normal." I was sure that was what my mother talked to the shrink about. When I was alone again with this psychologist (who had difficulty ejecting my mother from the interview), I was no longer receptive. (In fact, it wasn't clear to me what we were supposed to be doing. Someone needed to tell me that I was having difficulty and that talking to a professional outside of the family would help me, and then let me decide if I was willing to accept help or not.) So she asked me to draw and I refused because it didn't make any sense to me. We just exchanged banalities: "Are you getting along okay?" "No, I don't get along well with my classmates." She also asked me if I wanted to know how children were made but I was stubborn, and the climate of confidence faded. We didn't get much further. After that session, which I actually found very interesting because the psychologist treated me as a subject—as a person, I would have wanted there to be more sessions but my parents thought otherwise. My father said, "He's not crazy and the episode about the war, he's got to find a way to get over it!" (My father perhaps felt that if Pandora's Box were reopened my parents would have to reevaluate their own roles in my upbringing.) They thought, with good reason, that they had done everything to save me and that no one had the right to judge them, neither a "shrink" from outside the family, a bourgeois "intellectual," nor a fortiori their own son. My father, despite his political views, had not given up the traditional Jewish patriarchal model. This also strongly influenced his relationship with his younger brother.

Another "crutch" in this postwar period was ideology. Curiously, this revelation came to me (I must have been about six years old) during a speech by Maurice Thorez, an outstanding Stalinist leader, broadcast through loudspeakers hung from the trees at the L'Huma festival.[2]

Monsieur Thorez had a particular manner of delivery—I obviously understood nothing of what he was saying—but there was conviction in
his voice, certainty, a voice of great clarity, a tone that was somewhat
warm, that could denounce evil and that completely won me over. I
discovered that there are people armed with certainty—self-proclaimed
arbiters of truth—who are capable of speaking, accusing, exhorting,
leading. This is how individuals who have been traumatized and lost
their autonomy fall victim to the worst tricks. They can be led down the
path of least resistance, manipulated, and be made to do anything. This
particular ideology offered "salvation" and, therefore, perhaps a solution
to my personal problems. For me it served two purposes. On the one
hand it allowed me to leave my isolation behind because I found external referents, comrades, and also Jewish comrades (while avoiding Judaism!) with a common objective—to make revolution and share noble,
generous, coherent ideas with a sacred Soviet Union—and a face of evil
to destroy: Fascism, colonialism, et cetera. On the other hand it gave
me a chance to camouflage my personal problems behind speeches
and ideology. In short, it gave me a completely artificial and biased
Manichean worldview: cult of Stalin—the "People's Father"—a completely extraordinary great man whose portrait was pinned to a calen-
dar at our house. The Communist Party for me, as for many others,
operated as a religious sect. It created a closed world, secure and perverse at the same time.

In adolescence, in order not to suffer, I subconsciously again took
up the attitude I had during the war at Nana's house—that is, apparent
neutrality and emotional anesthesia in order to avoid getting personally
involved. From then on the world became viable for me since I had
only to bury the essential questions deep inside myself. As wooden language was an invitation to "think politically" while refusing the most
direct evidence in the name of ideological purity, this subjective indifference took the same direction. What better than a system of thought
that only acknowledges collective "man," man only as part of a social
class and denies him as an individual subject? Fortunately, I was honest,
and after 1956, as did a great many others, I saw a conflict between the
wooden language of the Party and the secular rationalist culture of the
"bourgeois" school. Being then engaged in the study of chemistry, in
the bosom of a very conservative engineering school, close to industry,
I was a militant in the Union of Student Communists—which was

beginning to show disagreement with the Communist Party—until the
end of the Algerian War. Through the labor movement, I clung tightly
then to the Communist Party line and its contradictions. I broke psychologically with this system in a somewhat curious way: I did an internship in cinema at a time when I had already started a thesis at
CNRS in structural chemistry, but this internship in cinema was about
creating a story, a screenplay. It involved the group from the Center for
Youth and Culture (MJC) and was staffed by professionals in the theater, militants of cultural action who challenged the absence of policy
in the Communist Party in their field. Ideology was no help to me in
creating something that made sense from the human point of view. I
said to myself, "That's curious. I have a political philosophy; I know
how to handle abstract ideas, but when it comes to imagining something alive, it absolutely doesn't work." You simply cannot make a film
with ideology. I had seen lots of films—Russian films and everything
imaginable as cinema goes. The Soviet revolutionary filmmakers knew
they could not compose a film worthy of the name with ideology; they
needed something concrete, psychologically acceptable, they needed
individuals. They had to portray people as they are, and there I had to
look at the system in which I was enclosed from the outside. I told
myself, "This is weird. Ideological discourse doesn't contribute to understanding the world and is incapable of convincing. The only thing
that counts when making a statement is whether it plays on the screen
or not." That's when I began to separate myself from wooden language.
I saw myself as alienated. And the definitive break came shortly before
May 1968; I rebelled against any kind of manipulation, of dishonesty.
When May 1968 arrived, I completely supported the movement, somewhat influenced also by my father-in-law, a former Trotskyite.

That said, I wasn't fully aware of the deep origins of my difficulties
and I still experienced difficulties, first and foremost in my professional life. I was incapable of competing. With an identity problem,
you can certainly learn but not resolve a problem or conceive a scientific strategy. It is essential in doing research to know how to situate
oneself: what questions are to be answered, what represents success
or failure of a process, how to have positive outcomes for various situations. If the external world is a "tunnel" into which you move along
on tiptoes, even guided by the hands of friends, you are in a bad
spot. What I lacked was the knowledge of people and situations. For

work that has a component of teamwork but relies on competition, that's a handicap.

In fact, I had disappointments, conflicts, difficult episodes in my work that I more or less overcame. At age forty, I started Reichian therapy, which allowed me to see that I had lost contact with my body (my body went one way, my mind another). I learned to reinvent my body from inside, to accept my emotions, and I felt an ongoing dialogue between my consciousness and the "living me." When I was separated from my parents at eighteen months, the loss of contact with the body was a way of deadening the suffering. It didn't miraculously disappear when the war ended.

With Reichian therapy, my condition improved. I still had an identity problem, but only in my relationship with others. I ended my first marriage, which was based on a misunderstanding and on two neurotics complementing one another. I was able to love another woman and to create a stable couple. She had been raised Catholic and was a divorcée with two children. I connected with something I needed while meeting her expectations. Despite my identity problem, I have been able to find a common basis for dialogue with my current wife. We can understand one another and build something together from there.

On the professional level I have gone on to discover my own intellectual freedom. To do that, I had to do a stint in the United States where I confronted the efficiency of the "American System"; the failure of my projects, the annihilation of my ego. To be "born again," one must first "die." Having hit bottom, I bounced back and from this experience. I learned what is important. It is the ethic of scientific truth, above and beyond the narrow personal horizon and its concerns.

I realized lately that my relationship problems were caused by a kind of amnesia. I understood that I was not responsible for it, so I was "not guilty." This discovery freed me from a spell under which I had been a victim. I experienced a feeling of hostility because of this lost time, these mistakes. I had not been the best of fathers. I had three children from my first marriage; my oldest son is schizophrenic and the second died accidentally after having gone through a wild stage. I cannot evaluate how much my own pathology impacted that of my two sons. I also have a daughter who lives with a partner and just had a child. I am, among other things, for her the father who read her Singer's story *When Schlemiel Went to Warsaw*, a book she gave back to me to reconnect us.

I would like to conclude by emphasizing that children inherit all the traumas and disappointments of history and that there is never enough done to help them internalize their experiences, both positive and negative ones. And when nothing is done, their descendants can be affected. On the collective scale, historical catastrophes generate new dramas, new conflicts because of the children born into them. If it is important to punish criminals, specific programs must also be put in place to help children and all who endure the modern genocides that get so much media coverage today.

It is true that much was done for us. For example, the Central Committee for Children (CCE) of the UJRE organized summer camps that helped us find a place to connect our experience as persecuted Jews with our identity as French citizens. Of course, these people had a Communist ideology and we children were held hostage in a political fight between them and the Zionists. Whichever way we turned, children were not the central mission but the means to their ends for these organizations. The survival of each of these movements among the Jews of the Diaspora was tied to their ability to capture the youth, because the youth are the future. Despite these failings, the organizations did a lot of good. They were devoted to assuring education for the children of the deported who were taught a trade, some even were provided higher education. (For comparison think of the way underprivileged children are treated today.) And these sons and daughters of the deported have been able to live in society, have personal lives, children, establish themselves in the society. The societal work was very important despite the fact that the individual problems of each child, whatever the family situation had been, deserved to be heard. It is true that the idea of the subconscious seemed like heresy and that, especially with the Marxists, psychology was not in vogue immediately after the war.

But that was only one aspect of a much wider problem, which was that the entire world generally hid the problems of the survivors. Thus those little ones who had been saved by the devotion of their elders couldn't a fortiori be taken into consideration. The matter was foreclosed with the statement by General de Gaulle on the steps of the City Hall of Paris that revoked the Vichy period with the slogan, "The Republic never ceased to be" and set a priority on reconstituting a national community to counterbalance the power of the Allies. And from that moment on, for political reasons, it was necessary to erase the dark, complex side of Occupied and humiliated France, to cover up the history of French Jews under the Occupation, even that of their being saved or of their contributions to the Resistance. However, my experience shows that what is left unsaid always has disastrous consequences. From the moment of birth, a child is a person.

FIGURE 3.1. Noël, age one, in 1942 with his brother
Benny, age six, and their mother, age thirty-seven.

# 3

# Noël Kuperman

**May 19, 2003**

*Noël Kuperman (son of deportees to Auschwitz, mother returned) introduces himself in this way: "Everything happened so fast. Ten years! The fall of the Berlin Wall, the end of the USSR, Rwanda, Yugoslavia . . . What some have called "the end of history," the end of ideologies? My brother's death, the suicide of his son—my nephew, the illness and death of my partner . . . My voluntary retirement . . . The second Intifada . . . September 11, 2001 . . . Fortunately, I still have that almost daily activity where, among my own kind, I listen and I look, I hear and I see stories of human beings continuously beginning again and yet each unique: the theater, and the students to whom I try to tell the same stories . . . My friends, my cats . . . ."*

*And he cites Kierkegaard:*

> *It happened that a fire broke out backstage in a theater. The clown came out to inform the public. They thought it was a jest and applauded. He repeated his warning, they shouted even louder. So I think the world will come to an end amid general applause from all the wits, who believe it is a joke.*[1]

KUPERMAN: I was born on September 26, 1940, at Rothschild Hospital in Paris in the Twelfth Arrondissement. We lived in the Eleventh Arrondissement, 77 rue des Boulets. I had a brother five years older than I, so there were four of us: my parents, my brother, and I. My father and mother were cousins; they had the same last name: Kuperman.

My father was born, as was my mother, in Szydlowiec, located between Radom and Kielce, in Poland. Both of them later returned to Poland since Szydlowiec is only about two hundred kilometers from Auschwitz.

My father's birth date is not exact, given the deficiencies in the Office of Public Records at the time; I think he was born in 1906. He left home in the early 1920s at the age of fifteen to go to Palestine. There were Zionist sympathizers in the family. He himself was a Marxist-Zionist and a member of Hashomer Hatzair. He spent five or six years working as a pioneer in Palestine, then left and came illegally to France.

My parents knew each other from their childhood because they were cousins. A few years ago I recorded my mother telling the family history. My maternal grandfather sold construction materials. My mother, born in 1910, lost her parents soon after and was adopted by one of her uncles. My grandmother died in an attack worthy of a western movie, except it took place in Eastern Europe. She sold food items and bought her staples in Krakow. One day while returning through the nearby forest, her carriage was attacked by bandits. The coach driver, who smuggled tobacco, did not stop. The bandits fired and my grandmother took a bullet in her belly and died—bled to death—before arriving at the hospital. I know nothing more about my grandparents, paternal or maternal. I didn't know them; they disappeared in Poland.

My mother came to France in 1927 at age seventeen. She had wanted to complete her studies, a difficult thing to do in Poland because of *numerus clausus*. She didn't complete them and learned tailoring. She arrived in Paris on the evening of December 24 at the Gare du Nord and was surprised when the whole family came to meet her at the station in long dresses and costumes. She didn't understand why she received so much attention, but it was simply because they were going to a dance, as they had back then, at the Hôtel Moderne. When she got off the train, my father introduced her to the others as his fiancée, which was a complete surprise. They lived together. My father was a leather cutter and my mother worked in tailoring; she was a finisher. They settled on rue Corbeau. There they lived in one room with the running water and the toilet down the hall and shared with other tenants on their floor. In 1935 my brother was born. Shortly before the war, my mother took him with her back to Poland to see the family. There were a few interesting people, not at all typical, in that family, notably my mother's brother who joined the Bund, and who, dissatisfied with the Bund, joined the Polish Communist Youth. He was noticed by the organization and sent to Moscow to the management school of the Comintern where he stayed three years and where one of his classmates was Léopold Trepper.[2] They were sent together during the twenties or early thirties to Palestine where they founded the Palestinian Communist Party, made up of Jewish, Arab, and Christian militants. My grandfather, who was very religious, was singled out by the community in Szydlowiec as "The Red's father." He wrote to his son to complain about this. My uncle answered saying that he was fighting for a new world, free from oppression, from obscurantism, from racism . . . The grandfather shook his head saying, "Yes, fine, that's a good idea but why take it out on me?"

When Stalin arrested the leadership of the Polish Party, which included a lot of Jews, my uncle was recalled to Moscow in 1938. This is the last time my mother saw him. He had secretly come through Paris, and they simply met in a street, each going along the sidewalk in the opposite direction. He disappeared into the gulag from 1938 to 1956 and was liberated in 1956 after the Twentieth Communist Party Congress. He died in 1957 in Moscow, still a Communist. He had two children: a son, Joseph, and a daughter, Maïa. I tried to find out about the son in Moscow, but I wasn't able to find him. The daughter—mentally ill, it seems—is institutionalized in Poland.

BAILLY: There was no other family in Paris except your parents?

KUPERMAN: Yes, there was my father's brother, a Communist. There was a lot of dissent and accusations between the two of them.

I was born September 26, 1940, and when my father went to register me at City Hall, I was a "beneficiary" of the Statute on Jews instituted on October 3, 1940, so I was born "stateless," not French.

BAILLY: Your parents spoke Yiddish at home?

KUPERMAN: Yes, Yiddish, French, and Polish. They were not known for strong political views. My father was Hashomer Hatzair, so he was a Marxist-Zionist; his brother was a Communist. I think they had a wide range of friends.

BAILLY: In any case, not religious?

KUPERMAN: Within the family or among friends, there were people who went to Spain during the International Brigades. But the full range of opinions was represented. My paternal grandfather in Poland, for example, didn't do any work. He devoted himself to the study of biblical texts, to the *pilpul*. A bit of trivia.

In May 1941 we were living in the Eleventh Arrondissement, beside Place Voltaire. One day my father was summoned to the Japy Gymnasium, with the famous green card. He had enlisted, voluntarily of course, in 1939 and had been decommissioned in 1940. The Gymnasium was near where we lived and he went in his French army uniform, thinking nothing whatsoever could happen to him. He was at the Gymnasium for two days. My mother went to see him the same day or the next to take him a suitcase with some clothing. This was perhaps the last time I saw him. I was nine months old. I have no memory of it aside from what I have been told. He left immediately, two days later, at the beginning of May for Pithiviers internment camp where he was detained for a year. I have reconstituted this chain of events later with my mother. She went to see him twice at Pithiviers, but I don't think I went with her.

My father had been imprisoned at Pithiviers for six to nine months when my mother developed peritonitis. There was a social worker near where we lived who helped us and took care of my mother. Seeing how serious my mother's condition was, she told her she absolutely had to be operated on. My mother refused; she didn't want to be hospitalized if her husband couldn't come to see her. And miracle! I don't know how, but this social worker got my father a week's leave, which was extremely rare. After the war, my mother never was able to find this woman who was clearly in the Resistance. At that time she worked at City Hall in the Eleventh Arrondissement.

BAILLY: Your father should have used his leave to get away!

KUPERMAN: Right. Obviously. But he returned to Pithiviers. My mother was operated on and got out of the hospital. Some time later, the social worker came to see her and asked:

"Your husband left for the country?"

"No. He went back to the camp. The French gendarmes made him sign a statement on his honor that he would return; if not, they would take hostages."

My father still had confidence in the French authorities at that time. Hostages—that could be family or other prisoners. So he returned, which no one understood. My mother saw him twice there and the last time must have been a week before his departure. He left with Convoy Number Four for Auschwitz in June 1942. We continued to live in the same place. We escaped the Vel' d'Hiv' Roundup, but my mother was arrested in December 1943. She went to Drancy where she remained a little more than a month before leaving for Auschwitz with Convoy Number Sixty-Four. A month or two after she got there, she met a friend of the family who, working as an electrical specialist at the camp, was moved from the men's camp to the women's camp. He told her that her husband, our father, was dead and told her exactly how he died. Returning from work detail, he was exhausted and fell. He was severely beaten by the SS.

The death factories were just getting started and not all the crematoria were functioning yet. Stunned but still alive, he was thrown into an open pit to be burned. He died like that. You can imagine how traumatic it was for my mother to learn about the death of her husband a month or two after her arrival at the camps in February 1944.

BAILLY: How had she been arrested?

KUPERMAN: In her home, at night—apparently from a list. (It wasn't the concierge who turned her in; she contented herself with pillaging all she could from the apartment.)

Before her arrest, at the beginning of December 1943, it had already become more and more dangerous, but she had continued to work. There was a neighbor in the apartment where we lived (rue des Boulets), a Catholic, who took care of us, my eight-year-old brother and me, age three, while my mother worked away from home.

BAILLY: She didn't want to put you out in the country to hide you?

KUPERMAN: Earlier, no. But later, yes. She has since told me that, aware of the general climate about that time, she had a kind of dream, a premonition one night. I think we were also helped by the Social Services for the Protection and Defense of Children, located on rue Amelot. Henri Bulawko, who is now secretary of the Friends of Auschwitz, was an activist there. With their financial assistance, my mother entrusted us to a neighbor, Madame Viamant, who knew us very well. She was a Breton so she sent us to her family in Bretagne. I have no memory of it, but that's what I have been told. My mother wanted to go with us by subway to the Gare Montparnasse. She was carrying me in her arms; I was three. Madame Viamant—who saved us—told her it had become too dangerous for the children in Paris, and because my mother wore the star and there were Germans in the subway, she should not come with us to the station. Apparently, I started to howl at the moment my mother resigned herself to handing me over to this neighbor. I made her pay for this "abandonment" later.

We were then hidden, from early December 1943, in Bretagne. I don't know where—not far from Quimper, I think, in the country, with country people who were fairly poor. They had a son; I don't know if he was a prisoner. They were extraordinary. I have no memory of it but my brother told me that they were very good. The lady was little deaf; she had an ear horn. They were simple country people; life was very hard for them.

Sometimes the husband drank a little (this explains why I never drink alcohol) and when he was drunk, he would open the shutters and say, "Tomorrow, I'm going to denounce them." We weren't very far from a *Kommandantur.* I was three or four years old and my brother was eight or nine. When the husband was in that condition, the wife had a solution. She would give him even more to drink and put him to bed and the next day there would be no problem.

I think denouncing us would have been equally dangerous for them. And they were extraordinary. Having heard that had some importance for me, I think . . . A year later, it had become too dangerous for them as well as for us. My brother and I left Bretagne and we went, always with the family of that neighbor, to Charente, near Cognac. The war ended and we returned to Paris in 1945. Some of the deportees came back.

BAILLY: During that time your mother, who had been picked up at home, had been sent to Drancy, then to Auschwitz?

KUPERMAN: At Drancy she experienced something absolutely "ignoble" (in quotation marks because it's easy for us, now, to judge). A detail about the context first: In certain cases the interned Jews would give some information to the French guards (gendarmes), hoping no doubt for privileged treatment or the possibility of being spared deportation. I think at the time, things were starting to become known. So a Jew asked my mother where her children were. She said she had abandoned them. She didn't say where we were. She was violently beaten. But until her arrival at Auschwitz, she managed to keep a photo of my brother and me, which was confiscated as soon as she arrived there.

My mother returned from Auschwitz.

My father died there under the circumstances I told you about, but my mother returned after several detours. She was at Auschwitz until the approach of the Red Army in February 1945; from Auschwitz, she made the "death march" (toward the west), which took her to Ravensbrück; and from Ravensbrück on to Neustadt-Glewin where she was finally liberated by the Red Army in May of 1945.

At Auschwitz, where she had seen Mengele up close, she had escaped selection twice, with a pretty amazing story. At the camp one day as she was coming from work or during a summons she heard someone call out to her in Polish. It was a Polish deportee whom my mother knew who was working in the camp kitchens. She had been a maid in the family! She gave my mother some food, some garlic, which helped her live for a while—to survive rather, to orient herself.

My mother had to do all kinds of work there; she worked in the Weberei—the textile mill where they made braids from old rags[3]—and with the metal recycling. She was sick—she had typhus; she was bitten on the leg by a dog. A French medical doctor treated her. I think it was February 1945 when she left on this "death march." So she was at Auschwitz from the end of January or beginning of February 1944 until the end of February 1945. After her liberation by the Red Army at Neustad-Glewin, she was repatriated to France.

BAILLY: Overall, what was it that let her survive at Auschwitz?

KUPERMAN: She wasn't politically connected, not part of any network. It was her strong constitution, her resilience that saved her. She was young at the time; she was thirty-three. But no one can say exactly why she survived. Today at age ninety-two, she is still independent. I see her very regularly several times a week. And she says to me, at least once a week, "Why did I return and not your father?"

BAILLY: Did she start a new life?

KUPERMAN: Yes. It was another chapter of her life story, as well as of ours. In 1949 she married again. He was a former deportee. She didn't really want to. My older brother persuaded her a bit and her friends said to her, "You'll see, he's a former deportee . . ." He had lost his wife and three children in the deportation. He was a deportee for a long time because he was one of the first to leave for Auschwitz. I called him "Papa." I was ten years old. It was good until the birth of my half brother; then it deteriorated. I have spent years trying to understand why. I love Shakespeare a lot but I don't particularly like *Hamlet* (it's my personal psychological work). It didn't go very well for the two of them, but they stayed together anyway. He died about ten years ago.

BAILLY: Did your mother have any aftereffects from her deportation?

KUPERMAN: Yes. She was given one hundred percent disability: lots of cardiovascular problems, bone loss, problems with sleeping, vision, and her lungs.

BAILLY: How did she get you back?

KUPERMAN: When she returned, she notified that neighbor I called "Nina," Madame Viamant (who has been dead for a long time now) and she had us sent back to Paris. My first memories aren't very early ones; I don't remember getting together, but I know my mother came to that neighbor's place when we returned from the countryside. She had spent some time in the hospital first but her hair was still very short; she was ill, very thin. She has always been small but she weighed only thirty kilos when she was liberated.

BAILLY: She went through Hôtel Lutétia?[4]

KUPERMAN: Yes, of course. When we were face to face—especially me, not so much my brother—I rejected her. I told her, "No, you are not my mother, you are sick. My mother was beautiful!" It was a year before I would live with her. To get even. I resented this whole situation as if she had abandoned me.

About ten years ago, I made a long recording of my mother speaking in Yiddish (I have always refused to practice Yiddish, but I have always understood it spoken). I express myself in bad German—I lived for a year in East Germany—and as I get older Yiddish is coming back, but that's another story. So I recorded her speaking Yiddish to tell the family history.

To be honest, my relationship with the entire family has always been very distant.

BAILLY: Including your mother?

KUPERMAN: Yes. I certainly have feelings for her because she's my mother, but that's all. These feelings are not "natural" and it's the same for the rest of the family. I spent time trying to understand all that. There is a whole time period that remains very deeply buried, repressed in me within a thick shell. I have tried to think it through because it is a subject that interests me on a personal level. I definitely think this distant relationship is tied to the feeling of abandonment I felt as a child.

BAILLY: Because your mother left you in the country with someone else?

KUPERMAN: Yes. I was three years old. My brother was eight; he had known our father. For me, at three, my mother was "taken" from me.

BAILLY: You held it against her?

KUPERMAN: I think I still do. Of course, I don't hold it against her any longer, but it is something that explains our relationship. When I tell this to my friends, some of them call me a monster. I am not a monster—perhaps I am—but I repeat, it's called "abandonment."

BAILLY: It is irrational, but it was your experience as a baby?

KUPERMAN: Yes, certainly. It was certainly not deliberate on my part or hers (even though she said at Drancy, when someone asked where we were, that she had abandoned us; that's completely different!). But for me it was abandonment. I believed I had a heavy burden to carry.

At the end of a year, in 1946, my brother and I went to live with her again. She started to work again. We found the apartment emptied, except what that neighbor, having broken the seals at one time, had amazingly been able to save and hide. She gave everything back to my mother when we returned.

BAILLY: Your mother, alone with two children, took up her sewing again?

KUPERMAN: Yes, 1946, '47, '48. Then I think she resigned herself to the marriage because she couldn't handle things alone any longer. She said it herself; it had become too hard for her. She did the maximum but there were food problems at that time. She put my brother and me in school. We felt entitled to everything, with a few incidents that explain my bad attitude. Here's one: during the war we had fake papers. Our name was Pernod (which is funny because ever since I have hated all the anise-flavored drinks; it took some time to understand why). My brother and I were then vaccinated with our fake identities. When things returned to normal, we took back our names. My mother tried to prove our vaccinations with the old papers. But the school nurse said they were invalid. So I had to have vaccinations again. And in spite of that, I still got diphtheria!

BAILLY: Why is your first name "Noël"?

KUPERMAN: It took me a while to figure that out. Actually, my name in Hebrew is Noah, Noïel in Yiddish, like my grandfather, that is

to say, Noah. I think there are several possible explanations for this first
name "Noël." First of all, when my father went to register me as Noah,
Noïel, Noé Kuperman, it was either somewhat redundant or the civil
servant misunderstood and heard "Noël." Another reason: Working
backward from my birthday (a certain September 26), it is nine months
after December 25. Finally, there is my mother's arrival in Paris, one
evening on December 24. It was evidently not by chance, even if my
mother . . .

BAILLY: Okay, now let's pick up the chronology again. Your mother
remarried, four of you are living together: your mother, your stepfather,
your brother, and you.

KUPERMAN: Afterward, it was a little difficult. She remarried in
1949. Then there was the birth of our half brother in November of the
same year. The family situation deteriorated. I was surely not an easy
child.

BAILLY: Already a fatherless child . . .

KUPERMAN: Yes, and with other things that it took a while for me
to understand. Up to the age of fifteen, I had the same dream every
night, with a sun—or a red disc—that appeared; it is a classic parental
image. I have to say that for a long time I waited for my father. Luckily,
my mother told us right away what had happened to him. She was one
of those who spoke quite early.

BAILLY: But you didn't want to accept it?

KUPERMAN: I waited for my father's return until age fifteen.

BAILLY: You didn't believe her?

KUPERMAN: That's right. With this same dream recurring every
night. There was a kind of continuous replay of the betrayal scene
(from Hamlet). My father was the big story of my mother's life; she's the
one who says so. Taking into account the difficulties, her health problems, she agreed to remarry and it quickly disintegrated—not only for
us, but for her, too, especially after the birth of our half brother. I was a
bit of a black sheep in the family. I was going on fifteen when I left
home the first time. I wasn't a runaway, but I went to see a girl from
school. I used to go to the summer camp of the youth center on rue
Amelot, at Berck-Plage, then to those of the CCE on rue Paradis. I was
also going to the youth centers of the UJRE. Charles Zelwer and I met
there. But at first, I went to the youth center on rue Amelot. At that time
there was no school on Thursdays. I went to this center with a lot of

resentment because on Thursdays the other kids played soccer or went to the movies, and I still had to go to "school." We were learning Yiddish, and what they called at the time "Palestinography" at this youth center sponsored by the OSE. I agitated some; I started some strikes.

BAILLY: Your family's desire to have you regain your Jewish cultural identity made you rebel against this kind of tutoring?

KUPERMAN: There were several stages. At first, it was a refusal of who we were, we children, because of what had happened to us.

BAILLY: You mean Jewishness, that curse?

KUPERMAN: Yes. Very soon afterward, I found my place more easily with the revelation of a much wider, political world that did not deny our past, but put it in perspective.

BAILLY: How did this revelation come about?

KUPERMAN: Being at the CCE youth center had already revealed to us that we were not the only ones to have lived what we had experienced. As Jews we were numerous, our personal story was in fact a common story, but beyond that, the broadening came about from coming into contact with the world, then with the collective endeavors, all within the framework of the UJRF. Some months later, I joined the Communist Party. I was fifteen years old.

BAILLY: So you were a rebellious youth, looking for an opportunity?

KUPERMAN: Rebellious inside the family unit because of conflicts with my stepfather and with my brother (he died of illness four years ago) who had chosen another path. He was responsible for "menial tasks." My stepfather, who worked from home, made leather clothing and my brother worked with him. My brother was his "secular arm" when he wanted to punish me. His youth was completely ruined. Our stepfather was frustrated and made my brother work twelve hours a day at the machine. It was not uplifting. It is also because of this atmosphere that I left home the first time to go to find this friend from the camp at Nancy that I spoke of. She was in the same situation as I with parents who had been deported. I came home from Nancy with the cops. My parents had found me—my mother, who opened my mail, had read a letter from this girl. Contrary to lots of children who cried when they went to summer camp, I loved it and cried when I came home.

During all these years, I went to school in the Tenth Arrondissement, alongside the Gare de l'Est. At the junior high level I took an exam in math to advance a grade and flunked it. I was then returned to elementary school and was put into a class that was called "pre-apprenticeship." We had ten hours a week of shop and I went on to complete junior high. Then I began to play hooky and to have a very irregular scholastic record, with subjects where I did well (French, languages, history) and other subjects where I did nothing (math, physics, chemistry). I selected my subjects at school and I began to skip the classes that didn't interest me. There was a math teacher whom we called "Führer"; he was Alsatian. I remember one day when he made me go to the blackboard for a quiz. I was incapable of answering. He asked me, "What do you want to do in life?" "I want to write." He then had this magnificent response: "Do cows write literature?"

There was also political activism. It was the time of the Algerian War. We sold *l'Avant Garde*, the newspaper of the UJRF, at the Gare de l'Est on Saturdays. (Charles was with us.) One day the English teacher came by and saw us selling it. I knew he was a member of the Communist Party. I saw him again not long after and he told me that in the faculty meeting Führer had said, "Yes, Kuperman, that dirty little Jew!" The teachers argued. The Führer came into the class, and said first thing, "Kuperman, outside!" Then I was sent into a vacant classroom with books. That's when I read the most. There was also a decidedly secular literature teacher, Monsieur Bonavita. A former Socialist Resister, he was an extraordinary guy who dressed in a corduroy carpenter's outfit and cleaned his ears with a safety pin. In tears, he had us read the text by Hugo about the man sentenced to death. I was doing some writing of my own. I wrote my essays in free verse, very influenced by the poet Jacques Prévert. There was a teacher called Arnaud who knew the people at *Lettres françaises*. He gave them my texts. They didn't publish them (I was only fifteen years old), but they found them interesting and told me I should continue. I left the school system fairly early; I was fifteen and one-half years old.

BAILLY: For you school was optional?

KUPERMAN: To a certain extent, yes. But the summer camps were for me the great moments of my life.

BAILLY: Your first loves, too?

KUPERMAN: Yes, sure. Furthermore, there were teachers who were absolutely stunning, mixtures of Makarenko, Korczak, and Piaget. Extraordinary people, Crypto-Communists or Communists. I met my first surrogate father, also a "hidden child," ten years older than I, who was a counselor at CCE, Gabriel Garran, the founder of the Théâtre de la Commune d'Aubervilliers. When I played hooky, I would go to his place. It was winter; we would freeze with the cold. I also found theater fairly soon, in the summer camps. After having left school, at age seventeen I left home for good. I had to earn my living. I was an apprentice typesetter, a career I had chosen. It interested me. I wanted to be a corrections editor. In the printing business, there were two branches: Labor and the Press. The corrections editors were the ones who worked the least.

I worked for more than two years as an apprentice typographer, and gradually became acquainted with Garran and this extraordinary universe of the theater, for several reasons. Much later I learned that my father had been fanatically passionate about the theater, opera, and exhibitions, that he loved live performance. He was a proletarian though. My mother told me that sometimes he would come home from work and say he wasn't very hungry. She understood immediately that he had tickets to go to the theater. There is also an anecdote about him that my mother is not very proud of. She noticed that he would get home late and leave early in the morning for work. One day, she followed him—to the workshop. He was teaching another worker to read and write, while my mother had convinced herself he was having an affair!

As for me, books contributed a great deal toward helping me live through this period. I read continually at home; I read at the table. Was I self-taught? More or less, because there were the centers where the counselors guided our choices. They were truly great teachers. Thanks to them I discovered Neruda, Hikmet, and other poets. There were representatives of every field among the leaders of the center. Above all, I was happy; I met Garran, the theater. So at about age eighteen, I gave up typography. At one time, one of the counselors of the camp was a painter and I became very attached to painting. I went to all the exhibitions, the museums; it was my first phase. Then, I had my film phase. I was going to movies several times a day.

BAILLY: Art was a path to freedom?

KUPERMAN: It was mostly the theater. This is still the case because I go at least five times a week.

BAILLY: Do you perform also?

KUPERMAN: No, I performed a little at the center but very quickly became interested in the technical aspects.

BAILLY: Directing?

KUPERMAN: No, technical direction. I began to work regularly in the theater. Then in 1961 the Théâtre de la Commune d'Aubervilliers and the Festival d'Aubervilliers were founded. I worked eleven years at Aubervilliers.

BAILLY: Full time, professionally?

KUPERMAN: Yes, that was my job. I did everything; I was technician, electrician, stage manager in other theaters. I did stage set construction, I put up all the sets and I was technical director of the Théâtre de la Commune d'Aubervilliers until 1971.

BAILLY: You were at Aubervilliers in May 1968?

KUPERMAN: Yes, I didn't move around much. Everything was on strike and I was busy finding gasoline for the personnel and the performances.

BAILLY: There was a lot of activity?

KUPERMAN: Yes. Lots of actors; various artists who had worked with us came to see us. They wanted to do a lot of things, to perform in the factories where there were sit-ins, and because we were very structured, we organized these performances with committees from the company and the unions. I was still in the Communist Party at that time. I left it in 1980 because of Afghanistan.

BAILLY: Before, in the Communist Party, you protested Hungary, Czechoslovakia?

KUPERMAN: Hungary didn't pose any problems for me; I was sixteen. Czechoslovakia gave me more of a problem. But what made me leave the Party was the intervention at the time of Afghanistan by Marchais on direction from Moscow, and the removal of the leadership of the Federation of Paris,[5] whom I knew from having worked there during major cultural and political demonstrations.

BAILLY: Did you keep this long fidelity to the Party as a substitute for a family?

KUPERMAN: Obviously. The Party was my family, my church, my school. I think there were several reasons for my fidelity, but among them, there was the desire not to be singled out, but to be a member of a larger totality, to be like everyone else, with a collective goal.

BAILLY: Did you marry?

KUPERMAN: I lived for about two years with Fiterman's sister, whom I met at the Center when I was a counselor. She was a nurse. Her name was Irène; she was four years older than I.

Much later, in 1961, I happened to be doing stage construction in a little theater in Paris with an Argentinean Jew older than I, who had come to France in 1949 at the time of Perón. He had been married and was separated from his wife and she and I started living together in 1964, after a major tour in Algeria with the Théâtre de la Commune d'Aubervilliers at the invitation of the Théâtre National Algérien where we performed Shakespeare's *Coriolanus*. She, too, was named Irène and was sixteen years older than I. It is not insignificant that I chose women who are older. We were together for thirty-six years—a great love—and she died from an illness three years ago.

BAILLY: You had no children. Was that intentional?

KUPERMAN: No. She couldn't have children. At the beginning, she was an actress with Louis Jouvet. I have a photo of her performing in Jouvet's production of *Tartuffe*. She was also a writer and wrote eight books. After living together these thirty-six years, she died, abandoning me treacherously, permanently. In a certain way, it is a kind of replay in my life, an echo of a previous abandonment. We had no children; we had cats. I've been alone for three years now.

BAILLY: If we now go back a few decades to when you started your career, your passion for the theater . . .

KUPERMAN: I was perfectly happy.

BAILLY: Financially, it wasn't always easy?

KUPERMAN: No. I left Aubervilliers in 1971. I took some time to "kill" my first substitute father. I have had others, even if I didn't know them; I'm thinking of the great authors like Shakespeare or Brecht. In March or April of 1971 we had organized, with two other theaters of the Parisian area, Saint-Denis and Nanterre, a production with the Berliner Ensemble of three plays by Brecht: *Les Jours de la Commune*, that we performed in Saint-Denis; *La Mère*, that we performed in Nanterre—it was the last time that Hélène Weigel performed, she died a month later in East Berlin—and *Le Commerce du Pain* at Aubervilliers. I took charge of direction and technical organization for the French side for the three theaters. It was a big production: one hundred forty people of the Berliner Ensemble took part. We were at Nanterre, at mealtime, in a little working-class restaurant. Hélène Weigel came and asked me if I was "Napo." (Napo has been my nickname since summer camp in 1955. Maybe I had grand ambitions then. I also wore my hair like Marlon Brando—*Julius Cesar, On the Waterfront* . . . and this nickname became my name in the theater.) She invited me to come to work with the Berliner Ensemble for a year. It was a fabulous dream—even if it was like the story the grandmother in Woyzzeck tells of the child who arrives on the moon and notices that it is a dead star. I left Aubervilliers and Irène and I went to spend ten months in East Berlin in September 1971. I worked as a trainee with the technical director of the Berliner Ensemble. I was perfectly happy, even when confronted with certain things that I didn't want to see. Like Mauriac, I liked Germany so much that I was glad there were two of them. In fact I needed *another* Germany, and Berlin was, at least partially, another Germany. (See the book by Régine Robin, *Chantiers berlinois*.) I met a lot of people, not just in the theater. I was happy, especially at the Berliner. It was a time when there was openness in politics, and it was also the time of the inter-German accords. For obvious reasons, since German is spoken in some places, I speak German. We have a common history. I know a little about German dramatic literature. I also like authors like Büchner, Kleist, and Brecht. I was very happy there for about a year. Then I returned to France.

On my return, I had several offers of work from people whom I had come across several times in my professional life, like Jourdheuil and Vincent of the Théâtre of L'Espérance, or Jean-Marie Serreau, with whom Irène had worked as an actress. She had left Jouvet to go to work with him. Then a young man I had heard about and who had brought certain performances to Aubervilliers that he had taken to the Festival at Nancy, Jack Lang, had just been named director of the Théâtre de Chaillot (it was in June 1972). I was the first person he hired at Chaillot. I was technical director for him, for Vitez, and for Dupavillon during the time they were at Chaillot, and even afterward. It was my highest position in the professional hierarchy. When Lang was fired by Michel Guy, I wanted to leave Chaillot, too, and not just to indicate my solidarity with Lang. But Lang and Ralite asked me to stay at Chaillot.[6] I stayed about a year, and then I left. From that time on, I never again took a permanent position in a professional theater.

BAILLY: What did you do politically after leaving the Communist Party in 1980?

KUPERMAN: I continued to be militant. In any case, between the extreme militancy (which Charles also experienced) and the time when the Théâtre de la Commune d'Aubervilliers was established, militant activism moved to the field of professional theater, because we were fighting for a different theater.

BAILLY: Did you ever have any connection with Gatti?

KUPERMAN: Yes. The history of the Théâtre de la Commune d'Aubervilliers actually started with Gatti at the MJC across from the Fort d'Aubervilliers where Gatti came to read *Chant public devant deux chaises électriques*[7] in 1961, prior to the Festival. It was a comfortable environment.

BAILLY: Did you take part in the whole adventure of the theater of the avant-garde?

KUPERMAN: Yes, more than avant-garde, the whole popular theater movement, of cultural decentralization. Aubervilliers was the first permanent theater to open in the outskirts of Paris. Then came Saint-Denis, Nanterre.

BAILLY: You were a creator, a theoretician of this type of theater?

KUPERMAN: Practitioner.

BAILLY: You are now teaching?

KUPERMAN: I very soon moved beyond the technical; I said so recently at France-Culture, on the program *Passage du Témoin,* with Lucien Attoun. At Aubervilliers I was technical director, but I was able to convince Garran and the administration that my going as a spectator to see performances other than those produced in our company was part of my work as technical director. The technical part interests me because of what it allows, as a part of the whole.

BAILLY: What do you teach at Nanterre University?

KUPERMAN: Introduction to technical theater, in the first year.

BAILLY: That doesn't involve a theoretical approach?

KUPERMAN: I am not at all a theorist. But there is another aspect of my work that is important. After Aubervilliers, with René Allio—who was first a painter, then a scene designer for Planchon, and later a film and television producer—I became involved with the conception of space and in the transformation of the former Festival area into the Théâtre de la Commune. In 1968 I met a group that had just transformed the Théâtre Sarah Bernhardt into the Théâtre de la Ville. It included two architects, Fabre and Perrottet, from the first multidisciplinary team to be formed in France in the field of architecture: the Workshop for Urbanism and Architecture. I worked with them as a technical consultant on theater construction projects from my knowledge of theater space. They remodeled Chaillot during the time Lang was there; they built Sartrouville, the Théâtre de la Colline, Ivry—twenty-some projects. At the end of the 1960s, I had three things going: technical work in theater and for political and cultural events like the L'Huma Festival, a little teaching (before going to Germany I taught for two years at the Université de Vincennes), and then in 1978 I joined the group at the Université Paris X-Nanterre, and finally this technical consultancy with the architects for construction or renovation of theaters.

BAILLY: What does theater actually mean in your life?

KUPERMAN: Why theater? When one is dissatisfied with the state of the world, what is more exhilarating, more inspiring than contributing to the production of these ephemeral prototypes known as theater productions? The theater was also my school. I have had several schools and at the same time, at about fifteen-sixteen years old, "crutches." At fifteen, I thought it wasn't worth continuing to live. I had quite a few suicidal thoughts. At the right time I found both political engagement (the Party, militancy) and theater activity. These two things have been my university, my family, and have even given me the possibility of conceiving representations of the world, of utopias. I haven't yet finished with all that. At the present time, happily, I have theater. When I was about fifty years old, in the 1990s, I had difficulties. My generalist sent me to a neuropsychiatrist who diagnosed me as manic-depressive and treated me very effectively for ten years with lithium. I stopped taking it in January of 2000.

BAILLY: Do you feel fairly well?

KUPERMAN: No, not at all. I stopped in January 2000 after having talked about it to the neuropsychiatrist who was convinced that I was in analysis because I talked about it. He didn't believe in analysis; he was a chemist. He retired and left me the address of a replacement. Things were going pretty well and after consulting my generalist, I stopped. I have not taken it up again since. So I am no longer manic-depressive, but simply depressive. I think it's connected to my partner's death three years ago. I feel a great solitude. I think the causes are multiple: age . . .

BAILLY: To what do you attribute this temperament? Do you think it is more "constitutional" or more "historical," given your family history?

KUPERMAN: I have no way of knowing if it is genetic. Clearly my mother shows no sign of anything similar. But for the rest of the family, out of sixty-four people there were eight survivors, in Poland or here, so . . . The neuropsychiatrist thought it was purely organic. He had me talk at first. For him personal histories have little importance.

BAILLY: The loss of your father wasn't relevant to him?

KUPERMAN: No, he thought it was all organic.

BAILLY: What do you think?

KUPERMAN: I think it's both. It's a heavy load to carry, even if I manage to do so. Around age fifty, I practiced a kind of primitive, personal therapy—if that exists. Theater played a role in it; a friend with whom I worked (my last play: *Le Prince de Hombourg*), a director from East Germany, Matthias Langhoff, wasn't well himself at the time. He staged a play at Bobigny, a collage entitled *Si de là-bas, si loin* with a poem of Hölderlin; *Hughie*, a little, rarely performed play by O'Neill; *Chimère*, a little play never performed by Lorca; and *La Dernière Bande* by Beckett. Several times Langhoff came to dinner with me fairly late in the evening, after the rehearsals. He is a brilliant intellectual trained by Hans Eisler (his father had been the equivalent to Gérard Philippe in Germany before 1933). He had been a refugee in Zurich, a creator of Brecht plays during the war, and had returned to East Germany to direct the equivalent of the Comédie Française, the Deutches Theater, in Berlin. One day I asked if he believed in self-analysis. After a long silence, he answered, "Yes, but that depends on the analyst . . ." This was not just a joke. I had never done analysis, but it is not a foreign universe to me. I did personal psychological work. I was a workaholic during the years of my career. It was an avoidance technique, but everything you think you have handled or that you think you can live with comes up again with age. There was this episode, at about age fifty, when I was not well and so I started that therapy.

BAILLY: This provides a transition to what I'm going to ask you now: what connection do you see between your most deeply held values as a middle-aged adult and those traumas tied to your hidden, ruined, scarred, fatherless childhood? What can you say to society about this? What lessons, whether political, moral, creative, do you draw from them? What message would you want to pass on to the next generation?

KUPERMAN: I believe the most important thing for me was the passage from the individual to the general, the fact of not being alone, of not considering my story as a unique story, but putting it into relation with history, with—when I'm well enough—a greater attention given to what happens in the world, including at the present time the Israeli-Palestinian conflict, something which, for me, is very painful.

BAILLY: Does your universality come more from your Jewishness or is the opposite true? How do you put the two together?

KUPERMAN: I declare myself to be culturally Jewish, only culturally, but not religiously, even though I spent a short time with the Jewish Boy Scouts of France. What I was looking for there was more the collective effort, being a member of a group more than the practice of a faith. I am an atheist. What does it mean to be Jewish, in these circumstances? What has been transmitted? What is my life story and what has it produced? In any case, judge me to be happy with my story because I have no other choice, so I make do with it. But as to how that helps me or doesn't help me live and try to understand how the world works . . .

BAILLY: Exactly, beyond the Shoah . . .

KUPERMAN: I don't like the word "Shoah."

BAILLY: It's better than "Holocaust . . ."

KUPERMAN: Yes. The title from Hilberg[8] seems to me the most appropriate.

BAILLY: The "Destruction"?

KUPERMAN: Yes. Even though I find the work of Lanzmann absolutely outstanding, I am strongly against regarding as sacred or memorializing the destruction of European Jews, and notably (belatedly as well) the use made of it in Israel. I read *Le Septième Million* by Tom Segev; there the manipulation is completely . . .

BAILLY: But then, beyond this history tied to the destruction of European Jews, when you say "culturally," is it a matter of distance, in other words, an individual Diasporic view, say of political battle, of solidarity, of rebellion, of aspiration for justice? How do you define this cultural Jewishness?

KUPERMAN: There are different moments. I think that as a child, I played on the pity, the pain, the victimization, and I had clearly understood how one could draw support from it. It was an excellent means, a crutch. That was over for me very quickly. What matters to me the most—and also because of this Germanophilia, this taste for the German language and for the German authors—is to try to understand how it was possible. Exceptionality certainly, but relative exceptionality.

I often come against this with members of the family. I have a cousin who was born in Palestine, whom I like to hassle because on her identity papers there is "Place of birth: Palestine." She is the daughter of my father's brother who was a Communist and who escaped deportation. He was hidden in the Creuse near Guéret. Every time I see her, at weddings or other events, I confront her, "Yes, okay, but how do you react in relation to Rwanda?" Maybe a pain that is too great makes one insensitive to the pain of another.

BAILLY: What about you personally?

KUPERMAN: I try to avoid making it personal and to put it in perspective, even if I know this history all too well from reading about it. Putting it in perspective interests me.

BAILLY: Does this past, according to you, give us a special responsibility?

KUPERMAN: Yes and that also involves communicating our story. It's something I do; I don't force it but I think that at the end of two or three classes at the University, my students know completely who I am, where I'm coming from. I speak freely about it.

BAILLY: So what is your message? What are the "lessons"?

KUPERMAN: I don't have a message; I am not someone who delivers a message. I think what is most important is never to be satisfied with the appearance of things but to try to understand how such events happened and how they could happen again.

BAILLY: The mechanics of Evil.

KUPERMAN: Yes. That's why I like, for example, the works of Braumann and Sivan about Eichmann: *Éloge de la désobéissance*. In *Si c'est un homme* by Primo Levi, there are two things that seem very important to me. At one point when he is at a camp, at the lab at Buna-Monowiez, he asks an officer, "Warum?" ("But why?"). And the officer replies, "Hier ist kein warum." ("Here there is no 'why.'") Primo Levi often spoke in Italian high schools before committing suicide, which bothers me a great deal. How is it that two men with different pasts, histories, vocations—he and Bettelheim—ended up in the same way?

BAILLY: Bettelheim, whose status has somewhat crumbled these days . . .

KUPERMAN: Yes, but it doesn't matter. What can be said about the method of suicide he chose: putting his head in a plastic bag and suffocating himself? He had been deported one year and released at a time

when the Nazis were releasing people because they knew they were
. . . That's also what happened to Langhoff's father, the author of *Chant
des Marais*.[9] The Nazis thought it was more interesting to release a certain number who would take up the political work and they could then
arrest even more people. That's why Langhoff went to Zurich on the
advice of the Party. He wrote the first book that came out about the
camps. Someone said to Primo Levi, during an interview after the war,
that the Nazis were monsters. To which Primo Levi said that some were
certainly monstrous, but that the majority were like all of us. Later, on
the other hand, there was the discovery (belated) of the gulag. How
could this great utopia produce the gulag? As Heiner Müller said, "Communism, a necessary utopia and one of the catastrophes of the twentieth century . . ." This question interests me, perhaps because part of the
responsibility is mine—even if I was not directly implicated—by the
fact of having belonged to the Communist Party: my own blindness. To
what extent, to different degrees, is each of us perhaps also responsible? Beyond the typical self-hatred . . .

BAILLY: Self-hatred: what do you think about that? Is it something
that follows you or is it a false problem?

KUPERMAN: I think it is a false problem concerning me. Self-hatred
exists, but to my mind it is not specific to Jews. Self-hatred can exist in
anyone just from being human, because life is difficult. And now is a
time when I am not feeling very well. There are enough certainties or
collective projects that are crumbling, and being alone—having lived
through one more abandonment at the age of sixty—is a little hard.
Mornings, I ask myself, why get up?

BAILLY: It's worth it, even just to tell all this; it is important!

KUPERMAN: When I am well, that is what I tell myself, and furthermore that's why this pedagogic activity is very important for me. I am a
little like Zazie; since I don't have children, I can mess up other
people's children.

BAILLY: So, in conclusion, what would you like to add?

KUPERMAN: One of my students called me today to ask me for a
quote from Shakespeare for some work she was doing about Heiner
Müller. I find the following quotation good in my present situation. (I
really like quotations, because they let us get to the point more quickly.
Why not use what others have said so much better than we could ever
say it?) It is from Act Five, Scene five of *Macbeth*: "Life, a tale of a

madman, told by an idiot, full of sound and fury, signifying nothing." It is a little depressing but right now, and temporarily I hope, I am a little depressed.

BAILLY: You're the one saying life is absurd! I beg to differ because what you have told us is anything but absurd.

KUPERMAN: Yes, but on another level, at my level, that's what I try to tell my mother who has been crying over the death of her oldest son for four years now (he was going on sixty-five): "Yes, but it's amazing! He might have left with a little cardboard label and a string around his neck in 1942, '43, '44. But it didn't happen. Yes, he died at age sixty-four, but he *lived* sixty-four years." It's the same story for me; I have lived until now.

BAILLY: You've created, left a mark.

KUPERMAN: I took part in things that have had a certain importance in the history of theater, it's true. I was lucky enough to meet people who helped me live and try to understand and discover things. Furthermore, I transmitted these things a little in my own way. It is a beautiful victory. If one considers the July 16, 1942 Roundup as a normal deadline, I have lived sixty-one years extra. It's amazing. As for my present disenchantment, is it genetic or tied to my personal history? Good question. It is true that there is a little sadness as I face the crumbling away, the end of major projects, which is not to say that the battle is over. With age, it's not bitterness but a little bit of realism perhaps. It is painful to think how few means are available to any of us to influence what happens in the world.

BAILLY: It's true. But for the future, you don't think one can act collectively?

KUPERMAN: Yes we can, even if this action has little effect. I took part in a great number of demonstrations for Chechnya—we were unfortunately only a thousand at Beaubourg two months ago—or against the war in Iraq. I continue to go to the theater; I think it is still necessary for me as I haven't finished my therapy. What has changed perhaps, relative to the time when I was sixteen, seventeen, eighteen years old, is that then I would say, "*I am* a Communist." Now I would say "*we*." Perhaps my partner later helped me to become lucid; she was very good at highlighting my contradictions, even if she also revealed her own. Now, I *try* to be a Communist.

BAILLY: Internationalist?

KUPERMAN: Yes, even if I am no longer a member of the Party, it doesn't matter. It is not the end of history or of ideologies. Can I use what I have experienced, which constitutes the essential part of my life story, to help me understand the world? And if I can't, what a waste!

I no longer hate my stepfather. In my naïveté I thought the experience of the concentration camp, in certain cases, could be a school, could help him understand how the world operates. When I was young, I thought that he didn't understand anything; he was racist, anti-Polish, anti-Arab. Now I can understand why he was like that, but at the same time, his blindness after his experience made me say, perhaps a little too harshly, that the Nazis had won with him.

BAILLY: They partly won maybe, but not completely.

KUPERMAN: One thing always surprises me, and yet I strongly believe it (it is even one of the reasons for my political engagement, even though it was at the same time a blindness): The camp survivors, at the liberation of the camps—whether they liberated themselves like at Buchenwald or by the arrival of the Allies—made a solemn pledge: "Never again!" Yet later the Soviet concentration camps were discovered (belatedly by some of us), there was Cambodia, Rwanda, and all the events that we have learned about recently! Even if the comparison is not exact, the repetition can't be measured in terms of millions of individuals.

BAILLY: Your lucidity and realism are tough . . .

KUPERMAN: A little bitterness, a little sadness.

BAILLY: With which one can only agree, but it doesn't erase the freshness and the force of your convictions. I think what's important is what one retains.

KUPERMAN: Yes, and other issues: how to make each individual try to understand how the world operates; how to demonstrate the right to open one's mouth to protest about specific situations in everyday language and not just in great revolutionary rhetoric? What do the lives of human beings in collectivity produce? With all that is possible, how do we go about refusing what is unacceptable? How is it that the unacceptable reappears in such varied forms—genocide, illegal immigrants, but also the humiliation of others in daily life? Of course, I am active on behalf of the undocumented; I had godsons, one from Mali, one from Mauritania. When they asked me why I was doing this, I explained to them it's because of what happened to me. Others did the same and even more for me and it is what has allowed me to be here, alive and speaking.

BAILLY: If you like, we could end with the positive sense of all these projects . . .

KUPERMAN: . . . that my malaise puts a perspective on just the same. To the Yiddish saying: *"s'ez schwer tse zaïn a Yd"* (It's difficult to be a Jew!), I like to add: "It's difficult to be a human being!"[10]

FIGURE 4.1. Francis at age four, in 1943 in Paris. This photo was sent to his father, a prisoner in a camp in Poland where Resistance fighters were held.

# 4

# Francis Bailly

**December 25, 2002**

*Francis Bailly is a researcher in physics at CNRS. He also has an interest in the epistemology of his discipline and has taken on union responsibilities and political commitments.*[1]

DANIELLE BAILLY: Francis, my dear husband, it's your turn. Can you tell us about your life, your war and its antecedents, going back as far as you can?

FRANCIS BAILLY: As far as I can? That's a long way!

My mother and father met in 1929. My mother was a secretary at the newspaper where my father was working, and from what I have been able to find out, it was love at first sight for the two of them. They dated until, having decided to marry and having had to surmount certain family obstacles that I will talk about again later, they decided to have me. They were married in June of 1938, once they were sure there was no going back, and I was born February 10, 1939.

My mother, born in Bucharest, was Romanian and Jewish. Her mother's maiden name was Zylberstein (her father was from Berditchev in the Ukraine), and she was born in Iassi, Romania, as was her mother (my great-grandmother), whose maiden name was Salomon.

My grandmother, my mother, her two brothers, and her sister had emigrated in 1913, because of the pogroms (significant anti-Semite movements had taken place in Berditchev and Bessarabia) and the difficulties of life in Romania. They had decided to go to the United States.

But I've been told that my grandmother's husband, who, I believe, was a tinsmith, was also an inveterate gambler. He lost the money that would have allowed them to continue the trip and he returned to Romania to earn money again. But he stayed there and never returned! His name was Cretsulescu, and the various names taken in France were Cretu, Cretzu, Kreitz, depending upon whether referring to my mother, my aunt, my grandmother, or my uncle. This grandfather certainly didn't have a good reputation in the family. My mother spoke of him very little, although she did keep a photo of him with her half-brother.

My grandmother arrived in Paris with four children: Joël—whom I've been told was from this grandfather's first marriage and who died young in Paris of typhus; my uncle Joseph, born in 1903; my mother, Ana, born in 1905; and my aunt Jenny, born in 1908. They settled in France in 1913. My grandmother was poor; she would go to the markets late in the day to get the cheapest food for her children. She cooked for other people as well and did some sewing to let her children have a little schooling. Early on my uncle entered into an apprenticeship to learn plumbing; my aunt studied tailoring and later married Bernard Starer, who was a furrier. My mother learned secretarial skills.

Originally, they lived on rue Roi-de-Sicile in the Fourth Arrondissement, close to rue des Rosiers and the *pletzl*, and later at 25 rue Hermel in the Eighteenth Arrondissement. I'll speak of this again, when talking about the final events. My aunt married in 1935 but didn't have children right away. In April 1940 she had my cousin Jacqueline. My uncle also got married about this time, to Esther (or Ernestine) Gross, but they didn't have children. This describes my mother's family as it was at the time.

Naturally, the children went to school. They quickly learned French and were well integrated into their school, earning the Certificate of Primary Studies. But at home they spoke Yiddish or Romanian because my grandmother had difficulty expressing herself in French to the point that, as a child, I spoke a mixture of French, Romanian, and Yiddish to communicate with her.

DANIELLE: Did she read Yiddish? Did she read newspapers? Was she religious? Did she prepare kosher recipes?

FRANCIS: I've been told she didn't know how to read or write but there were Yiddish books in her home. I don't know if she read them. She was more comfortable speaking Romanian. Furthermore, my father learned Romanian in prison from the Romanian prisoners so he could more easily talk with her. As for religion, my grandmother went to the synagogue at 80 rue Doudeauville. She had a reserved seat. I remember that the leader of the local community at that time was Monsieur Idessess, who was also from Romania, and that we were "part of the family." She used to prepare Jewish food, whether kosher or not, I don't know, but I know she observed the Shabbat and celebrated the holidays. Until the war, she would gather all her little family on Friday evening for the Shabbat meal. She "would do" the candles and she later gave the silver candlesticks to her daughters. My uncle rather quickly turned to Communist ideology. He didn't want to hear all those stories about religion. What little he did, he did to please his mother. He would come from time to time to the synagogue to say "hello" and he would come for the holidays, of course, because for him it was more a family occasion than a religious holiday.

DANIELLE: Your grandmother's apartment was small, I suppose? Two or three rooms?

FRANCIS: Rue Hermel was obviously a small apartment, on the third floor. The third floor is important for reasons I will explain later. We would go there fairly regularly, particularly after the war. My grandmother died in 1948 and there was a period I remember very well after the war. I would go to see her on Thursdays when there was no school because my parents wanted me to continue to have contact with her. I would take the subway to the Eighteenth Arrondissement to eat with my grandmother. And then she would often take me to the movies. I saw a lot of films at the neighborhood movie theater and she, who wasn't at all interested and who didn't understand any of it, would sleep peacefully. At the end of the movie, I would wake her and we would go home. That's what I remember.

DANIELLE: Your father wasn't Jewish?

FRANCIS: My father, Michel, who was quickly adopted by my mother's family, wasn't Jewish. He was even fairly nationalist before the war; he joined a nationalist movement called the Young Patriots but, despite being very Catholic, he didn't have a single ounce of anti-Semitism.

DANIELLE: Even though a lot of his family was anti-Semitic.

FRANCIS: My paternal grandfather—a university graduate—was more of a Dreyfusard; the rest of that family, yes. The women, in particular, were narrow-minded. But curiously the men weren't like that. Everything was fine with my paternal grandfather and my father's brother, Uncle Edouard, who used to come to the house.

So my father would go, dare I say "religiously," every Friday to my grandmother's for the Shabbat and later, in the letters he wrote from captivity, he would say, "I hope that our Friday evening dinners can continue." So he easily fit into and was well accepted by the family, which didn't always happen during those years, because not only was there anti-Semitism, but there was also, on the other side, the desire for cultural preservation, and it wasn't easy for Jewish families to accept mixed marriages either. As for my mother, other than her father-in-law, who was very nice, and her brother-in-law, she was rather poorly accepted by my father's family at that time.

Until the war, my mother followed my father in his career. He worked for some time as a medical journalist, some in advertising (always medical advertising). He worked at *Le Matin* and he founded at the end of the 1930s, with two collaborators, Dr. Guyot and a certain Dubois, *Les Échos de la médecine*, a publication that continued until 1972. Furthermore, Guyot conducted himself very well during the war, while apparently that was not the case with Dubois.

When my parents married, they moved into an apartment my father had rented on rue Antoine-Chantin. But my mother, according to the documents that I was able to see, remained the named tenant on rue Hermel and my father paid the rent there because he had a good job with the newspaper. Advertising paid well and that allowed him some breathing room. On the subject of money, the war proved to be revealing. When my father was taken prisoner, some of his clients from *Les Échos de la médecine* took advantage of the situation and left; others stayed on to help my mother as she replaced my father in making contacts for advertising. And after the war, some remained friends—for example, Monsieur Guillevic, who would frequently come, sometimes bringing a pheasant, sometimes a rabbit. He knew my parents from before the war and he used to invite them to his place in Marchainville to hunt. These people did right by my mother—others not so much. This is all just to give a context surrounding the time of my birth in 1939.

I imagine there were some fairly animated discussions at rue du Roi-de-Sicile, because my Communist uncle was known to be an ardent supporter of the Popular Front, and his brother-in-law Bernard was somewhat Leftist, so they got along. After the war that was certainly no longer the case. The Cold War somewhat moderated Bernard's opinions. And in the middle was my father—very tolerant, very open—but a man of the Right just the same who was, therefore, against the Popular Front. The discussions during the Shabbat must have been quite lively at times. It was a curious situation. My mother was mostly Centrist, with a social sensitivity. My father became Gaullist; the war was decisive for him. Before the war, he was simply on the Right. After the war, he was always Gaullist.

I forgot to say that my mother remained Romanian until her marriage, and that she became French only by marriage in 1938. Uncle Joseph remained Romanian like my grandmother, which, of course, had consequences later when, for the first time, a distinction was made by the Vichy regime between French Jews and foreign Jews.

The war came. In 1939, my father was mobilized. At the beginning it was the "Phony War," which lasted from September 1939 until May 1940, and my father, evidently secretly, found a way to tell my mother where he was. He sent postcards to her signed "Michelle" to make it appear to be one woman writing to another. My mother and I went to their encampment. All the officers, commissioned and noncommissioned, had a little party, and there was one captain in particular of whom my father often spoke, Captain Germain, who took a liking to me and held me the whole time. I must have been pretty little, less than a year old. Another anecdote: my father came home on leave in March 1940, and the last day—which would be when I was thirteen months old—I started to walk. I walked, walked, walked, all day long, not wanting to stop, from one room to another. My parents couldn't stop laughing and the next day I was so tired I refused to get up. My father was the one who told me this, and he was very happy to have seen my first steps.

In May 1940, he left for Belgium. It was a short war. June 1940: Dunkirk. My father, like a large part of the French army who had been protecting the English invasion, was captured. Still June 1940: Pétain signed the Armistice, giving himself full power. June 18: General de Gaulle called upon the Resistance. At the same time the "French State" was established. The first measures against the Jews were adopted in October 1940.

DANIELLE: Which required Jews to report for census?

FRANCIS: Yes. We still have my grandmother's census paper dated October 10, 1940, which my mother handed down to me along with some other papers from the war. My mother was French by marriage and she was also the wife of a prisoner and, as such, was somewhat protected, at least for a year or two, even though she was Jewish. It was more problematic for my grandmother and my uncle Joseph, who were both foreign Jews. Yet my grandmother went relatively unnoticed for a while since the apartment on rue Hermel was under my mother's name, Bailly, a typical French name. This did not prevent problems from arising very quickly for my uncle Joseph. Things became difficult. He was interned in several locations, notably in the camp at Gurs, then in the camp at Drancy. In both cases my other uncle, Bernard, managed to get him out!

DANIELLE: By what miracle did he get him out of Drancy? That was difficult!

FRANCIS: First he presented a statement from an industrialist in the water heater business claiming that Joseph was indispensable to their production; I think it was Chaffoteaux and Maury. He confirmed he was needed at the factory, the work wasn't possible without him, and it worked. Then they got him out for health reasons. Surreal, no? Uncle Bernard really had nerve. He spoke perfect German. He did his thesis at Leipzig on political economics and law. He approached the French gendarmes speaking German and that apparently impressed them. Finally they let Uncle Joseph out, and getting out of Drancy was no small thing. Furthermore, Uncle Bernard's conduct was faultless during this whole time. We have the entire dossier, and I will give more details on the subject because I think I am the only one of the family to have them and it would be a shame to slight him.

In April 1941 Uncle Bernard's furrier business was seized by the Germans who, of course, named an Aryan to be interim administrator. Then it became a can of worms because several interim administrators were named. Finally it came down to a certain Lucien Fabre. Incidentally, it is interesting to note that Fabre apparently performed ethically; although he had been the Aryan interim administrator, the records he turned over to the Liberation seemed quite accurate to my uncle when he regained possession of his business.

In September 1941 my uncle Bernard left to work in Lyon in the Unoccupied Zone and his family took refuge there. I remember my uncle Joseph was arrested and interned in the camp at Gurs. On January 13, 1942, he wrote to Uncle Bernard: "My dear Bernard, I have learned that I am certain to be sent to the residential camp at Gurs. In order to rule on my case they have advised me to get a certificate of residence at Lyon from my family there. With this certificate I could get out easier." There was an extensive correspondence between my two uncles about the camp at Gurs where Uncle Joseph was held.

DANIELLE: Guarded by French police.

FRANCIS: Yes. What's more, letters that passed through the censor were marked "Written in French." He was there until May or June of 1942. Later he would be rearrested and incarcerated, this time at Drancy, where my uncle Bernard would again get him out, which is completely extraordinary.

My aunt Jenny crossed the Demarcation Line in 1942. Heading toward Lyon, she was arrested at Angoulême and incarcerated with her little daughter Jacqueline in the prison at Angoulême. They wanted her to acknowledge that she was Jewish. She refused to do so. Finally, she was freed because the police had no proof against her. As for my mother, she stayed with me in Paris, rue Antoine-Chantin, relatively protected by her status, as I said earlier, and my grandmother continued to live on rue Hermel. It was at the end of 1943 that things became critical for my mother, but meanwhile, she stayed in Paris. She had to earn a living for her mother and me, so she sold advertising in my father's place. I remember she had good relationships with the people in the apartment building, including the concierge, the neighbor, and the Gouzy family on the fifth floor, whose father was also a prisoner.

DANIELLE: But what about this business of the anonymous letters?

FRANCIS: That was about something else. It was during the Aryanization of the businesses. Anonymous letters were sent to *Les Échos de la médecine*, to my father who was already a prisoner, denouncing the journal for not taking action against the Jews. Certain people suspected him of belonging, as one of these letters said, to "ein jüdisches Geschäft," a Jewish business that had to be Aryanized. Some medical doctors denounced a great many Jews in the profession. Two anonymous letters were addressed to *Les Échos de la médecine* to say, in substance, that the director hadn't carried out a good policy of collaboration. Yes, there was that.

On the other hand, in the apartment building there was no apparent anti-Semitism; my mother was at ease there. With the local shopkeepers, it went alright, too. When I was sent to the creamery, Madame Meyer, an Alsatian, would often add something. My mother, of course, took care of her own mother, and there were shortages during the war, but that was the same for everyone.

I have some memories of that time. I remember the trips on the subway where there were German soldiers, some who would give me candy (I would refuse). This was a strange situation. I was very blond and I think the German soldiers, completely indoctrinated on racial matters, must have thought I was a good representative of the Aryan race and were very nice to me. What do I remember beyond the presence of uniforms at the end of 1943 and the beginning of 1944? I remember the Allies bombing the Renault factories at Billancourt, and the residents of the apartment building taking shelter in the cellar to protect themselves. It turned out we didn't go down. I met the little girl from the fifth floor named Nicole. She was a little younger than I and her father was a prisoner, too. She was afraid that when he was liberated, he wouldn't be able to get into the house, so without telling her mother, she put the keys to the house in a little parcel her mother was preparing to send him.

DANIELLE: Oh, that's too sweet!

FRANCIS: It caused some problems! She must have been four and one-half at the time. Anyway, I remember very well making parcels for my father and taking them directly to the Gare de l'Est, coming and going by bus, the Number Thirty-Eight, with the bell and all that . . .

DANIELLE: You don't remember your grandmother wearing the star?

FRANCIS: Yes I do, very well. The anti-Jewish laws were still enforced; I won't go into detail, it's historical, and at the end of 1943, beginning of 1944, no one was protected from deportation. One day when we were at my grandmother's third-floor apartment on rue Hermel, the concierge came up to tell us, "Hurry! The Germans are here! They are on the sixth floor; they are coming down!" I remember very well that it was just before a meal; there were mashed potatoes with onions—there might have been at least one egg. We wrapped it all up very fast and rushed to the subway. My poor grandmother who had emphysema was all out of breath because we had hurried. That's how we got away from the roundup that took place in the building. There again, it was a concierge who warned us. As for my grandmother's apartment, it was sealed in January 1944, and all its contents stolen and taken to Germany in April of that same year.

My grandmother took refuge with us on rue Antoine-Chantin. And then it became very delicate because we had to make everyone think we weren't there—not everyone in the building because they saw us—but everyone in the administration, to the point that when the doorbell rang, we could not move; we could not make a sound so as to make the apartment seem vacant. I remember very well the tension and anxiety intensifying, because things were getting worse. Then there was the incident when three French policemen followed us without us noticing them. We were returning from the Place de Châtillon, a small public garden near where we lived. My mother was going on to run errands, and so she let me and my grandmother return home. Two of the policemen came up and simply ordered us to pack our bags. My grandmother said, "My daughter isn't here; she's coming back!" "Pack your bags and we'll wait!" they retorted. We were distressed. As it turned out, the third policeman had stayed in the street, seemingly to prevent my mother from escaping. But actually, he intercepted her and told her to go immediately to a medical doctor to get certificates of nontransportability before going up to the apartment.

We'll talk again about this policeman. His name was Monsieur Vaudrey. He was a brigadier at the time, and we have kept a copy of some of his testimony. So my mother, warned by him, went to Doctor Antomarchi, at the corner of rue Antoine-Chantin, to get these certificates. The doctor was courageous because he made them, knowing that he was taking a big risk. Then my mother and the policeman came back to our apartment. My mother was in a panic, seeing that we had been told to pack our bags. She showed the certificates of nontransportability and the other two officers said, "That's bullshit! We saw them walk up to the square and come back. You can't tell us that they are unable to travel!" and they started to take us in. My mother—I remember this scene—taunted the policemen, "Don't you have a mother?" And Monsieur Vaudrey said to his partners, "Look, let's not create complications. We're covered; they have certificates. If the chief tells us to, we'll come back, but for now, I just don't want to have any problems." The others, shrugging, agreed to leave.

DANIELLE: A miracle!

FRANCIS: Yes, but it's because of one person. It wasn't a miracle from heaven; it didn't come down like that. Needless to say, after that we absolutely had to get away. What was worse was how afraid we were of it happening again. Meanwhile Monsieur Vaudrey had false

papers made for us. We learned he had been a Resister from the beginning; he was in the Communist underground, and much later, well after
the Liberation, during the Cold War, he was punished for being a Communist despite my parents' testimony!

We stayed in the apartment because we had nowhere to go. My
mother worked hard to find an alternative, and that's when her friends,
my godfather and godmother, Monsieur and Madame Lauriol, were
wonderful because they let us use their apartment in Saint-Mandé in
the outskirts of Paris, which was vacant because they were then in the
Auvergne. I can't really say that we moved; we left rue Antoine-Chantin
in a mad rush to go secretly to Saint-Mandé until we were able to go
somewhere else.

Meanwhile Monsieur Vaudrey enlisted my mother to warn all the
Jews who were to be rounded up in her area during this same period.
She went to see each one. After the war Monsieur Vaudrey said that no
Jew had been deported because of him. It is true; he did warn them,
and I remember my mother carried the warning. Sometimes she was
even poorly received because they feared she was an agent provoca-
teur. There may have been people who stupidly let themselves be
caught by not believing her. We stayed several weeks at Saint-Mandé at
the Lauriols' place. My aunt Jenny came with Jacqueline to help prepare
for our departure to La Bourboule where she herself was in hiding,
after having first been in Lyon, then Angoulême, and so on. When the
false papers arrived, my grandmother was called Crestou, born in the
Basque region, to explain her poor French! We took the train to La
Bourboule, in the center of France, and Monsieur Vaudrey decided to
accompany us to reduce the risk. My mother was with her own mother
and I was with him. They were not to show that they knew us or we
them.

DANIELLE: What was your state of mind, as you remember it, with
all these strange things for a child four or five years old?

FRANCIS: I certainly remember an atmosphere of tension and anxiety from the moment the police arrived to take us. I remember this in-
termediate period of waiting when we could not move or do anything,
which was strange, but I understood perfectly that it was dangerous to
do otherwise. There was a real understanding of danger without actually understanding the nature of the danger. When we were at Saint-
Mandé, the atmosphere was more relaxed because my mother felt more

secure and she knew things were in preparation, so I, too, was more relaxed. I was evidently picking up a little from the moods and state of mind of the adults. And then later it seemed strange on the train not to recognize my mother and my grandmother, but given that Monsieur Vaudrey was nice and that my mother had confidence in him, I was quiet. I didn't talk; I didn't say anything.

DANIELLE: During this whole time, do you remember missing your father?

FRANCIS: Of course. Let me just say here that my mother spoke of him often and would show photos to me. There were some truly extraordinary things, because at the time of my birth (they were both religious), they had decided that I would be brought up in the Jewish religion. But given the circumstances that my father was a prisoner and was a Catholic, my mother decided to have me educated in the Christian religion to give him moral support. She had me learn the prayers, and I prayed for my father. She talked about him to me a lot. So as not to lose contact with Judaism, not only did we keep the Shabbat and the candles, but she bought a Bible game and I was supposed to learn the Old Testament this way. It was clever.

Going back to the trip, I remember very well our stopping at a station where the German police got on. Some were in uniform and some in civilian clothes, and they checked papers. My mother was saying to my grandmother (so she wouldn't speak, because of her accent): "Sleep, Mom, sleep!"

"But I'm not sleepy!"

"Sleep, Mom, sleep!"

These are little things, but in unusual situations. In short, they looked at our papers, which were, of course, false. I had no problems because I was with Monsieur Vaudrey, and moreover, he was a policeman. So we were not arrested.

We arrived at La Bourboule; I remember it was very, very hot! I think it was May 1, 1944. There was no transportation! And we had to creep along on foot over a long road; my poor grandmother who was in pain, my poor mother who was carrying the suitcases, and I who was hot. It was a rather painful arrival. We finally got to the farm where my uncle, aunt, and cousin already were. It was the farm of Monsieur and Madame Brandly, who put us up for a fee.

DANIELLE: The French farmers all knew who you were?

FRANCIS: Yes, of course. But they were alright. They took the money normally. Also they were anti-German. My cousin and I would hunt Colorado beetles in the fields because they ate the potatoes, and Monsieur Brandly would say, "Go! Kill them, those beetles, kill them!" because "beetles" was what we called the Germans. We would smash the Colorado beetles with rocks. From time to time my uncle would take us for walks in the woods up to Mount Charlannes to entertain us a little.

Right away, at La Bourboule from May 1944 until the Liberation, my mother joined the Free French Forces (FFI) and became secretary at the Command Post of La Bourboule for the Auvergne region. I remember she took me on an assignment with her to Clermont-Ferrand! At Clermont-Ferrand there were some other friends who provided a little cover for the activities. They were the Auchâtraires, old friends of my father, who were also very supportive. I remember being welcomed by the wife, Line—very nice—a French teacher. I then traveled once in a while with my mother because the Resistance said that a woman with a child could get through easier than a person alone. My mother later regretted the risks she had run by taking me, but in the desperate circumstances no one calculated the risks. The documents of that time are still around: a pass with her name, an armband of the Free French, and all that. We stayed there until the Liberation of Paris at the end of August 1944.

DANIELLE: Do you have any memory of the Liberation?

FRANCIS: At La Bourboule. Oh, yes! There were flags everywhere, there were parades, there was joy in all the liberated French towns. I remember there were festivities and games for the children for several days. The river that goes through there, La Dordogne, was very torrential and tumultuous. To frighten my cousin and me, and to discourage us from going near it, they told us horrible stories of children who had been carried off by the current; it seemed they would find drowned bodies all the time.

And moreover, it truly was torrential, especially for a child, who saw whitecaps taller than he . . .

DANIELLE: Did you get news of your imprisoned father at that time?

FRANCIS: My mother had managed to let him know that we had gone to La Bourboule. They more or less encoded a language between them. (I kept all the letters they exchanged.) During these moves, my father, in the early days, at first was transferred to Germany, and then they wanted to make him work for the Germans. Of course, he refused. Furthermore, he rebelled against the German soldiers, so he was condemned to five years of confinement. No one emerges alive from that prison, so it was fortunate that he was spared confinement there—thanks to an anti-Nazi German officer who deliberately "lost" him in another camp. Then because of his repeated refusals to work, he was transferred to a punishment camp in Poland because he had been judged to be "unworthy of remaining in the territory of the Third Reich." In 1942 he was sent to a camp for Resisters. It was a few kilometers from Auschwitz from where, he later told me, he could see the convoys of deportees in trucks or on foot. He remained there from 1942 to 1945. He corresponded with my mother on special cards that got past the *Geprüft* (censor). This is how he knew we had escaped and taken refuge at La Bourboule: "I hope you're getting over your illness . . ."

Shortly after the Liberation, we returned to Paris, but it was still a long wait until he returned. Because even though Paris was liberated in August 1944, the war wasn't over until May of 1945. And he didn't return until May 15, 1945. I had just turned six and had already started school.

DANIELLE: Did you get back the apartment on rue Antoine-Chantin?

FRANCIS: Yes. We had left the apartment on rue Antoine-Chantin completely as it was because it wasn't a matter of money—it was because the police were hot on our heels. We found it just as we had left it. However, at my grandmother's everything had been taken. The seal imposed in April of 1944 was still there. She was entitled to some personal equipment from the mayor's office—a whitewood table, two chairs, a bed—that's all. But for us, the war wasn't over. Because even if we were free in Paris, there were prisoners who hadn't come home yet!

DANIELLE: As for deported Jews, your family was lucky.

FRANCIS: Oh, very lucky! Even Uncle Joseph who had been at Drancy had managed to get out, which was truly extraordinary. Those who like us had been protected by Monsieur Vaudrey and warned through my mother's intervention could also get away, because they weren't surprised in their homes. I must also underline the fact that we were never denounced—not by the people on rue Hermel or by the people on rue Antoine-Chantin or by the people at Saint-Mandé. Moreover, the neighbors, seeing strangers like us settling into an empty apartment, could easily have denounced us. The French police came looking for us, it's true, but even so, the protection was relatively general. It is also amazing. That is why my appreciation for the behavior of these people and others is more nuanced. There were a lot of Pétain loyalists, no doubt, but to be loyal to Pétain didn't necessarily mean to denounce Jews. That's what is bizarre. That's how it was. There were no doubt some who supported Pétain who knew we were Jews, but even so they didn't tell—it is very strange.

DANIELLE: My family was denounced. It depended on the families.

FRANCIS: It depended. In May 1945 my father returned weighing thirty-seven kilos. A punishment camp is a punishment camp. But he returned; he knew what had happened, he knew a lot. The prisoners had built clandestine radio sets in their camp—things like that. He had written to my mother (from Lille, I believe): "I'm coming home." She had gone to the hairdresser and waited at the window for him all night! He arrived about six o'clock in the morning. He had with him two big sacks full of cans of sardines and other food he had collected along the route. Other people were getting rid of it because it was too heavy and he was picking it up. Picking it up, the poor guy, because he knew we were hungry. It was the first time I saw a can of sardines.

When he arrived, I was asleep. I heard some noise, I got up, I saw my mother in the arms of a man, and they asked me, "Do you know who this is?" Of course, I didn't hesitate. I was very happy; everyone was very happy. I have to add also that during the war, before our departure from Paris, we occasionally had a visit from my paternal grandfather who, himself, had taken refuge in Saint-Vaast-la-Hougue, near Cherbourg, with his family, and who from time to time brought us some food. Life was not easy for him either, but he made an effort to visit us and bring some products from the country. There was also correspondence between my grandfather and my mother.

DANIELLE: There's something I've never asked you: when you were in great danger and needed to leave Paris, did your Mom call on your paternal family for help?

FRANCIS: Certainly. My grandfather had no problem helping. Further, he himself helped the Resistance in Normandy, notably in preparation for the Landings. He would even be elected mayor of Saint-Vaast at the Liberation. But I think at the time there was too much tension with the rest of the family for her to ask. She preferred to approach friends who had already welcomed her. In fact, both the Lauriols and the Auchâtraires had accepted her into their circle, despite her being Jewish. Theirs was a mutual appreciation, so she had confidence. Among the women of my father's family she was not appreciated, to say the least. They must have thought she got my father off on the wrong track. In this regard, one has to read the letters to understand what happened. I think my parents always softened things so that I could have good relations with my grandparents and my uncles and aunts on the paternal side. Further, I believe most of them almost never came to rue Antoine-Chantin, except my uncle Edouard and my aunt Louise, who were more open. But with my grandmother and my aunt Marguerite, it was ostracism. Anti-Semitic? I never heard anti-Semitic talk. But it really must have been this idea of a mixed marriage that was intolerable to them. Maybe it would have been the same if it had been a matter of a Muslim or a Buddhist, I don't know. It was less so after the war, first because my father put a stop to it, but also because they were grateful to my mother for having waited, for having always been faithful to my father, which was not the case in many homes. There were dramas at the return, as you know.

Then, as we had good relations with the residents of the apartment building, my father didn't want to move. Later my parents bought the apartment.

DANIELLE: Your father was a Gaullist, but what about your mother?

FRANCIS: Less so. She had her memories of the Resistance, but she was naturally more Centrist, because of her social sensitivities—a foreigner, an ex-immigrant—and then there was her Communist older brother, and her somewhat Leftist brother-in-law. During the Cold War, listening to them talk about the different newspapers got so bad that when they were both in the car with my father, he would threaten to stop the car and make them get out if they didn't stop arguing.

DANIELLE: It was the same with my two uncles.

I would now like to ask you the questions that I ask everyone in these interviews. What influence or what connection is there between the experience you had during the war as a child and the way in which your values, opinions, and commitments were forged afterward?

FRANCIS: To be honest, it is difficult to answer because I am unable to say what of this experience as a child could precisely determine the nature of commitments I made later. It must have played a role, certainly, but to connect all that seems excessive to me. That said, I recognize elements in some of the values I have now that go back to the time of the war. Perhaps it has to do with a rational reconstruction a posteriori, but perhaps it also actually played an important, if not a determining, role.

What can I say? The first thing that seems important to me is the distinction between institutions and individuals. Institutions are made up of people, I know, but institutions have their own rules that they often impose on people. I tend to believe that while you can have confidence in people and find shared values, you must be skeptical when it comes to institutions, simply because their overall objective is more to perpetuate and reproduce themselves than to put themselves at the service of values, including the values for which they were originally established. I need no other example than how the institutions functioned under the so-called French State (the Vichy government) including the justice system, the police, the army, even a large part of the academy that accepted collaboration without much difficulty. This doesn't mean, however, that everyone who was a part of these institutions accepted it. Therefore the idea that one must mistrust the institutions and not think of them as representing values in and of themselves is an idea that comes from this period, even if it developed later.

The second idea that seems important to me is that in most circumstances where essential choices are to be made, belonging to something—whatever it is—gives no guarantee that one will make what I consider to be good choices. We saw some priests collaborate and others save lives. We saw judges go one way or another rather than straight ahead, because it was the judicial institution that was functioning (the special sections and other judiciary departments). We also saw medical doctors behave faintheartedly. In each of these cases, we saw cowards and spineless individuals as well as people who conducted themselves courageously, including some of the police, as in the example of Monsieur Vaudrey.

DANIELLE: Even so, may I make an observation here? I had an opportunity in the Cévennes region to speak with some Protestants. They explained to me that for various reasons within the Protestant tradition it seemed completely natural for them to come to the aid of the Jews during the war. Some of the reasons were curious, but most were of a historic nature and completely understandable. They explained to me that they felt a biblical closeness to the Jewish people who occupied an important place in their traditions, and that as a whole, or at least in a majority of cases, Protestants in France—former outcasts themselves—felt solidarity with the Jews, a phenomenon that doesn't exist in the Catholic tradition. So I would add a footnote to what you were just saying.

FRANCIS: That's an interesting point to discuss, but I think it is not so much the "Protestant" characteristic as it is the "minority" characteristic that played a role in that case, because, conversely, we mustn't forget that in Germany, Protestantism was the tradition of the majority! And it was a majority of the German population that brought the Nazis to power and supported them. This clearly shows that there is no guarantee of humanity tied to belonging to something. Further, you only need see how certain Jews in some places behave now to realize this. I think that each person is truly free and that the choices made are what constitute personal responsibility. I believe, given that each person's responsibility is made up from his or her choices, that this is what obliges us to reflect, to analyze, and create an alternative solution to what is often presented to us as inevitable or self-evident.

From an ethical point of view, I find it extremely narrow to think that membership in anything either determines the decisions to be made or denies responsibility and liberty. An illustration of this is how, between 1940 and 1944, certain people in the rural areas took sides for historic reasons, particularly because of the First World War—people who were relatively faithful to Pétain and the Vichy state, but who, at the same time could not tolerate treating a certain category of people badly, particularly children, and were led to protect them. The films *The Two of Us* and *Monsieur Batignole* testify to this, and there were obviously many others as well. So I believe in taking people as they are and trying to find in them the depth at which each of them is able to function in relationships. On the human level, this question arises each time we meet a new person, without having to categorize a priori people according to whatever ethnic, religious, social, or intellectual group they belong to. For example, I've met a lot of Communists of great human capacity, even though I consider the system they defend to be totally inhumane. It is also one of the elements that resonates in the times we are living in now, as well as in those times described by historians.

Of course, the fact of having belonged—and of having been treated as belonging—to a minority sensitizes one to the situation of other minorities and facilitates a commitment to people who are oppressed or excluded. But as we often see, there is no guarantee of this; it is only a choice.

Let's go further yet. I haven't forgotten that we were lodged at La Bourboule due to the efforts of my uncle Bernard, without going into what he did for my uncle Joseph, my aunt Jenny, his own brother, and his nieces that he managed to get to La Bourboule. This shows the important role family ties can play, remembering that in certain sad cases it may remain an ambiguous role. The family is an institution, but it is the institution where the closest and deepest relationships are developed. It can play the role of an institution of last resort when all other institutions have failed or have been marked by suspicion. In my case, we know the family ties worked in a beneficial way and have since then retained a value, no doubt, in connection with the experience of the war.

On another level, I also emphasize that children must not be overprotected so that they can learn for themselves how to resist in certain circumstances should they ever be caught in a situation where they must resist the pressures of the majority. If they are overprotected, I fear they will always defer to authority, whether it is paternal or institutional authority, and by so doing will give up part of their liberty and risk making later choices of which I would not approve. Why do I say this? Because although I was protected, I don't think of myself as having been "cocooned" and kept outside the events that were taking place. My mother protected me, but she also explained a number of things to me that I could understand at age five or six. I knew there were dangers. I knew that we had to pay attention, that I was obliged to go along with certain constraints, such as pretending not to recognize my family members when we were in the train, and so forth. I think she was right because it shows respect for the child and provides a way for the child to respect him or herself.

Those are the essential things I can say at this point. Afterward, one can develop from these core themes many values concerning commitments relative to colonialism, oppression, and racism. But let's not forget that these values are obviously shared by many people who haven't needed an experience like the Holocaust to hold on to them.

From a completely different point of view, what we went through may have engendered a kind of reflective, or intellectual second nature. Indeed, you must never be carried away by a given situation, but be able to objectify it enough to analyze and master it. You need the ability to abstract, because if you want to be able to survive, you must analyze. As a child, you realize that adults have to act this way, that they can't let things run on their own, and that if they don't take action based on analyses (right or wrong), they are somehow condemned. In a more general way this could also be what fed a large part of Jewish intellectualism. There is, of course, the tradition of scholarship, but also the fact that in every central European country where Jews were a minority, they had to find the means of objectifying situations, analyzing how to survive, and discerning the best strategies for avoiding problems either as a community or as individuals.

DANIELLE: Is the last point you made, in your mind, one of the components of a kind of "moral resistance" that hardship can engender?

FRANCIS: Let's just say that it is an obligation that hardship imposes on us. Then when we find ourselves in a critical situation, these intellectual values allow us to accept the idea of putting some distance between this situation and ourselves. So what you call "moral resistance" individually takes root, I believe, in this ability to distance oneself. By not thinking that everything that happens to you is essential, important—more important than what happens to others; by being able to regard oneself in a somewhat ironic and critical way so as not to be dominated by situations, behaviors, illusions, or intimidations. I believe that all this creates conditions that reinforce the fiber of moral resistance.

DANIELLE: From the affective, emotional point of view, can you say that hardship risks damaging the soul by a reaction, a hardening? Or does it rather contribute to openness?

FRANCIS: I think that hardship and having to face it doesn't necessarily harden, but rather shields. In this sense, it leads to objectifying what happens so as not to overinvest.

DANIELLE: Even facing the threat of death?

FRANCIS: Even facing the threat of death. Since the threat of death hovers over everyone, you have to realize that it doesn't take on a different importance because it is your own death. Convincing ourselves of this creates a kind of emotional shell. On the other hand, it doesn't contradict the fact that it sensitizes us; I think the two are even connected in my own case. We are thus empowered, if not by putting ourselves in the place of the other, at least by understanding what the other is feeling.

We create a kind of thick hide for ourselves and this hide works only for the wearer. When we see distress, it is intensified because of other distress we have experienced and had to overcome. I do not find these two aspects to be contradictory—on the contrary, they are complementary. We are all the more sensitive to other people if we know how to put aside some of our own emotions. This can take the form of empathy when it is a matter of emotion, but can also be a form of intellect when it is a matter of understanding another's experience. What another person is experiencing is both something of significance and something "lived." This is how the two aspects are connected. You have to be able to find good clues to protect yourself. At the same time, you have to be able to create a tough enough hide so that you are not affected every time something disagreeable happens.

DANIELLE: So let's put all these elements together: the intellectual part and the emotional part, the objective and the affective. In light of our war, what can you say about the construction of a personal ethic? Can you see in it a mode of operation reinforcing the individual's capacity to fight against injustice, to work for justice, to make oneself a "being of the world," more supportive of the collective for the sake of solidarity?

FRANCIS: In my opinion, that takes root in a term that is completely within the context—in the spirit of resistance, resistance to the status quo. The status quo then was collaboration, it was the Occupation, it was extermination. Resist all that. The status quo today is exploitation, it is alienation, it is domination, it is the jungle law of free markets. Resist all that. It is a matter of a double-edged determination, led partly by this sense of resistance that relies on the critical dimension, and partly by a sense of purpose since we believe it is possible to establish a more just society and to transform human relationships, including on the societal level.

DANIELLE: Between what the individual can sense and desire and the functions of the collective, how can this determination be articulated?

FRANCIS: That is a difficult question. I think we find ourselves torn. As I have already emphasized, in the collective ensemble we must always distinguish between the person and the role he or she is playing. And however hard we fight someone in the role he or she has agreed to play, whatever this fight requires, we must take the time to appreciate the choice the other has made in order to maintain respect for the person. There is the great difficulty. At the same time we know from experience that liberal institutions can, over time, become weak and use the collective as an instrument of oppression of the people. Once again, this means that we must not defend institutions as themselves, but only for the original objectives they were given. Institutions that once played a role in pushing for increased justice sometimes became, through historical evolution, a brake on increasing justice. They must then be resisted without fear. We don't challenge the reason they were put in place, but the way they are functioning now. In fact, the invariable that must be maintained is tied to our purpose and not to the means of implementing it. This calls for a kind of "permanent revolution," relative to institutions. What was put in place at one time to respond to our criteria but which now has deviated must be reformed. That was what was lacking in the Soviet Revolution, in my opinion. Very quickly it deviated and was not put back on track. So it seems to me that the critical spirit, the spirit of resistance, must retain priority at all times.

Finally, the principal idea is very simple: the people now are dominated by a whole ensemble of functions whereas it is the people who should be dominant. So what is called for is simply an inversion—a revolution—to put what is now dominated into the dominant role. For example, I can accept the idea of there being economic trade, a global market, on the condition that it be dominated by the needs of the people and not the reverse. A typical case right now is that of generic medications for the underdeveloped countries. If the laws of the market are in the dominant role, people will continue to die. However, if the needs of the people were to be put in the dominant role instead of the jungle laws of the market, mass-production of generic medications could easily be implemented. And so forth. The word "revolution" has real meaning in this way. In the final analysis, I believe that such an orientation would motivate all of history toward more justice. But to begin with, the aspiration toward increased justice you were speaking of takes root in a clear assessment of present injustices and, as it happens, of the extreme injustice represented by undertaking the extermination of Jews, Gypsies, and certain other minorities.

DANIELLE: And do you think the force of these convictions, a force fed by rationality, by a kind of rage before these wrongs, is enough to arm a person to brave the danger? When you are afraid—for yourself or your family—you are afraid, period!

FRANCIS: Yes, but being afraid is not in itself extremely serious. It only becomes serious when you start to feel overwhelmed by it and lose judgment. Otherwise awareness of danger is rather beneficial because you think, "Watch out! Danger ahead! There are steps to be taken to defend myself!" But if you allow fear to play the dominant role, and take the symptom—as with a fever—for the thing itself, it's not beneficial because you aren't treating the illness, only the fever. So in this case, treating the "illness" is to treat the danger. And you can do it in various ways. The most radical way is to say, "The worst that can happen is I might die. In any case, I will die. So what? Okay!" In such a case, you try to construct the situation so that if you have to die, it will be in a way that serves to protect your family. This is at the more emotional level, but I think that at a rational level, you have to use your ability to analyze because this allows you to distance yourself from the danger and begin to master the emotion that puts you at risk of taking the wrong path.

This can be acquired very simply through experience, even belatedly. I believe a person can be unaware of danger in two ways: either being overwhelmed by fear or by being stupidly reckless. What seems important to me is to get enough distance to permit critical thinking and analysis, which lets us attempt to discern the most rational and most efficient strategies to ward off or escape this danger. So for me the word "mastery," as it relates to self-control and control of events, is an extremely important term in these cases. I believe that if my mother had not shown a great deal of self-control as regards my grandmother and me, she would have certainly had lots of trouble escaping the roundups and even deportation. This certainly taught me something— never to underestimate or overestimate the danger, but to take it rather as something that can be handled.

DANIELLE: Is that courage?

FRANCIS: I think so. But to be courageous is not, to my mind, a value in and of itself; it depends on what use one makes of the courage. We've seen very courageous Fascists and yet I don't respect them. Further, I presume that based on the experiences one has had, there are some people who are more or less courageous in confronting danger or even pain. I would never cast stones at people who have had difficulty confronting danger or pain or fear. What I simply ask is that they make the effort to try to overcome this situation, to exercise their control and their liberty. I don't ask that they act like me at all, but simply that they keep a cool head so as to be as effective as possible. And I think that some people were thrown into inextricable situations mainly due to terror.

DANIELLE: Thank you for your testimony. Let's hope that the experience of the past can thus serve to nourish thoughts for the future and permit us to foresee and prevent repetition of this kind of traumatic situation.

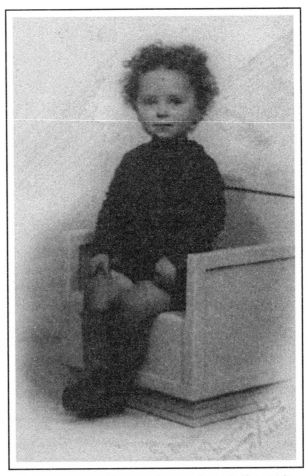

FIGURE 5.1. Arnold at age three and one-half, in 1942, in Paris. Serious expression.

# 5

# Arnold Rochfeld

**April 7, 2003**

*Arnold Rochfeld's father was deported; he never returned. Recently retired, Rochfeld spent most of his working life in the field of information technology. He alternately or simultaneously performed research, consulting, and teaching.*

ROCHFELD: I was born in Paris on June 29, 1938, so I'm going to be sixty-five years old. I've had a rather unusual professional life. Somewhat pressured by my family, I first studied accounting and started to work as an accountant's assistant, but that didn't suit me at all. Then I did my military service where I met the people who I ended up studying with at the Conservatory. After that I made a real change of direction and completed training at the National Association for Adult Education as an electronics technician, which was a huge shift to go from accounting to electronics. I went into information technology and began working as a programmer in 1962–1963 for a business. Then I joined the lab at CNRS because I happened to be working on a machine that interested the researchers there.

I began my studies at about age twenty-four. I was awarded one of the first master's degrees in information technology at the Blaise Pascal Institute while I was still at CNRS. Then, with my master's and the equivalent of an engineering degree, I spent two years at the University of Edinburgh where I worked in a lab. I returned to France in the early 1970s and I asked myself whether I should continue at CNRS or if I should look elsewhere. At the time there weren't many opportunities at CNRS in the areas that interested me, so I joined a private firm where I worked for seven years. I then joined the Institute for Computing and Information Technology Research where I worked for three years before going to another private firm, after which I started a service of my own. During my entire professional life, I have been successively or simultaneously doing research or consulting and teaching in various graduate schools like the School of Studies in Economics and Commercial Science, Télécom–Paris, and in particular, back at the Conservatory for almost fifteen years where I had the responsibility for somewhat specialized teaching in information technology. I was, in fact, one of the first practitioners—having published some books on this subject—to consider the process of computerization of corporations, thereby contributing to this discipline becoming a part of a university curriculum. I taught until 2002, and I decided to end my teaching career while continuing my consulting career. That's a little about where I am. On a professional level, by and large, I have had a good life. I have done what I wanted to do, the timing was right, and I really felt I was having fun, especially in comparison with the beginning of my life when I was completely messed up. There was quite a contrast.

BAILLY: We have you situated professionally. Now can we go way back? Where are you originally from? Your grandparents?

ROCHFELD: My origins are pretty straightforward. My grandparents, all of them, were Polish from Warsaw. My father and my mother, also from Warsaw, of course, arrived in France in the 1930s.

BAILLY: What do you know about your grandparents? Were they from a religious background?

ROCHFELD: Quite the contrary. My father and my mother were both part of Polish secular society. Neither side had a religious culture. But they came from very different social settings. My mother was from a relatively rich family. My maternal grandfather, if I can believe the family stories, belonged to the liberal bourgeoisie. He had a big leather business in Warsaw, he lived on the best street in town, and he had a second home in Zakopane.

BAILLY: Was it a big family?

ROCHFELD: Yes. It's difficult to know because, like so many other families, there were very few survivors—practically none.

BAILLY: They were exterminated in the Warsaw ghetto?

ROCHFELD: There or at Auschwitz. I have a photo from the 1930s that says a lot. It's a good sepia photo where there are some twenty people—perhaps not all family, some friends also. No one survived.

BAILLY: Have you learned anything specific?

ROCHFELD: From what I've picked up, they were part of the Warsaw ghetto and followed the typical "path." The only survivor of this branch of the family is my mother's sister, my aunt, recently deceased, who made it through. She was in the ghetto and then at Maïdanek. She survived there. I don't know when she was actually deported because the ghetto was there until 1943. She was perhaps among the last, the some fifty thousand who were still alive in 1943. She lost her husband and a child; that's typical. After the Liberation, like so many others, she was in a displaced persons' camp. She managed to get in touch with my mother—through the Red Cross, no doubt—and my mother arranged for her to come to France. She started a family here. I have three cousins. She remarried. Her children (three girls) didn't know that she had been married before. They found out only after her death. My mother knew. That's my maternal family. My paternal family is completely different. My father was from a very poor family. He was a Communist activist.

BAILLY: Already?

ROCHFELD: Yes. Actually, he was arrested in Poland and, like a character in some naturalist novel, he was illiterate. He was educated in prison. He had been arrested because the Polish Communist Party agitated for the return of the Ukraine to the Soviet Union, a position that was viewed unfavorably by the Polish government. For this reason he was arrested and condemned to death. His sentence was commuted because of his young age. He got all his political and intellectual education in prison and at the end of the 1920s, if my findings are correct, there was a short thaw in Poland. (I recently learned that in May 1926 the Polish Communist Party gave its support to Josef Pilsudski's successful coup d'état. The new president then freed the party members, including my father.) The Polish government authorized the various political parties, including the Communists, to present programs in the schools and (this is rather romantic) my father was sent to the high school where my mother was a student.

BAILLY: A Polish high school?

ROCHFELD: Yes. And they fell in love with each other. That was about 1929–1930. They left right away for France. My father went first and sent for my mother later.

BAILLY: In regard to your paternal family, was it social issues that caused your father to join the Polish Communist Party?

ROCHFELD: Yes.

BAILLY: What work did your paternal grandfather do?

ROCHFELD: I don't know anything about that. The only detail I have (very indirectly—from my father's sister who was the only one to survive the deportation in that branch of the family and who was brought to France during the Liberation) is that our paternal family was very poor. We learned nothing more—just some inferences through reading I've done. No direct information.

BAILLY: Including information about the eventual anti-Semitic pogroms and persecutions at that time by the Polish?

ROCHFELD: Yes and no. Historically, even though for a long time Poland had a tradition of sporadic but recurring pogroms (notably in 1881, in 1906, in 1918, 1919), during the 1920s there was a period of relative calm. Up until 1928, there was a certain willingness to integrate. For example, there was a Polish worker party that was relatively open and a fairly strong Jewish party, the Bund. It was a period with fewer tensions between the different sectors of the Polish population. The massive pogroms surged later, during the 1930s. There would still be some after the fall of Nazism, for example in 1947.

BAILLY: Your parents arrived in France in the early 1930s. Did they marry?

ROCHFELD: I think they married in France. They lived in the Nineteenth Arrondissement. They never really moved from there.

BAILLY: What do you know about their first home?

ROCHFELD: The situation wasn't all that rosy. Like other immigrants at that time, they had no work permits.

BAILLY: What work did your father do?

ROCHFELD: Home knitter. He had had dozens of jobs. He worked in the north as a miner, as a spray painter. He went to Belgium but was expelled and so he returned to France.

BAILLY: And your mom?

ROCHFELD: She followed along, more or less. My sister and I have talked about this some. I only know that my parents were expelled, that my father worked without a work permit, his coat over his arm, saying that he was passing through—the usual trick. These are typical stories, to a certain extent.

BAILLY: Was he active with the Communist Party right away in France?

ROCHFELD: No, not at all. Actually, he broke with them when he arrived in France—not ideologically but in practice. He was a Communist sympathizer but he wasn't active. Perhaps he had had his fill. He dropped out while remaining close to the Jewish Leftist community. But to my knowledge, he was not a member and he didn't participate in the Immigrant Workers Organization (MOI). He was completely out of it and played a kind of personal hand. He wanted to become assimilated so he gave up the political dimension while remaining sympathetic to the Left.

BAILLY: Did your parents tell you anything about the 1930s in France in general, about 1934 and the Popular Front?

ROCHFELD: Nothing at all. It's very frustrating. I don't know if this was all censured or what, but the story really begins with the war. My mother told us nothing special.

BAILLY: You were the only child at the time?

ROCHFELD: I have a sister, much older than I; she was born in 1931. I was born in 1938.

BAILLY: Did she go to school?

ROCHFELD: Yes. She was eleven years old.

BAILLY: She didn't tell you anything special about those years?

ROCHFELD: No, there is nothing in the family saga except that my father was taking food to the strikers in 1936.

BAILLY: So he nevertheless had some union activity?

ROCHFELD: Perhaps while he was working in that setting, but since he was on his own, at least at the end, it would surprise me if he had much union activity. From what my sister has told me, he took food to the strikers, if I remember it right. That brings to mind the big photos of the Popular Front where there are people sitting on top of the walls, pulling up the packages of food that people below were bringing them.

BAILLY: What street did you live on in the Nineteenth Arrondissement?

ROCHFELD: Rue Fessart, a street that has completely changed and been demolished. It was very much a working-class area. I lived in an apartment I will speak of later because it's an important factor in how places for us were arranged.

BAILLY: Were there a lot of Jews there?

ROCHFELD: No, none. It seems there were some in the area around us, but not in the building. We were the only ones. That's a part of the story that will unfold next.

BAILLY: These were working-class people in your building?

ROCHFELD: It was a working-class environment with an owner (a professor of medicine, Professor Augier) that we will come across again later. And also shopkeepers, people of modest means.

The apartment itself was small. It must have had three rooms, one of which had the machines. There was a room for my parents and one for my sister, but I don't think I had a room (I no doubt inherited hers when she left), and a kitchen. The toilet was down the hall.

BAILLY: A hard life for your parents? Long hours of work for your father?

ROCHFELD: Yes, no doubt. Typical.

BAILLY: So, a modest setting but not extremely poor?

ROCHFELD: I would say modest. My father had work at the end, but he had been a "jack of all trades." I don't remember feeling hungry or poverty-stricken, but we weren't rolling in dough.

BAILLY: In fact, he never became French? He would be deported before that?

ROCHFELD: He was deported as a foreign Jew.

BAILLY: We're up to 1939.

ROCHFELD: Yes. When war was declared, my father succumbed to certain community pressure, if only social, and joined a Polish regiment formed in France. His was a small story inside the big one; he fought the campaign in France, was at Dunkirk, was with those who embarked, went to Germany. He then wondered what he should do. According to my mother, he thought about his wife and two children and decided to return to France. He reentered at Bordeaux and came to Paris, doubtless in August or September of 1940, after the Armistice.

BAILLY: At that point, your mother was relieved to no longer be alone with the children?

ROCHFELD: Yes. In any case, he wasn't home long because he was among the first arrested. Being a foreign Jew, he was arrested in October 1941. Like so many others, he was called to the Commission for verification of identity and didn't return. He was held at Pithiviers. I remember very well seeing him behind bars. He was in civilian clothes; that is one of my first memories. I must have been about three years old.

BAILLY: You had gone to see him?

ROCHFELD: Yes. My mother had been told he was at Pithiviers.

BAILLY: By the way, do you know if she took a false name?

ROCHFELD: No, because we had very good relationships with the people in our apartment building. And furthermore, when it became obligatory for Jews, she never wore the star.

BAILLY: You felt protected by the working-class people around you?

ROCHFELD: Yes, and what follows will prove this. Everyone knew us, so it was impossible to change our name without moving. We didn't make a change; we stayed.

BAILLY: You learned, through Klarsfeld,[1] how long your father remained at Pithiviers and what happened afterward?

ROCHFELD: He left Pithiviers in March of 1942, as I remember. He was part of Convoy Number Eight for Auschwitz, direct. There, at first he survived but he died soon after from illness; he caught typhus. From what I've gathered, he must have died in July of 1942. So he must have been at Auschwitz for only a few months. At the beginning he had succeeded in not being selected. And further, he was among those relatively well prepared, in a certain sense; he spoke Polish and he even had a number of friends.

BAILLY: Was he part of a network?

ROCHFELD: Yes, I think so; a network of friends who must have helped him find a good *commando*, things like that which let him survive. But as his constitution wasn't particularly strong, he caught typhus and died.

BAILLY: After Pithiviers, did your mother learn he had been moved to Auschwitz?

ROCHFELD: She learned it later. It seems my mother had some information. She must have been more or less part of the network organized to save the children. This is how she knew in advance about the Vel' d'Hiv' Roundup in July 1942. She also had very specific inside information because among the tenants of the building, there was an Alsatian (therefore a "German") who worked at the Gestapo. He warned the concierge, Madame Lajoie, by telling her that he didn't want to see my mother around on July 16.

BAILLY: That was very unusual!

ROCHFELD: Yes, he warned her. To end the story of this Gestapo guy, he was arrested during the Liberation and my mother testified for him, which kept him from being condemned to death. She had been warned, it seems, by both sides and she spread the information a little.

BAILLY: She took her two children and left?

ROCHFELD: Not at all. As I remember, we simply spent the two days of the Roundup with the concierge and then the owner took us to his place. Our apartment building was, in fact, a little unusual (I alluded to this earlier). At the back was a house with a garden where the owner lived. That's where he took my sister and maybe all three of us. So we stayed in Paris two or three days longer. Then this apartment owner took my sister to Normandy where he had a summer place and entrusted her to a Catholic woman named Noémie Caniou. So my sister spent the entire war hidden in Normandy in a little village called Barenton. My mother took me by the hand and we went just outside of Paris to Milly-la-Forêt.

BAILLY: Just after the Roundup?

ROCHFELD: Three or four days later; it must have been July 20. My mother went to a little village near Milly, Noisy-sur-École, and went to see the mayor. She spoke French well and she asked him if there were any Poles in the village. He told her there was a Polish farmer. She went to his place.

BAILLY: A Jew?

ROCHFELD: No, a Pole who had immigrated. He had been there about ten years. My mother asked him if he would agree to board me. He accepted. My mother left again for Milly and I don't think I saw her again but once until 1944. This Pole was apparently part of the Resistance network. I remember meeting other children, so I was not the only one boarded at this farm.

BAILLY: He was one of those kindly anti-Nazi Poles who wasn't anti-Semitic?

ROCHFELD: Absolutely. I'm sorry not to have his name and for not having declared him as one of the "Righteous" because he undertook considerable risk. I remember later, in 1944, having seen soldiers at his place.

In any case, everyone who survived was lucky, and my mother perhaps happened upon a man who knew how to keep his mouth closed. I don't know who told me that this farmer, or at least his daughter, was part of a Resistance network that saved downed pilots and drove them to Spain.

BAILLY: Communist Resistance?

ROCHFELD: I don't know, but it's likely. Young Polish Communists, if there were any, other than miners. He himself was anti-German, period. He agreed to help because of his daughter. I think everything was done knowingly. It's difficult not to know what each other is doing within a family.

BAILLY: Do you have memories of this host family?

ROCHFELD: Yes, good memories. It was my only contact of any duration with the countryside. I have one memory—it would have been in 1944—of wandering in the woods. I have an anecdote about this. There was another child who was about two years older than I and we were very close. We were out in the woods and met some wanderers who must have been coalminers' sons. They invited us to eat some very good potatoes cooked with bacon over a wood fire. I remember spring, the awakening of nature. I have no bad memories of this time. I think these people were very kind.

BAILLY: Not missing your mother? Nothing in particular, really?

ROCHFELD: No. My mother had a story of her own; she was tending goats. She stayed in Milly. We were twenty kilometers apart . . .

BAILLY: Did she come to see you?

ROCHFELD: I seem to remember her coming to see me once and it so happened that the Germans turned up at that moment so she told me in Polish to clear out fast. That's what I remember. Other than that, I don't think I saw her for two and one-half years.

BAILLY: She did farm work in order to live?

ROCHFELD: Yes, it seems she tended goats for two and one-half years.

BAILLY: So you spent the war like that, protected?

ROCHFELD: Yes. Another good memory: It must have been the summer of 1943 because in the summer of 1944 I wasn't there any more. It was harvest time and I remember the reaper and playing in the bales of hay.

BAILLY: You went to church?

ROCHFELD: Never. And I wasn't in school because I was too young. I was at the farm.

BAILLY: You kept your name?

ROCHFELD: I don't know. This Pole no doubt introduced me as one of his family; otherwise it would have been too dangerous. I remember playing with the kids in the area, participating in the harvest and the fieldwork with other rural people, and living on that farm. That's what my life consisted of.

BAILLY: No agonizing recollections?

ROCHFELD: Yes, perhaps at certain times. I saw German soldiers, for example, but otherwise I don't remember feeling anguished, if it hadn't been for the war.

BAILLY: Were there bombings?

ROCHFELD: Yes. I remember seeing a downed plane, things like that, but I don't remember feeling anguished. Perhaps also because since then I have pretty much intellectualized my story, and in this way achieved a certain distance. Perhaps I have deeply buried my reactions, which would explain a certain number of things later, but in speaking about it now, I have no recurring memories of anguish.

BAILLY: You stayed there until 1944?

ROCHFELD: Yes. Actually, until August 1944. As soon as Paris was liberated, we hitchhiked. My mother came to get me right away.

BAILLY: Did she get your sister, too?

ROCHFELD: No, my sister stayed in Normandy quite a while longer. Contacts with Normandy were broken; she must have returned in September or October when they were reestablished. It's more a case of capturing family memories than of direct memories. So we hitchhiked. Apparently we returned to Paris in an American truck.

BAILLY: Do you have a memory of the Liberation?

ROCHFELD: Yes and no. The only memory that I have dates from May 8, 1945. I remember it snowed but I don't have any memories that connect the two. It is really very fragmented.

BAILLY: Is that when your mother did the research to learn what became of your father?

ROCHFELD: Yes.

BAILLY: And she returned to the old apartment, rue Fessart?

ROCHFELD: Yes. She came back to it; it hadn't been damaged or vandalized.

BAILLY: What did she do then to earn a living?

ROCHFELD: From what she's told me, I suppose she continued my father's work. He had left a number of sweaters. I also read a book about the life of the Jews during the Occupation where many lived precisely because of the fur or the wool they possessed.[2] I have the impression that my mother continued a while like that, but all that is still largely unknown to me. I don't have the impression that the business flourished much with my mother, who was not very gifted in business and who had no particular skill. I think she lived pretty much off the stock of sweaters left by my father.

BAILLY: Did she put you in school?

ROCHFELD: Yes. Here was the situation. When I had been hidden with the Pole in Normandy, I was on a farm, so I hadn't been unhappy, but when my mother came for me, she thought I was perhaps a little malnourished. As there were food shortages in Paris, she didn't want me there, so she sent me to where my sister was in Barenton with Mademoiselle Caniou. I don't know exactly how it happened, but I was in the country there. It was situated in the combat zone of the Liberation. It wasn't far from Avranches where there had been very heavy combat: the "breakthrough at Avranches" (my sister herself had been caught under fire several times). I stayed at Barenton the entire year of 1945–1946 and my first schooling was in a Catholic school. Mademoiselle Caniou, with whom we were staying, didn't especially pressure us, but she said there were two schools in the village, a public school and a Catholic one that was very good. So I went to the Catholic school. I think I was a choir boy. I remember walking behind a funeral procession. Then I returned to Paris for the opening of school in 1947.

BAILLY: In Paris, with your sister back in the apartment, did your mother put her in school?

ROCHFELD: Yes.

BAILLY: And she got by however she could. The three of you then spent several years like that?

ROCHFELD: Yes. My mother learned about the death of my father, and in 1949 or 1950 she remarried an observant Jew, which meant we didn't have a good relationship. He was a leather worker and had a shop. He had lost his entire family. He took refuge in Grenoble, in the Italian zone. His entire family was arrested. I don't think it was in the big Vel' d'Hiv' Roundup, but in a later roundup. His wife threw herself from the fourth-floor window and his four children were deported.

BAILLY: So they remade their lives. Do you have the impression that your mother rebounded in a way? Apparently she didn't give up?

ROCHFELD: I never saw her as particularly beaten down; I don't think of her as beaten down at all.

BAILLY: Did she speak to you of your father from time to time?

ROCHFELD: Yes, naturally. But at that time people tried to get away from it. I think there was even a culture of required resilience, by which people forced themselves to rebound.

BAILLY: Did you speak of the past?

ROCHFELD: Very early on, in our family, we spoke about the deportation. It was indirectly invoked when first my maternal aunt and then my paternal aunt returned from the camps. Then we had the opportunity to hear their stories. But this was not something we talked about a lot.

BAILLY: So you went forward, tried to rebuild?

ROCHFELD: Yes, life went on.

BAILLY: Even though you didn't have a good relationship with your stepfather you lived together?

ROCHFELD: Yes. My half brother was born in 1950. It was a relatively typical life.

BAILLY: You went to school and did your studies?

ROCHFELD: When I returned to Paris, I knew how to read and write and I was placed at my grade level in elementary school. My progress had been completely normal and I was one of the good students. But my mother made a mistake and missed the registration to get me into secondary school. But as I was a good student and didn't want to lose a year, she enrolled me in a final year commercial course in elementary school so I would then be able to go back to a regular school. Once I was on this track, I continued. I went to the Lycée Turgot where I completed a commercial course of study.

BAILLY: You didn't go to the Jewish youth centers?

ROCHFELD: Yes, I was at the CCE at 120 Boulevard de Belleville and I was at summer camp—always the same one, at Tarnos.

BAILLY: You blended fairly easily into this somewhat Yiddish milieu, all the same?

ROCHFELD: Yes, but with considerable reticence because I wanted to be French, while accepting that I felt myself to be a little different. On the other hand, I really liked the summer camp; I felt particularly at ease there. I was at the youth center and the summer camp until 1950. After 1950 I went to the summer camps organized by the National Federation of Deported and Imprisoned Resisters and Patriots (FNDIRP). We traveled to the "popular democracies." Already, at the CCE it was an extreme Leftist environment.

BAILLY: The Communist ideology?

ROCHFELD: More or less. My sister joined the Leftist Cadets. I read Leftist publications, that kind of thing. I began to discuss politics very early on; it was even comical. I think that at age twelve I'd had a row about our having to accept the Germans in the European Community Commission for Coal and Steel and was against the European Community Commission for Defense. From that age on, I was politically aware.

BAILLY: Was it your impression that you were continuing your father's orientation or was it completely personal?

ROCHFELD: It resulted from what had happened—my mother, perhaps. I didn't have the impression of being pushed; it was completely natural. I would say that capturing my father's personal history came later. It was really in adolescence that they told me what had happened, but at the time I don't think I knew much about it.

My mother must have had contacts with the CCE for a long time. She must have been a member because she had collected money after the July 16 Roundup; I think she was affiliated. So I went to the "popular democracies," to Romania, maybe at the time of the Korean War. I remember the military convoys leaving for the North Sea ports to supply North Korea. Then I went on to Hungary and Czechoslovakia where, even having a political awareness, I debated with people on the street. The Soviet "Big-Brother" and all that stunned me. I remember very clearly that one of the people who put us up bragged to us about the Prague metro. I said, "Yes, naturally, it's a Soviet subway." This person made a face and understood very well that I was not impressed.

BAILLY: So you fairly quickly became anti-Stalinist, as it turned out?

ROCHFELD: Yes and no. My commitment didn't at all imply this level of awareness, the proof being that I joined the Communist Party in 1956. Anti-Stalinist, yes, perhaps, but it didn't prevent me from being a member of the Young Communists even at the time of Hungary. I was back at L'Huma to defend it. I participated in the huge unsanctioned demonstration that started at the Colonel Fabien Square and stretched up to the Seventeenth Arrondissement. I didn't have all that much political awareness and lucidity.

BAILLY: During all these years of preadolescence and adolescence, did you feel that you missed your father, that you were missing his authority, or did your stepfather provide that despite everything?

ROCHFELD: Neither. I didn't particularly miss it. My mother had some authority, but I have a fairly rebellious spirit. I had rather unpleasant contacts with my stepfather. Outwardly, he was very religious, of Jewish culture, and that made me uncomfortable. I reacted very negatively.

BAILLY: As for this double identity—the one, normal, French, assimilated, at school and all, including with the French Communists; and the other, Jewish, with the history of the deportees and all that—through spending time at youth centers—how did you manage to combine these two aspects of your identity?

ROCHFELD: Very poorly. At that time I completely rejected the Jewish one; I did not think of myself as being Jewish at all. The youth center was a kind of transition, but I did not feel it concerned me. I was "French" French. I felt I was French with some peculiarities but my Jewish identity was totally absent. I was truly one of the Young Communists in the Communist Party and I had no problem there.

BAILLY: At the youth center there was nevertheless a Jewish specificity?

ROCHFELD: Yes, but I quit going after age thirteen or fourteen. I went there mostly during the summer camps. But I didn't see myself continuing because I didn't want to learn the Hebrew alphabet. They gave us courses in Yiddish; it wasn't my thing.

BAILLY: Your parents didn't speak Yiddish with one another?

ROCHFELD: Yes. Yiddish was spoken at home but it didn't interest me. It was even more complicated than that: I understood Yiddish very well but I answered in French.

BAILLY: It was a rejection?

ROCHFELD: Yes, it was subconscious. I didn't speak Yiddish. Moreover, it bothered me when my parents used it.

BAILLY: Like your sister?

ROCHFELD: Yes, virtually. My sister was ahead of me, but I took the same path independently, not because of her influence. She joined the Cadets and then went on to the Union of Young Women of France (UJFF). She was also always in the Communist Party. The only one who had a religious education was my half brother, who was the youngest. He had his bar mitzvah. It didn't do him any good because he turned Trotskyite.

BAILLY: So you rejected this Jewish aspect of your identity? It didn't give you any special problem? You continued down your path. What characterized your passage from adolescent to young adult was your political commitment, which followed its own course of emancipation from the Communist Party, I suppose?

ROCHFELD: Later. I joined the wave. The Communist Party was one of the political forces opposing the war in Algeria. This action coincided with the zenith of the Party and also with the beginning of its decline. I distanced myself much later, when I started at CNRS in 1965–1966. In 1965, I was still secretary of one of the large sections of the Party in the Nineteenth Arrondissement where there were two hundred Communists; I still had some responsibilities. Intellectually my commitment weakened after 1963–1964 at the end of the Algerian War.

At that time, while remaining in the Party, I began to spend time with other people; I questioned myself. Gradually, I detached myself from the Party.

BAILLY: So you got your *baccalauréat* at Turgot?

ROCHFELD: I never finished my degree. I got the equivalent by exam. I did a year of *lycée* and I took this exam and I began to slave away in accounting until my military service. When I returned, I started accounting again for a year, but it bored me so much that I took a different track, which led me to CNRS where I did my advanced studies without completing my *baccalauréat*.

BAILLY: In what year did you leave home and get a place of your own?

ROCHFELD: I think 1965–1966. I got married in 1967.

BAILLY: Was your first wife Jewish?

ROCHFELD: Half. Most of her family was Protestant but her father was Jewish and had been at Auschwitz. He had been arrested very late. He had done graduate work in business. He had a responsible position in a large firm that repatriated him in the Unoccupied Zone at Saint-Etienne and there, no doubt because of job rivalry, he was denounced in 1944. He was taken among the last convoys. He must have spent six or seven months at Auschwitz.

BAILLY: So you nevertheless looked for a wife who . . .

ROCHFELD: Not at all, it just happened that way. We were in school together. My relationship with the Jewish world came much later.

BAILLY: So there was your first marriage, then your second marriage, and your life continued. Because you yourself speak of this kind of late rediscovery, can we try to reflect a little on your values, to the extent they are inherited from your history as a hidden child?

ROCHFELD: I really have the impression of being just a statistic. I recognize myself in all the books I've read. I belong to the world of secular Jews, of the Left, it is clear. I have their values: a certain sense of history and—understanding that for me it is an epiphenomenon but very important—my relation to Israel, which was very belated. In the 1970s I really discovered Israel with a passion. I have the impression of having a relationship with this country that is a little unusual, even if belated. My mental block toward Israel didn't dissolve until 1972–1973 when they were bringing back the whole history of the Holocaust. I saw myself in the account given in the film *The Sorrow and the Pity*. Paxton's book about Vichy coincides completely with a rediscovery of a whole part of me that I had completely buried.[3]

BAILLY: In the preceding stage, would you say you were anti-Zionist? Anti-Zionism connected with the time you were still among the faithful in the Communist Party?

ROCHFELD: Yes. That was typically the Party's position. Furthermore, the Party put out some propaganda that did me a great military favor. At the instigation of the Soviets and in support of a certain number of sons of Resisters and deported persons, the Party made a big issue of the fact that a German general had taken charge of NATO forces. It had to do with Speidel. Party members refused to do their military service and I refused, too.

BAILLY: You were then considered a deserter?

ROCHFELD: Which I was not aware of, yes. But I was always lucky. I was a late signer of the petition, so I wasn't arrested because there were negotiations with the Party. That happened when Chaban-Delmas was Defense Minister, at the end of the Fourth Republic just before de Gaulle came to power. I had a bunch of pals who did time for having refused to go into the army to fight in Algeria, and others who did time because of this business that was, in my opinion, a Soviet red herring to try to break up NATO.

BAILLY: To get back to the anti-Zionism of the Communist Party, did it come from the fact that in their orthodoxy Israel's history is a colonial history?

ROCHFELD: Among others. At the time of the 1967 War, I was not an admirer of Israel so I was not in favor of it. Israel was not part of my story and I supported the Party positions. I was completely into the orthodoxy.

BAILLY: Afterward, you emancipated yourself from the Communist Party. You didn't however become strictly Leftist?

ROCHFELD: No, because my earlier experience made me unreachable. I had a number of friends who ended up Trotskyites or then "China-ites." I didn't adopt either ideology. I'm forgetting one episode: I had a certain number of friends at CNRS who had been important to my own evolution who were Trotskyites. I actually was, for two or three years—just before and just after going to Scotland—in a Trotskyite movement that was less rigid. I kept connections with these people because much later we were all together in the Socialist Party. I was a statistic, a marker. I went through it all and I admit to having followed the whole evolution of the times with a few somewhat personal parentheses.

BAILLY: So you say that later, through the bias of history, through this awakening, you found a certain sensitivity, something more balanced in regard to yourself, to this intimate part of your identity?

ROCHFELD: Exactly.

BAILLY: Can you say a few words as to the extent that this has influenced your ethics, what you want to leave to your children, your attitude with regard to society?

ROCHFELD: Yes and no. For me it is a question of a general ethics.

BAILLY: It's universal?

ROCHFELD: Yes, exactly. It is universal and furthermore, it is essentially secular with, in spite of everything, a sensitivity to Israel and the Jewish problem. I haven't had a fundamental change in values, even if I have acquired a little different perspective about things.

BAILLY: More balanced?

ROCHFELD: Absolutely. That's the right term. If you take a look at the politics of today, including that of Israel, I feel myself to be in a completely awkward position. I am relatively critical of the politics, while partly understanding it. All the same, I lived through the Algerian War; I have been in the army. The whole relationship with terrorism is not a simple one. If someone wants to say that Israel is in no way responsible, I can answer with the same thing that is said about Arafat: that he hasn't missed an opportunity to miss an opportunity. So I think the mistakes are shared. But for me, Israel's position leads to an impasse. All the same, I have a nuanced point of view when I consider that the Israelis are on the front line; that they have to fit themselves into an environment that is obviously not welcoming, even if I was agreeably surprised by the statements by the Prince of Saudi Arabia. Despite this nuanced perspective, I remain faithful to a certain number of universal values compatible with the fact that, with respect to my Jewish culture, I still have a historic memory. I am part of a history that I know much better now than I knew before. I read lots of books. I was very interested in the details related in the Hilberg book,[4] which seems to be a very detailed and comprehensive summary. In short, a universal culture, but with a certain number of specific sentiments.

BAILLY: Anti-Semitism isn't any particular problem for your descendants as well?

ROCHFELD: No. I have never lived in a Jewish milieu. My second wife is not Jewish. I have always lived with intelligent people. I've had some reaction from the Right, the Left, in the army or elsewhere, but not having a strong Jewish identity—my best friends are not Jewish—I haven't had dealings with anti-Semites.

BAILLY: You don't spend time in a Jewish milieu?

ROCHFELD: A little, but it is very artificial. In the late 1970s I joined a group of computer scientists from the Council of Jewish Institutions in France (CRIF). For me it was a chance to put in some money, as I do for Médecins du Monde. I don't try to buy myself back, but somehow I'm still willing to give money to groups I haven't given to before. But that's all. And also (this is somewhat anecdotal) my daughter and I took a course on Jewish culture with the liberal Jews, given by Rabbi Fahri, whom we had heard a lot about. The course was interesting to us but I didn't follow up on it. It was just a chance to be with my oldest daughter while we were there.

BAILLY: We are nearing the end of the interview. What seems important to you to connect between the past, present, and future concerning your deported father and your history as a hidden child? What do you want to leave to your descendants and society?

ROCHFELD: What I have begun to leave to my descendants is that I have talked to them; I have told them the history, the memory. What still has value for me as an individual is a strong sensitivity to all that concerns racism in general. When there are anti-Semitic movements, I react. That means something to me; I am sensitive to it.

BAILLY: That's evident. As for what you would say about racism in general, all the atrocities that can happen, do you have the impression that our history makes us particularly responsible to sensitize people on this question?

ROCHFELD: We are responsible because we ourselves have experienced atrocity. What is important to me is an openness to a certain number of phenomena. In the big demonstration I went to in 1995, under Juppé, I literally recognized myself in the slogan: "First, second, third generation, we are all children of immigrants!" There I met a lot of people I hadn't seen for years. That was our universality with an individual aspect to it for me, along with a growing awareness of the complexity of the world (which doesn't make things any easier). In fact, things are not simple; phenomena aren't interpretable through some preestablished prism, including my position on Israel. It is the same in other areas. We are in a world that is increasingly complex, where an increasing number of forces interact, and where there are fewer and fewer constraints. The disappearance of the filters, through which these forces used to pass, increases the number of possible outcomes and adds even more to the complexity of events.

BAILLY: So you try to be circumspect in making judgments, to take into account all these factors that interact?

ROCHFELD: Yes, despite everything, while watching for dangerous tendencies.

BAILLY: About social justice or injustice?

ROCHFELD: Yes, but considered with an awareness of the complexity of the world.

BAILLY: Alright. Do you have anything more to add?

ROCHFELD: No, I don't think so. When I read a book, I feel I am a simple marker, including a generational one. For example, when I read books about the generation of the Algerian War, I am right in it. And even after, from being in the Communist Party to belonging to the Leftist movement. For me, all that is no longer serious. I have a tendency to see it like an amateur performance. I am no longer an activist. I am incapable of being an activist now; it has passed me by. I no longer believe; I can no longer believe that anyone holds the truth.

BAILLY: Does that make you pessimistic about humanity?

ROCHFELD: Not at all. I've worked a lot on complexity, including on a theoretical level. That was part of my teaching at the Conservatory. I am not an unreasonable optimist, but I am not a pessimist either. I think we are moving toward an open society with all the dangers, possibilities, and liberty that it represents. I have been deeply into the technical, in information technology. I have worked a lot—including theoretically—on information technology, and that is also the reason I am not a pessimist. I think an interesting story will unfold—with lots of games. We are in a world that has never before been so open, that's obvious.

BAILLY: Knowledge, communication, and its exchange?

ROCHFELD: Yes, all that and even the disappearance of blocs. Politically, of course, people can engage in all kinds of foolishness and there are no counterbalances, but on the other hand anything and everything is possible; it's moving in both directions.

BAILLY: The game's not over.

ROCHFELD: No. I am one of the people who say that history is a blank page and it is written upon every day. This takes place with the values of openness in which I believe. For me, it is obvious; there are no problems, no ambiguities about that. The blank page is the open world.

FIGURE 6.1. Danielle, at age five, in 1942 at
Saint-Martin-du-Fouilloux (Maine-et-Loire),
with her teddy bear, Loulou, her companion
throughout the war.

# 6

# Danielle Bailly

*Danielle Bailly, now retired, was a professor of English at the secondary level and later at the University of Paris VII with specializations in linguistics and didactics. Her principal interests are in secular Jewish culture (Yiddish chorale, klezmer music, schtetl dance) and in the transmission of the memory of the Holocaust in connection with the values of the world of today and of tomorrow.*

I was born on March 23, 1937, in Paris.[1] My father was Polish and my mother, of Ukrainian origin, was French. My father, Thadée Schneck, was born in 1904 in Galicia—home of klezmer music—at Lvov. This military town, poorly governed throughout history, was Polish, then Austrian, and finally Ukrainian—first in the USSR, then in the independent Ukraine. It remains elegant, full of reminders of the Polish kings and rich with monuments, despite the Nazis having used flame-throwers to destroy some of the majestic synagogues. My father was proud of his hometown, of its great university, of its white stone Baroque architecture Opera House. He was also proud of his first name of Thadée, a Yiddish name (Tankhe) assimilated into Polish. My paternal grandfather was a tailor of considerable prestige, having created the uniforms with all the paraphernalia, parade weapons, and gold-buttoned embellishments for the Austrian army of Emperor Franz

Joseph, who was somewhat benevolent—even toward the Jews. My grandfather employed a large number of workers in a shop on the top floors of a building he owned. As a respected member of the Jewish community, he led a relatively easy life, enjoying good taste in art, meeting lots of people, and traveling. To my father, who loved and admired him, he was a *tsadik*, a wise and esteemed man, pious but open-minded, who treated his workers well and invited the poor to festivities. My great-grandmother—whose Hebrew name, Dinah, I bear—shared his commitments to charitable works. It was an observant Jewish family, but not fanatical, in contrast with the Hasidim—those "miracle rabbis" with their court and their beggars, exactly as Singer described them with their obscurantism, superstition, but also with an extraordinary mixture of ideas and discussions. Lvov didn't have a ghetto even though the Jews lived on certain streets, in the historic, rather well-to-do non-Jewish heart of the town.

Early on my father rebelled against religion, its rigidity and its resignation to social injustice. This is also one of the reasons France, home of the Enlightenment, attracted him. He would always be an unshakeable atheist and a secular activist, with clear Leftist tendencies. After his *matura* (equivalent of the *baccalauréat*) he couldn't go on to the university because of the *numerus clausus*, since anti-Semitism was rising in Poland. Seething with anger, he would tell us how the "Polacks" one day forced his father down on the sidewalk to humiliate him;[2] how another day they wounded his father trying to cut off his beard—little monstrosities that this dignified and respectable man had to endure in silence—a silence that was intolerable to my father. He despised the Polish, the sinister Pilsudski, the pogroms and injustices perpetrated by armed groups—against which the Jewish defense groups made up of butchers' assistants reacted. Furthermore, life after the First World War had become difficult and the family became impoverished. So in 1927 my father went to study in France, leaving his parents and his nine brothers and sisters. Eagerly arriving in France (France: land of liberty; Paris: the most beautiful city in the world), he found himself alone with no financial support, especially after the Crash of 1929, to study without help or mastery of the French language. He enrolled at the Sorbonne to major in physics, chemistry, and biology. He dreamed of majoring in cosmetology because he had an amazing sense of scent for perfumes, but he couldn't continue his studies. Handy with his hands, intelligent, resourceful, never defeated, he worked at several different trades. He nevertheless continued to be frustrated at not being able to become a perfume maker. That is why later he dreamed a single dream: that his children would perform brilliantly as students. My father would always have difficulty becoming integrated into French society and be disappointed not to participate easily in the intellectual life of the upper middle class. It was more a matter of milieu than of finances. Feeling himself superior to the tradesmen and small business proprietors but still not belonging with doctors, lawyers, and the like, he rarely joined with the Jewish community either. He remained on the fence—ill at ease on either side because of the disparity between his ambitions and his opportunities.

My mother, Jeanne (Haya) Népommachi, was born in France in 1907. My maternal grandmother, Bunia, was born in the Ukraine—then a part of Russia—into modest surroundings with a very pious carpenter father. She learned to read and write Yiddish and Russian at the *heder* and, orphaned, was raised by an older sister. She became a seamstress. She was a refined, lively, stable, and generous woman. My maternal grandfather, Moïshe, was a handsome man, but a little immature. Tack and saddle maker by trade, he never learned how to support himself or his family comfortably. After their marriage in Russia, my grandparents came to France in 1905, to flee—after my grandfather's seven years of military service—the Russian-Japanese War and the drafting of men into Nicolas the Second's army, which happened each time the Czar needed cannon fodder for war. It had been that way for a long time. In the preceding generation, problems had already surfaced. My grandfather's family actually owed their name, Népommachi, to that fact. It came from the Russian *niepomniaschy,* meaning "he who doesn't remember" because when, under the previous czar, my great-grandfather was called up for the draft, he wanted to be classified as unfit for service. He then feigned amnesia, and when asked his name answered, "I don't remember." Drafted under this name, he had to report for duty.

Later the anti-Jewish pogroms were raging. My grandmother told about the drunken Cossacks staggering during their hit-and-run raids in the *schtetls* during the Christian holidays or whenever, and the violent way they humiliated and killed Jews, slitting feather beds to make feathers fly around, and so on (exactly what is shown in *A Fiddler on the Roof*). My grandfather's parents had endured similar incidents, near Kichinev. I have a photo of them: According to the family history, my great-grandmother's anguished look results from her back having been broken during a pogrom. She was stooped over from that time on (with financial burdens, too).

My grandparents left clandestinely for America but stopped en route in Paris. They were simple, pious people—my grandmother never in her life broke either the kosher food rules or the Shabbat, even during the war—but they had a certain affinity for the Bund. They were relatively enlightened; they read the Yiddish press and often discussed issues with their friends. My grandmother very much wanted to see her family become integrated into France and her three children fluent in French, even though Yiddish would be the language spoken in the home and she did her shopping with her Russian-French dictionary in her hand.(My parents spoke French at home but Yiddish was their "hidden language." I understood simple Yiddish but not really literary Yiddish. In any case, I find the language moving. What Kafka says is true: "Everyone always believes he knows less Yiddish than he actually knows. . . .")

My grandparents rented a shop on rue Vaugirard; he was a cobbler, she sold shoes. Grandfather had even resoled Trotsky's shoes and those of his Russian revolutionary comrades who had immigrated to Paris. Chagall came also. All these people were poor and had but a single pair of shoes, and sat waiting in the shop until the repairs were finished. Grandmother made them a cup of hot tea, and this small society was happy just to be speaking Russian. It was a welcoming place, very Russian and very Jewish. Everyone talked a lot there.

The girls in these families didn't study; they married—period! My mother and my aunt suffered because of this. To their father, only the son mattered. My uncle became an engineer. On the other hand, my grandmother fought for the welfare of her daughters, who succeeded in obtaining commercial degrees. With their inquiring minds, they had wanted to continue their studies. They were interested in theater, reading, and the finer things.

This, then, is a little about my two parents for whom education became the priority because they both had been prevented from achieving their own educational aspirations.

My parents met in Paris, at a dance party. My mother was cute and shapely; my father had a way with words. They were married in 1935. To my mother, he was the love of her life. My father loved her a great deal as well. They became a close couple.

When Mama died in 1985, Papa was so stricken he lived only another six months. She was her husband's servant her whole life. I was put on a pedestal by him, but other than his daughter, women were nothing special. As a young girl, I was closely protected at home, which wasn't fun. No Girl Scouts, not much going out. My father was the fierce guardian of my virginity.

My maternal grandmother, who was strict with her family, took a dim view of my mother marrying a Galician (worse than a Russian) whose family was not in France. Knowing that my father was a nonbeliever, she tried to find out more about him before her daughter married him. At that time in the community, if a man were alone in France they wondered about him—if he was already married somewhere else, for example. My grandmother was finally reassured with the favorable information about my father's family she got from the rabbi. My father, a free spirit chilled by this distrust, never missed an opportunity to fulminate against the rabbis, and never really got along well with his in-laws.

To save money, in 1937 my parents shared an apartment with my grandparents. My father decorated berets to earn his living. He also tried several other short-term jobs. In 1938–1939, he finally got into his beloved beauty products business and rented a small place on the Champs-Elysées as a laboratory. He made perfumed face powders. (My brother has a treasured beautiful gold cardboard powder box labeled Poudre Thadée.) The war put an end to this experiment. Meanwhile, my mother was selling shoes.

In 1939 my parents rented an apartment on rue Saint-Claude, in the Third Arrondissement. That's where we were living when the war began. My father, having vivid memories of Lvov, followed the Nazis' rise closely in the press. He didn't need anyone to sketch it out for him; even in France Jews would face a threat sooner or later, he reasoned, and he warned his friends. Later, when the war began, he tried again to warn them and persuade them not to believe any patriotic myths and unrealistic, soothing assurances about the benevolence of France. Certain friends—who had already become naturalized French citizens—shrugged off the warnings. Later they were rounded up and deported, never to return. In September, rumors—at the time proven to be unfounded—circulated that Paris was to be bombed![3] Some of the capital's population wanted to leave. My mother, her parents, her sister, her fourteen-year-old nephew and I joined a group that "retreated" to the

province of Indre. Before leaving, she put the family's principal possessions in a trunk that she entrusted to the concierge, Madame F——. As
it turned out, this evil old crone stole practically everything we owned.
All of what she didn't steal (papers, photos of the family in Poland)
would be taken to be burned, leaving the apartment completely empty.
Germans? Collaborators? In 1942, she denounced the Jewish residents
of the building to Pétain's French police.

My father and uncle stayed in Paris. Wanting to do something to
help France, they had voluntarily enlisted and were awaiting their military orders. My uncle served to the end in the Foreign Legion at Sidi-
bel-Abbès, and was demobilized in Marseille in 1940. My father was
refused for military service because of an acute inflammation of the
throat.

Our little family tribe, after having lugged around all our necessary
personal belongings (I had my teddy bear, Loulou—my faithful
guardian against anxiety—clasped to my chest), arrived in Indre, where
we were cared for by the Red Cross. My grandparents were eating practically nothing—the food not being kosher—so my mother persuaded
the tribe to leave the "retreating" group. We then left, by taxi, for Angers
where some of my uncle's family had already taken refuge. Our first
little lodging in that city had mice and a big feral cat ready to chase
them. It was the dead of winter 1939–1940. The adults found odd jobs.
Then, after an exchange of letters with my father ("the most important
thing, especially for the child, is to obtain food"), my mother looked for
a job managing a food store. She was hired by Monsieur Châtenay, who
directed the chain of Brisset Stores in Anjou. He hired her to manage
the store at 12 rue des Lices.

In February of 1940 we settled in as a family. The store occupied
the street level of a strange two-story building where we lived—quirky,
antiquated, uncomfortable; destroyed today. Because my mother and
my aunt worked hard, our food was basically assured. In June my
father left Paris on a bicycle, in the wake of the exodus, and rejoined
us. He gave a boost to the commercial activity of the store, but my parents never engaged in black marketing.

On June 17, German bombings began over the area. I remember the
overall atmosphere of uncertainty—sirens, running for cover, gas masks.
On the 19th of June, the occupying forces entered the town. Between
June and October the collaboration was established. On October 16 my
father (Polish) and my mother and I (French) went to the town hall to

register as Jews, as required by the government—my mother fearful of any illegal situation. I became increasingly frightened by the whispered consultations between my parents. They said nothing in front of me that I might risk repeating or that might frighten me, but I saw very clearly that there were secrets that I complained about later: "You are hiding something from me!" Ill at ease, I could feel that they were hiding things from me to protect my peace of mind, but what?

In 1941 the atmosphere darkened. A nervous child, I began to be afraid of a variety of things. I was afraid of the Germans, whom I perceived as monsters or ogres. At night I was also afraid of the dark and of sounds. This big Brisset building had thirty-umpteen doors and windows and was poorly protected. Moreover, it was next to a charming twelfth-century chapel, Saint-Aubin Tower, and on the first floor of the house, at the back of a junk room, there was a door that opened onto the first floor of the Tower! I was afraid that bats, ghosts, or skeletons would glide over us from the dark corners of this place. Nevertheless life continued, for better or worse. Then came the laws prohibiting professional practice by Jews. The fragile equilibrium constructed with false bravery melted away. On June 26, we were obliged to leave management and lodging. Papa went immediately to ask Monsieur Châtenay to take us in, letting him in on the secret of our Jewish descent, but without success. This man showed complete solidarity, didn't betray us, and did what he could for us. He put my father in contact with the Angevin Resistance. They got us new identity cards based on our last false papers with the name of Tellier. They saved us. Thank you, Monsieur Châtenay! (I recently learned that Monsieur Châtenay was one of the leaders of the Resistance in Maine-et-Loire. I understand that he had to maintain his cover and couldn't risk breaking the law by hiring Jews.)

The family tribe broke up. My grandparents returned to Paris (unwise!), my aunt and my cousin went to join my uncle in Toulouse; all three were protected there by a wonderful priest named Buffières. My parents and I stayed in Angers and found a little lodging situated in a rat-infested building on a cul-de-sac (the building was later leveled). My parents again found odd jobs. I was four years old and was very talkative. I wrote my real name in pencil on all the walls that I also covered with drawings. I was scolded. My parents drilled into my head that my name now was Danielle Tellier, that I mustn't tell anyone my real name nor write it, because the very bad Germans didn't like it. I was furious because I knew very well that at my age it was good to be able to write like grownups and I didn't see why I was forbidden to do something good.

It was now 1942. Threats increased; "they" were beginning to arrest Jews. Anjou is very Catholic. I remember the grand processions in the town followed by a populace that was both devout and anti-Semitic. My impression was that it was a rather hostile environment.

(Today I know the figures. However if there were fewer deported from France than from other countries it is because, overall, people there contributed to protecting us. But my family met more people who were "not nice" than "nice." When we were at Brisset, for example, the customers didn't know that we were Jewish, so with us, they "relaxed" and expressed openly their position against Jews and in support of Pétain.)

At this point, "they" were arresting more and more Jews by going to look for them in their homes. "They" picked them up from lists, in alphabetical order. I lived in this environment, in secret, in fear, with a new identity, and I tried desperately to make sense of it all. I heard the whispers: "So-and-so was taken; so-and-so was picked up." It was a mystery to me, but the anguish was there, amplified by what was left unsaid.

Angers had definitely become too dangerous. In June there was a another census of Jews.[4] The first big roundups were July 15 and 16. That same month, fleeing cul-de-sac Saint-Denis, we took refuge thirteen kilometers away, in the village of Saint-Martin-du-Fouilloux, with our false identity cards (my parents' professions: "gardener" and "seamstress"). My father had made them himself from new cards filled in by Mama, an illegible stamp made with a five franc coin and violet ink, and a pseudo watermark of the *État Français* (French State) made with a little butter. The cards were, at most, only relatively believable.

My father worked in the fields. My mother did sewing, knitting with bits of yarn. Our landlady, an elderly peasant woman wearing a headscarf who knitted very fast, all the time, without looking at her work while walking around in her garden of flaming fuchsias, taught my mother to knit socks with four needles. Life was extremely simple. The people of the village were a little primitive. I played with the children of my own age. (For example, we made necklaces on steel wire and strung little violet pearls originally meant for funeral wreaths . . .) I learned along with the others to recite the Lord's Prayer. We lived discreetly, managing to eat—my mother's obsessive concern. Getting coupons for food was a tricky situation with false papers. Daddy would go by bicycle fairly far into the country. As we needed everything, including tires for the bicycle, he very efficiently rolled string very tightly around the metal wheels. Mama would anxiously await his return. The months passed.

It was now 1943. My parents were always anxious; my mother always sighing. We lived in two little rooms, high in an old house without electricity. To get up to it, we had to climb a shaky staircase with no handrail. We had to be careful not to fall into the stairwell. One day Mama was going up the stairs and, arriving at the top, she turned to say to my father, "Watch out for the little one!" and then fell herself, a fall of about three meters (which made me feel guilty later). She broke her heel bone and couldn't walk. The fracture was severe and she had to go to the hospital to be operated on. With false papers, it was dangerous for a Jew to be hospitalized, as well as for the French who "covered up" for a Jew. My parents managed to get Mama admitted to a clinic in Angers. She wore a cast and walked with crutches for a year, greatly handicapped. It was an untimely accident.

After a certain time, we learned that the village mayor, whom we knew to be a Pétain loyalist, had guessed, despite our false papers, that we were Jews. This mayor, Monsieur P——, with his beret, his big mustache, his fat belly, his brown corduroy trousers, and his suspenders, denounced us to the French police. Someone (who? thanks to him, in any case) warned my parents one day. We had to leave immediately because the police were coming for us the next morning. We cleared out at once—in September 1943—carrying a single small bag so as not to draw attention, leaving our residence and that village.

That same year, my grandfather, who was trying to make his living working with leather and moving around a lot, was picked up by the French police one day on the road between Paris and Angers.

(We were close, my grandfather and I. I remember strolling with him along the promenade that curls along the ramparts of the castle at Angers. From the top there was a beautiful view of the river Maine. Grandfather and I would take it in, me perched on his shoulders. He would also bounce me on his knees as he sang a Kazatchok. He would tell me stories. His French was very bad. For example, when he wanted to tell someone, "You are an imbecile!" he would say "A bissil af dir!" (Word for word in Yiddish: "a 'becile' on you!") His favorite saying was "I don't want nothing; I want all okay.")

My grandfather was taken to Drancy and deported to Auschwitz by Convoy Number Forty-Eight on February 13, 1943. He did not return. Later my grandmother would get word from the German authorities that her husband had died "of typhus fever." My grandmother, in Paris, went to live near her sister and her family.

(In my great-aunt's family, her daughter, son-in-law, and their twenty-year-old son, a gifted pianist, were deported. Only their daughter Renée was saved, thanks to a French policeman, Monsieur Barnabé (thank you, Monsieur Barnabé!) who got her out of Drancy within a week. She went to the United States in 1945 and, broken, never married. Our family losses include my father's parents and seven of his brothers and sisters who, with the other Jews in Lvov, died of hunger or illness in the ghetto, or were taken to be shot in the neighboring forests and then buried in common graves, or were forced to work to exhaustion breaking the family tombstones in the Jewish cemetery at the edge of town (where nothing remains from before 1948, as I saw for myself) to pave the roads to Lvov, or were deported to Maïdanek, Belzec, or Janow. Only three survived in his family; my father and a brother and sister who left in the 1930s for the United States.)

As for my parents and me, on the move again, what direction should we take? Well, it would be Grenoble where my mother's brother had found refuge. One memory of this trip is of a country family who put us up one night. The woman demanded as a gift for her children the little gray rabbit fur coat I was wearing. Another time we stopped at a farm with a large dirty barnyard, an odiferous dunghill, puddles of cow urine and chicken droppings. I remember the reticence of these French families who half-heartedly put us up. I later learned that we had to pay them a lot. I felt my parents' anxiety. My father always feared that his Semitic features and accent would give him away, his main concern being to pass as French, to be "a shade of gray." Since before the war, he had presented himself as Alsatian, inventing an Alsatian family, asking my mother to make sauerkraut. He was sure that they believed him! The poor guy, with his Polish accent and looking like Shimon Peres . . .

In short, we passed the former Demarcation Line at La Roche-Posay after a fairly long trip. Travel at that time was slow and complicated. By taking a train that was under surveillance, we risked being picked up. We had to change lines often, creeping along in little noisy local trains with hard benches and drafts of cold air.

(Ever since the war, I dislike trains. I hate stations. They bring me a sense of insecurity, of sorrow, and of desolation; something poignant, heartrending, that is completely idiotic. And what if we arrive late and miss the train? And if we were to take the wrong train? Or lose our luggage? And if we were to risk, despite all our efforts, being lost or falling into a trap somehow by some silly thing? What anger and shame I feel being overtaken for an instant by an irrational fear that is rooted in the dark years of childhood and returns in a perverse and burdensome pattern.)

And then there were the country buses loaded with miscellaneous bundles, poorly attached—equally noisy and smelly from the gas exhaust. We then traveled to the South. Armed with false identity cards, my mother's and mine with a different name than my father's (at that time we had several combinations of false cards), my parents had instructed me to act as if I didn't know my father. This was not easy for a six-year-old during a long trip with the three of us in the same compartment. Yet another lie! Finally, the controller passed us without a problem and it was over.

We finally arrived in Grenoble. My father found a poorly paid job as a worker in a leather glove factory. My mother worked at home, sewing woolen mittens. Our home was a tiny dark room in a venerable monument—the Duguesclin Tower—a tower dating from the Middle Ages, tall and narrow, with a marvelous and well-worn winding staircase. Inside our room were only the most rudimentary furnishings. It was freezing in the winter and stifling in the summer, with a small window placed very high in the enormous wall. There was just enough room to have only minimal necessities—a Spartan toilet down the hall. Our area, the Abbey area, was away from the center of town. From the Tower there was a magnificent view of the Alpine Belledonne range, which changed colors during the day. During the winter, I liked to play in the snow. Even in the most desperate times, nature is important; it offers freedom and beauty and contributes to inner strength. I didn't experience anything tragic; my parents did everything possible to create a world for the "little one." Sometimes we didn't have enough to eat but it didn't seem important. Anyway, I was never hungry, especially in the summer heat when Mama settled me at mealtimes on the landing of the Tower where it was cooler, with an overturned washtub serving as a table. As was the case everywhere in France for those not in the black market or in the country, necessity became the mother of invention. We would try our luck at buying food with false cards in the villages far from Grenoble, choosing a different village each time. Sometimes a city employee would get coupons for us or a vendor would help us out. The Resistance fighters came as we did for food (unlike Anjou, Isere was more pro-Resistance). My father also obtained, as did all the workers in the factory, a little plot of land outside of town and a set of tools. He would leave on his bicycle to cultivate our six square meters of garden. There he raised, at most, a kilo of Jerusalem artichokes. They were precious. Another day, my father brought home a little packet of pea seeds, completely dried out and as hard as pebbles. Mama, after soaking them, cooked them for four days. They stayed just as hard, completely inedible. We threw them out, laughing insanely.

I attended school using my false name. School was good. It was tranquil, distracting, entertaining—no sense of oppression. Of course at recess they made us swallow a spoonful of beef blood to fortify us. The hardest part was lying to my classmates about my name and my situation. I had to control myself all the time. I couldn't invite anyone to my home; this tiny room couldn't be shown to anyone. My discomfort with lying was dangerous, in and of itself, but we didn't know if my schoolmates' families could be trusted. Did the teacher and the headmistress know I was Jewish? I still have my birth certificate at home, the real one, where "Schneck" had been removed and replaced with "Tellier." But it looks awful! How could this messy forgery fool anyone? Did the headmistress guess everything and still say nothing while accepting my enrollment? If that was the case, thank you, Madame Headmistress!

Christmas was another memory I have of this time. My parents tried to celebrate it a little so I would feel like the other girls at school, wanting me to be happy, but with no money to buy presents. I believed in Santa Claus so my mother made clothes for Loulou from an old lace slip she had from before the war. "A present from Santa Claus," she told me. Unfortunately, I recognized the lace and said, "But Mama, Santa Claus took your slip!" My parents started to laugh and I to cry. They laughed at my candor. Needless to say, my belief in Santa Claus was over but I also felt a crack in the confidence I had in them. I held it against them. I so needed to believe them whenever they tried to reassure me. But in this situation, they would tell me anything in order to be less anxious themselves. But I was smart and their lies destabilized me. At the time, parents overprotected children by not explaining anything to them, but the children weren't fooled.

In Grenoble in 1943 and 1944, danger was increasing. In 1943, for example, the Resistance fighters came secretly to our neighborhood to get food. The French Milice and the Germans learned about it and they began to control the area. One day they came to our street, and on the next street—Washington Street (which people pronounced "Vaginton")—they examined the identity papers of every occupant of every house and apartment. Once again our safety depended on our false papers. Papa had an axe for a weapon in our home. He said that if they came to arrest us because they had figured out that our papers were false—what we most feared at that time—he would cut the guys in two. I was cautioned never to play outside and to make as little noise as possible. Quietly in my chair, I drew a lot of pictures with pencil and very little paper. I read the little storybooks I brought home from school. When you are confined, you fill the space and your mind with what little there is. Freedom of imagination helps you get through the dangerous times, month after month. Another season and yet another, someday the nightmare will end. We only had to hold on, the three of us, and to stay afloat without making waves. We didn't go to downtown Grenoble except when we had to, but who can survive in a city without leaving the house?

One day when my father and I were running an errand, we came upon the beginnings of a roundup on the large public square. We weren't taken, we were just at the edge, but we saw up close how quickly it happened. The uniformed, booted, and armed Germans assembled the people, put them in tight rows of three and checked their papers. The entire square was soon filled with the Germans' covered trucks. As they checked papers, the soldiers selected some suspect individuals and ordered them into the trucks. Then they searched a man in a tan trench coat (were they looking for weapons?). The poor man had a precious egg in his pocket and, of course, it broke and everyone could see it run down his coat. They took this man away. I still remember the silent consternation of the bystanders.

Was it the same day? Was it during a more or less random verification of papers? In any case, my father and I had to take refuge in a church. I felt uncomfortable there. Even if my family was not religious, I knew it belonged to a religion that was not that of my ancestors. At the same time, I intuitively felt we were in this strange place to escape a real danger and that we were safe there. It was an enclave both protective—because we could hide in the recesses—and hostile because the priests there didn't like us.

The fear of these well-organized roundups was constant—always unannounced so that people couldn't escape. These roundups, major or minor, were also a part of the exceptionality of the Holocaust. I refer to its overall conception of anti-Semitic and anti-Resistance persecution carried out on a grand scale, extremely organized, well thought-out, and intelligent (even if many of the individuals carrying it out were cretins). We Jews, unorganized and left to our own devices, within our families, without information, were always on the alert to avoid the traps, which were set where we least expected them. What anguish we felt, for example, when forced to move elsewhere! We took public transportation—city buses within Grenoble, local buses outside. The police also rode these vehicles; they could get on at any time, even if we had not seen them at the start of the trip. With the threat of arrest everywhere, the hazards of going out to buy provisions, and the difficulty of buying the least little thing with these complicated coupons; if one happened to become ill, it was a catastrophe. I often suffered stomach upsets. (My other curse was bed-wetting.) Was it psychosomatic? After the war, it stopped. I blame it on the war. I no doubt would not have had these problems if I had had a peaceful upbringing, without persecution. These things scar a child and the bad memories stay with you for the rest of your life.

(In telling this, I feel tremendous guilt complaining about these problems that are so minor compared to the grief of children whose parents were deported and who were then left alone in the world, or even those with one parent deported. But I still bear testimony about a terrible time that left deep scars on many of us: our war—a war that specifically and efficiently singled out the Jews, to hunt them down and flush them out wherever they were.)

One day when I was suffering one of these violent "acetone attacks," as Mama would say, she needed to go downtown to find an open emergency pharmacy to buy medication to settle my stomach. On the way, she was caught up in the beginning of a roundup. She had the presence of mind to say, "My daughter is sick, let me go to the pharmacy." They let her go. Her return home was a minor miracle. It was then that she said that the situation had now become impossible. It was urgent now to get me into refuge. My parents decided the next day to hide me. "And if I had been taken, what would have become of the little one?" Mama asked herself. While she was in town, I had been in bed alone with my nausea, with my father working from morning to night. Fortunately there was a charming Italian neighbor, Signora Berto, one of the "Righteous." When Mama came home, crazy with worry about what could have happened, Signora Berto told her that she would have taken care of the little one, that she would have protected her. Mama told this to Papa that evening, her eyes full of tears. And I asked myself, was it my fault (guilt again!) if we were in dire straits; with me being sick and having trouble lying?

In any case, fifty years later I understand why my parents at the time had to hide me separately from them. They looked for a family for me outside Grenoble. During the six months I was hidden, they also hid in Grenoble, sleeping in a different place every night to avoid the residency searches and roundups carried out by the French and the Germans, since our false papers were not all that credible.

So during the winter of 1943 and the spring of 1944, at the age of six, I was a hidden child in a little village situated in the mountains along the Isere River, not far from Grenoble. There I again savored the precious positive aspects of nature, its consoling beauty, the element of security I drew from it. In the spring, on the paths cut at the foot of the waterfalls with their moving sound, the pale pink wild roses bloomed so profusely they could make you feel faint. My parents had entrusted me to Italian friends of Signora Berto. It began well, but this family couldn't keep me—I don't know why—and they put me with another family in the same village, a French family this time, who agreed to keep a child as a boarder. And that did not go so well.

(I was hidden for only a short time, which is nothing compared with what happened to so many other children! I am ashamed of making such a fuss about so little! But after all, my experience, like all the others, puts the history of the hidden children under the magnifying glass.)

I was unhappy because I didn't know when I would see my parents and because this unmotivated couple showed neither understanding nor good human qualities toward me. The man drank and when he was drunk, he became aggressive and I was afraid. I wasn't molested, I wasn't even really ever hit, but I was poorly cared for. Moreover, I wet the bed every night, despite all my efforts. These people threatened me with harsh punishment if I kept it up because the woman was upset by all the bed linens she had to wash. So I cried a lot, which also upset them. At noon the woman would take my wet sheet and pretend to wring it out in my plate as if to give me this pee to drink. The man threatened me and was rude. I have memories of humiliation. I ate very little; I basically ate cooked onions every day. My parents couldn't come to see me. I was there with this enuresis which I couldn't control and for which I was punished with these people saying that I was doing it on purpose and that I was weak and naughty. Emotionally isolated, I went to school, still under my false name.

Yet at school there were times of beautiful serenity, a sense of escape from anxiety. As children, we needed very little to have fun. In Brignoud there was a small factory that made aluminum foil. These magnificent sheets of thin laminated metal were geometrically patterned with gradations of color. We were given some sheets of it, treasures that we stroked and traded during recess. The teacher let us cover the porcelain inkwells of our desks with pieces of this shiny metal. It was another consolingly beautiful vision at the time.

Another memory: One day, two French cyclists on loud motorcycles with black sidecars (very loud in this quiet village) came to ask my hosts, "Who lives here?" They quickly shut me in my room (a pre-planned strategy for when something might happen) and didn't denounce me. The cyclists left without looking further. What luck! And if they had searched all the rooms? I understood perfectly at that moment that they were searching for people; later I understood they were looking for hidden Jews or Resistance fighters. My hosts told me that the cyclists had been looking for me, but that they had said nothing about my being there. They had perhaps saved my life; nevertheless, my "thanks" is not forthcoming.

In June my parents took me back to be with them. That's it. In summary, my time as a hidden child was short, but the emotional weight of it remains with me. This is how the months went by in Grenoble until the end of the war. From 1942 until 1944, Mama had no news of my grandmother who stayed alone in Paris. She felt the full range of anxieties (arrest, penuries, bombings) and of guilt. At the last, battles took place around the city to dislodge the Gestapo and the Milice from their fiefdoms. People talked about it and kept score. News, some true, some false, was spread from person to person. My parents had no radio, no one around us had a telephone, no one read the disgusting newspapers, untrustworthy because they were part of the collaboration, but everyone followed the events, full of hope.

Finally Liberation came on August 23, 1944. My father—literally crazed with relief and joy—was exhausted and voiceless after having run for three days through the town in every direction shouting. My mother cried with joy. At the windows, she and the neighbors in the Dugueselin Tower displayed the flags of the four Allies they had sewn with the makeshift *schmates* of fortune. But the transition from war to peace was full of hazards. The gunfire between partisans and Germans or collaborators wreaked havoc for a few days in Grenoble and in the outlying areas until the actual liberation of the city, bitterly achieved after an extremely violent counterattack. I can still hear the whistle of bullets and the grenades exploding, not far from the Tower where we were ensconced. The Vercors Maquis was so close! The fighting would continue for some time. The flags were removed from the windows in panic as terrified people cried, "Look out! The Germans are returning!"

Finally the gunfire ceased. The flags flew again followed by unimaginable jubilation in the streets. I remember a huge crowd, a grand, if a little disorganized, parade of the French Resisters: the beloved "Fifi"—our affectionate term for the young members of FFI, de Gaulle's underground civilian army for whom we felt such tenderness and veneration—and the Communist Resisters of the FTP. General de Gaulle's kepi, higher than the others, emerged from the crowd. Perched on Papa's shoulders, I saw de Gaulle pass the flock of heads and advance slowly, noble and proud, surrounded by a large number of soldiers, who paraded as well as they could amid these people wild with joy to the sound of the Allobroges song. To this day it brings me to tears when I hear it. For us in Grenoble, it was the song of Liberation.

And then came the groups of German prisoners. They walked through the town well guarded and in rags. Those shabby-looking guys, limping or walking along like uncoordinated puppets, frightened no one. We were astounded. Were these the physically overbearing ogres who had terrorized us? The sound of their heavy boots, stomping in perfect cadence, that would resound in the ears of the Jews until the end of their days; I shiver at the mere memory of it. These guys wore only pathetic crumpled khaki hats, not the menacing helmets or the tall, rigid kepis the leaders wore that gave us chills just to see, even from afar. Clothes make the man. It was over, OVER! The people spat on them. My father unleashed a stream of abuse on them. He didn't yet know at that time that his family had been exterminated in Poland. No news was available. That would come later. But at that moment, relieved, enjoying liberty, we were completely alive, that's all.

The Americans, of course: jeeps, chewing gum, chocolate—our immense love for them. The United States would remain from then on a beloved country for my family. After the war, my American uncles and aunts would send packages to help us—a little family Marshall Plan—and I would teach English in gratitude to this nation that saved us. It was an extraordinary celebration. In the country divided in two, faced with the Pétainism—"à la Papon"[5]—of those French that I felt to be the majority, and I include here those cowards who put on a different face at the end of the war. One cannot overstate the vital importance of a heroic minority, resistant in spirit or actually linked to the Resistance of the modest and anonymous Righteous. How could we not express gratitude to the anti-Fascist beliefs, the organizations, the networks? In Grenoble, so many snipers had fallen in the streets, so many bouquets of flowers marked the spots! Later, plaques would be posted to commemorate the sacrifice made by these Resistance fighters.

In the summer of 1944 my family had neither attachment nor property in Grenoble, nor lodging or a place to land professionally in Paris. Mama received mail that reassured her about her mother, her sister, her brother and their families. She learned then that the others had been deported. My father chose to return to Angers to take up the management of the Brisset grocery store to insure income. My mother agreed. We left March 2, 1945. My parents began their life again with nothing. For example, in the bedroom over the grocery store, their bed was set on four beverage cases, with two doors placed horizontally on the cases to make a frame for a straw mattress. The Red Cross gave us some scratchy horsehair military blankets. I had a little iron bed and a straw mattress. We had no dishes or change of clothing. We lived that way a long time, but so what? My parents realized they had escaped extermination. They still intentionally masked the truth from me as if I were an idiot. We were alive; we felt we had been extremely lucky; we did not complain. In retrospect, I feel myself to have been extremely lucky to have kept both my parents. Nothing else was important; we were alive, we had courage, and we could start over. What that does to lessen the importance of material possessions!

My father later experienced the pain of learning about the loss of his family in Poland. At night, he moaned during his nightmares, or couldn't sleep at all. This upset me, since I slept in the same room as my parents. He never recovered from this loss. He would be somewhat misanthropic, bitter, closed within himself for the rest of his life. My mother would also mourn the loss of her deported father. Every Jewish family counted the members who were deported and did not return.

Despite all that, we took up a calm little life in Angers. To reconnect with life, my parents had a second child, my brother, born in 1946. He was a beautiful baby with big blue-gray eyes whom I doted on like a second mama. He made us very happy. We relearned what normal life was. In 1947–1948 I was awarded the Prix d'Excellence in my class at school. (Normal, wasn't it?) My father got in touch again with his brother and sister in the United States. We went to the theater or movies from time to time. With the first money my father earned at that time, he bought, even before thinking about buying a proper bed, an antique statuette. He was crazy about art, even if he was not a true connoisseur, and later in Paris he would attend auctions at Drouot's, to the extent his modest means allowed. In particular, he wanted to find silver objects like those his parents had owned in Poland and which had been stolen by the Nazis. An admirer of Jewish religious art in silver (spice boxes, *yad*, menorah), he also acquired, through the stores in Angers, some little objects that he placed in a window of the apartment we would later rent in Paris and that he never stopped looking at. "You see," he would often tell me while showing me a certain object, "this is exactly like the one we had at home in Lvov."

In October of 1948, we "went back up" to Paris. My parents weren't provincial people; they wanted me to do serious studies and my mother wanted to be with her remaining family members again. My parents worked hard at the grocery store—their career by chance, not choice, that they carried out, even if it didn't please them a great deal— with style, objectivity, and by taking an interest in the economical and ecological aspects. They resigned themselves and stayed there until their retirement (belatedly, given the meager pensions given merchants). Their new life after the war was focused on my scholarly success and later on that of my brother who did well, too, since he graduated in engineering after brilliantly completing studies in science.

My father had to rebuild his life emotionally, with the burden of his family's disappearance and the remorse of having left Poland without having been able to see them again, or help them, or prevent their massacre. He would be tortured all his life by these thoughts, along with his hatred for the "Krauts" and the "Polacks." My parents never had many friends and a number of those from before the war had been deported. I had very few cousins, uncles, or aunts. Our big family had become impoverished, stunted, and shrunken. Decades passed during which my parents tried to overcome this pain without ever forgetting or pardoning, silently settling their personal accounts with Catholicism, with a France they judged to have been too loyal to Pétain and to have betrayed its role as a land of refuge, with the non-Jewish world in which they no longer had confidence. Aside from that, things took their course.

And later on we, the young people of my generation, had to work at becoming integrated into French society. A certain number of us, including myself, took partners who were somewhat "mixed," so we had to deal with these problems. In the generation that followed, assimilation into France continued. Neither of my two children has a Jewish spouse. Despite this, my children are very vigilant that Jewishness be transmitted with the means at hand, and my son and my daughter-in-law are tolerant. What is to remain of Jewish memory rests with the grandchildren. It is not easy. It could be counterproductive for me to engulf them in these stories, and yet when the time is right I really want them to know what happened to us. So I distill a few softened stories of the Holocaust, watching that I don't traumatize them. I try to do it with tact. Do I succeed? I hope so.

What have been the consequences of a marked childhood on the rest of my life? Physically, I have none. Unlike my husband who lacked milk as a child and came out with bad teeth, I had enough to eat and have no nutritional deficiencies. Psychologically, I don't want to be overly dramatic. I have sporadic nightmares, which is not so severe.

(For a long time I had a recurring nightmare. I am in a closed room. Across from me there is a door that is apparently locked. This door, nevertheless, suddenly opens and a French policeman in a kepi and a cape, brandishing a nightstick, rushes in to grab me. I just have time to get to another door on the opposite side of the room. I open it, cross the room it opens into—the rooms are in a single file—lock the door behind me and look for another way out, terrorized. The scene begins again, from room to room with my frantic flight. The policeman manages to open the next door and I just have time to hurry into another room, and so on. Anxiety: I have less and less time to shut myself in and the officer will catch me soon. When he finally arrives in the same room as I (I don't have time to leave it or get it locked!) and is just about to catch me, I cry out and wake up terrified. Should this nightmare—which disappeared years ago—be attributed to the events of the war? I don't know. A psychologist might also say it's a sexual metaphor for fear of being raped, or some other things. I'm not a psychologist.)

What else? I tend to be afraid of everything and to imagine every possible danger for my children and my grandchildren. Can this be attributed to the anxieties of my own childhood? "Fear" indeed, is the key word of my childhood and that has stayed with me. Recently one of my grandchildren said to me, "Oh Grandma, you are always afraid of everything! Mama told me that you had an illness, the war illness, which made you afraid of everything!" I was not pleased with my daughter; I don't think I am pathological about it! But this family interpretation surprised me; I didn't realize that I signaled this kind of frequent and unreasonable anxiety to others in such a visible way. I attribute it generally to the war years that imposed a kind of second nature on me as a young child. If I reflect on this multifaceted fear I experienced while we were hunted and "camouflaged," what comes to mind first is that my young age limited my understanding, which then compounded the terror. Of course, I know that children older than I also had specific fears no less and sometimes greater than mine during those times. I only describe here those of a young child. Between the age of four and seven, I didn't really understand it to be a threat "of death." I could only tell myself that the bad Germans wanted to hurt me and my parents, and maybe take me away from them and their protection, or take them away from me. The only thing that was clear to me was that we had to avoid them, that we had to do everything we could to stay far from them, to be "good" so they didn't find us or punish us. To be "good" meant, above all, not to make mistakes about my name change, even if my common sense was unable to find any good reason for such a complication. This insecurity was connected to many changes in routine. It also meant being calm, not crying, not acting silly every time we had to move or change our daily routines or the food we ate (we had to eat what we could find), our surroundings, and our ways of sleeping. We could never make too much noise so as not to draw attention or alert the neighbors. How can a young child be calm when he feels his parents' anxiety? My parents' emotions showed on their faces as clearly as if they were an open book and a child, even a young one, sees this very clearly. She sees it even better being so young. To be very young and already involved in the delicate responsibility of sharing the family tasks of camouflage and optimal organization (a little local defense plan in the face of the permanent danger for such a long time) is a lot to bear. But the worst is what is left unsaid—the "phantasm-breeding" scourge that surrounded us because my parents wanted to provide complete reassurance to bolster their plan to defend the family. They naïvely thought that the bigger the lie, the easier it is for the child to believe it, and that it is best to impose silence on implicit and fundamental questions (Who wants to hurt us? Why? How can we escape? Who besides us is in this incomprehensible and absurd situation? How long will it last?), especially with little chatterboxes like me. This reasoning, of course, didn't resolve the problem of my fear. Fear is doubled when the cause is hidden, when it is undefined, when you don't understand the circumstances and reasons for its appearance, when the threat is arbitrary and unforeseen. You cannot build a rational system to master panic or anguish; you can't control anything. And speaking of aftereffects, I think that later in my life, each time I felt unable to analyze or control a threat or a danger, this little old rigid (psycho-rigid?) routine took hold as it did before and left me as helpless as a child.

One more thing: I am always apprehensive about people being anti-Semitic toward me or my family; certainly not because I would be ashamed, but simply because I am always afraid that will be the first reaction of a non-Jewish person toward us. It is a painful feeling. Not that I hide, but I always want to pass unnoticed in this regard. For example, I had a sense of relief dropping the name Schneck, which I found hard to carry, and taking on the name Bailly when I married. And yet, I'm very proud of being Jewish!

So be it. Let us accept this mishmash of contradictions. But let's not exaggerate; despite everything I feel mentally healthy and well balanced overall, even if very emotional and quick-tempered. I am still extremely hypersensitive and I revolt or become indignant over numerous bad turns, injustices, absurdities, or preferential treatments. Politically I spend my time wanting to right the collective wrongs.

(If I were to look at myself from the outside I might say about myself: "Danielle is too much!" I can overreact, become overly indignant or discouraged when I see something unjust or ignoble. It has something to do in some way with human solidarity and I always react strongly when I am confronted with negative activities in the public or private sphere. I get intensely involved emotionally, which causes me to get involved in a number of causes or positions to defend what I value as "good" or, on the other hand, to fight against what I consider to be "bad." These efforts are not necessarily useful or efficient, especially since I'm not engaged in militancy that would truly expose me, or worse, expose my family, but it is true that I never miss an opportunity to defend what I consider just. I follow current events and involve myself in the political debate. But it never gets any further. I simply think that Jews, because of having been through the Holocaust, should feel concerned at the first sign of any other dirty trick that happens in the world in the way of oppression or injustice. I see them as being insufficiently concerned and that bothers me a great deal. I have a sense of the absurd: "So what good did it do for us to endure all that? What did we learn about humanity?" Jews worldwide have pretty much forgotten the writing of Primo Levi, Bruno Bettelheim, and others. On the other hand, I feel just as strongly about the positive aspects of life, whether it be the *na'hes* (gratification) of children and grandchildren, the precious bonds of friendship, the beauty of the world, or art. During the war I also found help in certain small marvels of nature or beautiful things. What connection is there between a childhood during that horrendous war and an oversensitive nature, or a kind of internal emotional violence that contributes to the quality of my life even if it is somewhat tormented? The question remains open to me.)

Are these reactions aftereffects? I think that with all I have been able to do in a very active life, I turned out fairly well, with no real psychological handicaps. I kept my parents and I endured no real suffering, it is as simple as that. This is why at retirement I am able to take the testimony of my friends who experienced misfortune in the past—many of whom suffered more than I, and who still, despite all, succeeded, and admirably chose to remain upright all their life, and furthermore to devote themselves to causes. At the same time I wonder if being hunted down in childhood didn't also give me additional power, rage, and determination to fight for justice at the university, in the unions, the associations, the intellectual groups, and elsewhere.

As for my children, I don't think that having a mother who was a "hidden child" has traumatized them. They just have a Jewish mother . . . In any case, that's always a different mother—for better or worse—than a non-Jewish mother. Do they have the impression that my past was a little burdensome, that I was potentially and despite all my efforts, a mother with quite a load to carry (and yet in all modesty, my past difficulties were easy compared to those of the children directly impacted by the deportation), that my war gave my descendants the responsibility of conserving and transmitting the memory of it on to future generations? Possibly. I did not ask them, so as not to be counterproductive in terms of the work of transgenerational memory. But I think they are rather proud that their mother does useful work in her retirement, gathering and analyzing the testimony of hidden children. They understand the urgency of acting to prevent forgetting and revising history.

Have either my son or daughter inherited my excessive sensitivity or anguish? I don't think so. My husband, whose father is not Jewish, has watched to insure that our children are calm, confident, well balanced, at ease with themselves, French, and without problems. He has counterbalanced my tormented influence over them. Thus I think I can also say that our children don't have sequels to my story. They only have loyalty to the memory. So much the better. My four grandchildren, now between eight and twelve years old, are learning little by little with great surprise, what constituted Absolute Evil: the Nazi and collaborationist exclusion and persecution that is incomprehensible to the human logic or good sense of these little ones. This progressive awareness is apparently going well. I try to keep it from becoming an obsession. For them having a grandmother who at their own age had this strange history is still a little mythical, like a story from long ago and far away, exceptional in relation to the normal and banal lives of their friends' grandparents. They sympathize intuitively; that's all, even though I haven't yet told them every detail. I don't want them to know before they are ready. For these reasons, the matter goes slowly, as they get older and become filled with images from films or documentaries that they start to see on television or video. What images are going to strike them most? They know already, implicitly, the essentials: the fear we felt then and the inherent scandal of our having been persecuted for no reason. In history classes, the few lines that will later be dedicated to World War II will say more to them than to the other children. But above all, I think that for their generation one cannot speak of "sequels."

And now what connection is there between my values as an adult and my experience as a child during the war? I'm not going to analyze here the whole of my value system—commitment to the Left, secularism, overall questions of education, passion for linguistics, feminism—although there are some connections. But here I will simplify; I will deal only with my Jewishness. Having endured all those evils has never meant to me that being Jewish was a "flaw." It was just a pretext for a despicable injustice and not internalized by the Jews themselves. My parents transmitted to me their "cultural" Jewishness almost clandestinely. They were torn between their strong connection to their origins and the competing desire to become integrated—along with their family—into France, a modest Jewishness, that of the Ashkenazi tradition, excluding religion, but including cooking, klezmer, Russian, *tsigan* music . . . and, more importantly, a certain way of looking at the world—minority, protest-minded, distanced, "*pilpulesque*"; in short, a Diaspora perspective. This Jewishness is positive, full of pleasure and pride. By "pride" I don't mean a sense of superiority—that would be imbecilic—but the simple satisfaction of a tradition that is good, warm, tasty, colorful, intelligent, valuable. Anyone from any country or region feels the same sense of identity, I suppose. Except that for us, this collective identity is not attached to a certain territory. "Belong!" say the Anglo-Saxons. This collective identity empowers the individual if he doesn't seal himself up in a community. Personally I have built this identity brick by brick as best I could. It had to be essentially fantasized (as in the film *La Clepsydre* or as in the book by Finkielkraut, *The Imaginary Jew*), given that after the Holocaust so few traces of that authentic culture of the central European Jews have remained. For my father it was too painful to remember it and my mother, born in France, had already lost direct access to it. My parents, who were not religious, never observed any traditions. My grandmother, in contrast, always cooked traditionally for the holidays (gefilte fish, *umentachen*, and other recipes). From this background, I have forged over the course of my own life a secular Jewishness (which, I have theorized, can replace a religion that I like no better than my father did) from these two ingredients: memory and basic culture. By "basic culture" I mean a sociological content, something stemming from the best of what life in the *shtetl* must have been back then—idealized of course; the rest is meaningless and can be forgotten. That is why I take so much pleasure from singing with a joyful and humorous Yiddish chorale, from dancing the Hasidic dances with a secularized group, at memorable festivities. As for Jewish "high culture," I don't practice it all that much for several reasons: First because I have more important things to do; then because I have seen too often among the high-flying intellectual Jews a complete separation between their lofty ideas and their much less impressive daily practices in the professional or private sector. Did their Jewish mothers spoil them too much? As a feminist, that bothers me. Certainly I have read quite a lot of Jewish literature; I also read to my grandchildren stories of Khelm. But as for Jewish thinking in the strictest sense, I must say with a calm impertinence that I don't need mentors because I update myself with the trends of contemporary thought and forge my personal judgments, which to me are just as perceptive. This do-it-yourself Jewishness, which brings me invigorating and stimulating pleasure, suits me and I am zealous about it.

Memory, which is indispensable, is tragic. Culture doesn't have to be somber or nostalgic. If we want to transmit Jewishness and lure the younger generations (because it is no gift to convey only mourning and lamentations to them) we must, beyond the taste for study and intellectualism, also transmit the side of Jewishness that is "collective joy," a positive attitude about everyday life. We must counterbalance the burden of the memory we have to bequeath with the revival of an earlier way of life for them to savor (although most of it has already been lost forever).

I am not at all Israel-centered, or Hebraic-centered; I am Diaspora-centered[6] and somewhat Yiddish-centered. These things speak to my emotions. It is an eclectic and voluntary collection. Nowadays at my house, my husband and I celebrate the Jewish festivities of Rosh Hashanah and Pessah with my children, my grandchildren, and my brother. These secular holidays are when I make the traditional Jewish recipes I have studiously collected, Mama not having left me many recipes. Actually, she didn't even want me to come into the kitchen because, like Papa, she wanted me to be an intellectual. I am lucky that my husband, well versed for a long time in the study of the Kabala, can give a short and brilliant "lesson"—nonreligious but ethical—that transmits a little of the "high culture." In the same way, once a year we go as a family to the cemetery of Bagneux to put pebbles on the tombs of our family, and on the way back home, we have a nice Jewish picnic with the treats we love. One does what one can.

This personal Jewishness does not contradict my successful integration during the course of my life into French society. Further, during my work life, I never spent much time in the Jewish community because I devoted a lot of my time to the issues affecting French citizens and I met people accordingly. Having lived intensely the 1968 student uprising, I have also been an active member of a teachers' union and a member of quite a few feminist groups. I have lived the life of a very busy professor as the cofounder and codirector of the Institut d'Anglais at the Université Paris VII Jussieu—more progressive than the Sorbonne (where I also taught after having studied there), and assisted in the expansion of the Teacher Training Schools. I have lived an intellectual life with linguistics, philosophy, psychoanalysis, politics, symposia, lecture, writing, and seminars. All this took place far from the Jewish community, even if among the "activists" that I worked with a certain number were also Jewish. I have always avoided anything reminiscent of an enclosed ghetto, but I also often found Jews where I was working.

In truth, I have to say that after the first ballot of the French presidential election in April 2001 and despite the massive popular demonstration in reaction to it on May 1, I felt a slight rift with "my" France, at the idea that five million French were not sickened by their own vote for the extreme Right represented by Le Pen. This makes voters seem hopeless! So I felt like withdrawing into myself: Jewish first.

I suffer as does everyone over the situation in the Middle East. I feel close to "Amis de Shalom A'hshav" (Peace Now) and I am strongly anti-Sharon. I disapprove of the attitude of the Sharon supporters (seventy percent of the Israelis) who offer a pretext for a revival of anti-Semitism in the Diaspora—an anti-Semitism that, it is true, never needs much to revive, and so many times revives from nothing at all. I can't believe that Jews, having endured what we have endured, behave as they do toward the Palestinian *people* and their land. I don't put all the *people* of Israel in the same category as many Leftists do, and I remain unalterably pro-Zionist. But I am so sad that the anti-Sharon group is still a minority! So I'll stop here. I could continue to rant and rave forever, but I can also continue to sing, to dance, to read, to reflect, to discuss, to write. I would like, symbolically, to end on this positive note.

FIGURE 7.1. Danièle at age five in 1941 at
Laroque-des-Arcs (Lot).

# 7

# Danièle Menès

**February 2003**

*Danièle Menès' family is from Warsaw and the eastern area of Poland. Now retired, she first taught English at the Lycée Voltaire in Paris and later was a professor of linguistics at the University of Lille. A true European, she has always loved books and languages.*

I was born in September 1936 in Paris. My parents met in France, both of them having come there from Warsaw in 1927.

My paternal grandfather moved up a long way from his birth into a poor family in Brest-Litovsk. A photo taken about 1920 shows his father (my great-grandfather) bearded, with a cap and wearing a shapeless jacket. Maybe he didn't have another one.

By the 1920s, my grandfather Élie and four Jewish associates owned a renowned chocolate factory, Plutos ("wealth" in Greek—revealing etymology), in Warsaw. Several tea parlors also belonged to them; one on rue Nowy Swiat, one on rue Marszalkowska, another at Bialystok.

In photos my grandparents are dressed very upper middle class. He, with his head as bald as a billiard ball, is smiling and looks happy. She, with her lips pursed and her black hair skillfully crimped, wears jewelry and an expression of proud melancholy.

Respectful of tradition, they were observant, but not excessively so. Already well assimilated into the "good Jewish society" of Warsaw, they were patriots and therefore detested the Russian authorities. My grandfather insisted that only Polish be spoken at home but in his absence my father spoke Yiddish to his mother. Yiddish was the real *mame loshn*. As successful business owners, they lived outside the Jewish neighborhood. They occupied an entire floor in an apartment building on rue Natolinska. It was a short street, near a park—in other words, a desirable area at that time. I've seen the now vacant lot where the building once stood.

They had three sons. My father, Aaron, was the oldest. Because of limited opportunities for advanced studies for Jewish students, in about 1925 they sent him to Toulouse for three years to study radio and electricity. Several of his classmates were at the Institute for the same reason. His younger brother, Lazare, studied law and remained in Warsaw. Perhaps law was more open than other disciplines to Jewish students? The youngest son, Josef, left Poland as a teenager in 1938. I think he spent time in Paris with my parents. In 1940 he managed to travel to England and joined a Polish battalion attached to the Anders army. After the war, he married a very nice Scottish working-class girl and moved to Dundee, where he still lives. His sons started their families in England and Australia.

On my mother's side, it's a very different story. There was no religious observance at all—rather the more revolutionary Yiddishland. This is certainly true of my grandmother, born in Bialystok in 1890 and who at a very young age participated in the revolutionary movement in 1905. My maternal grandfather, Moshe Pumpjanski, was also born in Bialystok. Both of my maternal grandparents spoke Russian. My grandmother was fifteen when they married. As a dowry, she brought three or four half brothers and sisters whom she considered to be endangered by their father's remarriage. My grandfather accepted this entire clan, and my own mother was born in 1909.

My grandmother was trained as a cosmetologist. She made her own creams and lotions, and I remember her book of formulas, written in Russian or Latin. She never returned to Poland.

My grandfather and his brothers were photographers. He settled in Warsaw at 32 rue Nalewki, an address that is printed on several photos

I happen to have. I think he worked in his apartment. For certain young Polish writers, rue Nalewki has taken on a mythic dimension. A 1937 photo shows it lined with tall apartment buildings, jammed with people, buzzing with activity, covered with signs: the epicenter of Jewish life in Warsaw.

Later his business prospered enough for him to rent an apartment on Miodowa, in the town center. Although not rich, he also had moved up somewhat. From the windows of the apartment, there was a view overlooking the square of the Royal Palace (rebuilt during the 1970s) from where my seventeen-year-old mother and her four-year-old brother witnessed Pilsudski's coup d'état.[1]

My mother's family mostly spoke Russian. My mother, Raja, learned to read and write in that language; then Polish came in use again after 1918 when Poland regained legal status. She completed high school at the Herman Kalecki School for Girls and received her diploma in 1927. Miraculously, I still have the original document. The school was located in the Jewish quarter at 25 rue Nowolipki, and on Sundays she felt uncomfortable walking across a non-Jewish part of town with her satchel to go there.

My mother's younger brother was stricken with osteo-tuberculosis, and in 1927 my grandmother and her children left Poland to obtain care for him at Berck in the north of France. He had to spend five years on a stretcher. My grandfather stayed in Warsaw, but a young man had accompanied them on this trip. He was in love with my mother but the affection was not mutual. One day he introduced a friend from his high school, my father, to my mother. My mother, who had a good sense of humor, claimed he did it for revenge.

My parents were married in Paris in 1930. To please the groom's parents, they married at the synagogue, without faith.

In 1933 they had a son, but the infant, suffering from a cardiac malformation, lived only a month. I recently learned that my father's parents were hurt and shocked that their grandson had not been circumcised. That is why my mother wanted a daughter. It took me nearly a lifetime to put two and two together. It would be difficult to be further from Judaism than I was.

My father had a good degree, but in 1928 the situation for foreigners in France deteriorated. I believe he was, for some time, an electrician at a big department store, Bazar de l'Hôtel de Ville. In any case, he had work.

We lived in the Fifteenth Arrondissement, on rue Fondary, and then in Boulogne-Billancourt, on rue Tisserand. In May of 1938 I became a French citizen.

In August of 1939, my paternal grandparents came to spend some time with us in Boulogne. I was going on three years old, so I don't know whether they were there for days or weeks. But I remember them. My parents tried to keep them there, but were unable to dissuade them from returning to Warsaw. My grandfather was murdered at Treblinka in 1942. His wife, Esther, survived in the ghetto until 1943, along with her son Lazare. She was gunned down in one of those underground shelters where the last residents were hiding, shortly before the April 1943 insurrection.

My other grandfather also disappeared.

Lazare, my father's younger brother, helped by his Catholic fiancée and hidden in the sewers, was one of those rare survivors of the ghetto. Immediately after the war, the Polish government honored him and named him state prosecutor, but not for long. First, his dogs were killed; then he himself barely escaped an attempt on his life. He returned to his law practice and ended up overcome by paranoia. His children, born after the war, still live in Warsaw. But that's another story.

I'm going back to 1939, in France. In August my father received from the Central Recruiting Office of the Seine the following notice: "If you are a candidate for service for the duration of the war until the time of peace . . . you can come to . . ." He was to report August 17.

Activated into the Twelfth Foreign Regiment of the Infantry, he was "physically present" after October 7, 1939, and took part in the campaign and combat from L'Aisne to the river Gartempe. The discharge paper, signed at Cahors, carried the date of September 10, 1940. Only a few soldiers of his regiment were left, the others having been killed or taken prisoner. They traveled hundreds of kilometers after Sedan, mostly on foot. I still have photos showing them in uniform, garrison cap and all.

Arriving at Cahors, my father, extremely exhausted and covered with boils, decided to stop there. He could go no further. He found a job in a little radio store and rented a house without facilities at Laroque-des-Arcs, a village in the Lot River valley, five kilometers from Cahors.

During this time, my mother and I stayed in one or more villages north of the river Loire. I particularly remember a stay of several weeks on a farm. I have many memories, the funniest being that of my mother trying to milk a cow and the most terrifying being that of the killing of a pig. There were bombings; it was before the Armistice. I also was attacked by a big dog and rescued by a German soldier. I was three and one-half years old. Another afternoon, while I was taking my nap, a bomb was dropped at close range. I awoke with a start.

After that, I have difficulty putting the facts in order.

We returned to Paris, as many people were doing. My mother was friendly with the concierge of the apartment in Boulogne. She was an elderly lady called Marthe. She had a little house and a bit of land at Spéracèdes, a village above Grasse, in the Maritime Alps. In response to the "return to the land" urged by Pétain, she left Paris to go to her village and took me with her, saying I was her granddaughter.

After my father was demobilized and had found work and a house near Cahors, he came to Spéracèdes to take me home. I remember nothing of the journey back, but I do remember Marthe because I spent a year in the village later on.

As for my mother, she passed through the Demarcation Line with her own mother's future husband who was not Jewish. My mother was carrying only a handbag. The two of them acted like fiancés taking a walk. She finally rejoined my father at Laroque-des-Arcs and then he went south to get me. It must have been at the beginning of 1941.

In October 1941, I was five and started school for the first time. The school had two classes with very few students, but later filled with the arrival of refugees from Lorraine. The teachers, twin sisters names Pégourié, were ageless and had no life other than the school. They were excellent "soldiers" of the Third Republic for whom the school and the church were separated only by the width of the street.

The priest, Father Éreil, a very good person, then baptized me. My mother, an atheist, was not pleased, but she told herself that it could be useful. Her brother (the one whose illness had saved us from Poland and who had converted to Catholicism) was my godfather, and a pretty redhead, a friend of my parents, was my godmother. For one year I went to church. I perhaps went to catechism but I have forgotten. I was, after all, only six years old when my religious education ended.

My parents hadn't changed their name. In any case, they didn't hide. They were foreigners nevertheless. On their identification card the word JEW was printed in bold letters. I think we were the only Jews in the village.

At the beginning of 1943 (the Southern Zone was occupied after November 1942) there was an identity check. The roundups had begun in the South (August 26, 1942). It was no doubt a French gendarme who came. At age six, I knew perfectly well that I must not say I was Jewish. I never said so at school nor did I say it anywhere else for a long time. Telling would put me in danger of being killed; it could be a death sentence.

My father showed his card and I saw the word JEW on it. I jumped on the gendarme like a panther shouting, "No! It's not true! We aren't Jewish!" He was a good man, fortunately. But I feared that this episode was the end of everything.

Not long ago I learned from my uncle that we were protected by a certain Pierre B., a tall redheaded man whom I remember well, who worked at the prefecture of police and who had, as did others, his "good Jew" whom he protected. My father's friend had studied law and that enabled him to find employment at the prefecture of Cahors. He and my father had met during the debacle and had marched together. Arriving at Laroque completely exhausted, they leaned against the door of a house to rest for a few minutes, but the door was not completely closed. They ended up flat on their backs when the door opened and eventually became very good friends with the people who lived there, Monsieur and Madame C. In fact, Pierre B. became the lover of Madame C., a petulant brunette who looked a little like the writer Colette. Monsieur and Madame C. had a little boy my age, Pitou. We became inseparable.

My nineteen-year-old uncle rejoined my mother after several adventures. He and his friends had tried to cross the Demarcation Line but they were detained. He had his baptismal certificate and a letter from the priest who had instructed him. That saved his life. The others were all arrested.

Pierre B. said he could protect Menès, his wife, and his daughter, but no one else. Father Éreil, the priest of Laroque, advised my uncle to go and see the bishop of Cahors about his situation. The bishop sent him to the En Calcat Abbey in Tarn. There they told him, "We're full but go to the Monastery of Sainte-Marie-du-Désert." And there he was hidden for more than a year by the Trappists.

Now I'll return to our life in Laroque-des-Arcs. At the end of 1940 when my parents arrived, they were almost the only refugees. The population was truly welcoming. I'm not sure the word "Jew" meant anything in this secluded village. It really was in the most remote part of France. Even the most minimal of modern conveniences was unknown. The house my father rented had no water, no electricity and—it goes without saying—no toilet. My father put in electricity. For water there was a stream and in summer, quite a bit further away, there was a well. My parents stayed there until 1945. As for me, I was sent for shelter to Spéracèdes (again) from the summer of 1943 to the end of the summer of 1944. Then I had another year of schooling in Laroque, until 1945.

I left for Spéracèdes with my grandmother and her future husband in 1943. We spent more than a year in the Maritime Alps. Following the Armistice reached in 1943 between Italy and the Allies, the Germans occupied the Southeast previously controlled by the Italians. The consequences for the Jews were disastrous. Of course, I had to hold my tongue again and family ties were hidden. I called my grandmother "auntie." Louis, her companion, had forbidden her to speak to people because of her accent. I went to school. For a while, the kids nicknamed me "Parisian" although I had an accent of the Southwest, but this was not a real problem.

One family in a neighboring village knew the truth. The only time I ate meat was at their house. They had killed a young goat, which apparently was forbidden. So I was told it was a fox. Still we saw herds of sheep go by; hunters with a boar over their shoulders; the natives or at least the refugees had to content themselves with polenta (it is very nourishing) and some vegetables. My parents sent packages from time to time. We also had a little garden. The teacher, like many others, raised rabbits. For a sack of grass or a basket of peelings I could get coupons, and coupons were needed to get a workbook. This memory overshadows the rest of my life at school.

I would come home for lunch and sometimes the menu was really Spartan—chickpeas or soybeans. I had trouble swallowing it, but Louis, who was strict, insisted that I eat before returning to school. For me it was unacceptable to arrive late. With gulps from my glass of water, I swallowed the chickpeas. But it was not a sad time. One could see the sea, the islands of Lérins, and the river Siagne that ran below.

I remember returning to Cahors in August or September of 1944. Cahors had been liberated and my parents let us know that we could return. We could see, off in the distance, the bombing over Fréjus. The return by train must have taken quite a bit of time; some bridges had been bombed. We arrived in Cahors too late to walk the five kilometers between there and Laroque-des-Arcs, so Louis and my grandmother asked for shelter at the prefecture. We spent the night there. I slept on a big table and the next morning we started out on foot.

What is the emotional tone during this period? To tell the truth, apart from the episode of 1943, I don't remember ever really being afraid. Still I sometimes had nightmares. Fear was latent, buried, but it was there. The countryside was beautiful, the people hospitable, especially in Laroque, and yet what had children of my age known other than war? A faint smell of croissants and chocolate floated in my memory, a souvenir of what had been before.

I played war with the little boys of the village. As I was the only girl playing with them, I was the nurse. Furthermore, my father was respected because he was the only one for miles around who knew how to build and repair radios. A radio set could be traded for some eggs! The demand was strong and sometimes my mother, seated beside my father, soldering iron in hand, would also build a radio, duplicating what my father was doing. I was persuaded that the radio had been invented only to give news of the war, and that once the war was over, it would disappear. And of course, we moved little flags on a map affixed to the wall to trace the progress of the war.

From 1941 to 1943 and from 1944 to 1945, I lived at Laroque with my parents. It was happiness built on top of anxiety.

I have photos taken just before leaving for the Maritime Alps, during the summer of 1943. My mother is sitting on the steps of the house; I am standing beside her, dressed to leave for a party or for a trip. I am going on seven years old. Much later, I learned that when these photos were taken my mother was not sure that she would see me again.

I thought we were the only Jewish refugees in the village. It seems that others were more hidden than we were. In 1945, the mayor of Laroque-des-Arcs answered a letter from Rabbi Chneerson: "I helped a number of Israelites during the period they were hunted. I kept them at my house until 1943. But I know of no orphan and I understand your appeal too well not to respond." The author of this letter, Monsieur Calmon, had replaced the Pétain loyalist mayor, who was removed from office after the Liberation.[2]

My parents divorced in 1945. The war had postponed their decision. They had the good sense never to argue in front of me. When they didn't want me to understand, they spoke Polish. For me, happiness and danger remained permanently connected—a very tight Gordian knot.

During the summer of 1945, I left with my mother for Pantin near Paris. She remarried in 1946. The most difficult part was to leave the lovely countryside for the ugliness of Pantin and no longer hear the crickets at night. My new family had a business situated on the Eastern railroad embankment with all that smoke. Behind our house were huge flour mills. Sometimes we could walk along the Ourcq canal.

My father stayed in Cahors. He never wanted to leave. He also remarried, had two other children, and lived from hand to mouth. I was happy that my father was remarried. The idea of another mother pleased me, but she didn't accept me. Born in a Catholic family of the Bordeaux region (two of her brothers were priests), she had been rejected by the aforementioned family for having married a Jew, and moreover one who was divorced. Being Jewish was no doubt the worst. She was jealous of my mother and this was not totally baseless. My parents were in agreement that I should spend the two months of the summer at Cahors. Well, I could understand her hostility. She was not a happy person, to say the least.

Communication with my father was very difficult, once I was past the age for games. My stepmother made it next to impossible. She deliberately kept us apart. For a long time I thought she had behaved differently with my half brother and sister, but Martine, my half sister, later told me it had been the same for them. Our father seemed henpecked and depreciated. By the time I was twelve, the image of my father had been knocked off its pedestal. Martine had the same perception later.

In the family at Pantin, I was an outsider, too, and I can't say that I was very happy there. My mother slaved away and didn't have much time for me. I think she felt guilty because I wasn't her husband's daughter. However, my stepfather, his mother, and his sister accepted me very well.

In 1947 I entered junior high at the Collège Marcellin Berthelot. Latin wasn't offered there but the sciences were emphasized. The selection for secondary schooling took place in the first year of junior high. The boys at the school were educated only in the Cours Complémentaire, which ended after junior high. The girls came from the Northeast suburbs, from Drancy to Bobigny, but also from Pantin and Aubervilliers—in other words, a population of workers, salaried employees, and shopkeepers. There were fewer of us girls than in the *lycées* of Paris and we were well prepared. All of us passed the *baccalauréat* exams with honors. If one takes into account what the professional future for girls was in 1954, some of our successes were striking. One of my class-mates was the first woman to be admitted at Sup-Aero.[3] Two others became medical doctors; others professors or teachers. I was the only one of my class to study languages.

I was happy at school. I was a little talkative, but my good grades made the teachers tend to be lenient. For the girls with less success, there was a two-year commercial course after the eighth grade, which led to the Vocational Certificate (CAP) or, better yet, the *brevet*. At the time, work was easy to find.

At home (even the word seems incongruous to me!) there was no intimacy. My stepfather, his mother, and his sister ran two shops, one a café, the other selling furniture. The entire family worked there, includ-ing my mother, who also had to do the cooking for everyone. A member of the "tribe" got up at five a.m., another closed at midnight. To sustain his schedule and simply remain standing, my stepfather, who came back from Buchenwald, had to take ephedrine; otherwise he would fall asleep anywhere he was.

At noon, eight or nine of us ate in the café around a large table at the back of the room. I disliked doing that but the customers, who were workers from the railroad, women from the neighboring factory, workers and employees of the big mills, and butchers from the Villette slaughterhouse, were friendly and cheerful. My stepfather and his sister had a sense of humor and handled the slang with virtuosity. I still like working-class cafés.

It was a time of optimism, at least among militant communists. I was barely nine years old when the indoctrination began. The educational principles were very simple: be polite with adults, and serve the cause; exhibit a solid morality and a total absence of nuance. Everything was black or white. At the age of fourteen, going along with the crowd, I joined the UJRF. I organized a group at the school and I kept it going for a year. That provoked the ire of the principal (eighteen years before May 1968, understand!), and my stepfather sent her a threatening letter. She relented.

This intense militant activity culminated with the Festival of Youth in East Berlin in July of 1951. This festival lasted two weeks and was held every two years in one of the capitals of the "popular democracies." Tens of thousands of young people met there. I acted in a theatrical troop (theater of commitment, of course); I was also a delegate. I re-ceived a medal from Raymonde Dien (heroine of the fight against the war in Indochina) for having broken the records for the sale of our magazine. It was glorious. But the year had been so hard I had to abandon all activity other than my studies the next year.

At age seventeen, at the beginning of my last year of *lycée*, I was alone. My stepfather had health problems resulting from his deportation. The other man of the house, his sister's husband, a former prisoner, died of cancer eighteen months after his return. Everyone was overworked. They went to Seine-et-Marne, about eighty kilometres east of Paris, and sold goods in open-air markets. There, too, they worked like crazy. Without a car the place was inaccessible. They left me in a small flat in Pantin with just enough to live on. With my uneven upbringing, it wasn't easy. I had no scholarship but the rent, a very low one, was paid. Some teachers took me under their wings. I was like a little lost puppy.

Then I went to the Sorbonne on a scholarship. A great-uncle, a brother of my grandfather Pumpjanski, sent me something extra from time to time. For three years I led a rather pleasant life. Cramming was almost unknown (what good would it have done since we had already been selected?). I could go to the movies. Even today I have a happy feeling each time I go by the Champo movie theater.

Then I made the mistake of getting married. I had a son. I interrupted my studies for three years and taught English full time. The marriage was unbearable. I left with my child and I resumed my studies while still working. I earned the CAPES and then the *agrégation* degree. I taught in several *lycées* in the Paris region, especially at the Lycée Voltaire, until 1971. Then I was appointed to the University of Lille and I stayed there until 1996.

A few months ago, I became grandmother to an adorable little boy. It was a late birth, quite unexpected and was earth-shaking on the emotional scale—one of those events that adds meaning to the here and now.

As for my son, he more or less knows the history. Of Judaism I gave him nothing, alas. As I said, I was assimilated as much as anyone can be. My mother thought it best to just forget about being Jewish. This was understandable in 1945. Besides, she was remarried to a non-Jew. I went along with that, but fortunately, I did not completely forget. When I was about forty-five years old, I sensed that things weren't going well for us at all. The self-destruction was well underway. Of my Jewishness, I knew nothing. I had no sense of identity. I had always adapted according to the situation: Quercynoise Parisian, even Polish. But I had numerous memories of the war and those had not been eradicated. The core of my identity was intact. In the early 1980s I read *The Imaginary Jew*, by Alain Finkielkraut.[4] From then on, I began to find something other than the persecutions: the flavors, the aromas.

Much later I studied Yiddish. I had no difficulty learning to read it but it evoked nothing. I had never heard my parents speak it; it was a foreign language. If I were to go back to it now, it would seem more familiar—so droll, so warm. With time and work, one can create an affective memory. I find that fantastic.

As for deciding if my personal difficulties are more tied to the personality of my parents or to the war itself, the two are inseparable. I have no answer. My mother was an optimist; a gay, combative woman, not neurotic. But she lacked self-confidence, a characteristic that I took up in turn.

As for my father, there was something pathological. He was in his own world—inaccessible. I was never able to reach him. I pursued and attacked him verbally, never feeling he was really there. I regret having been so aggressive. He seemed to live in a mental fortress (*Le Désert des Tartares*, by Buzzati!). It's called "obsessive-compulsive syndrome"; his was severe. With the passage of time, he became increasingly senile.

As I said earlier, his parents came to France but returned to Poland just before the war. After learning what happened to them in Poland, he shut himself even more behind his walls. I think he felt a great sense of guilt, but was he aware of this?

It is only after the death of his second wife that I was able to make a kind of limited contact with him. If I had known how to speak Polish or Yiddish, I would perhaps have been able to have long talks with him.

In 1994, two years before retiring, I returned to Paris. My father had died the previous November and severe bronchitis and fever had prevented my attending his burial. Not being there cost me psychologically later on.

My father was like one of the living dead; nothing seems more difficult to me than burying a ghost. I started psychotherapy, then psychoanalysis, with a Jewish shrink about my age. After eight years with him I stopped, with his consent.

It is clear that living through the war has influenced my life; having learned at the age of six that we were in danger of being killed certainly shaped my life. I lived episodes of my private life clandestinely. That didn't bother me at all; it was second nature, a way of surviving. While I was clandestine, I was alive! And for that there was a price to pay; it could take many forms, but the price was high.

Here is a story I was told by a former Jewish classmate. She started at Sup-Aero in 1955. When we were fifteen years old, her father was seriously depressed. She was the one who took care of the store, so she studied by correspondence. She came back the next year. Her father took up his work again.

Her father's parents had come to France just before the war and then, like my grandparents, they went back to Poland. Her father was unable to stop them. Ten years after this period of depression, he killed himself. Guilt was obviously a part of his depression. I tell myself that if my father had not been protected by his obsessive defenses, perhaps he, too, would have killed himself.

## Testimony of Danièle's half sister, Martine Menès

*I wrote the first version of this text as a teenager, a rite of passage that would enable me to live. Born after the war, I was not a hidden child, but a child of that which was hidden. The most palpable memory I have is of silence. From this silence I had to be reborn, amid words that were stolen, created, accumulated, until I finally became a child of speech— and memory. This will be my testimony.*

## EX/IL[5]

Jacques Lacan, the Nineteenth Seminar; or worse, unpublished. Lesson of June 21, 1972:

> "*We are the children of discourse*"

From silence she learns that her father is a Polish Jew. She learns it from seeing him motionless, crying useless tears, confronting visions of ruin. She will never hear any of the accounts from which children ordinarily learn about war. Her father reduced to raw emotion, her mother turns off the television.

"Mama, what does the word 'Jewish' mean?"

"Just don't ask your father."

Should she from then on abstain from the ritualistic ceremonies imposed by her mother's religion during which she digs in the frozen dust and the scent of moist incense just enough to catch worried looks?

What is she doing in this chapel that commemorates a torture to which her father as a Jew is alleged to be an accomplice?

Yes, he must be guilty since he is so silent about it.

Strange persecutor, deaf to prophecy.

Her father lives as if buried, his eyes faded. No music echoes in his dreams. Besides, he no longer dreams.

She dreams. Naked, she crosses a closed room where people (who are they?) are dancing. Their eyes cast a sinister reflection. She stops, her numb arms dangling, before a bloody door. She suddenly recognizes the gas chamber.

"Don't go in," cries her childhood friend. "You are one of us, you are assimilated. Dance, dance, and keep quiet."

She no longer wants her father to help her learn to count. Over there, she says, the numbers are not the same.

How does she know without being taught that over there $1 + 1 + 1 + 1 \ldots = 0$?

They all died, one by one and together, while he somehow wisely chose France. In her hallucinations she hears their voiceless cries, an eternal wound.

And as for him, how is it possible for him *to be* except *to be* dead?

She knows how long she stood waiting for him in the corridors of her shattered childhood. She imagines the path of his flight: 1927 exile; 1940 exodus. She wakes up crying out: "Father, Father, why have you forsaken me?"

How long did it take for him to become this missing person seized in the grip of an unbearable memory, the silent responder to the questions she never asked?

What is forbidden to know?

She cannot continue as the only memory of a story he didn't tell. She cannot be the only one living from survival to survival without being able to bring a child into the world. She is as old as the oldest prayers. She awakens with her eyes turned inward, searching for her origins. Faint memories torn from eternity, convoys of death. She would drown in her own lake of tears if she didn't hold on to the lifeline of words.

But the words glide like the wind down the stairs of oblivion. Nothing to grasp at; nothing to hang on to. Unable to articulate the name she doesn't have, lost her quest for identity, she never knows who is who, what name to call out. Dead letters, letters assigned to fruitless attempts, inundated by what's impossible, unbelievable to (re)tell.

On her own she looks for the other side of the story: September 1942, deportation to Treblinka, her grandfather disappears; April 1943, uprising in the Warsaw ghetto, her grandmother is killed.

Without a past, the present destroyed, she lives in endless oblivion.

She cracks open the doorway to a renewal of ties; she lets go of her obsession and frees herself from her old ways of thinking to move on to a transforming future. But how long before history is overtaken? Hers is a hard-won relief that she cautiously tries to tame.

And what does she think every time someone says to her: "I won't forget you"?

"Mama, what does 'forget' mean?"

FIGURE 8.1. A drawing of Nelly by
her grandfather, the painter Moïse
Natanson, at Drancy. The lower-right-
hand corner bears his dedication:
"To my adored Nelly. Natanson.
Drancy 7/27/1942."

# 8

# Nelly Scharapan

**August 2003**[1]

*Nelly Scharapan is retired. She was part of the administration at the National Institute of Health and Medical Research. She is a militant activist in memory of the Holocaust (participates in school programs and pedagogical work). She is a member of a philosophical think tank. She loves Yiddish dance and choral singing.*

I was born on March 17, 1936, in Paris, three and one-half years before the declaration of war. My parents, Aline and Felix Scharapan, both born in Paris, were nonobservant, assimilated Jews and Communist sympathizers.

As for my grandparents, my maternal grandmother, Rajzla Witman, was born in Warsaw, Poland, of modest origins. She had brothers and sisters, but I know nothing about them. My maternal grandfather, Moïse Natanson, born in Odessa (part of Russia at that time) was an intellectual and a painter. He had studied at the School of Fine Arts and was well known. He specialized in painting portraits. A victim of the pogroms, he fled Russia and came to France—the land of liberty and the rights of man. In France he met my grandmother who was very pretty. They were not officially married. My mother, Aline, was born of their union.

My paternal grandfather was born in Moldavia, and my grandmother, whom I never knew, was born in Poland. My paternal grandparents were very poor. They lived on rue de la Forge-Royale in Paris. My grandfather was a cabinetmaker. They had fourteen children, two of whom died. My father was the youngest.

My paternal grandfather was a Communist, militant to the point that he would give his entire pay to the poor of the neighborhood, and his own children would have nothing to eat. His wife sewed all night long to feed their children. She was so unhappy that she committed suicide when my father, her youngest child, started to work. Having placed first in his district for the Certificate of Primary Studies, he hoped to continue his studies but that was impossible; at age fourteen he learned the trade of furrier.

My father and mother met in Paris. My birth was an unwanted accident. My parents put me immediately in a children's home and then with a nanny.

Such was my entry into life.

When I was very young, my father was called up for two years of military service. Toward the end of his service, rumors of war began and his company was not decommissioned. War was declared in 1939 and his regiment was among the first to be taken prisoner. My father remained a prisoner of war until the Liberation.

We're now up to 1940–1942. I am again with my mother, who was working at the Vichy-controlled UGIF as a stenographer. She had been told it would allow her family to be safe. We will see that this was not to be the case.

My maternal grandfather practiced his career as a painter in his home, rue de la Roquette. A precise, luminous, indelible memory is with me: I was four or five years old, seated on a chair with a doll in my arms, and my grandfather was in front of me, drawing my portrait. He was looking at me intensely, and to keep me from moving, was telling me marvelous fairy tales that he was making up as he went along. I have never found this drawing.

One day in July of 1942 he was doing the portrait of an old man who was posing as a model for him. There was a knock at the door. He understood. His little suitcase was ready . . .

He did his last two charcoal drawings of my mother and me at the Drancy internment camp. He rolled them up and fastened them with a rubber band. He wrote an address on them and threw them out the window.[2] These two drawings hang on my bedroom wall. (For a long time it was too painful for me to look at them.) Shortly thereafter, he was taken to Auschwitz to be slaughtered. He was fifty-nine years old.

My grandmother came to live with us. She sold hosiery in the open-air markets of the distant suburbs—Les Mureaux, among others. She got up at five o'clock in the morning and left, pulling a little cart, to take the train. She would come back about noon to take care of the house and of me. She made delicious little Yiddish cakes for me. This short period was the best time of my childhood. I always think of her as working very hard. She was small but very active and she never complained.

Then came the day when the first anti-Jewish laws were passed (October 1940) and my grandmother no longer had the right to work. She was removed from the Trade Register and had to get rid of all her merchandise. (I recently found the official document.)

Near us on rue Ordener was a dispensary. The manager, Mademoiselle Le Clézio, a middle-aged woman, was extraordinary. She helped my grandmother, as well as other people. Knowing what a good-hearted woman my grandmother was and how good she was with children, Mademoiselle Le Clézio made arrangements for her to take care of some children. My grandmother hadn't mastered French, speaking only Yiddish and Polish, and spoke very little. (I felt she was bearing the weight of earlier suffering that I could never decipher.) She lined up at the grocery stores with very young children in her arms. That is how she was able to slip through the nets of the Nazis.

My first humiliation came at the end of my first year in primary school, when the various prizes (Prize for Excellence, Honor, First Prize, Second Prize) were to be awarded. The children were called to the stage, congratulated, and kissed by the teacher and the headmistress. The family members in the room applauded; it was truly a big day. My mother was in the room. Finally the names of my class were called out. The Prize for Excellence was not announced—just the First, Second, and Honor Prizes. I listened carefully, certain that I would hear my name. My name was not called. The ceremony was over, the people got up. I felt mortified, humiliated. I had been forgotten! I didn't understand. My mother took me home with her in silence, and once there, she took a beautiful book from her purse. I can still see it—red and gold (I think it was La Fontaine's *Fables*; I never wanted to open it). It was the Prize for Excellence, the highest honor! I looked at my mother, questioningly. Why didn't they give it to me in front of everyone? My mother was silent. I know that it was hard for her to explain that I was a little Jewish girl who didn't have the right to anything. This incident followed from decisions that created the first humiliations concerning children. Some members of the teaching profession opposed them; others applied them zealously.

One evening in 1943 my mother didn't come home. The Gestapo had hunted her down at her workplace. I didn't get to tell her goodbye. I felt a general sense of anguish. I had learned to keep quiet but I understood nothing. I felt stupid in a world that was completely incoherent.

Later I learned that my mother had been taken to a German work camp in the Austerlitz train station in Paris.[3] Here the Germans sorted the valuables they had stolen from the Jews. I saw this with my own eyes one day when a man took me to see my mother at the camp at Austerlitz. He led me to the door of an immense room, saying he would come back to get me in the evening. There I saw (I remember the whole episode vividly because it shocked me so) beautiful objects, each one more fabulous than the one before—crystal vases, delicate china—set out on big wooden tables. I didn't understand. My mother was there, with other detainees, dressed in a smock. They didn't seem to be too sad. The guards did not maintain continuous surveillance. The women were energetically breaking the beautiful objects so the Germans couldn't profit from them! My mother didn't explain anything to me; she just told me, "Break all you can." I looked at her, perplexed; I still didn't understand and I was disappointed. I wanted her complete attention. I broke and broke but it didn't make me happy. I was, without knowing it, performing an act of resistance. That evening the man came back to get me. I learned later that it had been a great risk to take me to the camp because at any moment they would randomly take a certain number of detainees to the concentration or extermination camps, by way of Drancy.

After Austerlitz my mother was incarcerated at Drancy, where something else took place that I found out about later. Upon arriving at Drancy, my mother lined up to pass through the office where the new arrivals were registered. A young soldier was pacing in front of the line. Then he stopped just in front of my mother. Why her? It's a mystery. My mother was pretty. Very softly he asked her in French (Drancy was guarded by French gendarmes):

"Do you have children?"

"A little girl," answered my mother.

The soldier: "Say that you don't have children."

And he stepped away. My mother thought, "Why did he say that? Should I lie or not?" Finally it was her turn. "Name? First name? Do you have children?" "No," she answered. People didn't know yet what was happening in the camps and would voluntarily say they had children to get sympathy from those who were questioning them. It was later learned that all the children who had been named were sought for deportation.[4] I was saved by this guard because officially I didn't exist.

My mother was at Drancy a short time before being deported to Germany to the concentration camp at Bergen-Belsen as the wife of a prisoner of war. There was no gas chamber there, but it was a camp of slow death, usually from typhus.

So my mother had been arrested. I lived with my grandmother at 33 rue Ordener. I want to mention the concierge, Madame Pretet, a very good-hearted woman. One day the police came to our building and asked the concierge if there were any Jews (we were the only ones). She said no. Brave Madame Pretet! She immediately warned my grandmother that it was dangerous for us to sleep there. (I have recently tried in vain to find Madame Pretet.)

Mademoiselle Le Clézio, the manager of the dispensary, knew a woman who had a maid's room in a building near where we lived. My grandmother and I went there early in the evenings to sleep because we did not have the right to go out after the curfew. It was a tiny room that had only a bed that took up the whole room. There again, I didn't understand why we had to sleep in this tiny room under the eaves. I felt something abnormal was going on, but I was with my grandmother, so I wasn't completely lost. I didn't ask questions; I knew it was useless.

I remember a blonde lady, the owner of this room, who would sometimes come, smiling, in the mornings to give me a croissant. This croissant had an exquisite taste, the taste of compassion. I have never forgotten this lady whose name I didn't know. I can still see her, as she was then. As far as I know, she never knew the balm she put on the heart of a little girl who had no right to exist. In fact, memory is closely connected to affect; the slightest gesture, however small it might seem, took on an enormous importance and remained engraved in my memory.

Meanwhile, steps affecting me were being taken: Jewish institutions such as the OSE were established to hide the children because they were in great danger. For me, as I recently learned, this came about through the intermediary of the Fathers of Zion (Catholic priests).

So one day in 1942—I was then between five and six years old—a man whom I didn't know (I learned later he was named Monsieur

Landeau) came to look for me and took me by train to place me on a
farm in the Sarthe region, west of Paris. I was in a state of shock. Moth-
erless, with no explanation, without saying goodbye to my grandmother, I was pulled from my surroundings. I had never been in the
country. I felt abandoned, alone. My mind rejected it, blocked it out,
and I have no memory of this terrible trip. During the entire war, my
lack of understanding anything that was happening would be very destructive to me.

I arrived in Sarthe, at Écomoy (I recently learned the name of the
place and I went back there). The farm belonged to Madame Pousse. It
was her brother (I learned much later) who had come to Paris to look
for me and other children to hide on farms. He had a large farm where
he lodged some ten people, adults and children (he was recently given
the Medal of the Righteous for his actions). I wasn't lucky enough to be
there with him; there wasn't room for me. He then insisted that his
sister, Madame Pousse, who was about thirty years old and whose husband was a prisoner of war, put me up. She no doubt did not want to.
She completely ignored me, never spoke to me. I was alone, disori-
ented. She had other concerns; in fact, she was a German soldier's mistress. In the woods, not far from there, was a German base. One had to
be careful because it was in such close proximity. She went to join him
at night. She had a son, a year younger than I, whom the neighbors
took to their house. As for me, I was nobody; I stayed alone.

I had never been in the country and I had never seen animals in my
life. I was extremely afraid of the cows, but I was supposed to take care
of them. However, I had a bed, I ate (obviously, but I don't remember).
As I didn't go to school, I was left entirely to myself. That's where my
real trauma began. I was in total isolation. No one spoke to me or paid
any attention to me. I had no structure, I had nothing to hang on to—
not reading, not drawing, not speaking; complete nothingness, psychic
agony.

I was thrown like that, without explanation, into a place that was
foreign to me, an environment that I felt to be hostile. There were
horses on the farm. I remember that one day as I walked by a tethered
horse, I gently caressed his muzzle. I must have tickled him because he
suddenly opened his mouth as if to bite me, and I was frightened. I
pulled my hand away at once. I remember thinking, "Even the horse
doesn't like me." I never approached a horse again.

Time passed in this way with me left to myself. For a child, it is important for the day to have a rhythm: waking up, breakfast, school.

Instead, I had the whole day before me with nothing to feed my mind, no real memories, only emptiness. No one came to see me, not even Monsieur Landeau. I had no identity; I lived in fear and total isolation. (I learned recently that before my departure from Paris, I was given a false name, "Gillier," but as no one spoke to me or called my name, I didn't know.)

Slowly I lost my sense of self. So I searched unconsciously for anything that was positive. One little happy memory, for example: at Madame Pousse's farm there was an employee whose daughter I found again not long ago. She was a poor woman. One day she came to me and said, "My dear, you are unhappy. Here!" and she gave me a little cake. I didn't see her again, but these simple words warmed me.

This situation lasted several months. And one morning, no one was in the house! Madame Pousse had left permanently to join her German lover. She left her son alone also, but his grandmother took him to her house. As for me, I wasn't native to the village; I was unimportant; no one came for me.

The country helped me to survive; it was aromatic, the grass was abundant, the air was refreshing. I remember picking berries, they were my treat. I also ate apples fallen from the tree. I don't remember being hungry. I certainly ate very little, but this wasn't the worst part.

Madame Pousse left; so did her son. I don't know how long I was left all alone (my memory wasn't functioning). I was about seven years old.

I don't know how, but I ended up on another farm, and this was a slide toward the worst. I was with very rustic people, on a farm without modern conveniences—no water, no toilet. This was torture for me because I could never manage to go and the urine ended up flowing by itself; such embarrassment! It was a second marriage for the farmer and his wife. There were two daughters, a little older than I. They were unhappy. Their stepfather was alcoholic and violent. He was always angry. He beat us with a whip, his stepdaughters and me, too, if I didn't manage to escape. This couple had taken me in to be their servant. I had to sweep, serve the table, and tend the cows.

Not a word was exchanged. I stayed quite a long time. My descent toward emptiness and despair was accelerated. Physical deterioration was added to my psychological deterioration. No one said a word to me except to shout orders: "Go get the cider in the cellar!" I used it as an opportunity to take a drink. I thought it was good. In this way I tried to glean a few sweets. I didn't sit at the table with the farm family; I just served them and gathered up the crumbs. I had no bed; I slept in the haystack, which bothered me since I was accustomed to a clean bed. At Madame Pousse's house, at least I could wash myself, I could eat, I could sleep in a bed. But these farmers were terribly crass. One time, on impulse, I went to one of the daughters and said, "I would like to go to school." "You? To school! Are you crazy?" These are the only words I ever said to them. They were unhappy themselves; they often cried, but they still had their mother. They showed no pity for a little girl of no importance.

My situation became serious. My physical and emotional degradation was intense. I never washed. Scabies covered my body and lice had invaded my hair. I became a cipher. I no longer felt emotion or had memories. I was incapable of reflecting, of understanding, of hoping. Somehow, however, deep inside, something remained. I remember once I heard, coming from far away, a faint sound of music. And all alone, instinctively, I sketched movements of dance.

I was there at least two years. Fortunately, I escaped serious illnesses, other than a little pulmonary problem (discovered later), which has given me a bronchial weakness throughout my life. Once I hurt my arm badly, but whom could I tell? It healed by itself.

My memory has reconstructed certain flashbacks. For example, there were seasonal workers and once one of the young guys chased me. I was completely naïve, but I sensed danger, without knowing why. I started to run because I wanted to get away from him. I was afraid, and there was good reason to be afraid. I still have this memory. My instincts still functioned. I was still alive!

I didn't understand anything about my life, but slowly I grew up. I heard the voices of the farmers, the words "war," "Germans," "Jews." I understood that to be Jewish was bad, but what was it to be Jewish? I felt somehow guilty without knowing why, always with fear in my gut. My emotions were tangled. Happily, there was no mirror on this farm because I could not have been a pretty sight; I hadn't washed myself for months. I wasn't developed, wasn't prepared for life. I could have fled but where would I have gone? How? I didn't even think about it. Everyone seemed hostile or indifferent.

Nevertheless, neither blows, nor hunger, nor the discomfort in which I lived caused me to suffer as much as this emptiness—this total absence of human warmth.

The Liberation came at last. Madame Pousse's brother then took steps to save me (this also I learned later). He telephoned the OSE to have someone come to pick me up. The OSE was authorized to take in all the hidden children and for that purpose had requisitioned the Méhoncourt Château, at Le Mans—which I visited again not long ago and which now belongs to the anti-riot Security Force.

This is when one day I saw an American truck arrive. I was afraid—everything that had happened to me up to then had been negative, so I didn't expect anything good from this truck, parked at the farm, which had come to pick me up. I got in, anxiously. Other children were also sitting inside. To my surprise, an American soldier smiled at me and handed me a piece of chocolate. I did not react. He insisted. I timidly took the chocolate—delicious! They first took me to a hospital. Upon hearing this word, I was seized with fear. The word "hospital" frightened me. "I don't want to go," I cried, but they forced me. I was malnourished, infected with scabies, repulsive.

The hospital was operated by nuns. They bullied me but cared for me conscientiously. And I had a bed. A bed! With sheets! After eight or ten days, a tall man came to see me. He was the director of the OSE home at Méhoncourt Château. He took my hand in his and said, "You are coming with me. Other children are there." At last someone looked at me with kindness! Someone spoke to me! I could say nothing, but something in me slowly lit up. He took me to the Château.

A new period began. I took on a human face. A large number of Jewish children who had been hidden arrived at the orphanage. I later learned that these children stayed there one or two years. Research was conducted for each one of them until at least one member of their dislocated family was found. The children who remained as the sole survivor were sent to America where there were families ready to adopt them.

At the Château, everything had to be organized on an emergency basis: camp cots to be set up, children to be fed. There were not enough personnel. The older children took care of the little ones like me. Much later I had a chance meeting with one of the older girls who had taken care of me. She recognized me because of my family name. She told me that she had thought when I arrived at the Château, "What a pretty little girl! Too bad she has so many pimples!" She described my face as a child for me. I had not known what my physical appearance was. I knew nothing about myself. I would not have even recognized myself.

And such joy! I went to school with the other children, two by two. Of course, I would have been happy if I could have told someone about my school work, that the teacher had congratulated me. I remember one teacher who used me as an example. I quickly learned to read.

I was neither aggressive nor rebellious. I was still devastated. But something was growing in me. I remember one evening when we were in bed in the dormitory for the little children, a little girl softly sang the Guardian's Song. I have never forgotten this melody. I heard the children crying in their beds, children torn from their parents, each remembering his or her own suffering. For months, and even though there was enough to eat, these traumatized children hid food under their pillows! I did not do this because I no longer had the capacity to act on my own behalf in any way. In that regard I was dead.

My grandmother had stayed in Paris. At the time of the Liberation, there were no trains; they were replaced by military trucks. My grandmother came to get me in a military truck. She didn't speak French well and she had no money. She had looked for Madame Pousse but had not been able to find her. She continued to search until someone told her about Château Méhoncourt. One day I heard unusual activity in the Château and loud voices. "It's a grandmother looking for her granddaughter!" They called me. "Your grandmother is here!" I was dumbstruck. I had a hard time understanding. I went to the courtyard and saw my grandmother.

I recognized her at once. But we had suffered too much; we couldn't celebrate. My first act must seem a little stupid, but it indicated something. I was wearing a piece of material as a skirt, held at the waist with a large safety pin. Automatically, I covered this pin with my hand. I wanted to hide the poverty that I was ashamed of. My grandmother covered her face with her hands and cried.

I must have been the first one to find a family member. Emotion showed on everyone's face. I will never forget this scene. This event showed the others that maybe they, too, would find at least one person from their families.

My life changed direction again. I was no longer going to America; my grandmother took me with her . . .

So I left the Château Méhoncourt with my grandmother, heading toward Le Mans. We waited on the sidewalk for several days for a truck heading for Paris, but very few went by. Lots of people were waiting. At night we went to sleep in a shelter with street people who were often drunk. But it didn't matter to me. I was with my grandmother! I was completely oblivious to all the rest. I had found my lifeboat. Finally we arrived in Paris.

I was nine and one-half years old! My grandmother took me to a clinic to get the care I needed. Life slowly started up again. I went back to school.

Neither my grandmother nor I could say it, but I knew she loved me very much.

In Paris a social service system was put in place. I remember standing in line with my grandmother for an entire morning at the City Hall to get a pair of galoshes.

Several weeks passed. No news of my parents.

It was my second year of elementary school (I had finished the first in Paris, just before leaving for the Sarthe region). I had gaps but the teacher helped me. Evenings, she took me to her place with several other pupils to catch up on what we had missed. School was my salvation. I needed to try to organize my inner chaos. It was important for me to gain knowledge, to have points of reference, to try to understand. I seized upon the resources of the school to make sense of my life. The more I learned, the better I felt. I did well at school but always had this fear of other people. I was unsure of myself. Sometimes the teacher would ask a question of the class. I knew the answer but would not say anything, afraid that I was mistaken. It would turn out to be the right answer. This inferiority complex gnawed at me. It stayed with me for years.

Despite this, the teacher liked me because I had a lot of enthusiasm, even if I didn't answer the questions. I was very attentive, eager to learn, even if I didn't express myself. No one knew my story.

I loved reading. Little by little I even became a compulsive reader.

Then my mother returned!

One day Mademoiselle Le Clézio knocked at the door, out of breath, and said to my grandmother, "I have a telegram. Your daughter has escaped and she is coming home!"

Here's my mother's story:

The Americans and Russians liberated the camps. The Nazis panicked. They evacuated the survivors from the camp at Bergen-Belsen to transfer them by train—the "ghost train" heading for Czechoslovakia. The deportees were sure they would be exterminated. The train often stopped. The SS were less vigilant because they were afraid. During one stop, my mother and four other deportees got off the train. They saw a wooded area and the five women decided to run for it. It was madness. What would they do in the woods, without water, without food, without a way to orient themselves? They nevertheless made their unbelievable, unimaginable escape (this is the escape I wrote about for the Amicale de Bergen-Belsen Association).

So one morning, very early, my mother appeared in front of me. "You are so tall!" she simply said.

The first words my lips formed? "I finally have a mama!"

But alas, my mother was in a sad state, physically and psychologically. She couldn't care for me; she needed someone to care for her.

A few days later it was May 8, 1945, Armistice Day. Everyone was in the street. An aunt came to our house and persuaded us to join the festivities. We walked with the crowd on the Boulevard Barbès. Several buses carrying the last of the prisoners rolled slowly by. In one of them, my aunt recognized my father. "Félix! Félix!" she cried. "A woman has found her husband! Stop the bus!" voices from the crowd cried out. The bus stopped, my father stepped out and saw his wife. I was beside her but he hardly looked at me. I said, "Bonjour, Monsieur." I was nine and one-half years old and had practically never even seen him. My parents and I got on the bus to go to the Hotel Lutétia where the survivors from the camps and the prisoners were assembled. My parents, who had been separated as a young married couple, had found each other. And I felt all alone again.

I tried to tell my parents what I had lived through, but my father silenced me, "You were out in the country; you have nothing to complain about!" So I remained silent.

I learned much later that my father suffered from paranoia. I became the scapegoat for his neurosis.

My parents, who themselves had suffered, left for Divonne-les-Bains to regain their health. I was once again alone with my grandmother. After a few months, my parents returned, rented an apartment, and started to work.

Life began to take structure. I managed to have good moments, especially at school, but a suffering that was unconscious and never expressed persisted in me. I did not exist for anyone, least of all for myself. My internal wounds couldn't heal. I needed time to recover some of my intellectual and emotional abilities, but it wasn't easy in this environment. I could have recovered fairly fast with a little love.

Even though I had only two years of elementary school, I passed the entrance exam to the secondary level. What was extraordinary for me was that especially the French teacher, Madame Mainé, appreciated me. I think she would have been willing to listen to my story as a Jewish child, but I was sealed off. One day she had us listen to a recording of Chopin's *Grande Polonaise*. For me it was the discovery of music that I have loved ever since.

At the *lycée* I flourished. But after the fourth year, I had difficulties with certain teachers. I always acted guilty and was therefore accused. In such cases, I didn't respond; my past trauma reappeared. One history teacher in particular (it's understandable that I might have a block in this subject) took a disliking to me and I didn't defend myself. She did me a great injustice when she put a "zero" on my record for the *baccalauréat*, which meant I was not to receive the degree, even though I was a good student in the other subjects.

After writing a good *baccalauréat* exam, I met with the examiner at the oral exam, which was obligatory at that time. I was mute when the history teacher asked a question. Seeing my good grades and the zero in history, which was very unusual, the examiner understood there was a problem. She shared her surprise with me, offering me a chance to explain. Nothing came out of my mouth and I never got my *baccalauréat*.

After this failure, everything fell apart for me. I was depressed and I was the only one who knew it. I stopped speaking and eating, lost a lot of weight, but no one noticed. I felt I was in danger so I started eating again; my life force was still functioning.

My father thought he had an idiot for a daughter. There was no question of my repeating the last year of *lycée*. I was completely discouraged. Under these conditions, my resilience was gone. What saved me was reading. During my vacation, I read the great French and Russian classics. I learned everything through books. I got better because of them. I discovered that beautiful feelings existed within me. Books built me up and gave me hope.

I decided to take another route: work. At the Jewish Center for Continuing Education, I took an entrance exam equivalent to the *baccalauréat* and earned a diploma in management. It was not what I had wanted, but I needed a way out. I had given up my dream to teach because of my lack of confidence. Then I began to work. At the same time, I joined the Young Communists.

On the emotional level, my inferiority complex handicapped me. I thought I was ugly and stupid. If a young man appealed to me, I ran away. I had an extremely negative self-image: "It's impossible for anyone to love me; the good things in life aren't for me."

At age twenty-four I met an attractive young man who came from Israel and courted me. I was surprised and won over. I married him, had two children in a short period, and was divorced. All my life, in extreme situations, I reacted by moving on. I took the initiative to divorce and raised my children alone. After some professional work experience, I finally got a permanent position at the Institute for Health and Medical Research.

My two children also had difficulties; their father ignored them and I, their mother, had not recovered from a painful past. I tried to sensitize them to what had happened during the Nazi occupation, but I was unable to describe it. But children sense what is left unsaid. My son finally wanted to know what it meant to be Jewish. Today he lives in Israel. He is married with a family.

My daughter, intelligent, extremely sensitive, an artist, too lucid about this world, became mentally ill. At age thirty-four, she ended her life.

Four years ago I retired.

Driven by a strong need to understand, I decided to make sense of my past. I had promised myself never again to set foot in Sarthe. I nevertheless returned there for the first time, at age sixty-five. I did research to recreate my erased childhood. I was largely able to put together the puzzle of my story within the history. I learned that there were four hundred fifty Jewish children hidden in Sarthe. It turned out to be a good place to hide children, given the numerous isolated farms there.

I could also understand the farmers. Many of them were accustomed to taking in children from Health and Social Security Services for pay. When they were brought little Jewish children, for better pay, they didn't ask questions and they certainly weren't aware of the risks.

I also learned that there are today, in the archives of the *département* and closed to the public, letters of denunciation intercepted by the postal service.

I take part in the activities of the memorial organizations: The Association of Hidden Children and the Association for the Remembrance of Deported Jewish Children.

We, the former hidden children, are among the last witnesses of the Nazi era.

I speak in the schools to explain what the Nazis were like. I tell my story, adapting it to the age of the students. I try to make them understand that no one has the right to humiliate, torture, or kill human beings, neither physically or mentally; I urge them to reflect and be vigilant. I tell them that in France many children were saved, partly because of the actions and the courage of a certain number of people. The worst and the best people coexisted. There were the "Righteous" and those who denounced the Jews; there were people who took interest and were good-hearted . . . and also those who were indifferent!

Today as well, terrible things are happening. Children are suffering and dying. In telling my personal story tied to the Jews, I also refer to history. I always emphasize how Nazism is unlike any other genocide.

I have taken a psychological path within a therapy group of the Association of Hidden Children. I discovered the concept of "resilience" by reading Boris Cyrulnik,[5] whose books have been of great benefit to me. I belong to a philosophy group to try to understand something about this world. My fight to survive, to overcome unhappiness and failure, has given me the strength to continue and to hope.

I attach great importance to the arts. I think that art is essential. It is a transposition, a means of expression beyond words. For a number of years I have sung with a choral group that means a lot to me.

As for drawing, I have never been able to take a pencil in my hand. It is with my grandfather, a painter, that I wanted to learn to draw. The Nazis killed him; for me drawing died with him.

A few years ago I discovered Jewish culture. I was captivated by Jewish humor and the literature, which mixes tears and laughter. I love the music that moves me and fills me with enthusiasm. I recently joined a Yiddish dance group, which brings me great joy. Atavism reemerges.

I remain estranged from any religious Judaism. I am deeply secular. My Judaism is a Judaism of reaction; it is because we are Jews that they did "that" to us. It was madness! I feel myself to be marginalized everywhere. For religious Jews, or even traditionalists, I am not Jewish. For non-Jews, I am Jewish.

Even though during the course of my life I have kept myself away from all Jewish life, for the past few years my path has taken me toward the secular Jewish institutions on the political Left (the Cercle Bernard Lazare, for example). Even if I have been able, after many years, to rid myself of my fears, of my feeling of guilt and shame, if I have been able to have self-confidence, there remains with me always a hypersensitivity and anguish before a separation.

Times change, but not human nature. Technology progresses but cruelty, obscurantism, and indifference remain. I still want to be optimistic. Humanity can and must change. Hope is the motivation for life. Life is still, above all, fascinating.

FIGURE 9.1. Éliane at age ten in 1944 in Ballainvilliers during one of her mother's few visits to the boarding house.

# 9

# Éliane Séravalle

**August 2003**

*Éliane Séravalle is French and Jewish. Retired from the National Educational System, she has spent time in Israel. She is a member of a group called Memory and Vigilance.*

I was born in 1934 on August 16. The incidents I experienced during the war were minor compared to the atrocities suffered by thousands (millions) of human beings. This no doubt explains why it was only two years ago that I realized that I, too, had been a hidden child. Despite numerous conversations and interviews I had held on this subject, I was unaware of it until then.

My family was well integrated into French life. My father was born in the center of Paris on rue Jacob. He was raised by a very pious father and attended a yeshiva on rue Jacob for a long time. He ended up as an atheist.

My grandfather had come from Istanbul, Turkey, when he was about twenty-five years old, after having been a tailor for the Sultan. He tailored magnificent suits. I saw his admirable work myself because he also sewed for my parents. As much as he wanted it, he was never given French citizenship. I have part of a handwritten letter dated July 4, 1899, to some official. It is a touching letter in which he explains his situation and reminds him that he had made a request ten years earlier.

My grandfather married a young woman from Lorraine about whom unfortunately I know nothing except that she was a beloved and caring mother. From rue Jacob where my father was born, the couple moved to 37 rue Censier in the Fifth Arrondissement. The couple had two children—two sons who became French only after serving in the military and being mobilized during the First World War. My father used to say that he felt doubly French because he had wanted it and he had paid for it. In fact, he had been gassed and had contracted tuberculosis, which kept him in a sanitarium for a while. Then he took up his usual activities again.

The family's financial situation must have been comfortable, because every year my grandmother spent a month at Dieppe with the children, and grandfather would come on the weekends. Life was good.

For several reasons my family ties on the paternal side are now strained, and I am only in contact with my mother's family. She was proud of her family and often talked to me about them. In 1870 they all left the Alsace region, where they originally came from, to avoid becoming Germans and moved to Paris. Some were lawyers; one was a notary, and another was a stockbroker; still others were in the military; and relatively recently one of our cousins was even elected to the Académie Française.

My parents lived in Paris. In 1937 they moved from their apartment on Boulevard de Belleville in the Eleventh Arrondissement to a single-family house with a garden at Rueil-Malmaison, a suburb inhabited by narrow-minded petit bourgeois. My early childhood, other than being a little solitary, was happy.

I don't remember the declaration of war. I went to the big school located a good kilometer from our house. I would cross the field to school with two other children in complete safety. School was no problem. I learned to read very quickly, skipped the first year of primary school, and moved directly on to the second year.

My school years passed happily, calmly, and without problems. Being an only child, I was no doubt extremely spoiled by my parents.

The war had begun, but I didn't yet feel the anguish. At least at the beginning. I have no memory of those troubled times. And yet, I have found a letter from the management of the Postal, Telephone, and Telegraph Services. It is dated December 14, 1940. I was six years old. The Chief Engineer and Director of Telephone Service of Paris was writing to inform Madame Séravalle: "In accordance with Article 7 of the Law of October 3, 1940, Jewish employees covered by Articles 1 and 3 will terminate employment two months after the passage of the law . . . I hereby inform you, on behalf of the administration, that you will cease your employment on the evening of December 18, 1940." The letter added, "Your retirement rights will be validated proportionately." The letter was signed by the Chief Engineer and cosigned by the Office Head.

I have also found, dated October 30, 1940, my parents' identity cards with the red stamp "Jew" and "Jewess" (required after October 22), stating "dark brown eyes" for my father, "dark blue" for my mother—although they were rather light—and skin color "dark" for both my parents—even though they both had very pale skin. The civil status officer must have assumed the stereotypes of the times.

In 1940 there was the exodus. I don't remember it as being frightening. I remember leaving for Bordeaux in a little Simca automobile with my maternal grandmother, some aunts, an uncle, and some cousins. We once had a small family party. Was it to celebrate a baby cousin's circumcision? It all remains very vague to me. My parents came to meet us on a bicycle. My mother's little red bicycle, a vestige of that past exploit, slowly rusted in our garage for many years.

My parents must have protected me a little too much, because I am surprised to have no memories of that anxiety-laden period. My father had been a sales representative for paper and cardboard products for a long time and we had an easy life. I no longer remember the obstacles he had to overcome in order to do his job. I learned later that he was not allowed to make contacts in some parts of France and that traveling put him at risk. He then had to resign and take odd jobs, which compromised our financial situation.

The anti-Semitic laws and harassment were developing but I don't recall having suffered during this time. We no longer had a maid, but a family friend took care of me. From my point of view, she was an improvement.

My parents carefully explained to me that the problems were becoming serious. In fact, I knew very well that we were at war and that the Germans had invaded France. My father had tacked maps on the wall that showed the enemy's advances in Europe. I was not to talk during the BBC broadcast of *The French Speak to the French*. The windows were covered with long strips of craft paper in case bombs shattered the glass. New dark blue drapes of rather poor quality were drawn every evening because of the curfew. It was better for us not to light the lamp. Food became scarce but we lived near Montesson, a suburb adjacent to Paris now, but then, open country. I would sometimes go with my father when he went on his bicycle to the truck farms to buy vegetables, but we had to cross the bridge spanning the Seine near Chatou and always ran the risk of meeting a German patrol. I still remember the boxes of potatoes that had to have the sprouts removed regularly. Our garden became a vegetable garden. No more flowers, but vegetables—tomatoes, leeks, salad greens, potatoes and their beetles! To this day I can still taste and smell the flavors of our garden. I wasn't hungry during those years, but I nevertheless remember the rutabagas we had to choke down and the little cakes with raisins my mother baked for special occasions when we sometimes invited friends and family. That's when we would sacrifice a rabbit. The shed at the back of the garden was a hutch for the litters. I would feed and pet the rabbits every day after pulling some grass in the surrounding fields. These rabbits were adorable, but we were hungry and had to kill one from time to time. My father was unable to do it, so a neighbor did it. We dried the skins just in case . . .

While I don't remember being hungry, I do remember suffering from the cold at the time, and for many years afterward, and even now. Some parts of the house were off-limits. We did everything in the kitchen, the only heated room of the house. The coal stove was always going—warming us, cooking the meals, heating water for the hot water bottles—with its oven heating the bricks that warmed our beds.

From time to time the silence of the night would be broken by sirens and bombs that exploded like thunder. When I was afraid, I would run to my parents' bed and, when an alert was sounded, we would go down to the cellar. With the passing years, we learned to recognize the sounds, and by 1944 we were able to tell whether it was a V1, V2, or just an alert. Like our grandparents before us, we had started using oil lamps and installed a Bunsen burner in the kitchen. This was very useful when the electricity was off.

May 29–June 1, 1942. Jews were required to wear a yellow star after declaring themselves "Jewish." One day my parents showed me a six-pointed yellow star that carried, in black gothic letters, the word "Jew." This star, which we had to wear, counted against our clothing ration points. After that day, some specific images remain engraved in my mind, but I am unable to date them.

At what point did I understand that I was different from the other children? At that moment, perhaps. The episode with the yellow star permanently transformed me. My mother had carefully cut it out and partly hidden it by sewing it under the lapel of my coat, hoping to have it go unnoticed. I was, up until then, an open, laughing, noisy, and rambunctious little girl, it seems. The shortages had no doubt affected me a little, but I thought the war would only last a while. I looked on the good side of life, unconcerned, without worrying too much.

Events reduced my family to just the essentials. In our family, now very French, my father was not really concerned about the Vichy laws. My mother was. To my father, Pétain was still the World War I officer who had known how to lead in battle and earn the respect of his men. My mother, however, saw things more clearly and was worried.

We never spoke about religion at home. I had been to a church several times, but never to a synagogue. I had put pennies in a statuette representing Baby Jesus when I was in Auvergne with Henriette, my first nanny. Baby Jesus nodded his head to thank me, which delighted me. That was the sum of my religious instruction. Santa brought me toys; I would go to admire him in the department stores and I believed in him completely. Hanukkah? Kippur? I had never heard these words. We observed no holiday. I had been taught morality but not religion. And now someone was making me wear a yellow star imprinted with the word "Jew" in gothic letters because I was not Catholic like everyone around me! This star was my first harsh contact with Judaism. Above all, I was not to talk about it to anyone. I risked being arrested and killed. I had to wear the star, but under the lapel of my coat. I was never to turn the collar up, even if I was cold, because I would be in danger of death. If in the street I were to see someone arresting people wearing the star, I was to discreetly move away and not go home until everything seemed normal, or I was to hide with the neighbors.

What did this mark of disapproval have to do with me? It was the mark of society's rejection of me. I was carrying a kind of incurable disease that generated fear, anxiety, what was left unsaid. I did not understand at the time all that it signified, but I remember feeling strongly the mortal danger around us. I suddenly understood the word "death." The awareness of death was immediately followed by the fact that it was linked to Judaism. From then on I felt I belonged to a stigmatized race but I didn't know why. I was afraid, of course, but at the same time in a vague way I felt superior. Beyond that, I knew what the words "silence" and "secret" meant. I don't think I received other explanations about the Jewish religion from my parents, even at that time.

Although they hadn't been arrested, life had become increasingly difficult for my parents. My father lost his job. My mother was dismissed from the telephone company. Her cousins, the Lévys, gave her work in their optical factory and then she was hired by the bank, Crédit du Nord. I remember she sold sewing supplies from our home to make it to the end of the month. I saw things like spools of thread and embroidery floss.

We had little food, very little heat—like all the French—and furthermore, the Germans submitted the Jews to all kinds of humiliation. I only know of one which my parents told me about later. They spared me all they could. One Sunday the police came looking for my father and other Jews to take them to the center of the town, to Place de l'Eglise. They made them clean the urinals as people were coming out from Mass.

Above all, we resented our isolation. The neighbors across from us knew we were Jewish. My parents had entrusted some things to them, like a grandfather clock that they returned to us regretfully after the war. The house to the right of ours had been recently rented by a German who said he was Greek. Living with him was a woman who, although rather coarse, treated us normally as neighbors. She entertained a lot of Germans. A little pool had been dug in their garden and from behind our barely opened upstairs shutters, we watched her bathe with loud shouts and outbursts of laughter. My parents said they felt rather reassured by the presence of German neighbors. Was that to keep me from worrying? Even so, they were worried, because it wasn't always mere curiosity that made us watch from behind our closed shutters.

There was a little wooden house out in the garden. My father would go there often to sleep at night because it would allow him to leave quickly through the back of the property. He could then stay with our neighbors at the edge of the garden and disappear in case they came to arrest him. We only feared for the men. The women and children, it was thought, were not at risk. Little did we know at the time.

One day, no doubt in 1943, I was home alone as usual. I went to the mailbox for the mail and I opened an envelope. It was a summons to appear at the *Kommandantur*. I remember the panic that spread over me although I scarcely understood what it was about. For the first time, I thought they were going to take us away to kill us. In my childish innocence, I had been living as remotely as possible from the surrounding terror, but even so I had internalized everything. I stayed in the house until my parents arrived. They reacted calmly. My father assured me it was just a normal summons and it wasn't necessary to go as a family. His confident and normal manner calmed me. He went without further comment to the *Kommandantur* and we anxiously awaited his return. I think at that moment I truly realized what was happening; I had just reached a new level of understanding. Nothing was ever the same after that. Even today, how could I not tremble at the thought of all that those Jews endured—deportation, beatings, torture, murder—if I, at that time, was already terrified by the mere sight of a summons? How could I not be ashamed of my attitude then, when I see the reports of children violently torn from their parents with complete indifference?

Things became more and more critical and dangerous. My parents decided to better protect me. One day they came to get me at school; this had never happened before. They came to talk to my teacher to assure themselves that she would not hand me over in case the authorities came to the school to arrest the children. This would have been easy because I was the only Jewish child in the class. The teacher told them that she would never resist governmental authority and would not hesitate to point me out in such a case. Obviously my parents didn't want to take unnecessary risks, so they made a quick decision. A short time after this interview, my father was waiting for me again when school was out, a suitcase in his hand. We didn't even go by the house. We took the train to Paris and I was placed with the Vasner family on rue de Tolbiac in the Thirteenth Arrondissement. Monsieur Vasner, whom I didn't know, was a printer. He had had a good working relationship with my father. I spent the night there, and the next day I was taken to a convent of the nuns of Saint-Vincent-de-Paul on rue Geoffroy-Saint-Hilaire, in the Fifth Arrondissement. This address had been given to us by the Démonet family who also worked with our cousins, the Lévys.

Within hours, I left the relative comfort of a protected life and found myself surrounded by strangers. I was behind a metal fence that seemed extremely high. I must have arrived at this house on a Saturday afternoon. I remember an enormous dormitory where there were at least fifty beds lined up in three rows. Curiously, I don't remember the feelings I had about leaving home. I must have been in an anesthetized state or else my parents had been able to explain it to me calmly. In the evening I was shown to an empty bed where I must have fallen asleep immediately. I only remember awaking the next morning; it must have been a Sunday. The dormitory was completely empty. I was alone. No one had awakened me. The morning hubbub hadn't bothered me. I still hear my own anguished cry. Did tears fall as well? I had just realized that I was to be alone, completely cut off from all affection, abandoned. A young girl came to comfort and reassure me. It was the last time in the course of those years that I freely gave in to my fear, at least in a visible way. Much later when I regained my calm, I still felt the shame of having let my anguish be seen that way. I promised myself to hide forever my deepest feelings. I succeeded a little too well.

How long did I stay in Paris, rue Geoffroy-Saint-Hilaire? A very short time—one night, no doubt. I was soon riding in a truck. A nun with a cornet was driving while another recited prayers, using her rosary. I was eating cookies. The trip seemed long, and yet we went only to Ballainvilliers, a large suburb of Paris. At that time it was still rural. I saw an impressive building and lots of children.

Only a few images remain of the first few days I spent in the new environment. I see myself in a courtyard, in the middle of a large circle, dressed in a brown wool dress decorated with yellow mohair embroidery. Henriette had knitted it for me; I had been very proud of it but it had gotten much too short and I was uncomfortable. And all these wicked girls were making a circle around me and chanting while pointing their fingers at me and viciously insulting me. I was very unhappy about this cold welcome and that evening in my bed, I swore that never again would I allow anyone to mortify me. Curiously, I don't remember any feeling I had after that. The reception must have hardened me for a long time. All that remained were the enuresis crises that I usually managed to hide. These crises lasted several years after the war and complicated my life when I went to summer camp. When did they end? When I regained my self-confidence, no doubt.

Vainly I try to recover the feelings I had at the time. It must have been a traumatic time because I knew there was life-threatening danger for my parents. I knew they were trying to protect me and that the only real refuge for me was in this convent with the nuns. As for visits from my parents, I had a few during the year I was there, but they were always very short. I knew that communication was difficult. I knew that I could no longer see my family. A photo clearly shows my need for affection, which must have tormented me but which I never wanted to reveal. I learned to hide everything. I can't even imagine the danger my mother took to come to see me. Now I greatly regret that I never again spoke of these times with my parents.

I have some memories of this period. Time spent there didn't seem too difficult for me. I must have had, as did the others, a great capacity to adapt. I think most of the boarders were poor children of the area or even orphans. I remember the tension, the taunts about influence with one of the girls of my age. I quickly learned that she and her sister were refugees, just as I was. We ended up getting along and playing our role of little leaders without too much difficulty. What became of her at the end of the war? I don't even remember her name. I remember Sundays, which were holidays. We would dress in clean outfits to go to Mass in the chapel. We sang hymns, some of which I remember today such as:

> It's the month of Mary.
> It's the most beautiful month.
> To the cherished Virgin,
> Let us sing a new song.

I still know two prayers by heart: *Hail Mary, full of grace* and *Our Father, who art in heaven* . . . I happily recited them like everyone else. I remember the month of May in the country and the rosaries that I recited while carefully counting my beads. I went to Mass without being forced. I liked the ambience of the chapel and the odor of incense there. I dreamed. I prayed to Baby Jesus and St. Anthony of Padua, he who returned everything, St. Michael the Archangel who brought down the devil, the Holy Mother dressed in blue, the big St. Teresa, the little St. Teresa, and all the saints. I knew the adventurous lives of them all and the martyrdom of some of them. I prayed sincerely to them to end the war. I became pious; I wanted to be baptized and take communion.

The communicants were dressed in beautiful white organdy dresses as in the photographs typical of the time. Alone at a table covered with a white tablecloth, they savored a special meal that day. The nuns were wise enough not to grant my wish to be converted in that situation. They told me I was too young and that later, if I still wanted to do so, I would be accepted. I had to wait. Now I don't know which I regretted the most—the dress, the meal or . . Even so, I was sincere. I still have today, in the bottom of a drawer, a tiny crucifix. I had chosen it from among other baubles as a prize for a game I won. Why keep it? I can't explain. However, I was incapable of giving or throwing it away. And yet I can't stand the sight of a cross, whether it is in a church, on a hill in the middle of a town, or as jewelry. Whenever these crucifixes attract attention, no one doubts that Jews killed the "son of God." This cross calls for vengeance. So why did the nuns refuse my conversion? Was it a realistic assessment of my desire, or the fact that end of the war was near and that my parents, who were regularly paying my room and board, would not appreciate it? After all these years, I am grateful to them for never having tried to add me to their flock.

Activities and entertainment were not lacking at the convent. We would sing at the top of our voices "Maréchal, nous voilà!" I remember running in the woods on nice days. I remember walking in the fields. We would pull spears of wheat to make chewing gum. I can still taste the raw cabbage we pulled up when no one was looking. Still, I don't remember being hungry. The simple fact of our rushing to the nearby fields during our walks to eat cabbage leaves and grains of wheat or fruits doesn't mean we were hungry.

All in all, what happened there seems fairly minor now. I remember being very cold. We had to line up at the wash basins very early in the mornings and wash ourselves with water that seemed freezing to us. I hardly ever worked in class and the ruler marks that covered my hands didn't leave too harsh a souvenir—only one faint mark on one finger reminds me of it today. This incident allowed me to spend an hour in the infirmary and soak my hand in a soothing liquid instead of being in class. I was not a good student. I didn't want to work. Why would I? Only once when it was a holiday, Mother's Day, I decided to do my school work well. It was the only present I could offer my mother. The nuns seemed surprised that I did so well. A letter accompanied the work. I found it recently. It was a nice letter.

I was not really unhappy; I had my little group to lead, I got along well with the leader of the other group, and I didn't do any chores. My parents told me afterward that they paid my room and board and that only the poor girls without resources had to scrub the floor and help with the upkeep of the place. Personally, I would have liked to peel potatoes!

Not all the nuns were nice. I hated one of them; I loved another—Sister Antoinette, very tall, very plump, an imposing figure with her big blue gown, her big, very white apron—starched like her cap—and her long rosary that swung as she walked. She hugged me sometimes, which was perilous because of her cap and glasses. How old was she? She seemed very old to me.

Now in 2003, sometimes I feel like contacting the main abbey of the convent, which is fairly close to my apartment. I still haven't taken that step. For more than fifty years, I have brushed aside this memory of a convent.

One final memory of my stay at Ballainvilliers: It was the end of the war. There were tanks in the streets of the village and Americans everywhere, passing out chocolate and chewing gum. We had yellow corn bread to eat because the importer thought the English word "corn" meant wheat. The government had ordered tons of it. I thought it was delicious.

And then there is a black hole. Everything is locked away. Even today, I am surprised that such remarkable events could have vanished from memory without leaving a trace. I don't know how I left the convent; I don't remember when or how my parents came to get me; how I took up everyday life and my place in the family cocoon again. It was as if nothing had happened. Not entirely, however. I started classes again at my former school. Madame Trincot, a teacher whose husband had been imprisoned, gave me, along with her daughter, private tutoring so we could pass the entrance exam into junior high school in Paris.

Life went on, but I had a hard time getting into it. I worked only at what was of interest to me. Only one history teacher, Madame Ache, interested me. I was told she had taken part in the Resistance. I thought she was wonderful, but I was unable to perform in class. I contented myself with talking with her after class, near her desk. She mentioned this to my parents who spoke to me about it, but didn't take it any further. I wasn't timid or isolated, because for several years I was elected class leader. I was not afraid to go to talk to the dreaded assistant principal when my schoolmates found the rules too severe. Taking up a role, a duty, to speak for others about subjects that I understood, didn't bother me. I had several good friends at the *lycée*, but we couldn't get together often because we lived too far apart. Solitude didn't bother me because I couldn't forget the command I had so often been given: "Look out, don't speak, you are risking your life. Especially don't tell anyone you are Jewish; it's too dangerous." It was like an incurable illness that I couldn't get over. Since then I have always kept a certain reserve when I meet a new person. People tell me, even today, that I seem cold at first meeting. I have only recently understood one of the reasons for my difficulties in expressing myself with strangers: I need to scrutinize them. I'm waiting for them to reveal themselves.

Somehow I continued my studies at the *lycée*. At home, I kept to myself. The heroes I found in my father's numerous books kept me company and let me dream. This is how I spent my adolescence—not particularly happy, but not unhappy either—surrounded by the love of my parents.

My mother had started back to work for the telephone company on rue du Faubourg-Poissonnière in Paris. My father had lost his job and he was worried. He was noticeably losing weight. We didn't know that a cancer was growing. My father felt the need to change direction. I saw him then in military uniform. Why? I had learned not to ask questions. I knew he went regularly to the Hôtel Lutétia and then left for several months in Alsace, always in uniform. I learned later that the rapport between my parents had become strained. I didn't notice anything. When he returned, my father again worked at odd jobs and life took up its usual course.

I led the life of a high school student, then as a student at the Sorbonne. That was when I wanted to join Jewish movements. At home we never spoke of the war, of the anxiety and the abuse suffered, but I had kind of an indelible mark that kept me from connecting with potential new friends. I signed up to eat in a university Jewish restaurant where the food was especially distasteful. I joined an organization for Jewish students. Outside of one friendship I had with a delightful young woman, in truth I must admit that I never felt a connection with these young people who, for the most part, came from North Africa and only wanted to enjoy Parisian life. I knew nothing of Judaism except that it had ruined my life. When anyone asked me if I was Ashkenazi or Sephardic I didn't know what the words meant. And at the Hillel Center on rue Vaugirard, near the Sorbonne, I discovered once again one of the aspects of Judaism: they all wanted to live, to have fun. I wanted to, too, but I didn't feel ready. My years of isolation and the little bit of spending money I had didn't prepare me to confront life as a casual student.

It was then that I discovered Israel. I thought vaguely about moving there, but after my father's death in 1955, I decided to stay in France near my mother. Then I started my professional life and I had to work hard to try to regain the easy life of before the war. I didn't meet many Jews in the French milieu, into which I didn't feel completely integrated either. I would never have married a non-Jew. Late in life I married a Jew from North Africa who was nonobservant. My husband helped me a great deal. I immediately felt in harmony with him and his friends. Those were happy years. Occasionally I dared to reveal, without complexes, my Jewish origins. But my husband died in 1979.

In 1992 one of my friends, originally from Poland and later naturalized as an Israeli, talked to me for the first time about his childhood in the ghetto at Krakow, and later in various concentration camps before his liberation from Auschwitz at the age of eleven. I had known him since we were twenty and our friendship had been continuous. I had seen the number inscribed on his arm, but I had never dared to ask him about it. He had never brought up the subject either. One day, when he was going through a particularly difficult time in his life, he swore to me that he was living a second Holocaust, and he opened up and began to tell me about it. I recorded what he said. Later he spent half his time in American universities talking about these horrors and his unwavering hope for human nature. He belonged to an assimilated family. He had paid a high price for being Jewish, and he decided to appreciate the Jewish culture.

I, too, have decided, rather late, I admit, to discover the culture, to learn Hebrew, to go again as often as I can to Israel. I acknowledge that even if I have not become religious, I now appreciate my Jewish identity and take satisfaction from it. What will it be like for my daughter?

FIGURE 10.1. Rachel, at right in the photo, at
age eight, with her sister Louise, age thirteen, in
1942 in Paris. Photo sent to their father interned
at the Beaune-la Rolande camp prior to his
deportation to Auschwitz.

# 10

## Rachel Jedinak

**August 2003**

*Rachel Jedinak, an orphan of the Holocaust, is retired from a career in fashion merchandising. She dedicates much of her time to speaking about the Holocaust in elementary and secondary schools, and holds responsible positions in several organizations associated with the memory of the Holocaust. Her work in the schools includes placing plaques memorializing the school's former students killed in the camps. She has received the national award for merit (Chevalier du Mérite). She is a member of a Yiddish chorale and a Jewish theater group.*

I was born on April 30, 1934. My parents were both originally from Warsaw, but they arrived separately from Poland in the 1920s when they were very young. They met and married in Paris. My sister Louise was born in 1929.

I knew my paternal grandparents and several of their children—my uncles, aunts, and cousins. They all lived in Paris except for one uncle, his wife, and their son, who disappeared in the Warsaw ghetto or at Treblinka. Almost all those who were living in Paris were deported and did not return. A single family was spared—my father's oldest sister, her husband and their four children. My youngest aunt was sent to her death with her four children. Her husband met the same fate shortly thereafter. My father's oldest brother and his wife, still living when their two adult sons were deported, died of grief.

My mother came from a large family. Most of her family still in Warsaw disappeared in the ghetto. My very religious maternal grandparents immigrated to New York with three of their children in the 1920s.

My mother and one of her sisters—who had planned to rejoin their parents in the United States—traveled through Paris on the way, met and married their husbands, and the trip stopped there. They disappeared at Auschwitz with their husbands and a young cousin.

My paternal grandparents left Warsaw to escape poverty and the virulent anti-Semitism. Their children had them come to France. Their travel was delayed for almost two years in Duisburg, Germany, where things were still difficult for them in the mid-1930s during the economic crisis.

My grandmother, who took care of me for four years after the Liberation, told me the stories that now allow me to retrace this period.

In my father's family, the political tilt was to the Left. An image of my early childhood often recurs. I am sitting on my father's shoulders, in the middle of an enormous crowd. Was it during the Popular Front?

We lived in the Twentieth Arrondissement of Paris where many immigrants settled. I played in the street with the other children because traffic was light—if not nonexistent—at the time.

My father worked in carpentry and cabinetmaking; my mother did not work outside the home. My early childhood was happy in a family of modest means. That certainly helped me get through what was to follow.

We lived in a two-room apartment and my father worked in the Twelfth Arrondissement, near Faubourg Saint-Antoine, in the furniture manufacturing sector. My father came home almost every evening at the same time. I would go down the street and when I saw him, I would jump into his arms. There was a strong bond between us. We would often sing together in Yiddish, French, or Russian. He had a beautiful, warm, and resonant voice.

I didn't like going to nursery school; the walls were gray, the smocks we wore were black or gray, and the afternoon naps, on dingy mats, were compulsory. I always thought I had started school a little later than the other children but recently, when I had the opportunity to copy from the registration records of that school the names of the Jewish children who died during the deportation, I learned that I was enrolled there at the age of two years and five months on October 1, 1936—a year in which a number of significant events took place.

My parents, especially my mother, spoke French with a strong accent. They often spoke Yiddish, but my sister and I would answer in French. We had been declared French citizens. Our parents, still foreigners, had applied to be naturalized, but then the war started. Their social life was centered on family and friends. My father liked to organize get-togethers with friends. Both of my parents sought companionship. They knew what was happening in Germany. Close friends would come to talk about it in the evenings. I sometimes felt the tension, but I was too young to understand.

My father read the French newspapers and the New Press (*Naïe presse*), a Leftist Jewish newspaper. Sunday mornings he would take me with him to walk to Belleville to meet with friends and acquaintances. I was thrilled to go with him, but even though I understood Yiddish, their adult conversations were incomprehensible to a little girl as young as I was.

More than once I heard the words "Dirty Yid!" Then I would fight like a little wildcat. The other Jewish children and I couldn't stand this insult. There was a kind of anti-Semitism within the French population that was very different from the State anti-Semitism that we would soon confront. The children were only repeating what they had heard at home, and my pain from these insults never lasted very long.

When the war started I was five years old. I remember the big posters attached to a wall: "General Mobilization." I could read the words but didn't understand them.

My father volunteered and was assigned to the Foreign Legion, as were many of his friends. He certainly felt the need to defend France, his family, and his values against Nazi Germany where Jews were already being persecuted.

I remember the day we went with him to the train station as he left for war. My mother and sister were crying, so I cried, too. I know he fought in the battle at Ardennes because I wrote to the Foreign Legion to ask about his service duty. He was discharged in September 1940.

During this time my mother did odd jobs to keep food on the table.

Then there were the alarms that sent us rushing, day or night, to the bomb shelters in the apartment building or to the metro station

Père-Lachaise. We heard German bombers flying over—until we left to join the exodus. In fact, an uncle, an aunt, and their four children (who later died in the camps) had fitted out a truck and came to get my mother, my sister, and me while my father was still at the Front. We took to the road along with many other families who were fleeing the German Juggernaut.

I have precise memories of this because on the way we were attacked. People were yelling, "Are the Italians shooting at us?" The planes flew very low—we could clearly see the pilots in their leather caps who were strafing us. I saw two people lying on the grass, bathed in their own blood. Despite the fear we felt in the pits of our stomachs, we continued playing as children can do in the midst of danger.

The Germans had trapped us en route, so my parents decided to return to Paris.

Then there were the iniquitous laws of the Pétain government; the necessity to be counted as Jews; forbidden to have a radio, a bicycle, a telephone. I remember hanging on the fence at Père-Lachaise Park to watch my little friends at play, but I was forbidden to enter. A sign, white with black lettering, stated, "Jews Not Allowed."

Meanwhile, my mother received a letter from her family locked in the Warsaw ghetto and she broke into tears, fully comprehending their situation. I think she had a premonition about the future.

My father was discharged and came home in September 1940. I was happy that we were together again.

On May 14, 1941, my father received a summons—the infamous "green letter"—ordering him to go to a certain location for the so-called identity check. I remember his kiss and his smile. It was very early in the morning and I was still in bed. He went with a friend of his. The trap closed. He was sent to the internment camp at Beaune-la-Rolande, near Orléans, until June 27, 1942, and then to Auschwitz on Convoy Number Five. My parents managed to write to each other, even though their letters were censored, during his thirteen months of detention in France, and we got permission to visit him. Getting to Beaune-la-Rolande was a real expedition—by train and then by horse-drawn cart to the entrance of the camp, which was guarded by French police. They took my mother's identity card for the duration of the visit and we were allowed to be together for only a few hours. My parents argued and I learned much later from my sister that my mother wanted him to run away with us across the fields to try to find refuge but he refused.

He said, "As long as I am here, nothing will happen to us." Or so he thought.

I have recovered four photos of my father as a soldier and in the internment camp from my aunt because I had none. In these photos of him, the physical degradation resulting from those thirteen months spent in the camp can be clearly seen.

I started elementary school in October 1940. That pleased me. Some other little girls had seen their fathers leave for the Front. Some said that their fathers were prisoners in Germany. In June 1942 we had to sew onto our clothing the infamous yellow star inscribed with the word "Jew." We not only had to pay for these stars, but two clothing points were deducted for them. It was difficult to deal with people's stares, with the mockery of my little classmates at school.

Then came July 16, 1942, and the Vel' d'Hiv' Roundup. My mother must have heard about the arrest of women and children predicted for the following day. She took us to our paternal grandparents who lived nearby in an unheated sixth-floor room without running water. At dawn, a loud pounding on the door made us jump. Two officers, one in uniform, the other in plainclothes, ordered both of us to dress quickly to join our mother. On the way one of them said to us, "Your concierge turned you in." When we got to our apartment where our mother was, she was very upset to see us. I remember the rough way they told us to finish packing quickly. They hurried us along and we went downstairs. In our courtyard, then in the street, coming out of other courtyard gates, I saw families—women and children—herded by police, heading on foot to rue Boyer in the Twentieth Arrondissement. On the way I saw the faces of the people crowding the sidewalks or at the windows, watching us move like a herd of animals. Some made the sign of the cross, tears in their eyes. Others pointed at us, grinning, and as young as I was, I understood that the Parisians were not all of one mind.

We were taken to an empty movie theater, La Bellevilloise, where the seats had been removed. We were pressed together. My mother had only one thought in her head at that moment: we had to get away. She went from one acquaintance to another saying, "No, we won't go to Germany to work; we can't with small children." I was eight years old, but there were some who were two, three, and four years old. One mother came up to mine and whispered that Léa, her fourteen-year-old daughter, had gotten out the exit door and that the policemen on duty had turned their heads so as not to see her leave. So my mother ordered us to go back to our grandparents, telling us, "And if they come to look for you again, try to run into the street where they won't dare do anything to you!" I didn't want to understand; I clung to her dress. Then she slapped my sister and me to make us obey. This slap, the first of my life, was hard to accept because at that moment I didn't understand it as an act of love and wrenching sacrifice on her part . . . Yes, she was a "Mother Courage." My sister took me by the hand and we headed toward the fire exit. The two policemen on duty turned their heads. Léa was waiting for us and we left, running down rue Menilmontant and the next street over. Out of breath and exhausted, we returned to our grandparents in tears.

Our sixteen-year-old cousin Paul was one of those taken in the Roundup. My mother had begged him to run with us but as a stubborn and proud teenager, he wouldn't listen. In 1943 his parents received a postcard from him, mailed from Auschwitz-Birkenau: "I am well and I love you." The Nazis sometimes made the young people write to fool everyone. He disappeared in smoke, as did his older brother, Maurice, twenty years old, deported to Auschwitz on the same convoy as my father.

I don't know how we learned that my mother was interned at Drancy. She was there for thirteen days before being deported July 29 on Convoy Number Twelve. Louise and I went to Drancy several times to try to see her from afar, in the upper floors of the camp where there weren't windows yet because the building wasn't finished. We were behind the barbed wire and we were able to see her once because someone lent us a pair of binoculars. Other people were there alongside us, trying to catch a glimpse of their loved ones, but the French police officers chased all of us away.

On the morning of July 29 we went to Drancy. Buses were passing in the street and Louise told me, "Let's go home." I objected. Later she confessed to me that she had seen our mother on one of the buses and that she had signaled for us to leave. This bus was headed to the Bobigny Station—the last stop on the journey to Auschwitz.

I found the names and numbers of the convoys of my parents as well as all my family in Serge Klarsfeld's *Memorial to the Jews Deported from France*[1] in 1978, and it was only then that I could begin to mourn. And I do mean "begin . . ."

Our lives became very difficult after my mother's deportation. There were six of us hidden in the one room my grandparents had, including our uncle and aunt P.—the parents of Paul and Maurice who had been deported. Every day there was the rush for food. Jews were allowed to shop in the grocery stores only between three and four in the afternoon, but at this time of day, during war and shortages, the shelves were empty. I remember counting the pieces of potato on the others' plates for fear of not having my share. Potatoes were a rare commodity. We lived in continual fear of the roundups. I grew up all at once. My conversations with schoolmates were superficial; I distrusted them. It was 1942 and I had seen the Milice brutally arrest people in the street. I had seen the teams emptying the apartments of the deported families. They took everything but papers and photos, which were thrown into the gutters. So many lives, so many memories washed away with the sewage of Paris.

One day I came home from school for lunch and ran up the six flights of stairs. Surprise! A team was emptying the apartment next door to my grandparents; the people who lived there had been deported. I quickly ran into our apartment; my family was terrified. Shortly after, there was a knock at the door. I was sent to open the door because I was the only one who had been seen; the others were hidden behind a recess in the room. I don't remember if the man behind the door I opened was in uniform or not. Speaking with a heavy accent, he mockingly offered me a gift—a roach-infested sack of beans. He returned several times with spoiled food, and each time I met him at the door to accept it. We were terrified. Finally the moving men left.

I returned to school in October of that same year, 1942. A number of little Jewish girls were not there; some had been deported, some were hidden. There were only four or five of us there. The headmistress got us together in her office and told us, "If one of the women working here comes to get you, take your things and follow her quickly without saying anything to the other girls." Two or three times, we were taken to the building's cellar because the police were coming to search for us at school. I pay tribute to the courage of this headmistress.

This is how we lived: shut-in, cloistered, until February 11, 1943—the day of the roundup of the elderly. That night, fortunately, my uncle and aunt P. were not in the room with us. I think they had gone to sleep in an already stripped apartment in the same building, with the help of my grandparents' concierge, a courageous Italian woman.

At dawn two policemen knocked loudly at the door and the scene already played once was replayed: "Come on, hurry up!" My grandfather, suffering from hemiplegia, couldn't walk. They left him alone on his bed. I still remember the heartbreaking goodbyes my grandparents exchanged. My grandmother, Louise, and I were taken to the police station in the Twentieth Arrondissement on Gambetta Avenue, now the mayor's office. It was very cold and dark. I had chicken pox.

Once there, the policemen opened a trap door and ordered us to go down into the cellar where there were already other frightened, shivering, crying old people. We were the only two children arrested that night in the area.

The police took people down to the cellar and then went back up. Overhead we heard voices and noise. Louise told me, "Let's go up behind the cops." We followed them up the steps and started to come out into a room. Only our heads and shoulders were visible because we were still on the cellar staircase. The people in the room who had been arrested that night for various offenses suddenly became aware of what was happening in the cellar. Seeing us, they started calling the police names and cried out, "Shame on you, arresting children!" These people were under arrest for various reasons, but their reactions seemed unusual to us because so few people reacted to the roundups. The police chief and the other policemen, visibly annoyed, told us, "Get out of here!" Louise had time to say that our grandmother who took care of us was downstairs. As it was night, she asked (innocently?) if a policeman could walk us home and this was done. I stayed with my grandfather and Louise went over to another neighborhood where my aunt and uncle K. were hidden to warn them. A short time later a police officer brought our grandmother home. It was a miracle!

After that, we realized it was no longer possible to stay there because we were in constant danger. My grandmother left with our uncle and aunt K. Louise and I were taken to a UGIF center for Jewish children where we stayed for a while. However, aware that the Germans could carry out roundups any time because they had the addresses of these centers, my aunt and uncle got us out and I was sent to live with different Catholic or Jewish families, a few days with one and then another, sometimes precariously. Separated from my sister, I moved several times. My grandfather died in October 1943 at Tenon Hospital.

My uncle and aunt K., along with my grandmother, were hidden in a private home in Surenes, with the couple who lived there. My aunt and my uncle, a tailor by trade, made clothing that the homeowner delivered to businesses. This is how he made a living for the household. I don't think the little bit of family still alive was in contact with the Resistance networks. A few months before the Liberation, my oldest cousin, Josépha, got false papers for me. I became Rolande Sannier. She took me to Château-Renault, near Tours. Her two younger brothers and her sister were already hidden there with a nanny they had known for years. The nanny then placed me with her mother-in-law, and my uncle paid my room and board. My sister, arriving a little later, was placed as a maid with a young couple and their new baby. My caregiver lived with her husband and their daughters. The oldest was retarded but sweet; she herself had four children. At the time, white bread was considered best so her children had white bread and I did not. I needed a schoolbag with notebooks and pencils. I don't remember now through what means I told my aunt about this, but when I received my schoolbag by mail it had the name "Rachel Psankiewicz"! Imagine! When my caretaker opened this schoolbag and read my name, she began to scream, "You lied to me, you are Jewish!"

I stood up to her, but at age ten I really didn't know how to defend myself. I was threatened; I was sometimes hit. I withdrew into myself and I almost never spoke to the point that when I was able to go see my sister, she was shocked. Her employers were good people, Monsieur and Madame Proust (I'm not making this up!). They alerted my cousins' nanny who took me out of there a month before the Liberation, and I was placed with her sister and brother-in-law, Monsieur and Madame Saillard. Because of their kindness I was able to enjoy life a little again, to speak and smile again. Their teenage daughters sang songs to me. Conversely, I have blocked out the name of my first caretaker.

An anecdote: During my stay in this town, a little girl, Chantal, had organized a party to baptize her doll. I was invited (why?) along with about twenty other children for this occasion. I found myself in a wealthy household where an immense table had been set up in the garden with rich foods with names and flavors I had forgotten. We did a pretend baptism. I wore a hat that was too big and I had a missal. I remember looking at these children—I knew some of them—but I had nothing to say to them; I couldn't tell them anything. I had to remain silent about everything, and at that instant I truly understood that there was a complete and irreparable disconnect between us. My childhood had been stolen, and I was no longer their age.

Then there were the bombings. At the station the Germans mounted machine guns on a train for the wounded. The American planes returned fire and I saw wounded and dead men, all of them German soldiers.

I never betrayed myself. No one knew that I was Jewish other than my cousins' caregiver, my own caregiver, and Monsieur and Madame Saillard.

In July 1944 we learned that the long-awaited Americans were finally coming. The German convoys, fleeing the advance of the Allies, passed in front of us. One event comes to mind. I was with a group of children on a ball field playing leapfrog. On the road alongside the playground a convoy of camouflaged German trucks was passing. They stopped and several soldiers laughingly aimed their guns at us. We were paralyzed! Our counselor said to us, "Keep playing and jumping as if you don't see them." And the trucks finally started down the road. The reaction came afterward—children wailing . . .

Some of the town's Resistance fighters were killed. Near the end of July, a young man arrived running and crying out, "The Americans are here!" I started toward the main street with some other people. A few American jeeps had just passed and a German truck came along firing at them. Somebody flattened me to the ground and when I got up, no one was there. The Americans set up camp for a while. All of us children went to their camp to get chocolate and chewing gum. There was no real celebration in the town because of the killing of the Resistance fighters.

At last Paris was liberated on August 25, 1944.

Shortly thereafter my uncle K. arrived to take his sons and my sister back to Paris. My aunt came the following week to get her daughter and me. We started back, jammed into a truck full of apples rolling around. Trips were still dangerous. The war wasn't over; they were still fighting in the east of France.

At last we arrived in "Free Paris." My sister and I were reunited with our grandmother, and the three of us decided to go back to my parents' place. We tore the seals from the door and went in. There was nothing left—nothing. Those who had emptied the apartment had even pulled out the electrical wiring to remove the ceiling light more quickly, and we lived without electricity for a while. We used an oil lamp for light because we didn't have the money to pay an electrician.

This empty apartment—without furniture, without belongings, without photos that would have allowed us to remember those who were gone, to reconnect us to our parents—made us cry. The loss of our memorabilia was even more painful than the loss of our material goods.

We had to get mattresses, a bed, a table, some unpainted chairs, but I don't know who helped us with that; was it my aunt and uncle K. or was it an aid organization?

My grandmother was worn-out, tired, greatly aged. She gave me a handkerchief that had belonged to my father. It's all I have of his.

My aunt gave us some photos of our parents. I would look at them sometimes, trying hard to remember their faces. But at that time we still had hopes of seeing them again. The three of us lived almost without means, in extreme poverty. At the time there was no social or psychological assistance as there is today whenever there is a crisis. My aunt sometimes sent her children with a shopping bag of food for us, and our grandmother sent us to ask for help from certain organizations from time to time. This was difficult for me.

France was liberated but the war continued in the East, in Germany. The children who were able to stay with their parents didn't have the same difficulties we had in getting the basic necessities.

When I felt the need to talk, to tell about my suffering, I was told, "Let it go, let it go. Let's talk about the future. We don't want to talk about that, it's over!" No one was ready to listen to me. People wanted to get past that dark period, but no one can forget such a catastrophe.

I started school again in October 1944. It was a very emotional experience. Many little Jewish girls were missing; they had gone to meet horror and death.

Some of the teachers and children embraced me. We sang "La Marseillaise."

Then came the Armistice. People danced in the streets for several days. The hope of seeing our parents and family again was strong despite the alarming news we received. The rare survivors from the camps arrived at Hôtel Lutécia. We went to greet them with photos of our parents to try to get news. Arriving there, we saw these deportees who looked like expressionless, skeletal ghosts. No words came from their lips; it was terrible! We felt the unspeakable horror they had experienced.

A young Belgian cousin was repatriated to Paris from Auschwitz at the beginning of May 1945. He looked for the family. His father had died at Auschwitz; his older brother, at age twenty-one, had been tortured and put to death in Belgium and thrown onto the public square. He told the older family members of the horror, the gas chambers, the crematoria. I heard, and yet I couldn't resign myself to the idea that I would never see my parents—that they had been slaughtered.

My uncle L., deported in 1943, whose wife and four children had been taken to Auschwitz in August 1942, knew he would never see his family again. We received a telegram from Odessa saying he was returning to Paris. Three weeks later, a returning deportee came to visit us and told us that our uncle had died of exhaustion.

I made up stories at night in order to go to sleep, persuading myself that my parents had perhaps been liberated by the Russians, that they had temporarily lost their memories. I clung to this hope for a while, and then I had to accept the evident: I would never see them again.

I lived with my grandmother and Louise. Life for the three of us was difficult. We had only a minimal amount to live on. My grandmother often cried. She had lost almost all her children and grandchildren.

I completed elementary school and then was put in the classes that would end my primary education because no one was looking out for my future. School being obligatory until age fourteen, I asked my teacher if I could try something else. She got me admitted to the Alternative Program for entering secondary school, along with my childhood friend Fanny, who still had her parents. We were the first two students admitted to this program from the Twentieth Arrondissement. I attended this school situated on rue des Pyrénées, which is now called Collège Dolto. I would have been happy to stay there, but the circumstances dictated otherwise.

Louise, at sixteen, entered an apprenticeship with a leather worker. Then at age nineteen, she hastily married a man ten years older than she, a Polish Jew who came to France in 1947 by way of Germany. His mother and several of his sisters and brothers had died in the ghetto in Bendin, Poland. After their marriage, they lived in my parents' apartment and my grandmother left to live with her daughter, my aunt K. I didn't know where to go. I was fourteen years old, so Louise decided to take me to Belgium to the home of a cousin of my father whom I didn't know. Her husband had been deported, one of her sons shot, and the other—whom I spoke of earlier—had returned from Auschwitz.

I would get up at dawn to go around to the markets with her to sell small items. It was very cold in the winter. I didn't know anyone; I was isolated, without contact with other young people, my hope of continuing my studies dashed.

Meanwhile, Louise and my brother-in-law decided to leave for Israel in 1948 and asked me to join them. I came back to Paris to the home of my uncle and aunt, where three of their children and my grandmother were also living. I slept beside my grandmother one night, but there was no room for me there. But where was I to go?

My aunt, the only one of my father's sisters living comfortably before the war, had kept in contact with the former maid of my uncle L. (whose family had all been deported). This wonderful woman agreed to let me live with her while I waited to leave for Israel. She lived alone, her little girl having been placed with a nanny because this woman worked from morning to night. We shared the same bed because the small room was crammed full. She showed me how to do the finish work on garments. We worked all day in a little space on rue des Poissoniers in the Eighteenth Arrondissement of Paris.

I joined an association to go to Israel. I was able with my small salary to buy myself a bag and some clothes. After about six months, I received notice to join a group in Marseille. I arrived at a center where I found hundreds of children and young adolescent Sephardic Jews from Morocco or Tunisia. These young people were going to a kibbutz while waiting for their parents to join them.

I, a little Ashkenazi orphaned by the deportation, arrived there with my sad story. These young people knew nothing of what had happened in Europe and didn't understand anything. There was a world of difference between us. At night I was given a place in a dormitory full of girls who sang in Arabic. We really didn't understand one another at that time. I felt like I had been transported to North Africa that night. Afterward, I got along well with the counselors who were over twenty years old and who were closer to my state of mind, which was not that of a normal, carefree fifteen-year-old girl.

Six weeks later we boarded a boat. We slept on hammocks in the hold; the cabins were reserved for families. Rats ran everywhere, so we took our blankets and slept on the deck. The crossing took six or seven days. When the boat reached Haifa, I saw my sister, her two-month-old baby in her arms, waiting for me alongside her husband.

They lived in a room with no facilities on the first floor in the out-skirts of Tel-Aviv. The heat was unbearable that August of 1949.

The pioneers who had emigrated in the 1920s and 1930s tried to find people from their cities or villages of origin, knowing that most had been put to death. Before I arrived, my sister had contacted the husband of a family who, in his youth, had known our father in Warsaw. This family—the parents and three children—accommodated me in Tel-Aviv. At night they put down a mattress for me, and two days after I arrived they found work for me. I made lampshades and sold them on a main street of Tel-Aviv. I stayed with these nice people for about four months. Then my sister wanted to return to France. She couldn't stand the suffocating climate and the hard life. She had lost a lot of weight.

At that time in Israel it was a little like the Tower of Babel, each speaking his native language. There were many unfortunate people, most of whom arrived from the displaced person camps all over Europe, who had often been submitted to abuse and persecution. They formed tight communities, making it difficult to form relationships among the people of different origins. Of course, all that was quickly settled later.

I decided to go back to France with my sister. We left together, Louise, her baby, and I, in November 1949. In Marseille we spent a night in a disreputable, but inexpensive hotel, and my sister went to sell her wedding ring so we would have enough money to buy our return tickets to Paris. My brother-in-law sold their furniture and joined us a week later.

At last I was back in Paris, but what now?

Louise, her husband, and their child stayed at several places before obtaining, for a fee, a room overlooking the backyard on rue Lancry. The miniscule kitchen was transformed into a nursery for the baby. Running water and a toilet were out on the landing.

And I, where was I to go? Again I was up against a wall. Someone who worked for my uncle and aunt K. took pity on me. She herself had known the horror of Auschwitz. She lived in the Tenth Arrondissement. Her elderly mother and two of her three daughters were living with her. She welcomed me warmly, her humor softened the situation. We slept three to a bed. One of her daughters, Monique, later married one of my cousins.

I worked at odd jobs—apprentice milliner, stock clerk. I even sold men's underwear and long johns. I then enrolled in an intensive course and earned a stenographer's certificate.

My uncle and aunt K. opened a ready-to-wear store in Bourges. I lived with them and my cousin Hélène, who was two years older than I, for a few months. I took care of ordering and selling and some of the bookkeeping, but I didn't like living in this small town. In any case, at that time I felt ill at ease everywhere. I didn't fit in anywhere.

When my sister and her family left Paris to settle in Lyon, I moved into her tiny place on rue Lancry. My cousin Hélène also came to stay with me for a time. I was only sixteen and one-half years old.

I worked making women's clothing. I did the finish work and at the time we were paid by the piece. The work was seasonal. By the end of the month, money was tight.

My cousins lived in Paris and I was a friend to my cousin Maurice's wife. At the age of fourteen, she and her sister had been arrested in a roundup in a Vichy-controlled Jewish Youth Center and deported to Bergen-Belsen. She had survived typhus in the concentration camp and had miraculously returned.

I took care of my cousin's children twice a week after work in the evening, so I got two free meals. I was left to myself, but I was determined to pull through. I read a lot in the evening or during the weekend.

At age twenty-one, I married a childhood friend of my cousins. His parents and two younger sisters had also been deported. He still had only his two older sisters. He had been arrested, along with his parents and two younger sisters, in the Vel' d'Hiv Roundup. At the time of the arrest, his sister's eighteen-month-old daughter was being cared for by her grandmother and this child had been taken along with the others. My husband's mother had cried out, "This child isn't mine, look at my family record book." So the police pointed at my husband (he was fourteen years old) and said, "You, take the baby to her parents and come back here."

Of course, his sister didn't let him go back. She kept another sister, too. They went to the Unoccupied Zone. My husband worked with the Resistance in the Vercors Maquis at the age of sixteen.

After our marriage we both worked making clothing. My daughter—my happiness—was born and I had a family again. One day, at age four, our funny and happy little daughter said to us, "You are both naughty! The other children have grandmothers and grandfathers and I don't!" We began to answer her questions gently, trying to tell her, but she was traumatized by the lives the two of us had led.

I was widowed at the age of forty-one. I was working in a ready-to-wear store at the time. My daughter continued her studies and married. They have two sons. My son-in-law is like a son to me.

After I was widowed, I had the opportunity to take night classes for several years in literature and other subjects. In the evenings I would work on these courses. This helped me restructure my life. I discovered will power I didn't know I had. In this way, I was able to partly achieve intellectually what I lacked emotionally.

My oldest grandson at an early age began to ask me questions about my life. He has been suggesting for a long time that I write my testimony, his younger brother listening as he asked questions.

When they were children, on my days off I often took them to the Louvre, to Beaubourg Museum, to the Musée de l'Homme, and numerous other places. I wanted to give them the opportunities I never had. Our relationship remains special now that they are university students.

When the store where I worked was sold, I found myself out of work at age fifty-eight. That's when I began to take courses in history at the university.

I joined organizations of former deportees and the Mémoire juive de Paris Association. We organize photographic exhibitions in the city halls, taking as a key theme "Jewish Immigration and Integration in France from 1880 to 1948." The enlarged photos that we exhibit trace the lives of immigrants in their native countries and their life stories in France after their arrival: work, sports, school, artistic life, the scientists, the intellectuals, including, of course, necessarily, the war, the roundups, the Resistance, and the deportation.

In this organization I met my partner; we share the same work and the same values.

In 1997 a former student from the school on rue Tlemcen (Twentieth Arrondissement), along with some friends, wanted to put up a plaque at the school, in memory of the children who went to school there and who had been deported and murdered in the death camps.

Being a former pupil at the school, I was contacted and we created an association, together with the teachers who did a great job helping us research the archives.

The mayor of Paris gave us the green light to extend this initiative to all of Paris, and many associations were created in the other arrondissements and now in other cities. We cross-check our lists with the valuable *Memorial to the Jews* by Serge Klarsfeld,[2] and when we are certain that our list is correct, we put up a plaque outside the elementary or secondary school citing the facts, and another plaque inside the buildings with the names and ages of the children who were put to death. The ceremonies are exceptionally emotional and include elected officials, representatives of the national educational establishment, former deportees, and combatants.

Furthermore, we talk to the young people in the elementary and secondary schools. We explain to them as former deportees, Resistance fighters, and hidden children how the country fell so quickly into horror, stimulated by racist propaganda, anti-Semitism, xenophobia, and exclusion. We talk to them about the tolerance that is indispensable to understanding others. In this endeavor we are supported by their teachers whose advance preparation for these presentations is excellent.

To judge by the letters, art work, thank-you notes, and poems I receive from children and teenagers, I am certain we are doing real educational work. It is not easy to speak about a painful childhood, to explain how it feels to be a child in a secular and democratic school one day and to be a pariah the next day.

These young people understand us. Today some immigrant children have their own stories, often painful ones. It is disturbing, but we think it is of primary importance to make the youth of today aware of this unspeakable past. During the ceremony of unveiling the plaques, the pupils recite poems, sing songs learned for the occasion with the devoted help of their professors, and it is very moving.

I have also involved myself in an association with the same objective: the Joseph Migneret Committee (Righteous Among the Nations) in the Fourth Arrondissement.

At night, I still have nightmares; images of the war superimpose on each other . . .

I have been a member of a Yiddish chorale for years and that gives me a needed respite. I now sing with my grandsons like I used to sing with my father, in French or in Yiddish. I also take part in a community theater workshop where plays from the Yiddish traditional repertory are performed in French.

In this testimony, I would like to express my appreciation here to the team from the Center for Contemporary Jewish Documentation (CDJC) for the help, efficiency, and friendship with which they honor me.

My conclusion is a call for vigilance. Let us remember what Primo Levi wrote: "It happened once. It could happen again."


## Response from Kevin, Rachel's Grandson

March 26, 2002, at City Hall in the Fourth Arrondissement in Paris at the awarding of the Chevalier dans l'Ordre National du Mérite to Rachel Jedinak:

My dear Lalo,

When you asked me to speak today, I didn't have to ask myself whether I would do so. I had no hesitation whatsoever. On the contrary, the words carrying images and memories surged up in me. What I want to say is not at all formal because it is about you, and about us. I say "us" because my brother's voice echoes with mine.

The work you do every day with memories of your past comes not from a sudden decision, but rather as the culmination of what you told us when we were still in the sweet peace of childhood that was denied to you. Early on, almost naïvely as children do, we started asking you about your own childhood, your own youth, about your parents, about your grandparents whom our mother never knew. With extreme gentleness, you elaborated your answers.

With the two of us leaning against you, you told us of your stolen childhood, your childhood brusquely taken; you told us about fear and flight, running from the authorities, the perpetual state of danger.

Gently, courageously, however painful it was for you, omitting nothing, using direct language, you let us see the harsh realities that made you what you are. Silently, we listened to the story of our Lalo, your story, your personal history—our own now because it is inscribed on Alan and me. At the age of eight I became the heir of this living memory. It is integral to my perception of existence and my understanding the of the world. Through flashes of insight, bursts of understanding, we heard your story. Huddled together, the three of us would weep as we savored the joy of living in peacetime together. We would sing Brel, Brassens, Piaf, and Boris Vian. We would hum Yiddish songs. I remember our long strolls through Paris in the spring on the Saint-Martin Canal, in the Buttes-Chaumont Park. With you I discovered the Musée de l'Homme, the Louvre, Beaubourg, Orsay.

Today I, the young man of whom you are so proud, tenderly treasure those privileged moments, this childhood that you took such care to give importance to, this childhood of which you were and remain a major part. You are always the attentive observer of our successes and our doubts and we, in a way, are your compensation as we pursue the studies you were denied. It is difficult for me to have an objective view of this life that was yours and that of so many others. For me, history at school is too intimately associated with you. I have the deepest admiration for you, for your work with remembrance, and for your work as a witness of history—a history that some would like to deny.

I am so happy to see you here today with Ernest, your "singing sunshine," as the poet Éluard says, to receive from the French government recognition for the work you and the organizations to which you belong are so courageously accomplishing. To me, this recognition not only honors you, but it also marks your rehabilitation in the name of the French government and, through you, returns dignity to your parents who so ardently wanted to "belong," and who today would be so proud to see their daughter, their little Rachel, thus honored.

FIGURE 11.1. Daniel, at the right in the photo,
at age seven in 1939 with his older brother
Maurice at Sauvelade (Pyrénées-Atlantiques)
outside the farm where he was
hidden during the war.

# 11

# Daniel Krakowski

**April 1, 2003**

*Daniel Krakowski (mother deported—never returned; father a Resistance fighter) is retired. Self-educated, he succeeded in rising socially. He worked mainly in electronics at France's Atomic Energy Commission. He has always remained faithful to his early political commitments. He also is a very active member of various organizations, is interested in issues affecting citizens, and loves to read and repair things.*

KRAKOWSKI: I was born in France, in Paris in the Twelfth Arrondissement on April 26, 1932. I will be seventy-one years old in a few days. I am culturally one hundred percent French, having lived at home very little and having scarcely known my parents. I heard my parents and other people speaking Yiddish but I never learned it.

BAILLY: Can we go back as far as possible? Where were your parents from?

KRAKOWSKI: My parents were both Polish. They met in France. My mother was born in Warsaw and my father at Zunska-Wola, a rather big settlement not far from Krakow. My wife, Annette, my brother, and I

209

went there a few years ago. We saw what a village, a *schtetl*, might have been like at the time because there were still some old houses, including apparently the one where my father was born and lived as a young man. The experience was very moving.

BAILLY: What do you know about your grandparents' time, either from what your parents told you or from what you have been able to reconstruct? What work did they do? What social groups did they belong to?

KRAKOWSKI: Actually I don't know much. My family didn't talk about that. I had already left my parents before the war, as my mother had tuberculosis and had to go to the sanatorium. I learned later that I had had diphtheria. I had short stays in rest homes and in summer camps. I spent several years of my childhood, before 1939, in the country on a farm where I returned as a hidden child when the war broke out. I never knew my grandparents. They stayed in Poland. My paternal grandfather had been a baker like his father, but later became a gardener. I think the occupational restrictions placed on Jews prevented him from continuing to work as a baker. During the Holocaust he was tortured, despite being eighty years old, then deported by the Germans, as were other members of my family. My maternal grandfather was an accountant in a cousin's cookware factory. He had six children. When he died, his wife began selling wood and coal.

BAILLY: Do you know what their convictions were?

KRAKOWSKI: My paternal grandfather was very religious. This was not the case with my father, who very early in life was a Communist. He fled Poland partly because he didn't want to do military service, which was long and risky for a Jew, and partly because he espoused revolutionary ideas. I know he was pursued, and I think he escaped through a window when the police came to get him. He ran away to Germany where he continued his studies until he again had to flee because of his political activities.

BAILLY: That was an early commitment, but not particularly tied to a family tradition?

KRAKOWSKI: No, I don't think so. But no one talked much about those things at home. I think there were religious people in my family, but I don't know if it was my grandfather's generation or an earlier one. That was not unusual at the time.

I don't know much about my father's childhood either. He never spoke to me about it. Like most men, he didn't like to talk about himself. Moreover, it must be said that parents and children talked together very little. I didn't know my father very well. When I returned from hiding in the country after the war, I spread my wings and took off. I didn't work with him. He communicated very little and today I find that I don't know much.

My parents became acquainted in France in the early 1920s after coming there separately. They were married at Montgeron in August of 1926. My brother was born in 1929 in Paris.

BAILLY: Is there more you can say about this Polish past?

KRAKOWSKI: My parents were of modest means but not poor. My mother trained to be a hairdresser. She had several brothers and sisters. The sisters were very independent, which was not always the case for young girls at the time and especially not for Jewish girls. I later knew two of them. One, who worked as a salesperson of fashionable clothing in Warsaw, came to France. The other, who was a wigmaker, left for the United States. They were "thinking" women who had learned a trade. My parents met in Paris at a party. I think they were introduced to one another. It was perhaps an arranged marriage, but this was often the case in the communities and among minorities.

BAILLY: A Jewish community, but Jewish Communist?

KRAKOWSKI: I'm not sure if they met in a Jewish Communist environment. You can be Communist and still go to social events with others in the community. My father was a tailor and a very dedicated union activist. It may have been a union party or a Jewish social. My mother, as far as I know, was not politically connected.

BAILLY: So there were two sons, your brother born in 1929 and you in 1932. Was your family living as a middle-class family?

KRAKOWSKI: No, not really. My mother did people's hair at home, but she became very ill and had to stop. She went to a sanatorium in the Ain region. My father worked from home as a tailor's helper. It was a difficult trade. We lived in successive tenements, in the Eleventh, then in the Twentieth, then in the Fourth Arrondissement in an unhealthy area. It was charming because it was along the Seine, but there were rats and the toilet was down the hall.

BAILLY: The poverty of the past . . .

KRAKOWSKI: That's how it was. People today can't imagine. For example, my brother and I, at the time of the Liberation, had chilblains because we slept in a very cold entryway on a folding metal bed. There was no heat, nothing to burn, so we picked up pieces of wood in the streets. One of my rare memories of before the war is that our whole family—my parents and their two children—lived in a one-room apartment where the running water and toilet were out in the hall. My parents worked there and slept in an alcove.

BAILLY: Their home was also their workshop?

KRAKOWSKI: Workshop? What's that? By five or six a.m. the sewing machine was running. In the evening, with me and my brother in bed, the machine continued to run. We endured fatigue, stress, the lack of privacy. I remember a childhood spent in very tough circumstances but not unusual for the time. After leaving Poland, my father had stayed in Germany for some time—in Cologne and Bonn where he took up his studies again, probably general education, but also tailoring. He came from Germany with one suitcase. He was skillful at his work but he also worked very hard all his life. Being a tailor who worked at home subjected him to the worst kind of exploitation. Home workers were rarely unionized. They worked all alone, sometimes with their wives and children. They probably worked twelve to fifteen hours a day, Sundays included. They were paid by the piece, and at delivery time the inspections were very rigorous.

BAILLY: You were in school during that time?

KRAKOWSKI: Before 1939 I spent several years away from my parents, in the country, in the Basses-Pyrénées (today called Pyrénées-Atlantiques), in a village near Lagor called Sauvelade, thirty kilometers from Pau and about twelve kilometers from Orthez. It is tiny on a map because it has only about one hundred inhabitants.

My mother was in the sanatorium, and my brother and I had been placed by the Health and Social Security Services in this house to improve our health. I went to school at Sauvelade as soon as I was old enough, and I also worked on the farm. I was little when I went there. I was very well treated and as the baby of the household, I was even spoiled, so I didn't suffer there. On the contrary, I have good memories of being there, which allowed me to be welcomed back with open arms when in 1939 I had to be hidden. I returned later to this welcoming place where I was known and had friends.

BAILLY: When did your parents take you back? Did your mother get well?

KRAKOWSKI: I don't know much and I don't remember. When you are young, at least as it applies to me, you are unaware, you don't notice. I wasn't very curious and didn't ask questions later, so things are now very vague in my mind. I saw my mother again in 1938 and at the beginning of 1939 when I went back to Paris, for a year, no more. Then I went back to Sauvelade.

BAILLY: In 1938, 1939, your parents took you back to the little room where they worked. But you know nothing more of this time; you were too young to have any perception of the years of Hitler's rise to power?

KRAKOWSKI: Yes, in 1939 I was only seven years old. Taking into account my poor memory and my probable lack of awareness, I have no recollection of it. So I'm not going to elaborate; I might repeat things I learned later and that are not my personal memories. I have a very vague recollection that, at school in Paris, I must have been treated as a "dirty Yid" but nothing more; perhaps there were some blows exchanged. I am not by nature aggressive, so it didn't make much of an impression on me, but it must have happened. It was a state school in a working-class neighborhood. Anti-Semitism was quite commonplace. They would say things but it didn't have a great impact on me, probably because I didn't know what it meant.

BAILLY: Your parents didn't tell you much either?

KRAKOWSKI: No. Maybe because I didn't tell them what was happening at school. Anyhow, my father was slaving away.

BAILLY: You said your parents spoke Yiddish to one another?

KRAKOWSKI: Yes, fluently. My father's French was not good. My parents didn't speak Polish. Both of them knew it, certainly. I think it was simply that their culture was Jewish and that they hated Poland and the Polish so much that they didn't want to speak Polish. They spoke only Yiddish, which my father read and wrote fluently.

BAILLY: Do you remember anything about the declaration of war?

KRAKOWSKI: No, nothing that I can place. Everything that I know about that time I learned later.

BAILLY: Your parents sent you back to the country in 1939 for safety, because of the war?

KRAKOWSKI: Yes, it was in 1939. I don't know the exact reason. I don't rule out the possibility that my mother suffered a relapse, because she returned to the sanatorium about then. That's why I didn't see her during certain periods of time. I think that must have hastened the departure of my brother and me to the country. I was taken by the Health and Social Security Services through the normal administrative process, apparently not as an emergency.

BAILLY: Between 1936 and 1939 was the period of the Popular Front. You don't remember anything about this kind of people's liberation movement?

KRAKOWSKI: No. I wasn't in Paris much. My brother remembers more. He remembers having ridden on my father's shoulders in a demonstration in 1936. It doesn't surprise me because my father was an activist. I remember him speaking about 1934 as a major event that he personally experienced. Knowing him, when he said "Fascism," it was something he felt strongly about.

BAILLY: Do you know any details about the responsibilities or activities of your father as a union delegate?

KRAKOWSKI: I know he had responsibilities in the Tailors' Union. He often went to the Trade Union Center, and I would often see him writing and sending meeting notices. He also wrote in Yiddish in the *Naïe presse* (*New Press*) but I didn't know that until much later because he never talked to us about it. Others who knew him well told about it, for example in his eulogy.

BAILLY: So you and your brother returned to the country. It must have been hard for a child of seven to be separated from his parents again, especially his mama?

KRAKOWSKI: I don't remember. I'm not sure it was hard because I left with my brother and went to people I already knew, to a nice country place with animals, surroundings that meant something to me and that were very pleasant.

BAILLY: Did this family know you were Jewish?

KRAKOWSKI: Yes. I wondered about this for a long time without wanting to ask them. I recently asked people who told me that everyone knew it. Sauvelade was in the Unoccupied Zone but Orthez was in the Occupied Zone, about fifteen kilometers away. That's where the Demarcation Line with the Germans was. I crossed it several times completely unaware in order to go for the medical checkups required by the Health and Social Security Services. I would go by horse-drawn carriage; we would see Germans, and for my part I thought nothing about it.

BAILLY: Didn't your host family tell you not to give your name? Did you have a false name?

KRAKOWSKI: They didn't tell me anything. No one paid much attention there. They knew there were Germans, but we wouldn't see them all year, even though they weren't far away. It was a village without electricity; there was no machinery, no radios either, and no cars. There were very few newspapers at the time and I don't remember if the people subscribed to a weekly or monthly newsletter. We were away from everything; we lived in autarky because the villagers raised chickens, hunted, and fished. They lived self-sufficiently. Other than the trip to Orthez, they never went farther than a few kilometers. I stayed at

Sauvelade during the entire war, until 1945. My brother couldn't stay with me at that farm and that was a big dilemma. When we returned in 1939, there were already three other little Parisian Jewish children there, and there wasn't room for my brother. As I already belonged in the family, they kept me. So we were separated. My brother Maurice was placed elsewhere, with a sister of my foster mother, four or five kilometers away. It was difficult for him. He was sensitive. He had been separated from his little brother, he was with people he didn't know, and furthermore, in a house where the son was a prisoner of war in Germany. When he arrived there in 1939, he was already ten years old and he worked hard, like a man. I didn't know about it; he told me later. It was also difficult because of the particular geography there—hills, with snow in the winter, storms from time to time, and steep slopes. My brother went back to Paris earlier than I, near the end of 1944. I stayed more than six months longer, but I was eager to return to Paris.

BAILLY: Do you know what your parents were doing during the first part of the war? Did they declare themselves Jewish at the time of the anti-Jewish laws?

KRAKOWSKI: I don't know much. I was away, with no telephone, no radio. You have to consider what the situation was then. It is perhaps difficult to imagine; my father was living clandestinely and my mother was in a sanatorium.

BAILLY: Was your mother safe in the sanatorium, as long as she didn't leave?

KRAKOWSKI: Yes, one could assume so, but she made the mistake of returning to Paris by clandestinely crossing the Demarcation Line. She was arrested in January of 1942. She had returned to Paris a few months before. She probably wanted to be with my father. She was arrested simply while going to the police station to have her papers validated because there was a big campaign in the newspapers telling Jews to make sure to have their papers validated. She was one of those credulous people who believed it.

BAILLY: Your parents were still Polish citizens at the time?

KRAKOWSKI: Yes. Ill-advisedly, my mother went to the police headquarters and never returned.

BAILLY: So between the time when she came back from the sanatorium and when she was arrested, she was with your father at home?

KRAKOWSKI: I think so. My parents must have lived together a short while. I don't know exactly how she left the sanatorium or how she returned to Paris.

BAILLY: Afterward, your father went underground. Was he in a Communist network?

KRAKOWSKI: He was in MOI. I can't figure out how he lived.

BAILLY: Did he take part in the Resistance with MOI?

KRAKOWSKI: He didn't talk about it and I was too stupid to ask him . . . He was also an activist in the Jewish organization Solidarité, which became the UJRE in April of 1943. I know only that he was responsible for distributing the leaflets translated into German and placing them on the pavement to be picked up and read by soldiers walking along there. It was all aimed at demoralizing and frightening them by telling them things that they didn't know. He used a set of letters generally intended to make rubber stamps to print little pamphlets. I think he typeset short texts with three, four, or five lines in this way. He would go to the little bookstalls and when he saw German soldiers ten or twenty meters away, he would swiftly put the pamphlets down on a bench or among the books so they would see them. What he was doing was very risky and one day he was chased. He ran home. We lived on Quai des Célestins at that time. Fortunately, at the back of the building was a door through which he managed to get out again. The Germans searched the building but they didn't find him. He would also go and meet with defenseless or skeptical Jewish families to persuade them to flee or to hide, in anticipation of the roundups. He lived under the constant threat of being tracked down. I remember once he came to see us in the country. He was extremely thin, like a skeleton. We thought he probably didn't eat enough. He was already naturally thin. I remember vaguely that he  seldom wrote to us and that he never had the same name or the same address. He was in various hideouts. That's all I know about the underground work of my father.

BAILLY: He came out of it?

KRAKOWSKI: Yes, he survived, but he and I did not communicate very much, for all kinds of reasons.

BAILLY: You said that your mother didn't return from the police headquarters?

KRAKOWSKI: They arrested her there. She went to the Tourelles prison, then to Drancy.

BAILLY: You later obtained papers that retraced her path?

KRAKOWSKI: I got some dates from the Center for Contemporary Jewish Documentation (CDJC). My mother's sister, also now deceased, sent her packages and went to see her at the Tourelles prison. My mother was then deported to Auschwitz by Convoy Number Seven on July 19,

1942. After that I have no details, but taking into account her fragile health and her age, she must have been selected for death early on.

BAILLY: Did your father find out what happened to his wife after her arrest?

KRAKOWSKI: No. At the time there wasn't much detail. It would surprise me if he learned anything since there weren't any witnesses. Furthermore, no one talked about it at that time. We speak much more freely about it nowadays than we did back then.

BAILLY: Do you attribute this silence, all that was left unsaid, to the culture of that time?

KRAKOWSKI: To three things: first, to the very great and very real lack of knowledge at the time; and secondly, to the fact that my father was a discreet man who kept to himself and who didn't talk much; and finally, to us because we were too inattentive and too taken up with our own stories.

BAILLY: Let's review the chronology. From 1939 to 1945 you were in the countryside, you went to school and worked on the farm, and during the war, your dad was active in the MOI. Is that right?

KRAKOWSKI: Yes. For me, he quickly became clandestine. He didn't come back to his apartment until the Liberation, which means that before that, he didn't live at his place; he lived with other people. I recall an incident he later told me about: one day he was in a hideout in a building with a garden on the ground floor on rue Saint-Julien-le-Pauvre, very near the church, in the center of Paris. One or more Resistance fighters were arrested and shot right before his eyes in that same garden that evening. He saw the whole thing from his window—he had a room high up under the eaves. He said that if he had had a weapon, he would have fired. He probably owed his life to the fact that he didn't have a weapon that day.

BAILLY: Liberation came. Do you have any memories of it? Did the village where you were celebrate?

KRAKOWSKI: No, it happened in a very ordinary way. In the country it wasn't like it was in the city. It was a small village—scattered—without a real town center.

BAILLY: Before we leave this village, located in this very southern region—was it a village that supported Pétain?

KRAKOWSKI: Not much. On certain occasions they sang "Maréchal, nous voilà!" The townspeople knew I was Jewish but I was adopted; I was the family's child. The village's protection of my brother is more surprising because he had changed towns. I was younger than he, I had a history, I was a little kid; no one would have dared to denounce a little kid. Whereas he arrived there at age ten. He told me an anecdote that proves that the people knew he was Jewish. They couldn't help but *know* with the name he went by, and by the fact that even if the parents were never seen, they were talked about; so he couldn't have been an orphan. In other words, people weren't crazy; they understood.

BAILLY: No one from the village denounced you then?

KRAKOWSKI: No. They had a tradition of solidarity, of hospitality. Were they Pétain supporters? Some probably were.

BAILLY: Did they sell on the black market?

KRAKOWSKI: No, they didn't need to. The cities were far away and there were no cars. They lived self-sufficiently. They had everything they needed at home. For example, they grew grain, took it to the mill, and got bread in return. They got water from a nearby spring—I was the one who did that—because there was no running water. We ate well, we had everything, thanks to the garden and the variety of what they grew and the animals they raised. Each family would kill a pig. So during the years I spent in the country, before and during the war, I was very well taken care of in this home where there was no poverty. I had, until my return to Paris in 1945, a normal, protected life without deprivation.

BAILLY: Do you want to reveal the name of the family who cared for you?

KRAKOWSKI: It was the Bonnassies family. I took too long before returning to visit and, unfortunately, there is no descendant. In a lot of ways, I belonged to the family. I was the "little brother" since there was a "big brother," so to speak; their only son had been called up for the Obligatory Work Service (STO). He went to work in a youth camp. One day he didn't go back to his camp from leave. I learned later that he had deserted and was hidden. To my knowledge no one ever came to look for him at the house. The village was located far away from everything—the big cities, the administration. Things were probably less difficult there than in many other places. The Pyrenees weren't far; it was fairly easy to hide. There were many scattered little villages without any bigger towns nearby.

BAILLY: And now it's 1945; your dad takes you back. Did he come to get you?

KRAKOWSKI: No, I left as I had come—with the Health and Social Security Services who had placed me there—with a group of children returning to Paris. When I arrived in Paris, in the Fourth Arrondissement, I was the little country bumpkin. I was dressed in the corduroy outfit that was the uniform for children cared for by the Health and Social Security Services. I spoke with a strong accent that made me different.

BAILLY: From then on you lived with your father?

KRAKOWSKI: My father was back in his apartment, which had been looted. He came across people wearing coats made of fabric pieces from his reserve . . .

BAILLY: Did he find family photos?

KRAKOWSKI: Yes. My father kept photos that I got when he died, but without knowing who was who. Recently I showed them again to an older cousin, and she was unable to put names with the faces. There are handsome bearded men and elderly women dressed in the Polish style, often seated in artificial settings. They seem to be my grandparents and their kinfolk.

BAILLY: The three of you were together—your father, your brother, and you. Your father was very stricken by the death of his wife, I suppose?

KRAKOWSKI: One would think so.

BAILLY: Do you know if he looked for information at the Hôtel Lutétia or elsewhere when the few deportees returned?

KRAKOWSKI: My brother told me they went to the Lutétia when the convoys arrived. I wasn't there at the time. We spoke very little about it. My father went there and sent people to at least look at the lists, but I don't know what importance the loss of my mother had in his life.

BAILLY: So your father tried to start over. He took up his work as a tailor, just as before the war?

KRAKOWSKI: Yes, with my brother helping him. He was already out of school at the time. He had passed the Certificate of Primary Studies (CAP) in the country but he did no further studies. Reluctantly, he had to help my father and do the pressing, which was very hard work. He had to use a very heavy iron and work very long hours, and for a teenager that's not a very exciting life. He left for the United States in 1945 when he was fifteen or sixteen years old. He still lives there. In fact, he went in place of a female cousin that an American aunt was willing to take in. The papers for this cousin were ready, but she decided at the last minute not to go so she could stay with her mother and sister. Her father had died in the deportation. During the war this cousin was an active member of the MOI in Grenoble. She was eighteen years old.

BAILLY: You continued with school?

KRAKOWSKI: I went to school.

BAILLY: Do you remember your father as beaten down or did he, for example, throw himself into the work of the union? What was his state of mind at the time?

KRAKOWSKI: That's when I learned that he was an activist, because I didn't know about it before the war. I was too little and I didn't always live in Paris. So when I speak of his life as an activist and a militant, it is after the war. I think it was not the war that led him to be militant; it was in his nature. He had always been that way. The memory that I have of the years after 1945 is that he worked very hard, both at his trade and for the union.

BAILLY: Did he bring another woman into his life?

KRAKOWSKI: Yes. There were several attempts. The last was the most fruitful because he lived with her for quite a long time until she died. But I saw several women pass through our house.

BAILLY: Do you remember anything about your teenage years? Naturally, life wasn't easy, but youth is still youth.

KRAKOWSKI: Yes, all the more as people were coming out of the war and as I myself was coming out of the country. I don't know if you can imagine someone coming from a place so deprived of amusements, a God-forsaken place with only one dance a year. I had to go to mass three or four times a year because it was almost the only distraction. So can you imagine someone leaving such a life, so sheltered and restrained, to life in the city with the "qualitative leap" it entails?

BAILLY: By the way, in the country, did you allow yourself be open to Catholicism?

KRAKOWSKI: No, I rarely went to mass, but I was with people who were not really religious. The family's son wasn't, and even the husband, despite being the village gravedigger, didn't go to mass. The women did go to church but they weren't overly religious. Religion was totally left in the background.

BAILLY: Let's go back to your adolescence in Paris. You discovered the city. You had friends?

KRAKOWSKI: Yes, I made friends. I reacted against my father's ideas and activism, which took far too much of his time. Moreover, I had just come from an area where I was completely unaware and bored to a city where there were crowds and events, demonstrations, reconstruction, organizations, political parties, unions. I remember having had a slight reaction of defiance and mistrust. Fairly soon after I returned, at about age fourteen or fifteen, I felt like rejecting the serious political questions. Some youngsters resist their parents at a much earlier age, but I couldn't, and so that's when it happened. There were probably other reasons for my reactions. Anyhow, I was always going to school and my father and I didn't see each other much. Also, I did the errands for food; we had to eat. My brother often did the cooking. I couldn't be completely independent like the other young people I saw around me. That's how it was. Plus the fact that my father spoke Yiddish in his shop; he spoke very poor French.

BAILLY: There were employees in the shop?

KRAKOWSKI: Yes, there was a finisher—a neighbor who sewed—and a "presser" (an ironer). They worked in our home. My father lived in this environment. And for me there was school or errands, getting away, taking walks, because I didn't want to be tied to the shop like my brother was.

BAILLY: How old were you when you left school?

KRAKOWSKI: In the country, although I had been a good student, I couldn't get permission to sit for the exam for the Certificate of Primary Studies (CAP). So I went to elementary school in Paris for one more year until I was fourteen years old. I had an unusual schooling. I am mostly self-taught—one of those individuals whose education alternates between work and studies and for whom the absence of a recognized diploma requires going to vocational schools and night courses. I never even considered working in the shop with my father. I needed to get away from this confining situation of working at home that was very tiring but not very rewarding. So once I had the Certificate, I decided to be an electronics technician (called "radio-electrician" at the time), whether in aviation—considered then to be the highest niche—or as a sound technician. A necessary step for me was to obtain the CAP. I started my career at the entry level, checking radio and television sets at several firms. It was perhaps my dismissal after a month's work for going on strike at one of the firms that accelerated the pursuit of my studies. I chose the school known as "École de la rue de la Lune" (from the name of the street where it was located). I earned my spending money doing repairs, home installations, and as a salesman in various trade shows for a business in the neighborhood. Later I studied at the

National Conservatory of Arts and Crafts and did a lot of things that allowed me, all in all, to get along fairly well, with stops and starts along the way, but always working.

BAILLY: If your mother had lived, do you think she would have encouraged you to continue your studies?

KRAKOWSKI: I can't extrapolate. It's true that mothers are often the ones who worry more about their children's future. That wasn't my father's thing. He had his own life. He left me alone. He neither helped nor hampered me. Maybe he helped a little. I don't think we ever talked about it. In sum, you see, I took a path that is unusual. It may seem strange, but I never set foot in a *lycée*. I move among professionals, teachers, and people in middle management who talk about their schooling, of the good or bad teachers they had, and so on, but I don't even know what a Latin or philosophy lesson is. When I took up my studies, I was with people who had the *baccalauréat* degree. I had to struggle because I clearly wasn't at their level. That didn't prevent my having, throughout my life, the good fortune to specialize in fairly specific areas, to work in important, technologically advanced public services where I had challenging equipment at my disposal. I was with the Atomic Energy Commission for thirty years. Being conscientious, I always took my work very seriously and, in turn, I was taken seriously, which allowed me to become an engineer. That's how I was given assignments for which I was not a priori academically prepared: testing electronic components and measuring devices, studying specification notices, gaining expertise and developing new products, performing reliability studies, managing a research bureau, determining qualification of suppliers, reporting at international expositions and conducting training. I also had the opportunity to organize my time fairly freely. I have always liked my work. It was varied and it permitted me to meet all kinds of people—clients, suppliers, partners, French and foreign colleagues. Looking back, I think I performed with what was required to have self-respect but without any real ambition. I don't like blowhards and careerists, even if a little ambition does no harm and is an excellent motivator. I have sometimes tried to see myself the way others see me. I must have within me a hidden "shrink." I was probably influenced by an idea I had of "Man" since adolescence—of the "New Man" perhaps—serious, straightforward, honest, faithful, modest. Was it an ideological model or pure romanticism or a combination of the two, with perhaps also the unconscious desire to gain recognition? In any case, it seems healthy to me to live up to the ideals one adopts, so they become more than just theories. I see it as an excellent way to gain self-respect and to bring together passion and reason. In my responsibilities for quality control as well as in my life, I have often practiced the "WWWH (Why? Where? When? How?) Method." This involves mistrusting the obvious and imagining alternative solutions, discovering as many different responses as possible. Can this be called the "dialectic method"? My close colleagues and friends may simply see me as a contrarian. I am always questioning—maybe not enough in politics—the arguments and words that are too simplistic, too reductive. By reading and traveling, one learns that things are seldom as they seem at first glance. History teaches us to stand back and take measure, to consider that in the game of public relations there is that which is an excellent intellectual exercise, and my grandchildren are good guinea pigs to continue this game. And when lacking a partner, it is perhaps home repair that has helped me ask the questions: "How does that work?" "How can I fix it?" You take whatever victories you can, and pride in work well done is perhaps the prerogative of hard-working people. This is the calm, fatherly side of me. But there is also the "committed" side. At the present time still, the rise of the Right Wing, the developing violence and its consequences, the recent war in Iraq—all that which is at stake for civilization and makes us fear for the survival of the planet—is enough to make any citizen actively stay in the game, and I am in it. From this point of view retirement, like the working life, is not a long, tranquil river.

BAILLY: Let's go back for a minute to your adolescence. Was it then that you joined the Communist Party?

KRAKOWSKI: No, it was later. I joined in 1950, at age eighteen. Even so, I wasn't very committed to the Communist Party. I don't think I went to a single political meeting for several years. Contrary to what everyone thinks, even at that time, people easily joined and left the Party, despite its strongly centralized organization. They no doubt sent me mail about coming to meetings, but for a long time I didn't go. On the other hand, I rather quickly became active in a Jewish youth organization, the Cadets, also of Communist inspiration, which brought together children of the deportees at the initiative of the UJRE, where my father was active and with which he was well acquainted. Early on, I left for summer camp with them. We had excursions and cultural activities. There were two or three meeting places for the Cadets in Paris. For example, we sometimes went to the Charles-Dallery Center in the Eleventh Arrondissement, not far from Place Voltaire. We met there to take part in all kinds of activities; I probably sang a little in a chorale, but I don't think I belonged to any theater workshop. We got ready to participate in frequent demonstrations for May Day, Bastille Day, the commemoration of the Warsaw ghetto uprising or the 1871 Commune, events like that. There were sometimes political confrontations. I remember having carried petitions and collected money to establish the State of Israel. At that time it was fairly difficult for the State of Israel and in addition to the Zionists, it was often the Leftist organizations that agitated for the Right of Return for Jews to Israel. Stories like the one about the boat *Exodus*, for example, mobilized us. We also sold door-to-door *Droit et Liberté*, the publication of the Movement Against Racism and for Friendship Among Peoples (MRAP).

BAILLY: For a young man without his mother it was somehow a milieu that served to balance you—a little joyful, active, gregarious?

KRAKOWSKI: Yes. I met my wife Annette in that youth organization.

BAILLY: How old were you when you met?

KRAKOWSKI: Fifteen or sixteen years old. Her parents were very kind to me. I would often go to eat with them. They had a little house in the woods not far from Paris at Sénart where I spent my weekends with them and sometimes my summer vacations. I didn't spend leisure time with my father. I led my own life; I was more often with Annette and her parents than with my father. This is another reason why my father and I were never very close to each other.

BAILLY: So that's how your adolescence ended, a period that was certainly difficult. When you earned enough to live on, did you move out of your father's place?

KRAKOWSKI: No. I stayed in the Fourth Arrondissement, Quai des Célestins, with my father until I married.

BAILLY: What year did your father die?

KRAKOWSKI: In 1978. He was born in 1895. He was sick and tired.

BAILLY: During his life, were there times when you were close?

KRAKOWSKI: Hardly ever. He used to invite us sometimes on Sundays but we never talked about our relationship, out of a sense of modesty. He liked to see his grandchildren.

BAILLY: You never talked about your mother either?

KRAKOWSKI: No. I never even questioned him about her and neither did my brother when he used to come back from the United States (which was rare but, even so, he did come from time to time). It was a silence, a blackout, a systematically established reticence. Now, on the contrary, people say that we must speak and that we have to deal with the facts about the Holocaust.

BAILLY: It isn't healthy, in any case, to have been an orphan of the Holocaust and not to have been able to talk about it to someone close!

KRAKOWSKI: No, but it was common in our milieu because we lived according to our common culture. The people I knew, the fact that we went to the UJRE, all worked to keep us among Jews. I didn't feel Jewish, however. I have never felt very Jewish, but even so I was in a milieu of Jewish youth. A lot of things were implicit, not stated. The word "Holocaust" wasn't a part of our vocabulary. We were all turned toward the future; that was our strength.

BAILLY: So what did Jewishness mean to you at the time?

KRAKOWSKI: Nothing at all except that I was in a tribe that had suffered a lot but of which I didn't know the history, the culture, or the language.

BAILLY: You were completely secular because your father was?

KRAKOWSKI: Yes, and I have remained so all my life.

BAILLY: You didn't have a bar mitzvah?

KRAKOWSKI: No, and I am not circumcised.

BAILLY: So getting back to the chronology, you left your dad's apartment only when you married?

KRAKOWSKI: We got married in 1955. Young people didn't live separately from their parents at that time. We did go to camp together, Annette and I. Even the last year when Annette was pregnant, she and I went to a Youth Hostel where we were separated like at school. (I never went to a coed school.) It would have been out of the question—however old we were (we were about twenty)—for us to live together before we were married. We had to hide to bill and coo. We were twenty-three when we got married. Annette's parents, who liked and respected me a lot, would have probably been shocked if . . . while they trusted me completely. For me, they were my real family. There was never a cross word between us. They were charming people, and I was accepted and welcomed.

BAILLY: Was Annette as much of an activist as you were?

KRAKOWSKI: No. She discovered politics later, especially during her first year at the university. She came from a more middle-class milieu than I. Her parents weren't at all politically involved. The war had forced them to make choices. Her father was never openly politically minded. He would go to public meetings but never carried any political card. He was a sales representative, very independent, a little religious or superstitious. They were an average middle-class French Jewish family, Left-leaning, concerned about justice, voting Communist Party, but not militant.

BAILLY: Now we are going to jump over a long period. After your marriage, you had two children, then grandchildren?

KRAKOWSKI: Two times two.

BAILLY: The two of you were then very active in the Communist Party and you are still faithful. What connection do you make between your being an orphan of the Holocaust and your beliefs as an adult—universalistic, Communist, very committed—since you belong to several associations that involve you in many local issues as well as other, more broad-based issues?

KRAKOWSKI: I owe a lot to the Party; I learned a lot from it. It gave a sense of purpose to my life, it socialized me, it opened me to the world. The two aspects of my life—professional and political—have played complementary roles. But I am also in a variety of organizations that are not political!

BAILLY: But that have collective concerns?

KRAKOWSKI: It's the need to meet people, and nowadays everybody is overly urbanized. The social connections seem to me to be stronger in the cities.

BAILLY: But this is not how everyone feels!

KRAKOWSKI: Annette and I are not people who can sit around doing nothing. Is it a certain fear of emptiness?

BAILLY: Beyond that, do you or do you not see a connection somehow between this commitment and your dramatic childhood, this drama of the Holocaust that touched you by depriving you of your mother? Do you see a connection between your ethical values, your general convictions, and what happened to you during the war?

KRAKOWSKI: In hindsight I feel that is obvious.

BAILLY: It's different for each of us.

KRAKOWSKI: In *Astérix*, there is a character who fell into the pot. Today I think my being the son of a deportee, of modest origins in the context of the war, makes it rather natural that I would become Communist; staying one is something else. I have the impression that to become Communist after the war was a common phenomenon. There were values born of the Resistance that were widely shared; there was the force of the Left in its diversity; the Communists were involved, but they weren't the only ones. In France the Left was the majority for a long time; the values of democracy were very strong; radicalism as well as secularity was dominant for a long time. I think that for progressive Jews, secularism—that is to say, the separation of Church and State—is a very important aspect. Another is respect for the culture with cultural access desired by and desirable for everyone! It's out of this respect that the desire to know and to understand was born in me. Moreover, the fact of having suffered probably developed in me a greater sensitivity for the suffering of others. That must be true, even if it is not automatic.

BAILLY: No, it's not automatic. For some people, it induces the opposite reaction—withdrawal.

KRAKOWSKI: There can be an element of rejection. I must have felt it myself for a few months when I came back from the country and discovered the city. I came from a place somewhat cut off from the world, and suddenly I discovered a father going to meetings, a world bubbling over: the existence of two blocs, the electoral confrontations, the big strikes in 1947, the Rosenberg affair, the colonial wars, and also social injustice. For me the "tomorrows that sing" made sense as we were both descendants of the ghetto and the heirs of Stalingrad. This rejection, for me, didn't last long. Maturity came fairly soon; I became aware of who I was—that it was not luck but circumstances that had allowed me to survive. By listening to what others were saying, I learned all at once more than I had in the ten previous years. I came out of my cocoon.

BAILLY: You seem to be saying that, having endured the suffering we endured, it was natural for us to turn to others who were suffering and show not only compassion, but real solidarity. Now, as I told you before, I have noted more than once among Jews who had this same past, a kind of "tribal" retrenchment—which is easily explained but which has hardened them and closed their hearts to empathy toward those suffering in other genocides.

KRAKOWSKI: I don't think that was the case with the people I was with after the war. Remember, we were in an Ashkenazi milieu that was very political and very secular. The synagogues were not full and we didn't talk about kosher food. There was a Jewish culture, certainly, but very secular and very French. The Jewish "tribal" retrenchment of which you speak came much later.

BAILLY: This open culture you describe is typical of the Diaspora in a certain way. How would you characterize it in contrast to a religious traditionalism that we know well, very community oriented? It is difficult for the younger generations to put a definition to this idea of "Jewish culture, secular and open to the world."

KRAKOWSKI: Personally, during my childhood, I was not influenced by the Christian culture because I wasn't in a very religious milieu. Religion was foreign to me, and it appeared useless and irrational to me. So I lived outside religion and I have always been able to do without it very easily. I didn't look for a cane to lean on. It is still the case today; I am interested in religious issues because they call into play ethical and social issues, history, and the values we have in common; it is the history of society, the societies of the world and of France that are intertwined. I look at it a little as a scientist and not as someone who would like to escape reality or who has inherited some religion or another, neither Judaism nor any other. My father was very hostile to religion. He really saw it as "the opiate of the people" and the enslaver of many among them.

BAILLY: You spoke of a "cane;" one could say "crutch." Without making comparison with religion, would you say that the Communist Party was a "cane" for you in the sense that it was a substitute for family, a solid set of convictions upon which you could rely?

KRAKOWSKI: Social life, whether one wants to admit it or not, is always a bit of a crutch—the need to be with others, to share values. One can either play the hermit, go to Africa, hide out in the Larzac mountains or elsewhere, or seek common values in an existing community that allows you to both develop and enjoy. Both aspects are at work at the same time. The older I get, the less I can imagine being an activist simply for the sake of being an activist. I did it because I wanted to, not because I had been obliged or ordered to do so, but so that I could understand. I think, in fact, that one can find pleasure doing anything, including an unrewarding job. I've been lucky to have had a job that interested me and that I enjoyed doing; I also wanted to be an activist for pleasure, which is not at all easy, and which one can't always do. But can you conceive of undertaking any voluntary activist commitment, unselfish and unconstrained, if it didn't somehow also bring satisfaction and pleasure?

BAILLY: You have never been disappointed, never been disillusioned with the vagaries of ideology?

KRAKOWSKI: Yes, but not to the point that I wavered or took the opposing side of my earlier convictions, although I have sometimes suffered from them (you are wounded yourself when you feel and share suffering). But I was lucky enough to find answers that allowed me to cope. This is not easy but it is necessary and desirable.

BAILLY: Looking at the non-Jewish French milieu and its behavior in connection with what happened to us, and rethinking the war and after the war also, do you have, overall, a positive or negative impression of the role of this milieu?

KRAKOWSKI: Neither one. We can't say "overall"; we can't speak in these terms. A life is too complex; there are both positives and negatives that coexist and everything can quickly change.

BAILLY: You didn't experience anti-Semitism after the war, for example?

KRAKOWSKI: No, one has to remain lucid and calm—that's the most difficult. Anger is a bad counselor. I have gotten angry or agitated; I usually regret it because in these cases, you can miss the truth. Anti-Semitism exists; it has to be fought, but it isn't the only avatar of society.

BAILLY: You prefer not to pass judgment?

KRAKOWSKI: But I do, all the time! The only thing we can do is to avoid making judgments that are too rash or too simple. You have to analyze the reality of situations because things are often much more complicated than they seem. Let's avoid the amalgams and preemptory opinions.

BAILLY: What message would you like to give to your children and grandchildren for later? What of your personal history seems to you the most important to pass on to your descendants, to society?

KRAKOWSKI: That's a little difficult; messages can seem pretentious. One always has to be modest, being careful to pay attention when speaking to someone and not start out with "In my day . . ." We have to avoid putting ourselves up as models—we are not models, we are witnesses who are not ashamed of what we have done, who have nothing to be ashamed of. We have to transmit things without imposing them and without giving definitive value judgments. This helps others grow.

BAILLY: So let me form my question this way: what do you really feel strongly about?

KRAKOWSKI: Dignity, respect for others and for one's own dignity. A very simple example: I detest bad words, insults. I am not able to treat anyone in a rude manner (I've probably done it and must have regretted it), and yet there are days when I want to. I am the first to blame. We need to stop and think a long time before judging others so as to have as little as possible to reproach ourselves about as to the way we judge society. We also have to keep in mind that we are social beings who share life in common with other people, while insisting they tolerate and respect our values in return.

BAILLY: So respect, self-control, holding back before spouting off?

KRAKOWSKI: It's not holding back in a defiant sense; it's prudence in the sense of not making too definitive a judgment so quickly that one falls into stereotyping. Take a side too quickly and you miss seeing how difficult, complex, moving, evolutionary man's intelligence is.

BAILLY: For you, this is one of the universal values?

KRAKOWSKI: Yes. I think rationalism is an essential value, but it's not all black or white. There is a lot of gray and many nuances. Nothing is ever definitive; the proof is in how we look on the past differently today from how it was seen ten or twenty years ago. The mentality has changed, we've gotten older, there are other documents, another history, there are questions and answers that were not available earlier. Those who pass definitive judgments at a given time risk being very unhappy later when they have to retract them.

BAILLY: Is this connected in any way to the war, to us as children during the war?

KRAKOWSKI: It marked me deeply. I have read many articles about the war, not only about Jewish martyrdom. War is always monstrous, full of the unexpected. And we ourselves evolve. For example, today I see the American General Schwarzkopf speaking out against the war in Iraq, when he was the one who led the war there in 1991!

BAILLY: But the harm done to us *is* absolute; it is beyond nuance, isn't it?

KRAKOWSKI: It is absolute, but leaving it at that makes no analysis possible.

BAILLY: So how do we overcome this drama?

KRAKOWSKI: For example Lanzmann's film, *Shoah*, was said to be the definitive film. His film was certainly very good; it was rather complete, but if you leave it at that, it means abandoning everything else— literature, thinking. Now new films are being made, they are interesting, modern; their writing and analyses are different and they are equally useful and necessary. I also take pleasure in watching the dozens of books coming out today, written by people who dare to tell what they have lived and who didn't do so before, and by new historians who help us better understand. Of course the war marked me a great deal. I see this in comparison with other people. I have the peculiarity of being a Communist and a Jew at the same time. It is not always as easy as you might think.

BAILLY: Did it mark you by making you more sensitive?

KRAKOWSKI: Yes, for example, about the problems of Israel. Whether I like it or not, I am of Jewish origin so I can't treat it lightly, nor can I fall, as some others easily do, into stereotype. This is also true for other issues, including some far removed from me. I *have become* of Jewish culture, without even noticing it, and I think it contributes to my way of looking at things, to my perception of the world, and perhaps to the modesty I'm trying to talk about. But it is also part of my wealth of references.

BAILLY: Do you mean that you have noticeably recaptured, over the course of time, a little of the Yiddish or Ashkenazi culture?

KRAKOWSKI: Yes, although the word "recaptured" is a little strong in my case. Let's say "rediscovered." The events themselves have caused me to reflect, and whether I want it or not, I am somewhat obliged to place myself in relation to my origins without proclaiming my Jewishness. It exists without being exclusive.

BAILLY: You are not "Jewish first, French after"?

KRAKOWSKI: No. I am a French Communist of Jewish origin.

BAILLY: Of origin only?

KRAKOWSKI: Yes. Do I really have Jewish culture?

BAILLY: When you see Annette and me dancing and singing in the klezmer festivals, what do you feel?

KRAKOWSKI: I like it a lot, but you adore it. I'm glad for you because I see you are thrilled, but I personally have the same feeling in non-Jewish environments. You sparkle, but I see it also with others who are not Jews. It is more other people or events that remind me that I am Jewish, but it doesn't give me too many problems.

BAILLY: You feel no need to recover Jewish culture, even secular Jewishness?

KRAKOWSKI: I am seldom among secular Jews who are not assimilated. I am a member of different organizations. I recognize the Jewish culture as being particularly rich, with strong emotional content for me. That's all. I see around me a number of people who are bored, who don't read, don't go out. Often it is because of their social status, but they don't get out of it. Jews have suffered so much that they tried to pull through and they have. (I am tempted to add, not necessarily in the best way . . . ) In general, they get away from isolation and despondency through culture, through a certain withdrawal into their community and also in reaction to events. That's why when I say, "not necessarily in the best way" I mean by a way that sometimes takes them in unfortunate directions.

BAILLY: Your children are married to non-Jews; your grandchildren are "mixed" also. What of their Jewish origin is important to you that they keep?

KRAKOWSKI: I don't know. I don't think about that because I know they will retain very little of it, and also because I can't decree what they must or must not retain. What is important is that they know that they have Jewish origins and that those origins have been heavy with meaning and danger, not only in a general way, but for their own parents and grandparents. It is not about the neighbors; it is in their direct family line, and afterward it's up to them to take it up, according to the circumstances. Our history is a world in itself, but it is only a part of the history of the world. It must help them choose peace, democracy, respect for human dignity.

BAILLY: Are they depositories of the memory?

KRAKOWSKI: Yes, but that's not decreed. I have a son and a daughter who are very different from one another. My son is fairly sensitive to Jewish problems but my daughter, not at all or very little. Perhaps as they get older they will be more interested. Like many grandparents, I notice that the grandchildren are perhaps more interested. That is tied to a number of things. One of my granddaughters is now fifteen years old. I talked to her about the Holocaust because she is curious. I speak to her more freely than to either of my children, who have never asked me questions. I didn't ask questions of my father and I was wrong because it was a whole life experience that was not transmitted. But my children have their own lives, their children, their problems. There are no lessons I can give.

BAILLY: What more would you like to add?

KRAKOWSKI: Don't volunteer to transmit a message, stay modest, don't use yourself as a model!

BAILLY: There's a risk of being counterproductive?

KRAKOWSKI: That's right. And it could give a self-image that is not the one I want to give. If possible, I want to give the image of a free man, an independent thinker, despite his political commitment. I see that my children seem to share my democratic, secular, human values—that's what counts. Whatever they become really is not for me to judge. I won't be there to appreciate it. So with a great deal of modesty is how I must live at my age, I think.

BAILLY: Among the other values that seem important to you, you were speaking also of your reading, of its importance for you?

KRAKOWSKI: On second thought, it's not only about reading. We lived during times of deprivation, our own and that of those around us. When I was in the country, we had everything needed to live except the superfluous. I didn't know what a birthday present was. I once got an orange for Christmas and it was the only orange of the year. We lived like that, and mine was not an isolated case. What I still have is this rejection of present-day consumerism. I am of a generation who went without and didn't live with abundance, and I continue to be with people who don't throw away a crust of bread, who get angry when someone throws something in the street, when someone doesn't respect the work of others. I think that among the values to transmit there is also the respect for work without making this into a sacrament.

But to return specifically to books, when I was a kid in the country, without a telephone, without television, without radio, with very few newspapers, I would read any slip of paper that came my way because I felt I had to read; it is how we discover the world. I would read the rare book that fell into my hands. Books have become sacred for me; they are the tools par excellence for initiation. Reading has helped me find answers. It can change lives. I also noticed that my father, who had difficult times, always kept his books and photos. When you consider the history of the Jews who came to France, they came after they had discovered liberty—through Rousseau, Voltaire, Victor Hugo. My father, who couldn't read French well, held Victor Hugo above all other mortals. I think he had read him in translation (in Yiddish perhaps), but to his eyes he, as well as the Encyclopedists, represented the essence of the spirit of liberty. Jews in Europe used to say, "To be as happy as God in France," and that was probably true for many of them. I believe what let them think that were the books, the culture, and the French Revolution. I still can't part with a book. It's irrational. Books take up space, they turn yellow, but I can't help buying them. The love of books is an affliction that can never be cured, but it's not deadly.

FIGURE 12.1. Willy, in 1991

# 12

# Willy Swiczka (1931–1999)

**October 12, 1987**

*Willy Swiczka, born in Strasbourg, died at age sixty-eight. He was an independent thinker, a multilinguist fluent in eight languages, an activist with a strong personality and an extraordinary sense of humor, whose Leftist political commitment never wavered.*

I was born of Jewish parents in Strasbourg in 1931. I was among those who left Alsace in the first exodus in 1939. Later, the Alsatians who were not Jewish returned saying (not all of them, of course), "We are going home; you Jews stay where you are!" It was the real breaking point—the point of no-return.

My family settled in La Châtre.

At first I had no problem. I enrolled in the *lycée* in La Châtre, by myself. My parents didn't know about it. When I started eighth grade, there was a small problem. Filling in for my father, I said, "My father will come to see you." The principal was a nice guy from the southwest and we made a deal. The school provided the books, and the principal saw to it that I had a supply of notebooks. No doubt there was a budget for that. So I completed elementary and junior high school there

235

and I lacked nothing. My parents didn't have to pay. They didn't know anything about it.

My schooling was irregular, but I easily caught on.

The first mad dash took place in 1942. My parents had to send me away. They sent me for six months to Talloire in Haute-Savoie. I went there during the month of June, and I returned right before Christmas. I had been taken there by my guardian angel, a Red Cross nurse. We traveled by night and I rested my head between her beautiful breasts.

I went to school in Talloire and then I returned to La Châtre a few minutes before Christmas—just in time to be deported. All the Jews were rounded up.

We were sent to the internment camp at Agde. All our family was sent there, including my little sister born in 1941. It was October, after the beginning of the school year. There were atrocious scenes of husbands and wives being separated. The camp at Agde, guarded by French gendarmes, was something like a concentration camp. There were also Spanish Republicans in the camp.

As children we could get through the barbed wire. We managed to have money. My older sister and I brought back things to the camp for my parents and others to eat.

My father was with my brother in a camp facing ours. The wives could see very little of their husbands. I was with my mother, older sister, and baby sister.

We stayed there about two months. A decree from Vichy stipulated that foreigners whose children were born in France could not be interned, so we were freed. This decree was soon abrogated.

When my sister and I left, I with a raging case of measles, we took the train from Agde to Périgueux, where my mother's sister and my father's brother lived. We passed through Béziers, Montpellier, and Mazamet. Travel was not easy . . .

We finally arrived in Périgueux and my sister and I were immediately taken to the hospital. We were very happy there because we had sheets. After the hospital I went to my uncle and aunt's house. My father made the trip between La Châtre and Périgueux, a big city where there was an entire Jewish intelligentsia.

My father soon decided to settle in Périgueux with his family. He then went to La Châtre to put his affairs in order, and the guy at the office of Jewish Affairs in La Châtre told him, "You are crazy to go to

Périgueux. Here you are more or less protected; you should stay here."
My father understood immediately. He returned to Périgueux and told
us, "We're going back to La Châtre." We all howled, but he persisted.

So we returned to La Châtre, which saved our skins. Even so, there
were roundups at La Châtre and a number of Jews were deported. My
father was passed over; he had a hideout. When he heard rumors of a
roundup, he would hide, sometimes for a week or two, without showing up. He lived an underground life. He must have been active in the
Resistance but I don't know at what level. He didn't say much; he didn't
want to be a hero. He was an antihero, that man.

At La Châtre, I picked up on my schooling again, which had been
interrupted for two months. Then I went to La Bourboule, again accompanied by the same young woman from the Red Cross.

In 1944, I was sent to Servières-le-Château, in Corrèze, fifteen kilometers from Argentat. It was hell there where only a small number of
Jewish children were hidden. Some children—not Jewish, it seems—
had been there four or five years and hadn't seen their parents in all
that time. About twenty children—bed wetters—had been put together
in the same dormitory. Of course, it was a disgrace. I stayed there for
about six months. Life was far from easy. Now and then, when I got
really fed up, I would fake an asthma attack, which I was very good at.
It was very impressive.

The big kids bullied the little ones. It was really like the Mafia. I was
a little bulldog and I protected myself pretty well. I started bullying. I
got by.

It was a very, very hard routine. I got through it because I went regularly to school in the village. Very few children went, and it saved me;
it gave structure to my life. Every time I made the effort to go to school
it always was beneficial.

My aunt and uncle from Périgueux were deported.

Then, for us, the war ended, even though it continued on the Eastern Front. My parents were able to take me back. We then all returned
to my parents' home; suddenly there were seven children to care for:
my older sister, me (my younger sister had died sometime earlier), and
five orphaned cousins we had taken in. My mother did a fantastic job
raising these seven children.

After the war, my family stayed a short time longer in La Châtre, and
then returned to Strasbourg.

## After the War

In Strasbourg, my father started up a metal recycling business. He worked like a madman and earned a lot of money. He had a fairly large operation. He cut up tanks; he bought a lot of things to cut up with a blowtorch (after the war there was a shortage of all kinds of basic materials). We hardly ever saw him. He made long runs, first with one, then later with two trucks.

The oldest of my cousins quit his studies, married, and took care of one of his brothers. There were only the little ones at home. Then my older sister married.

Since La Châtre, I had been very impressed by the Communist Partisans (FTP) and about the same time, at about age fourteen, I joined the UJRF. At fifteen and one-half, I was responsible for the publicity. We had evangelized the crowds! I wasn't very Jewish at that time. And then there was Israel. This brought me back into Judaism. During the war we went fairly regularly to the synagogue. I made my bar mitzvah.

After the war, I was a very committed Communist. At that time the Communist Party was not anti-Zionist. It became that later. I became a Zionist a short time before Israeli independence. At sixteen or seventeen years old, I stepped into Hashomer Hatzair. I quickly became one of the leaders of the movement in Strasbourg. The national movement sent me to Israel in 1948, and I left on a boat with immigrants.

I arrived in Israel, still a little juvenile, wanting to be a soldier, this and that. They calmed us down. We learned Hebrew and psychology. There were lots of courses that were very interesting for a guy of seventeen. It was prodigious!

We also worked on the land. We did lots of things. After a little training, we were sent to a kibbutz.

But during this time, I was becoming conflicted. We saw difficulties arising with the young Arabs that we met. We saw that if the State of Israel did not integrate the young Arabs, there would be problems. It was obvious.

After a year we returned to France. We were political Zionist leaders. We held a lot of meetings, camps; it was a little like Boy Scouts. Even so, there was this serious problem of having to break with the West. We had to break all philosophical, moral, intellectual ties with the West and dedicate ourselves to Israel.

And we didn't quite agree. I was half Communist, half Zionist.

And to complicate things there was a split within the Communist Party at the same time . . .

With the stories about the Arabs and these difficulties, I ended up breaking with the Hashomer Hatzair. I continued, however, with the Communist Party, and then at age twenty I left for Paris where I took up my studies. I earned the *baccalauréat* degree and then threw myself into Advanced Studies in Social Sciences. I wanted to go into politics. In fact, I didn't know exactly what I wanted to do . . .

I also wanted to study medicine, but I didn't. As a result, I foolishly studied humanities part-time while working, but never under the best circumstances.

By this time of my life, the Jewish milieu was completely missing from my life. At the time of my bar mitzvah, I had been completely in the game but I hadn't experienced any kind of revelation, though I was still full of goodwill . . .

After the war, my father also abandoned all religious practice. He was an agnostic. We no longer went to the synagogue on Saturdays. I am still interested in Yiddish. Back then in Israel, I was already seeking Yiddish more than Hebrew.

The interview stops here. Willy died in 1999. His testimony remains incomplete.

ERNEST                                       ÉDITH

FIGURE 13.1. The Moskovic family in Hungary in 1934: grandmother, parents, Édith—age three, on her mother's lap, at the right of the photo; her brother Ernest—one and one-half years old, on his father's lap, at the left of the photo; and their seven brothers and sisters.

# 13

# Édith Moskovic[1]

*Édith Moskovic is retired from banking administration. She volunteers in various benevolent associations. She took a seminar at Yad Vashem at the International School for Teaching about the Holocaust (Jerusalem 1999) and then dedicated herself to numerous causes associated with transmitting the memory of the Holocaust across France, in schools, at the university, and on radio, television, and in the press.*

*In honor of Marraine, Maman Marie, Papa Philippe, and the unknown young man who, one day, took me by the hand.*

I have no memory of my grandparents, so I rely on those of my older sister Szidi. My paternal grandfather Bendet died before I was born, at only forty-five years of age. My father often told us about my grandfather's difficult working life in his village of Olvös, Hungary. He was a cobbler and had to feed his wife and five children. He was extremely pious, very attached to "The Book" and to the Rabbi. After his death, my grandmother (born Ida Farkäs), following the Jewish tradition, came to live with her oldest son, my father. From the family of ten that we were, we grew to a family of twelve because my grandmother brought with her my father's youngest sister Hélène. My grandmother always dressed in black and had a prayer for every act of everyday life. In 1935, she refused to follow us to Belgium, fearing the loss of her religious points of reference. In 1941, at age sixty and hospitalized, she refused to eat. She was afraid that the hospital food was not kosher.

After her mother's death, my aunt Hélène joined us in Belgium, where she married Alexandre Klein. He died in the deportation, leaving a young wife and a two-year-old child. Abraham, my father's youngest brother and also the most religious, lived in Anvers, Belgium. He was married and had five sons. The two youngest were twins and were only a few weeks old when the father was deported, then slaughtered at Auschwitz. He was hung on a butcher hook because he refused to work on Saturday. He was twenty-nine years old. His wife Rivka was deported to Teresin. She survived and came out alive from this showcase camp and was repatriated by the Red Cross and was able to find her children for whom my father had found a place to hide as well as for his own children. The twins were taken to a nursery created by Queen Elisabeth of Belgium.

My mother's family lived at Tehépé in Hungary. My mother Fanny, the oldest, had three sisters and a brother: Anna, Rosa, Franck, and Dora. She was eight years old when her own mother, Régine Schönberger, died. My grandfather, Mena'hem Lebi, then thirty years old and owner of a flourishing inn in Tehépé, was unable to take care of the children so he sent Uncle Franck and Aunt Rosa to the United States to his wife's family. Mama and the other children were taken to their maternal grandparents in Sòlös. After a few years as a widower, my grandfather remarried and had four other children: Alex, Sarah, Herman, and Elizabeth. In 1944 Herman was arrested by the Hungarian Nylös[2] and shot. He had stolen a German army uniform and had freed some Jewish detainees. My aunt Anna and her husband, Uncle Paul, were deported from Hungary in 1944 with their five daughters. They were killed at Auschwitz with their youngest daughter Judith, six years old. The four other sisters survived and were taken in by relatives in the United States, where they started families.

After the death of my father in 1957, my mother went to spend several months with my brother Nicolas who had settled in Canada. Secretly, he had also invited Uncle Franck and Aunt Rosa who lived in the United States—he in New York and she in Pittsburgh. This is how my mother saw her brother and her sister again—after fifty years of separation! Such emotion . . .

My brother and sisters and I traveled to Los Angeles and San Francisco to meet our four cousins who survived the Holocaust.

In 1996 I enrolled in Judaic History and Civilization at the College of Arts and Letters. This is when I wrote the following text. It was also the first time that I expressed myself in public. This explains the first lines of my narrative.

Night and day, so many memories come to me! I have no talent, neither as a writer nor as a speaker. I already know that, as soon as I turn in my composition, I will regret having left out certain things. But how do I bring back this life, this flight while trying to escape the Nazi barbarism?

The pain of abandonment, the solitude, the fear, the incomprehension . . . the incomprehension . . . Are there words to describe it?

I was only nine years old when on May 10, 1940, Germany invaded Belgium. I am now sixty-six, and it is still incomprehensible.

My name is Édith Moskovic. I am Ashkenazi, born in Hungary in 1931. There were ten of us in my family: my parents and their five daughters and three sons. I was the next to the last in this "Thirteenth Tribe."[3]

In 1935 my parents decided to leave Hungary to settle in Brussels. My father was a tailor. He went a year before us to prepare for our arrival. He was a good man, honest and generous. He was marvelous. From 1935 to 1940, we lived modestly, but free and happy, in an ambience common to large families.

From the first day of battle in Belgium, my father organized our departure for France. I remember that morning perfectly. I was awakened by the sound of the sewing machine. My sister Livia was making a cape for each of us with our name on it. My brother Ernest woke up singing, "I will wait—day and night . . ." (He was seven years old.) I told him, "Stop singing, it's the war!" A week later we left Brussels.

I remember taking the train. We were crowded in with other refugees. There were numerous stops in the open countryside. From time to time, volunteers distributed a little food to us. Our journey lasted for days, and then one evening we arrived in a village at the end of the trip. I now turn the story over to my "little brother" Ernest who, despite his young age, has an extraordinary memory of that time.[4]

**[ERNEST'S STATEMENT]**
Imagine a family of nine (my sister Zora stayed in Belgium because of illness), tired, worried, eyes red from lack of sleep, with each of us

carrying a bundle. It was night and we were out in the country. We were sitting on very low benches along a wall outside city hall.

We didn't know it yet but we had arrived at His!

This little town was to be a little paradise for us! The residents had been invited to come see and help those who were already being called the "refugees." I envision this scene again in great detail. I had just turned seven. We were all sitting in a row, pressed against one another, and the people of His passed in front of us. I still remember this sense of shame, because I had the impression that we were being appraised like a herd of animals.

In fact, these kind people were wondering what they were going to do with us, and today I understand why! At the urging of the mayor of the time, Monsieur Albert Rives, and after a short conversation, Léonie Abejean, Juliette's grandmother, said, "I'll take them with me to my house."

The house didn't have enough beds, so the first night I slept with sisters Boué and Léontine Bordeneuve. I think that despite the fatigue and anxiety, we were happy to find ourselves in a bed at last, this first night at His. I remember the canopied four-poster bed and the rosaries on the walls. I had never seen that and then, little by little, our life organized itself alongside the residents of His. My father and my brother Bélā, both tailors, began to mend the residents' clothing and often turned their worn-out coats. To do their work, they were given a little spot situated beside the city hall. They sewed what there was to sew and in exchange we received food. The village council gave us ten francs a day per person so that we had a little money. We children went to school in the class of Catherine Barbouteau. I especially remember gardening and tidying up around the school. We even waxed the dining room floor and got a cookie and a little glass of wine in return. It was a special school and we were very happy to go there. My mother spent most of her time cooking, cleaning the house, and taking care of the laundry for the whole family. Little by little we were assimilated in with the other residents, and life was happy. So as not to distinguish ourselves from the others, we even went to church on Sundays.

Obviously, given my age, I didn't completely understand how difficult it was just to survive. But I know today that a number of people helped us. How can I forget Madame Denjean, who always saved eggs and butter for us, and who, with her regional accent, would say to others, "I don't have any more, my dear." To us she would say, "I don't have any eggs to sell but I'll give you some." Every morning a basket of eggs, butter, and milk was left on our doorstep. We are sure today that she was our generous benefactress, along with the grocer, who often said to us, "You can pay me later." And Madame Lucienne Téchené whose authoritarian manner so frightened us and hid her enormous generosity toward us. We stayed with her until leaving His. I will never forget Marie and Pierre, either, and my place at their table where I was treated as one of their own children.

But the town of His was also something more. It was a miracle. We came from the big city of Brussels and were suddenly plunged into the wide open countryside. To eat cherries, we only had to pick them, and it was the same with plums and apples. We even had a vine on the balcony of the house. Every day after school I would go to herd the cows and sheep in the fields with my friend Roland. He would tell me fantastic stories that amazed me. It was he who taught me how to milk a cow, to herd a flock, to steal apples in the orchard, and especially to swear in dialect like they did in His. We took part in harvest and we stomped the grapes, barefoot, in a big tub. We collected the honey from the hives. How can I forget all the friends we made: Paule who constantly recited her catechism before Holy Communion; Lily who rang the church bells; Juliette who was always dragging her little brother behind her; and all the others! We experienced reaping and harvesting and all the life and camaraderie they bring. We also have memories of joy and amusement as when Hilarion and Étienne crossed the village, one dead drunk, the other singing, "With pompoms, with pompoms, with firemen." We followed them down the lane, shouting with laughter. I was also impressed with Eugène, the current mayor's father, who traveled the lane at full speed on his superb bicycle. The château of Madame Gazel was always open to us and we would go there to play with her grandchildren. Of course, it wasn't always so simple and easy, but we only want to keep the happy memories of His. We stayed a year in this haven of peace, happiness, and liberty for us. And then . . . and then . . .

First, my father and brother were detained at Saint-Cyprien,[5] but they were soon able to return to His. Then early one morning everything changed. Gendarmes as black-hearted as their black coats came to get us. At the time, we were staying with Madame Téchené. Without a word, they loaded us into black cars—Citroëns, I think—for an unknown destination. We were torn from the town of His that had been for us a little paradise. After long moments of anxiety, we ended up at Récébédou internment camp.[6]

Most of the people there were Spanish who had fled Franco's regime. We were held in wooden huts and we slept on the ground on straw mats. The food consisted mainly of rutabagas. The winter was very hard, and I remember also being caught in a snowstorm. We were guarded by French gendarmes and every evening there was roll call. Jean Raspaud, whom we called Jeannot, came several times to bring us food. After a while, my father fled the camp to go to Belgium to see what was happening. In Brussels the situation was calm in 1941. In fact, however, the Germans were letting us doze.

My father judged the situation to be basically safe in Belgium and came to get us at the camp at Récébédou. Coming and going was possible because of the complicity of some of the guards. This complicity was rarely free. We decided to leave. We left one night after curfew, always with the help of the compliant guards. After walking a long way across the fields, we saw a light. We were dead tired, hungry and thirsty. The light was actually a little country bar. We opened the door and we found ourselves face to face with two of the camp guards who looked at us, as surprised as we were. Frozen with terror, we were stuck to the floor. I see them now, leaning on the bar, turned toward the entry. Brusquely they looked at each other and turned their backs to us as if they hadn't seen us. God bless them! Today we know that if we had been taken back to Récébédou, it would have then been to Drancy and finally to Auschwitz. For the Jews, Récébédou was the antechamber for the gas chamber . . . With the help of a smuggler, we got across to the road that would take us to Belgium. We walked at night in the mud a few meters from the Germans. We couldn't cough, speak, or sneeze. My father carried me on his shoulders. My sister Szidi left her high heels in the mud and finished her walk barefoot.

We crossed the Demarcation Line at Abbeville. This alone would make a novel. We passed, one by one, with all kinds of people in the most unimaginable situations. I crossed the line in front of the German guards with a young man barely twenty years old who pretended to be my father. I was only eight years old. My brother Béla went between two guards whose backs were turned. The Germans, who were about two meters apart, were inspecting other people's papers. Slipping between them, he calmly walked about twenty meters, turned to us and waved. If he had been seen, he'd have been killed on the spot. Our

return to Brussels, in the beginning, was so uneventful that we wondered if we had been right to leave there in 1940. What happened next
made clear that we should never have left His.

The German attitude toward Jews changed abruptly. From one day
to the next, they forbade us to go out after eight o'clock, to go to the
movies ("no Jews, no dogs"), to do business, to practice a profession.
We all had to wear on our outside clothing, on the left side, a yellow
fabric star marked with a "J." It was the beginning of the end. All of us
being on file because of all kinds of schemes, the Germans only had to
pick us off like ripe fruit. One night in September 1942, every street
where Jews lived was blocked. The one where we lived was miraculously spared. We spent the night on our balcony watching the SS load
up their victims. We will never forget the cries of the women and children as they were thrown into the trucks lined up one after the other.
The men were pushed along with gun butts and the women who didn't
move fast enough were dragged by the hair. Even today, I ask myself if
it was not just a bad dream. Unfortunately, it was real. It was what they
called the big roundup, comparable to that of the Vel' d'Hiv' Roundup
in Paris.[7]

We once again escaped death.

The next morning we decided to hide separately. In the course of a
single morning a family of ten split up. With the help of neighbors, we
all went in different directions without knowing where we were going.
Furthermore, none of us were to know where the others were so that
we wouldn't reveal their hiding places in case we were arrested. My
parents first found an attic where they could hide. One of my brothers
ended up on a farm where he worked as a servant all during the war.
He had to steal food, sleep in the stable, and work very hard. To make
him do extra work, the farmer would promise him food. After having
worked, he would ask for what he had been promised. The response
was, "Shut up, dirty Jew. If you don't, we'll turn you in to the Germans!"
One of my sisters was lodged in an institution for mentally handicapped children. Another found refuge in a convent. The oldest of my
sisters was employed as a caretaker in an institution. I was taken in by
kind people who were very poor, and one of my sisters went to their
daughter's house. I was nine years old.

Can you imagine what it was like to be from a family where there
were ten of us every day at the table—with all that means to life, to
one's surroundings, with the special ties that connect large families—

and then in a single day to be taken from all that at age nine when a child most needs his parents and the warmth of the family to develop? Can you imagine that at age nine, someone would look you in the eyes and say to you: "From now on, your name is this, you are alone in the world, you have no brothers or sisters and your parents died in the bombings; no matter what anyone says to you, no matter what anyone does to you, you always say the same thing or they will kill you"? The psychological shock that I felt that day was such that I started to wet the bed and did so for four years!

This was my first day of war. Despite all the kindness of the people who hid me, I was hungry. That's when I learned to beg. I worked it out so that every day of the week, I had someone give me one or two pieces of bread and butter. One day it was the doctor, then the pharmacist or others who took pity on me. On the days when no bread and butter came my way, I snatched fruit from the store displays. I would run by at full speed, and in the crowd by the fruit stands, I would sneak my hand in and grab an apple or a pear that I would eat in secret before returning home. The people who hid me never knew I was begging and stealing because they were doing all they could and I didn't want to make them feel bad. In 1945, on my school medical chart was written, "Child of twelve and one-half years, underdeveloped; general state of health: looks to be seven years old." What I am telling is a summary of my life, but each of my brothers and sisters could tell similar stories. Imagine for a moment the anxiety of my parents. My father was the only one who knew where we were, and he spent this entire time, until the end of the war, going from child to child to see how we were getting along and if we were still safe. I think his early death was not unexpected given what he endured during the war.

When you are in this situation where there is no hope—because you don't know if this is going to last for one year or ten years—if the days are difficult, the nights are atrocious. Everything goes around in your brain like a bad dream, and it is your pleasant memories that give you the strength to continue and want to live. For my family, the images were of the return to family life and the marvelous times we had lived at His. The two images were always superimposed in my head during this time. I would see again as if it were in a film: Roland with our outbursts of laughter, Noël and Jeannot with their kindness, Madame Téchené, Juliette's grandmother, Eugène on his cycle, school, the Château, Madame Loubet, Madame Marie-Louise Abejean, Juliette's mother and her little brother Pierre, Hilarion and the others. During these moments, the most common scenes of everyday life took on great importance and value. As I plunged into the night of despair, His became for me a little opening through which I could see the blue sky and the sun—in a word, His became a source of hope. We idealized the place and the residents of His.

### [BACK TO ÉDITH'S TESTIMONY]

Now I would like to return to Récébédou Camp, where we stayed about six months, to complete what my brother Ernest said about it. Like all the internment camps, it was horrible and inhuman.[8] The hunger, the cold, the promiscuity, the filth, the roll call—outside in all kinds of weather—were interminable. Our survival was a miracle, but unfortunately, for me the worst was yet to come. In the camp, we were together, Mama was there.

As my brother explained above, we were able to flee and return to Belgium. We started school again until the day when the principal took us into the courtyard, and when our names were called we Jewish children were to step out of line. As usual, my friend Madeleine was holding my hand. When I heard my name, I tried to step forward but she held my hand very tightly, refusing to let me go and followed me in the line of the undesirables. This caused a terrible scene. They forced her to let me go. But why me? What difference was there between her and me? I didn't see one, except perhaps it was the yellow star sewn on my checkered smock that was otherwise identical to hers. Until then I didn't know that being Jewish meant being different. What I felt when we had to leave school is inexpressible—the shame, the sorrow, the humiliation. During the desperate times that followed, I thought a lot about Madeleine—our games, our lives as happy children, our closeness. She was fair-haired, always well groomed.

Alone, in my attic, I would talk to her. I would even laugh at our silliness. I never saw her again, despite having searched. I am indebted to her for enabling me to dream and escape my loneliness as a hidden child.

When the film *Au revoir, les enfants* of Louis Malle was shown, I told my eleven-year-old grandson about the episode of being taken out of school, which I wear like an open wound. He listened to me to the end and only asked me, "But Granny, why you?" The only answer I

could find was that I was "on the wrong side of the line." It is the only
time I spoke to him about my past.

After the roundup of September 1942, the ten of us took different
directions. Some generous neighbors agreed to help us. This first day as
a "hidden child" is still one of the most painful for me. From the
moment I entered the house of Maman Marie and Papa Philippe, my
Calvary began. I was immediately taken to the attic. There was a
window covered with a heavy curtain, a mattress laid on the floor, and
one table and one chair. The door was locked for fear, no doubt, that I
would come down and cause a problem in the apartment. Today as an
adult I understand their fears. By hiding a Jewish child, they were risking their lives. But I was ten and one-half years old; I was very afraid, I
was living a nightmare.

Sometimes in the late evening, I was allowed to share a few moments with my benefactors and wash myself. Soon after, I was back in
my attic, without light. The sound of the key in the lock was terrible; I
was again alone in the dark. I gently pushed back the curtain to see a
corner of the sky. In the morning I would put the curtain back before
Maman Marie brought my breakfast. Slowly I lost the concept of time
and other things. I didn't understand why I was there—alone, abandoned, forgotten. I dreamed that Mama would open this damn door
and take me in her arms. I wished it so much that sometimes I would
see the door open, but no one would be there. I also thought about my
classmates, about Madeleine Bulens and our neighbors who must certainly be worried about us—a family of ten who suddenly disappeared!

I don't know how long I stayed with these people. Several months,
perhaps. How many days, how many nights, hours, minutes, seconds? I
don't know, but I am forever grateful to Maman Marie and Papa
Philippe for the risk they took to hide me with them.

One morning my few belongings were put into a bag. A young man
came to get me. He took my hand. We were walking rapidly. I remember having a problem with my eyes. It seems I was crying, perhaps because of the light or from happiness of being outside—I don't know.
We took the train. He spoke very little and only in a low voice. In case
we were questioned, I was not to answer, but to let him speak. He
made me repeat my new name a few times: Éliane M. I was his sister;
we were going to meet our parents in the country. The trip was long
and difficult because of frequent stops. The train was full of German

soldiers. They didn't pay attention to us. I was tired, I was hungry and thirsty, and finally I fell asleep.

We got off the train at the station in Ottignies, some twenty-five kilometers from Brussels. We walked a long time. It must have been summer because I was very hot and my legs hurt. Finally we got to a house. A lady came toward us, smiling. She hugged me. My head was spinning; I thought I was going to faint because it had been so long since I had been hugged!

The young man gave me my bag. He squeezed my hand and turned away without a word. I never learned who he was.

I remember this first day in Ottignies perfectly. I wore a corduroy dress with a little white design. In the room where I was taken there was a phonograph playing "Having a good friend is more faithful than the world . . ." I had arrived at the place where I would be hidden until the end of the war.

Le Joli Coin (The Happy Place) was an institution for mentally handicapped children and adolescents. There were about eighty of us, twenty-five of whom were Jewish children. The directress, Madame Jacqmotte, had help with the cooking from Paula. Every morning we would go to mass to avoid arousing the suspicion of the residents and the villagers. The woman we called "Marraine" (Godmother) gave classes. The meals were very meager. I remember being hungry and cold. I was eleven years old and, along with the other girls, I took care of the younger children. In the evenings at bedtime, they would cry and we would stifle our own sufferings to try to console them. We never said the word "Jew." It was strictly forbidden to talk among ourselves about our situation or the reason for our presence in this institution.

I remember vividly a young blond boy, very handsome, whom I liked a lot. I knew he wasn't Jewish. Marraine recommended that I not spend too much time with him; in an unguarded moment I might confide in him. Imagine the consequences!

The non-Jewish children had visitors, but the danger was too great for us. My father, who was the only one who knew where we all were, still traveled from one child to another until the end of the war. He actually came to Ottignies twice, I think. He was dressed as a farm worker and he carried a scythe. I couldn't go near him. We were unable to exchange a single word. I couldn't hug him. A child's sorrow—a father's pain.

My life took shape; I was no longer alone. We could play, even laugh and sing. Despite this, the situation remained incomprehensible to me. Why was I here, separated from my family? Where were my parents? My brothers and sisters? At night I tried to remember my earlier life. I wondered if it had even existed. The emotional suffering of being separated from my family became a physical suffering. I would talk to Mama; I would ask her to come and get me. And then one night, I heard her say to me, "Faïgele, you must pray . . ." I prayed, but nothing happened. I confess that as soon as I entered the church, I would feel a presence and I would hope again. Days passed, but nothing changed; I became desperate.

And then one morning, a morning like any other, I felt as if I couldn't breathe. We were in class. I leaped up and out into the courtyard and I began to scream, "Mama, my God! I want Mama!" Marraine hurried to me and placed her hand over my mouth, whispering to me that I was being bad, that I was putting everyone in danger. After that day, I didn't scream again, I didn't cry again, I didn't pray again. I refused to go to Mass. But I had to follow the others. And then the miracle happened . . . and once again, it is my brother Ernest who, with his sensitivity, relates this part of the story.

**[ERNEST'S TESTIMONY]**

My parents, having had to flee their hiding place on a small street in Schaerbeek, appeared before me one morning in Ninove, where I was lodged. My father begged my benefactors to keep my mother for three days . . .

She stayed there six months until the Liberation.

I was greatly surprised when my mother announced to me one evening, "Tomorrow we are going to Ottignies to see Édith!" Édith is my sister, born eighteen months before me. It was April 1944. You can't imagine the trip that this represented. Take the local train "NI" to Ninove and then on to Brussels. There, take the streetcar to the Luxembourg station and then the train again on to Ottignies. The trip alone took more than four hours because of the frequent stops in open country. Finally we arrived at the right place. My first surprise was to learn that my sister Édith had become my sister "Éliane"! The place where she was staying was none other than an institution for mentally handicapped children. Some Jewish children were hidden among them. The woman who dedicated her life to these children was an admirable woman. All the Jewish children she kept were saved. They called her

"Marraine" (Godmother). At the age of ninety-six, she received the medal of the Righteous, in Brussels. When my sister saw us, she almost fainted. It had been two years since we had seen each other. For two long years she lived among what I at the time called "the crazies"! You can imagine the joy when we met!

After the first emotional moments, I saw there was a certain excitement in the institution. In fact, the same evening the children were putting on a show for the town of Ottignies. Just being in that room, in the middle of the war, was itself unbelievable. And then came the magic of the play . . . This was performed by the Jewish children because they alone could do it, given the other children's situation. For my mother and me this was a happy moment!

And then, suddenly, it was completely dark in the theater. The stage was in total darkness. Music was heard, coming from I don't know where. It was *La Mort du Cygne* (*The Dying Swan*) by Camille Saint-Saëns. And then in the light of a spotlight appeared a little girl, in a white tutu with white wings on her back and a crown of the same color on her head. She came out on stage on her toes, moving her arms as if she would take flight. The secret had been well kept, because this little girl was my sister Édith.

For my mother and me, our emotion was at its peak. I think we stopped breathing for a moment. Our throats were closed as if in a stranglehold. It was like a fairy tale, as if it were outside of time . . . a little Jewish girl, in 1944, performing a classic dance in a theater, under the nose of the Germans. Today, more than fifty years later, the memory of this image still moves me.

Caught up in the ambience, we didn't notice time passing. And yet, suddenly, reality set in and my mother whispered to me, "We must go." Broken-hearted, before the end of the dance, we quietly got up and slowly moved toward the door. We were sitting in the first row. Our departure couldn't escape the notice of my sister who was still turning on toe point in the middle of the stage. We made a small sign with our hands; she slightly moved her head to signal goodbye. We were leaving one another for a long time—perhaps forever! As we turned to look at her one last time, we saw that she was still dancing, tears streaming down her face. It was a heartbreaking moment for us as well, and we silently cried. We weren't there for the final moments of *La Mort du Cygne* but I know that it ended with her lying on the ground, shaking with sobs. On this particular evening in 1944 reality overcame fantasy!

The lives of the "hidden children" are scarred with these wounds that even time cannot erase.

**[BACK TO ÉDITH'S TESTIMONY]**

The situation seemed to change. Marraine was nervous, preoccupied. We dared not question her. Food was becoming rare. At night the air raid warnings kept us going down to the shelter because of the bombings—sometimes several times during the same night.

One night we were in bed and Marraine made all the Jewish children go down to the cellar. The Germans were in retreat. A large number of them had stopped and set up in the courtyard and in the park. Fortunately, they did not enter the house. At the front of the house, Marraine had put up a big flag of the Red Cross (to which she belonged). On it was written that the children inside were tubercular and, as the Germans were very afraid of the disease, they stayed outside. However, they camped around the house for several days. We were hidden just under their feet; a few steps separated us. If one of them had been curious enough to go down those steps, it would have been the end for all of us.

During those days we neither drank nor ate. We were forbidden to cry, to cough, to sneeze, to move—forbidden to live. Marraine was a marvel of courage, of calm. How many days of Calvary did it last? I don't know. One thing impressed me deeply—Marraine was barely recognizable. She was severely tested by this tragic episode. Furthermore, she had deep wounds in the palms of her hands because the Germans had made her hold a basin full of boiling water. She more than deserved the Medal of the Righteous awarded her by the State of Israel.

Liberation took place in September of 1944.

After that, things moved quickly. Very soon, our parents came to get us. Some children's parents were missing—taken away in the catastrophic events. Each day all of us Jewish children would cluster outside the house, hoping that it would be our turn, or that our happiness would be tomorrow . . . We had waited so long!

I remember very vividly the day that my father finally came. He was running down the little road that led to the house. I saw him from afar. It was unreal. I was so afraid that it would prove to be another figment of my imagination! (I ask you to forgive me for not describing for you the moment of our meeting. It is beyond my ability to express.)

Another miracle took place; all ten of us were still alive! We were together again under the same roof! We didn't explain anything to each other, each sealed in silence concerning what he or she had lived through. And what could we say, compared to those returning from the camps? Faceless, lifeless people, numb with fatigue. Faced with the unspeakable, we remained silent, ashamed to be there alive, not daring to look directly at all this pain. In *All Rivers Run to the Sea*, Elie Wiesel posed the following question: "If I am alive, who died in my place?"

We carry this devastated childhood with us to the end.

And yet we had to reconstruct everything. There were, of course, priorities. The Jewish organizations got to work. They helped us materially. The adults started back to work; but we, the hidden children, curiously, we have been forgotten during this "reconstruction" . . . There was nothing visible about the sufferings that had marked us, and we resumed our normal lives as children. I was fourteen years old; I started back to school. I led an active life. I married.

I have a daughter who today is thirty-nine years old. She knows nothing of the burden under which I have been living since childhood. She has never asked me questions, and I, accustomed to remaining silent and not wanting to add anything to the problems of today, have told her nothing. In 1965 I suffered from serious depression. My ex-husband, wanting to explain my situation to the doctors, told them, "My wife is Jewish (he wasn't); she was a child during the war, you understand?" They tried to make me talk, asked me questions about that time, but no sound—not a single word—came from my lips. I had become completely mute. This lasted for a year. Then they gave me a sheet of paper so I could try to express myself by writing. I made a drawing— the attic, the covered window, the mattress on the floor and the locked door.

Here I am, evoking a very dark part of my life, unknown by all until today. I had never intended to write or speak about it. I am doing so today because I have been asked to do so, and I can see more than fifty years later that the old pain has not disappeared.

During all these years, one feeling has never left me. It is my gratitude for all those "Righteous," known or most often unknown, of modest means, who took the unreasonable risk, in peril of their lives, to hide Jewish children. Because of them, these children were able to survive and become free adults.

FIGURE 14.1. Nicole at age eleven in 1943 in Corn (Lot).

# 14

# Nicole Eizner

**August 28, 2001**

*Nicole Eizner, an orphan of the Holocaust, is a researcher in sociology at CNRS. Now retired, she was active in various causes without being politically affiliated with any particular organization. She opposed the war in Algeria, Pinochet, the Greek generals, and she supports the researchers' union, the Ateliers de Mai, the Association for Taxation of Financial Transactions for the Aid of Citizens, and the League for Human Rights.*

EIZNER: I was born February 10, 1931, in Paris. I am a sociologist. I worked for CNRS and, other than during the war, I've always lived in Paris. My father was an officiant rabbi at the synagogue on rue des Tournelles in the Fourth Arrondissement of Paris, and my mother, who came from a family of small business owners, was a housewife.

My maternal grandparents were born in Belarus and came to France at the beginning of the last century. My grandfather left Russia because he couldn't find a job, but originally he had been a blacksmith. He came to Paris very early on, perhaps in 1899. All his brothers emigrated; some of the family went to the United States, and he came to Paris with another brother. He set up on rue Basfroi in the Eleventh Arrondissement—I don't know why, the family story doesn't say—and little by little, like in a *Reader's Digest* story, he began as an iron worker and after fifteen years had his own factory. When I was born, he headed an enterprise that manufactured metal beds with thirty to forty workers at Fontenay-sous-Bois in the Parisian suburbs.

My father's side of the family was Polish from the Poznan region near Germany. My grandfather was a Hasidic rabbi, but I never knew anyone on my father's side of the family. I only know my father went to do rabbinical studies in Berlin, about 1920. I don't think he went for any ideological reasons; I think he was simply attracted by the city lights. He lived there six years. Then he came to Paris, and during a dinner at the home of my grandparents—who were already well established—he met my mother, and that was it!

BAILLY: What languages were spoken at your grandparents' house?

EIZNER: At my paternal grandparents' house, obviously Yiddish, and also on the maternal side, except that my grandfather took evening classes and after a few years spoke perfectly good French—better than good actually—as if he had been born at Fontenay-sous-Bois. My grandmother was illiterate and remained so. She knew just enough to read her *sider* in Yiddish and she always spoke Yiddish. She absolutely murdered the French language. When she took me in after the Liberation I was irritated by this. Young kids don't understand anything.

BAILLY: Was there a language your parents used between the two of them?

EIZNER: Yes. My mother attended French elementary school and had her primary degree. My father first spoke perfect German, Polish, and Yiddish. He learned French and he spoke it very well also. The language they used between them was Yiddish. I could understand it but I never spoke it.

BAILLY: You were an only child?

EIZNER: Yes.

BAILLY: And did the rest of the family come to Paris, too?

EIZNER: Yes. My maternal grandfather sent his younger brother and my grandmother sent her younger sister. And then these two married, so my great-uncle and my great-aunt are doubly so. They worked in the family factory where some cousins had also come. My grandparents' house eventually became a little like an Open House. Everyone landed there. In the living room there were always three or four mattresses that could be put down whenever anyone arrived from who knows where. I lived in this atmosphere of "Russian hospitality" that was not limited to the Jewish community, but was also open to the French.

My parents and I lived in an apartment on rue des Tournelles next to the synagogue, and every Friday evening I went to the service. My family was religious, but it was an extremely liberal form of religion. My father didn't wear a beard; he wore a hat outside but not in the house, and if he wore one in the street it was because everyone else was wearing one. We sort of ate kosher, but when I got good grades in school, we would eat in a restaurant that was not. I think my father would be called "liberal" but he was a very strong believer.

BAILLY: So it was sincere, wasn't it? Did people come to consult with him?

EIZNER: Yes, especially German Jewish refugees came to us during the 1930s. He helped them find jobs and get their papers in order.

BAILLY: Did your parents sense the rise of Nazism at the time, at least through hearsay?

EIZNER: I was little at the time. They were careful to keep me away from all that. In the 1930s, I was four, five, six, seven years old and my parents were very concerned that I have a normal childhood, so I was not at all involved with all the political preoccupations. No one talked to me about that. I didn't even get bits and pieces.

BAILLY: So no anxieties. And you don't remember any French anti-Semitism during that time?

EIZNER: Not at all. On the contrary, my integration into elementary school was very good. I was very proud to be among the best pupils. The teachers loved me and they always used me as an example because I didn't have lice while the others did—no problems. I was a true Parisian elementary school kid. But at the same time, there was the synagogue and all that, so I always lived a double life. I mean that for me, these things had always coexisted. My religion was just different from that of the others, that's all.

BAILLY: In any case, there were other children like you, with the same cultural life, weren't there?

EIZNER: Yes, especially since I went to school in the Fourth Arrondissement, Impasse Guéménée, where there was no shortage of little Jewish children.

BAILLY: So you had a sense of good integration, a good psychological base?

EIZNER: Yes, I don't remember having had the least problem with that. Furthermore, the synagogue on rue des Tournelles was a well-established Consistorial synagogue. I liked seeing the beautiful brides. It seemed very normal to me. I was Jewish and others weren't. They were Catholics. That was all.

BAILLY: Did you get news from the family in Eastern Europe from time to time?

EIZNER: Certainly, but I didn't know about that either; I was too much of a kid. My parents showed me photos of my grandfather and grandmother but that was about all. They would tell me, "You see, you have a grandfather and a grandmother there." They hardly ever spoke about the family that went to the United States either.

BAILLY: Okay. So what else would you like to mention about the time before the war?

EIZNER: Well, curiously, the main thing I remember is that we were very poor. My parents were expected to entertain a lot and we really didn't have much money, to the point that my father had to become a wine salesman besides being an officiant. Moreover, there was an economic crisis. I remember, for example, my mother complaining because she had a hard time making ends meet. She reproached my father. But there was another reason they weren't close: my father was a womanizer. This is unusual for a Jew, but he was like that. He really liked beautiful women. But since I was the greatest wonder of the world to him, I didn't suffer much, but my mother felt forsaken. So I have on the one hand this memory and on the other hand wonderful memories because of all the members of my father's religious flock (in any case all those who became friends with him) who would bring me candy, gifts, and cakes. I was the little girl who was spoiled rotten. So about the time before the war, I can say that these are the two main memories I have, but nothing very connected to the fact that I was or was not Jewish. It was so normal!

BAILLY: So this Jewishness, if you can summarize it; it was religion and also social status because your father was a leader respected by the community. From all that, did you get a certain perception, a kind of pride?

EIZNER: Pride, no, I don't remember that. Children don't think like that. I would say that I had a childhood before the war that was completely calm, in any case at the level that is of interest here.

BAILLY: Do you remember your schooling? No doubt you were a child who read?

EIZNER: Yes, a lot, strongly encouraged by my mother. She wanted to push me as far as possible. Her problem was that she didn't have a career and she absolutely wanted me to have one. She always raised me with the idea that I must not depend on a man. She succeeded with that. My father, however, didn't want me to have a career. He wanted me to marry well, but my mother, no matter what I would do later, wanted me to do advanced studies.

BAILLY: Do you remember the Popular Front?

EIZNER: No. My father read *L'Œuvre* (*The Worker*, a left-wing newspaper). From that I conclude that he was somewhat on the Left, but I don't think ours was a political family.

BAILLY: Did he also read books in German, things like that?

EIZNER: Yes, and perhaps books in Yiddish, but not a newspaper. To be honest, I don't remember. In any case, it's not part of what impressed me.

BAILLY: You've told me that during this period before the war your relations with the rest of the family were good? I'm asking that to find out if these good relations changed later during the ordeal. In some cases, the relations with the rest of the family could be very good before the war, but broke off at the time of the war when it became "everyone for himself" and there was less solidarity.

EIZNER: No. With us, it deteriorated only after the war.

BAILLY: Okay. So now can we get to 1939?

EIZNER: My father, already a French citizen, having been naturalized before my birth, was mobilized.

BAILLY: No particular problems with the naturalization? It wasn't too complicated?

EIZNER: I don't know. But in any case, what I can say is that later on when I needed an identity card or anything else, it was done in three minutes because my father was listed in the register of naturalized citizens before my birth, so I could prove that I was French. He was then mobilized as head of a French family. He was an "officiant minister" so he was an infantryman. I don't know where or in what regiment. I have a photo of him in a very fine uniform, combat cap and all.

BAILLY: He was a French patriot, with conviction?

EIZNER: He was anti-Nazi. The stream of German Jews coming to our house was enough to make him anti-Nazi.

BAILLY: You were saying that your parents protected you from worries about the rise of Nazism in Germany, but you also know that your father was aware of it.

EIZNER: I know it now, having put things together. At the time, all these Germans who were coming rather amused me because I had noticed that they always said, "Ach so!" and I would go around also saying, "Ach so!" This was me at six or seven years old, living in my childhood universe. I didn't know what the other worlds were like.

BAILLY: Your father slipped into the role of French soldier without panicking your mother, who was now alone?

EIZNER: Not exactly. My mother, my aunt and her children, and I left for Beaugé in Maine-et-Loire. I didn't understand very well why I was out in the country. They told me, "It's the war, Daddy is at the front." All that seemed strange to me. He was near Alsace, along the Maginot Line in the East. In Maine-et-Loire I continued my life as a child. Our neighbors were Armenians—refugees like us. We played together. I went to school. That's where I went to the movies for the first time and saw a John Ford western, *Stagecoach*. That I remember.

BAILLY: You weren't especially singled out as being Jewish by the people there, were you?

EIZNER: Maybe, but no one cared about that at the time. I didn't perceive any anti-Semitism. I had the arrogance a city kid has among country kids. I had the impression that they didn't know anything. I went to school normally. Every week there was a letter from my father. Every week I had to write to him. My letters always started with "Dear Daddy, I hope you are well. I am fine."

My mother and I lived on my father's salary, which continued to arrive while he was mobilized. The Consistory paid it. We rented a little place in the country that wasn't expensive, especially at that time. I must say that I remember this as a very pleasant time with my aunt, uncle, and cousins. We had no difficulty obtaining food; on the contrary in 1939 there was enough.

BAILLY: Your mother was content, even having left your belongings in Paris?

EIZNER: Oh, it was only the furniture. We locked the door, that's all. No one expected anything dramatic to happen. It was like a long vacation in the country. Afterward, there was a time when we had to leave there, no doubt because of the advance of the German army. We went to La Palisse, near La Rochelle, in Charente-Maritime. Once there, I understood what war was because the train that took us there was bombed. There I saw dead people; I saw atrocious things, and that was the turning point for me.

After the "Phony War" my father was demobilized in 1940 in Toulouse after he had almost been taken prisoner. In the widespread demoralization, he was walking along with the guys from his regiment when at one point they all stopped to stupidly wait for the Germans to come and take them prisoner. Suddenly my father grasped the reality of their situation and said, "But this is crazy!" and all of the soldiers took off into the countryside.

BAILLY: In fact, they deserted. But didn't that cause problems for them later?

EIZNER: No. You have to remember how demoralized people felt at that time. They didn't know what to do anymore; you can bet the officers had already taken off!

So we went to meet my father at Toulouse and then we returned to Paris to my grandparents' place, because at the time there weren't any particular measures taken against Jews.

BAILLY: Why did your father and mother decide to return to Paris? As aware as your father had been of the rise of Nazism since the 1930s, wasn't he alert to the present political danger?

EIZNER: My parents didn't know what to do. It was normal to go back home! And they must have stayed six months in Paris. It was because of the census of the Jews that we left. Then we crossed the Demarcation Line and went down south to Cannes.

BAILLY: No problem with the Jewish star?

EIZNER: I never knew about that.

BAILLY: False papers?

EIZNER: Not then, but later.

BAILLY: So you crossed the Demarcation Line under your own names?

EIZNER: I don't know. There must have been smugglers.

BAILLY: It wasn't through the Resistance. Was it perhaps through the Jews?

EIZNER: At the time, there wasn't really a Resistance yet. I think it was the guys who were making a little money like that, that's all. Speaking of crossing the Line, I remember taking a boat. So we must have crossed the Line at a place where there was a river. I think it was near Vierzon. I also remember walking a lot, in the woods; I was getting tired, I groaned.

BAILLY: You don't remember Germans or French on the way—policemen, the Milice?

EIZNER: No. Nothing happened. It was calm. We got to Cannes. That was where the Consistory had appointed my father. I think there was a time when they decided that they needed some of the rabbinate to go into the Unoccupied Zone where a lot of Jews had recently arrived. Before there was an Occupied and an Unoccupied Zone, there had been very few Jews in the South. My uncle, who was a rabbi at Lille before the war, was named rabbi and my father officiant at Cannes.

BAILLY: So the Jewish institutions protected their officiants?

EIZNER: Yes, but it was not just a matter of protection, it was also a redistribution of responsibilities in the whole country because there was now a large Jewish community in the Southern Zone.

BAILLY: Yes, they needed to be taken care of, of course. So in 1941 you were in Cannes. You were there in an official and open way as Jews, as "professionals," so to speak. So how did that go? Did you rent a house?

EIZNER: Yes. And the Protestants lent us a place for the Jewish group. They showed a special understanding for us. What I can tell you is that I was a Unionist "Bluebird" (because there were only the Protestants and the Catholics) and the pastor in Cannes was a member of the well-known, upper-class Monod family. I remember that his wife, who was the leader, wrote a Christmas play about the birth of Jesus, and one day I cried because I didn't have a role, so she told me, "My dear, I would gladly give you a role; I just don't want anyone to think that I want to convert you." For all the big Jewish festivals like Rosh Hashanah and Kippur, the Protestants lent us their church. And they had an old pastor, a Hebrew scholar, who had endless discussions with my father and my uncle. It really was an extraordinary welcome. So in Cannes I did not experience anti-Semitism because when there were problems after the arrest of my parents in 1943, it was the principal of the school who saw that I had false papers.

BAILLY: For now, in the interview, we are still in 1941.

EIZNER: In 1941 the main problem we had, of course, was anxiety about the war.

BAILLY: At this stage you were aware? The people around you couldn't hide things from you any longer, could they?

EIZNER: No, because we listened to Radio-London every evening. But what interested me most was my friends . . . it was to go swimming, and it was . . . I don't know how to tell you. At the same time I knew that it wasn't a joke and I knew there was war, I led a life where I discovered music, where I took dance classes. And then there was nothing to eat in Cannes, at the beginning, because it wasn't an area that produced much. So the Baron Rothschild, on his property in Cannes, bought two cows and gave us a liter of milk every day.

It was a strange life and my father, who didn't have a lot to do, played a lot of bridge in a bistro. And I remember that in this bistro there were bands with singers. I was nine or ten years old and I fell in love with one of the singers. I tried to go to the bistro as much as I could.

BAILLY: Did your father still take care of his flock?

EIZNER: Yes, but he went to play bridge between three and five o'clock. It was another way of taking care of his flock because he saw everyone there. It was the equivalent of Deauville after the war.

BAILLY: And the French people of Cannes were mostly nice?

EIZNER: I can only speak of the people at school. They were okay. The teachers, too. In fact, I don't know if I have a mental block, but I don't think I ever experienced any anti-Semitism directed at me.

BAILLY: Did you have Jewish friends?

EIZNER: I had both kinds of friends, not just Jewish. And I can say that even later in life I never felt that what I didn't achieve was because of anti-Semitism—for other reasons, yes; from being a woman, yes.

BAILLY: In 1942, in Cannes, all the same it was a dark period?

EIZNER: A lot of things happened. For example, my father, who despite his lack of concern was aware, had gone to Vichy and returned—don't ask me how—with all the papers to leave for Spain. With a real passport, in his real name. My father had connections. And we started toward the Spanish border in 1942 at Tour-de-Carol, and it had been closed two days earlier! We learned that we could enter Spain anyway, but that we would spend a week in prison there. And my father stupidly said he didn't want his wife and daughter to spend time in prison! So we returned to Cannes, and then . . .

Then there was the Italian occupation in 1942–1943. That was a big joke because the Italians didn't seem to be interested in waging war, and they all seemed to be related to someone in Cannes. They spent their time selling chocolate on the black market, swimming, and chasing girls. They didn't worry about the Jews at all! The Germans came later, in 1943.

BAILLY: What were the French police doing all this time?

EIZNER: I don't know. In any case, they weren't worrying about us.

BAILLY: So you and your family still had your real name, your income, your few belongings?

EIZNER: We didn't have any belongings at all. We had clothes, that's all. In Cannes we were in a furnished apartment. To eat, we had to go to the black market, that's for sure, because in Cannes there was nothing except dates and figs.

We felt the trap close later, when the Germans arrived.

BAILLY: Your schooling wasn't interrupted? Except for going and coming back from Spain?

EIZNER: That was only for a week. Then I went back to junior high at Collège Capron, the girls' school in Cannes. Also there was the headmistress' daughter who crossed the Spanish border with us and who came back, too, but I didn't know her; I didn't learn this until later. And then the Germans arrived.

BAILLY: In Paris, 1942 was the terrible year, but for you, in Cannes, it was 1943?

EIZNER: At first there was a tragicomic aspect. In Cannes there were my father, my mother, my uncle, my aunt, my cousins, and then my great-aunt, my great-uncle and their children. There were all these people, except my grandparents who remained in their house at Fontenay-sous-Bois where there was a garden in front and a garden behind. They always had a suitcase ready, and if the cops were to come the neighbors would take them in immediately through an opening that had been made in the back garden. And they lived the life of Jews wearing the star, having turned in their radio and their telephone. And nothing happened to them! While *we* had problems and would have been better off to have stayed in Fontenay-sous-Bois. It seems no one was arrested at Fontenay because the employees of City Hall systematically destroyed the dossiers of the Jews and told the Germans that there were no Jews. It came down to simple things like that. These people belonged to a Resistance network. I believe it was just the employees themselves—not Communists, not Gaullists, not whatever*ists*; they were people who couldn't stand the Germans.

BAILLY: Alright, it's something to emphasize. In fact, it's about the French who saved the Jews!

EIZNER: Yes, I mean that if more than half of the Jewish population was saved, it is thanks, in a large part, to people like that, people who said "*niet*" in their own way. In any case, for me it was like that.

So in 1943 the Germans arrived. One of my cousins had gone to run an errand in Nice and was taken in a roundup. He was arrested and held in a hotel where they were detaining the Jews they had rounded up. He spent part of the day there, and then he told himself he was going to take an all-out risk. He left the room where he was, he acted calm, and he went down the stairs and got to the door and out into the street! So that was a first alert.

The second, unfortunately, was much more serious. One day, a Gestapo car stopped in front of the door of the house where we were living and arrested everyone—my father, my mother, my aunt, my uncle, and my cousin. They had been denounced, no doubt, by someone French. We never found out who the denunciation came from. The Gestapo was looking for the rabbi and the officiant. My cousin and I, who were at school, weren't arrested because we weren't at home when the car was there. There was another uncle who had come to see us who was also arrested. It was in September 1943. They were taken directly from Cannes to Drancy, the French internment camp near Paris, and were deported from Drancy to Auschwitz in October.

BAILLY: So you were at school during this arrest. You didn't see them again?

EIZNER: I was at school. I didn't see them again, and when I got home at six o'clock, the neighbor was waiting downstairs for me and my cousin to tell us not to go up because she was afraid there were still Germans around. So we both stayed with her.

But we still had an uncle, an aunt, and another cousin, who seeing what had happened, decided that it was time to leave Cannes, and they took us all to the Lot region, further north. That's where we went with false papers that the Resistance fighters in Cannes made for us, thanks to the headmistress of the school who was part of this network and who got the whole thing together for us. Furthermore, this headmistress, on the day of my parents' arrest, kept us at the school until everything could be arranged. These people had very strong secular and tolerant convictions—they were more or less moderate "centrist socialists."

BAILLY: You could never have guessed that . . . well . . .

EIZNER: No, impossible.

BAILLY: So you told yourself that you would go to live for a while with the rest of your family, you would soon find your parents, your parents would find you . . .

EIZNER: Yes, I believed that. I never returned to that house. I was then in school in Figeac; it went on like that until the Liberation.

I used the name Nicole Esnault and said I was born in Coude-kerque, near Dunkirk.

It so happens that the uncle I left with had a comrade from his regiment who owned a factory, Ratier Propellers, which made aircraft propellers in the Lot region. That's why we went there. He had a family home in a village called Corn, which he put at our disposal and we lived there. To go to school, which was fifteen kilometers away in Figeac, I had to cross the woods and hills and then take the train two kilometers from the village. I was afraid because I had to leave at six o'clock in the morning; I was afraid of the animals . . . So I told my aunt that I preferred to be a boarding student.

BAILLY: Did you know that your parents had been sent to Drancy?

EIZNER: Yes, because I had gotten one letter from the train, and then another. You know, people would toss letters outside. Someone picked up the letter and sent it to me. I kept these letters for a long time. Unfortunately, I no longer have them. Those two letters fooled me. My mother wrote me that everything was fine, that they were in good health, that they were going to work in Germany, that I shouldn't worry and that they would return after the war. We would see each other.

BAILLY: How long were they at Drancy? Do you have information about their movements from Serge Klarsfeld?

EIZNER: Yes. At Auschwitz, my mother went immediately to the gas chamber and my father committed suicide on the electrical wires.

BAILLY: Were they together in the same convoy? Which convoy?

EIZNER: I don't know. It was a convoy that left Drancy on October 27 or 28, 1943. But that's not all. While I was a boarder at the school in Figeac, I was surprised one day to see my uncle, with whom I had traveled, in a nearby courtyard filled with men. And you know, in that region there was the infamous Panzerdivision Das Reich that spread terror, the ones who were responsible for the Oradour-sur-Glane massacre. There were also many Resistance fighters, and in reprisal for the actions of the Spanish Resistance fighters, the Germans had arrested these men, just like that, randomly. My uncle was in Figeac where he was running errands and he was taken in the roundup, and then the headmistress of the school—it was the second or third day that these men were detained in that courtyard there—said we should take them something to eat. She proposed bread and jam. So we carried food to these men. I saw my uncle there and I ran to him crying, "Uncle!" He pretended not to recognize me, and that saved my life, because the day they had him take his pants down, he was deported. So that was a tragic episode.

One day at school there was a geography test and I, not thinking, wrote my real name. Later, when the teacher returned the papers, she gave my grade with my false name and told me to come to see her after class and gave me a lecture about how I needed to be more careful. When she saw that I had written the name "Eizner," she knew that it didn't sound very French and she understood everything.

I have many memories of this time as a boarding student at Figeac. I was eleven years old. There were extremely nice friends, one of which was a girl named Wisot whom I learned after the war was from the Wisotski family of furriers. There were a lot of people hidden there with false names, and also one friend who was from the village where I was. We would go back there Saturdays. Her parents were farmers and they would sell us food. It was a funny little village. The writer Roger Martin du Gard was also in this little village. We didn't talk about that among my Jewish friends separated from their parents. We talked more about girls and boys; we were preadolescents. I find it hard now to understand how, amid all that, I managed to lead a normal life. Was it in self-defense? It was also because I couldn't believe that I would never see my parents again. In some ways I was entering the age of revolt, and I felt somehow liberated not to have to report to anyone. I'm saying it as bluntly as I think it. I also was discovering the country—a milieu that I didn't know at all before.

BAILLY: Do you think that led to your later career in rural sociology?

EIZNER: Certainly. The freedom of myself in my own body—free to run around, to ride bicycles, to swim in the river . . . Even so, I had good relations with adults, at school, and with my aunt and my cousins. I had a cousin who was exactly my age and we lived the first bloom of our adolescent life. I don't mean that I was ecstatic with joy. It's simply that I don't have any memory of having lived this period of time in terror. But I was afraid of the Germans. I didn't see them in the village, but I saw them in Figeac. I was frightened by that, of course. I was afraid at certain times, but I wasn't frozen with fear all the time. The other life, my normal life continued. It was after the war when I realized all that had happened and was surprised by my own attitude.

BAILLY: No immediate trauma?

EIZNER: None at all. Fear, I would say, ordinary, normal.

BAILLY: And enough concentration to continue your studies? You were in school?

EIZNER: Yes, but I wasn't studying seriously at all! All things considered, I must have been somewhat traumatized. For instance, the necessity of using a false name humiliated me a lot. And then I had to act Catholic. That, too, was very strange because when we got to this little village, my uncle and my aunt decided that we had to inform the priest, which they did. And this priest, who was a very good man, said it was absolutely necessary that we come to mass so that people wouldn't think we were Jews. This was not at all with any idea of converting us, of "seducing" us. He was a good old guy. So I went to mass, I remember, with my cousin. We would burst out laughing; we did everything backward. The priest was obliged to say, "That's what secular children are like! They don't know anything." You see, he was super nice. This kind of thing shows the gap between the harshness of the reality and my perception of it as a child. There was always a gap between the two that I am unable to explain.

BAILLY: And your relative detachment from scholarship didn't make you give up the idea of getting the *baccalauréat* degree?

EIZNER: Oh, at the time I didn't even think about it. I was in junior high. I hadn't abandoned anything except that I thought school was of secondary importance; it wasn't at all among my major concerns.

BAILLY: And your aunt, your cousins—it was truly a close family, a replacement?

EIZNER: Yes and no. I didn't like my aunt much. Furthermore, after the war she didn't react well. But my cousins did, yes. Later on they were the only members of my family that I continued to see. My aunt was partly authoritarian and partly extremely egotistical. Well, I would say that she was kind, but . . . She was very frivolous; she loved beautiful clothes so she absolutely had to buy me dresses, lots of things—especially at that time when I was a little tomboy; all that stuff didn't interest me at all. So my relationship with my aunt was neutral.

BAILLY: So your adolescence was not a crisis, but not very easy either?

EIZNER: I had my real adolescence after the war. I think that not being able to revolt against my parents during those war years gave me a very strange adolescence.

BAILLY: We'll come back to that. For now, you've gotten up to 1945 in Figeac, until the end of the war. Before the Liberation, you have nothing more to tell about life there, either factually or emotionally?

EIZNER: I remember we spent a lot of our time making fun of the country folk, their actions, their way of life, and especially of the fact that there were light-years between us. I mean we were totally in modern times and they had an unbelievable lifestyle. Later I often told my students how backward life in the country was at the time. They couldn't believe it. I mean, the chickens that jumped on the table, the eternal soup that was boiling, the grandmother who stank and whom the family left in a corner—all that. And for me, that was an unbelievable discovery!

BAILLY: But it wasn't all negative? There was also the wisdom of the elders, rapport with nature—all that, right?

EIZNER: No, I didn't see any wisdom of the elders. I met some nice young people and nature, yes. But I never got over my fear of animals.

Even so, I very much felt the sword of Damocles over my head. I think I always had a little gift for seeing the bright side of life, but I think at the same time I learned harsh lessons; I was harshly educated and I gained an understanding of a lot of difficult things during this time, not especially tied to Judaism, mind you. It gave me a depth of life that helped me later. For example, I completely lost the faith that never really had a strong hold on me. You see, before the war my faith had been very "social." It was part of what existed. In fact, my parents, who in their continual contradictions were at the time both inside and outside the Jewish religious observance, didn't help faith get a strong hold on me. But that's how it was.

The Pétainism of the time made me laugh, even in Cannes. I had a literature teacher who was very loyal to Pétain and who made us sing the hymn "Maréchal, nous voilà!" I decided I wouldn't sing it because I was against Pétain. So I was aware that there was Good and Evil and that Pétain was Evil. My parents transmitted that idea to me.

BAILLY: Did you think the French population was more supportive or more disgusted by Pétain and the Vichy government?

EIZNER: That depends on when you mean. By 1944 they were more disgusted.

BAILLY: Wasn't it just opportunism because they saw that Germany was going to lose the war?

EIZNER: I don't know; I wasn't political. I really wasn't into that kind of thing. What I saw was that I got constant support and that there was a series of little miracles for me, one after the other, due to these average people.

BAILLY: What did you do on the weekends?

EIZNER: First we would torture my little cousin, we older ones, and then we would play, ride our bicycles, go out to take care of cows with my farmer friend. We would go swimming in summer, as I told you; I did what all kids do. I made cakes, all that; we had stuff to eat there, bowing and scraping to the country folk.

BAILLY: And it didn't seem like a long time not to see your parents? It had been a year since they were taken.

EIZNER: Yes, it seemed like a very long time. But it was also extremely full of discoveries of life. I lived all the contradictions at the same time. I would cry sometimes at night, of course, but I would also have moments of unrestrained laughter. I don't know if I can say which predominated. In any case, it wasn't dereliction, that's for sure.

BAILLY: You weren't overwhelmed; you were protected by your young age, by these little miracles and all that. By the awareness of these little miracles?

EIZNER: Yes, I didn't have bad people in direct contact around me. So I lived like a kid. I cried because my Mama wasn't there to console me anymore when I had things I needed Mama to console me about.

BAILLY: Especially when you are an only child. A cousin is not like a brother or sister.

EIZNER: This cousin was, because we had practically been raised together. He was two months older than I, and even before the war we spent every weekend together. Now we don't see each other much.

It was in this context that the Liberation took place. I remember some things. First, it was the Resistance fighters who liberated Figeac. It was joy—it really was joyful—and I remember that all of us kids in Figeac were on our little bicycles to share in the jubilation, and that I was sure I would see my parents in a few months. Then I went back to Paris after the connections between the Northern and Southern Zones were reestablished.

BAILLY: So along with your aunt and cousins, it was decided to return to Paris to take back your apartments and try to get information about your parents.

EIZNER: To my apartment alone, no. In August 1944 I went back to live with my maternal grandmother whom I found in her house in Fontenay. I stayed there until 1953–1954.

BAILLY: And there you started waiting for your parents.

EIZNER: Like everyone else, I went every day to the Hôtel Lutétia.

BAILLY: I don't want to appear to be the "voyeur," so simply say what you wish about this period.

EIZNER: It was very hard, that's all I can say. Then there was a time when it was over, when no one else was returning. I understood. I didn't even have what some people had—that is to say, the dream that their parents were somewhere and that some day they would reappear. When I saw the faces of the deportees who were returning, I didn't need anyone to spell it out for me. Then little by little, I got accustomed to the idea that I wouldn't see them again, and after that I had a pretty simple life.

Immediately after the war, things were difficult for several reasons. On the one hand, there was my parents' absence, obviously, but there was also the fact that between my grandmother and me there was a generational gap, so we couldn't communicate. In some respects I detested her because she was very *frum*, in an old-fashioned way. I'm not talking about my grandfather. He died of grief six months after the war ended because my grandparents had lost all three of their children. My grandmother held on to raise my cousin and me.

BAILLY: Your cousin was at your grandmother's, too, so at least it was someone close?

EIZNER: Yes, but not all that much either, because everyone was always lecturing me and I wanted to send them packing. I was very rebellious—completely rebellious—first against my grandmother who didn't understand anything about anything. About twenty years ago, I at last understood my grandmother, because I had to get older myself to understand what motivated her. But at that point, I didn't know how to talk to her. For example, she would say to me—I'm telling you this anecdote to show you the light-years that separated us—that I shouldn't wash when I was having my period—I mean things from the nineteenth century to a kid in 1945, you see, and I won't even mention the psychological aspects! In fact, she was a good woman; she did all she could. But that's how it was. She couldn't stop saying to me, "Du bist eine Aristokrat!"

BAILLY: Yes, that says it all. Was there also a class difference between the two of you?

EIZNER: But it was *she* who belonged to the bourgeoisie! She owned the factory; it was her husband's, she played the role of granddame in her milieu. During the war there was an Aryan administrator. He, too, was an honest administrator who returned everything at the end of the war. Then it was my aunt who took over the factory and she made a fortune, because metal beds sold very well after the war to hospitals and schools. And to think that she left us almost starving to death because she figured that she had just a little pension to spend on people who weren't working in the factory! When I told you I didn't like this aunt, I had reasons for that, after the war. My grandmother did all that she could. I went to the Lycée Hélène Boucher, but I spent my time in the caves of Saint-Germain-des-Prés, at the Lorientais (a night club where New Orleans–style jazz was played) and other places, and I dreamt of nothing but getting away.

BAILLY: At that time you were already in high school. Had you gotten interested in studying?

EIZNER: No. I had to repeat a year, but I don't know if it was because I didn't have an interest in studying or if the schooling in Figeac wasn't quite at a level to allow me to move to the next level at Lycée Hélène Boucher in Paris. Afterward I was a very brilliant student in all the subjects that I liked and a complete zero in the others. It was literature, philosophy, history, and Italian that I liked.

BAILLY: School was not really the center of your life. You had friends, boys and girls?

EIZNER: Many, many of them, both boys and girls. I was at Saint-Germain-des-Prés all the time after school, in a French milieu, but there were also lots of Jews who were reacting as I was—with an enormous desire to live. And that's why when I was at a Jewish lecture one day much later on at the Rachi Center, where the psychiatrists explained to us—*to us*—that we somehow felt responsible for the death of our parents, I took the floor almost shouting because, on the contrary, I think the message my parents left me was: "Carpe diem!"

BAILLY: Yes, coming from them, this "survivor guilt" stuff was really perverse!

EIZNER: And all that, in a fit of pity, of unbearable dereliction, of pathos . . .

BAILLY: You reacted in a healthy way.

EIZNER: I reacted by throwing myself wholeheartedly into life, and especially in all that appeared, suddenly, in this restrained family context, as prohibited; that is to say, let's admit it, sexual relations, dance. I was a fanatic about Sartre, Merleau-Ponty, Dostoevsky. I read like a madwoman, I never stopped. And my grandmother didn't like that. It wasn't good for a girl to be too educated . . . a girl had to find a husband. My grandmother had the *shathen* come every Sunday who would propose doctors or lawyers to me, and I would receive them with onions on my breath so they would give up . . .

BAILLY: Did that make you reject the Jewish community completely?

EIZNER: I never knew there was such a thing as the Jewish community. In my life I wasn't acquainted with it. I was with Jews a lot; I was with a lot of them, but I never had the feeling of belonging to a specific community.

BAILLY: So did you especially plan to marry a Jew, or especially not to?

EIZNER: Rather not to. Even so, I wasn't completely crazy. I planned, if I were to marry one day, to marry a man I loved. I didn't care if he were Jewish or Patagonian. More from that perspective. It was all the same to me.

BAILLY: And for building your career, the fact of being orphaned by the Holocaust gave you a "moral armature," I mean by that a special drive?

EIZNER: No, I have never been obsessed with success. I don't care about it at all. I simply studied psychology by chance, with concurrent studies in sociology, and afterward I needed to find work. For certain reasons, I met some people who offered me a job and I worked on motivational studies in a private office for almost ten years. And then I met my partner who said, "What! You are working in the private sector!

That's disgraceful, it's disgusting!" "Well, what should I do?" "Well, come
to the CNRS!" Good enough. I made an application and went there. At
the time that's how it was. It was by chance. I was motivated and I still
am—it's a constant in my life—by the desire to understand what I am
not. I mean, for example, for me the country people are the absolute
Other and that is what interests me.

BAILLY: No direct connection with the trials you lived through, your
situation as an orphan?

EIZNER: No.

BAILLY: This is intellectual in fact. Is it also emotional?

EIZNER: Yes. It correlates with the fact of my being Jewish.

BAILLY: Yes, of course. Can you give more details about this?

EIZNER: The interest in the Other, for me, is one of the Jewish
values—to try to put oneself in the place of the Other, but it is perhaps
something I fantasized about.

BAILLY: Why is this a Jewish value?

EIZNER: Because historically, I don't believe the Jews, who, as you
know, were rejected, shuttled off from one country to another, could
have survived without understanding what others were like. It is not an
instinct for assimilation, but at certain times connected to survival there
is an interest in other ways of thinking and being that are not Jewish.

BAILLY: You think it is an acquisition in the memory of our history
as a people?

EIZNER: I don't think we are a people. I think that is something historic; I think it is lost now. I think that for the young generations, because of the existence of Israel and the total normalization, it's finished.
Historically, it seems to me that the Ashkenazi were unable to survive
as a specific people because they were at the same time both inside
and outside of the societies where they lived. And in order to be
"inside" one has to understand the Other, one has to be able at least to
pretend, one has to play the game in some way. It is not the only thing.
I wrote a little article about this that appeared in Izio Rosenman's publication, *Plurielles*.

BAILLY: That's an important point. Do you have other points like
that—about the Jews' personal situation in relation to their environment, especially after the ordeal?

EIZNER: Listen, I've always had the feeling . . . I feel very Jewish
really, and I have never understood very well why.

BAILLY: Yes, and yet it doesn't tie in to religion!

EIZNER: No. But I believe, in the final analysis—it's what I wrote in my paper—that in my head, in any case, the absolute value is knowledge. That is why I reject the peasant values, notably the possession of land. That's all. For that reason I also reject the Zionist values. As for knowledge, the Jews aren't the only ones to be like that, but I think we have been a lot like that—the objective of our parents was always to move ahead through study. The lowest ranking peddler or hat maker, as soon as possible, had his children study. And also, knowledge is transportable; wherever you go, you take your knowledge with you.

BAILLY: Would it be the same with art, from this point of view?

EIZNER: There is that. I also often wonder why the Jews, after the emancipation, for such a long time remained Jews. After all, it was easy to meld into the population! To me this is proof of an extraordinary courage.

BAILLY: Well, we're up to where we talk about values. I have some questions (treat them however you want): How did the trauma of the war forge your values? How did this situation as a child of the Holocaust determine your ethical life? Did you develop more fear or rather a special moral fiber? What responsibility—citizen, activist, or other—did these ordeals induce in you? What is your message to society in this regard? And what can be done so that it happens "never again"? What is the place of the "duty of memory"? What role do you see for a Jew of the Diaspora?

EIZNER: Only all that? Well, it is clear that my activism is entirely determined by the Holocaust because I have been militant all my life. I do not tolerate injustice. I do not tolerate ordeals as tragic as those that happened to us happening again to others. This experience, in any case for me, made me understand—putting it in very simple terms—that if we don't fight evil everywhere, it is the same as admitting that evil will always exist. I could tell you that in political terms, but I prefer to say it this way. So all my life I have sworn not to tolerate people being killed, persecuted, humiliated by dominant forces. That has often taken the form of the anticolonialist fight with me, obviously, but I also believe that I have been in all the great struggles that have occurred.

BAILLY: But what relationship do you see between this particular sensitivity and a general, principled, theoretical, philosophical doctrine of universal values?

EIZNER: There is no contradiction. I do this in the name of universal values. Communitarianism interests me even less now that it has become the pet theme used to explain everything and its opposite. I am beginning to be very afraid of reclaimed identities. It seems to me (but I say this with a lot of question marks) that for people, whatever their basic myths are, to attach themselves to an identity that, in fact, no longer exists—is no longer alive, has become a dead thing—it's the same as our talking about community when there is none. And I will go a little further: I am beginning to wonder if this importance placed on memory is not a way of hiding the absence of creativity in the here and now.

To speak specifically about Jews, I wonder if their historical role, in Europe for example, is not over, either because of total assimilation or because of the existence of Israel or because of a withdrawal into religion. By the way, this doesn't just concern the Jews. In any case, nowadays I don't see anything creative in reference to the Jewish tradition, but I don't see anything creative ahead in our society in general either . . . By that I conclude that we have become like everyone else.

BAILLY: Let's go back to little things. Due to the fact of your parents' absence, I suppose that a certain number of very humble traditions of ordinary Jewish life were not transmitted to you—Jewish cooking, popular music, certain delightful customs?

EIZNER: Of course they were, by my grandmother. That was transmitted and I enjoy it.

BAILLY: These are unpretentious aspects, but strong in one's emotional identity.

EIZNER: I'll cook something Jewish for you, if you want . . .

BAILLY: Okay! That is also part of the memory to transmit, because it carries—with limits—joy and balance. It could even nourish a modest form of creativity, serving up a diet of youthfulness in the twenty-first century.

EIZNER: Let's go back to the example of cooking, even if it deals with trifles . . . What do I see around me now? More and more often the Jewish kosher restaurants are Chinese restaurants, are restaurants where they serve Peking duck! The connection to Central Europe is disappearing from modern Jewish restaurants in Paris.

BAILLY: For example, the *schtetl* folk dances that we try to revive with feminist humor, or the jazzy klezmer music, or the chorales where we sing the stories of earlier times, or sociologically stylized episodes of the Old World, these are things distant but alive and pleasing.

EIZNER: Of course.

BAILLY: But all in all, for you, first, not much is left of the old times and, secondly, it's not worth the trouble to make a fuss about?

EIZNER: No, but it's worth the trouble to do it for pleasure. Why not? I am very much for that . . .

BAILLY: But for you it's not a soil rich enough to nourish a creativity worthy of the name; it doesn't free either the mind or forces of joy that would be valuable?

EIZNER: The forces of joy, of course! When I hear the Yiddish singers Talila and Ben Zimet and their followers, I dare say I am charmed. I feel completely in harmony, I very much respond emotionally. But I also respond emotionally when I hear the old French melodies! As I wrote in my article, I always tried to place myself in the juncture between bœuf bourguignon and gefilte fish . . . It is extremely satisfying to have several identities at the same time!

BAILLY: And if one joins the positive fragments of identity to a political creativity, what does one do with them at the present time, given the general context? Where are the strong points?

EIZNER: There is no political creativity. I am a pessimist.

BAILLY: That is surprising, given your past commitment. Do you rebound each time because you keep making commitments here and there?

EIZNER: I rebound because I am an optimist. But right now I am very pessimistic.

BAILLY: And as for intellectual creativity, in your professional field?

EIZNER: In every field. Do you know of an absolutely transcendent philosopher living today, a writer whose book you would give up everything just to read? A painter who is a genius? In every field, I find that . . . Finally, it is connected to the marketing and media society; things are born and die and last only two or three years in the best of cases.

BAILLY: Yes, but is your message colored with this pessimism?

EIZNER: I don't have a "message" to transmit. My personal optimism resides in the fact that each time period has its basic contradictions. But for the last ten years I have had a hard time, like people of our generation, working through the basic contradictions. It is likely that one day they will take form around the antiglobalization movement or I don't know what. But for the time being, it is all formless. I don't want it to be. Even if I wanted to attach myself to a movement—which I don't—I wouldn't know which one.

BAILLY: So what will you do with your vitality, your strength, your sensitivities, and your convictions?

EIZNER: I live with them. I live with them in everything I do.

BAILLY: So all in all, you don't want to suggest Diasporic roles for Jews?

EIZNER: No, nor a "mission," not even universalistic nor "messianic." Especially not messianic, nor political, nor ethical. It's over for me. I don't believe there are Jews who are capable of bearing that. Or rather they are buried in their problems of territories down there in Israel, which is the opposite of Judaism. Or up here where they are, I was going to say like in a cocoon where each one returns to his gated community, the Jews also. As for universalism, I don't see much. I hope I am wrong. But the return of religion frightens me.

BAILLY: So the question, "What to do so that *never again* becomes a meaningless phrase?"

EIZNER: We haven't stopped having that *never again!* Whether it is in Vietnam, or Cambodia, or Rwanda, in Chechnya, or wherever. If you want to look for horror, it's not like we don't have it now. I know very well that the Holocaust is still something different from everything I was just mentioning. But at the end of the day, there are different ways to massacre the innocent. I would be willing to do something against that, but what?

BAILLY: In conclusion, have the ordeals you endured, among the most atrocious one can endure, caused you to try to simply be happy in your daily life while, of course, being openly generous to others? Or to continue to try to fight?

EIZNER: No, listen. I've spent my whole life fighting. Now, I am still willing to fight but I don't know where. I can't invent it. I don't feel any movement. I'm not saying that there isn't one, but for the moment . . . Perhaps there are groups organizing in undetectable ways. I don't know. But I am panic-stricken by the things people are praising to the skies, stuff that lasts a month or two, a year, two years, and afterward they move on to something else. This really prevents our getting to the core of problems.

BAILLY: And what about knowledge? Does it remain a rich, consoling value of refuge?

EIZNER: Yes, but it is not a part of the collective action; it is strictly individual. I can't go beyond all that, even having had a traumatic experience as a Jew, and even carrying behind me centuries of messianic and universalistic aspirations mixed together.

BAILLY: A final word?

EIZNER: The final word is that I hope humanity will find the strength to prevent barbarianism from becoming permanent.[1]

FIGURE 15.1. Odette and her star. Age twelve, in Paris
in November 1942, two months after the deportation
of her parents.

# 15

# Odette Kozuch

*Odette Kozuch, born in France, an orphan of the Holocaust, was one of those children who married too young and had to grow up fast, and then rebuild her life alone. She realized her adolescent aspiration by making her alyah in Israel. Now retired after married life (twice widowed) and professional life, both difficult, she remains very dynamic, dividing her time between cultural and volunteer activities.*

My name is Odette Kozuch. I was born Odette Diament. We were a family of eight: my parents; my sisters Suzanne, Simone, and Fernande; my brothers Isidore and Georges; and I. What led me to speak today is the fact that in a few years there will be no one left to say "I was there" or "I lived it." I believe we must leave something for posterity beyond, of course, the writings of the historians who personally lived the horror in the concentration camps and have told about it very well. In my case, I was not in a concentration camp, but my parents were deported, never to return, as was one of my brothers and one of my sisters. The French police had come to arrest them.

My father had arrived from Poland by way of Germany in 1923. He had spent six months in Berlin earlier but he had not liked the atmosphere there. As soon as he found work and housing in Paris, Mama joined him with their oldest children, who were born in Poland. We, the three later ones, were born in France, in Paris. I was the last of the six children. I arrived in 1930. This is important because being a child of immigrants was really not easy during those years. Some people always exploit others—there will always be that—but there was great solidarity among the Jews, and overall there was a great deal of human warmth within the group. From this perspective it was amazing. We lived in the Tenth Arrondissement of Paris, between Belleville and République, in an apartment building about eighty percent inhabited by Jews. Everyone knew each other and everyone helped each other.

I can say that my childhood was difficult but happy in this family of modest means. Papa was a cutter in the shoe industry; Mama didn't work, she cared for her six children at home. We lived in a tiny two-room apartment. It was warm. I was a spoiled little girl. Well, okay, I didn't get my first doll until I was seven years old, but I had rag dolls and I knew how to amuse myself with a lot of little things—with a piece of string, for example. In fact, we were poor but happy; we had what we needed. Of course, my parents, like everyone else of that generation, dreamed of seeing their children pursue studies. My brothers and I went to school and we were very good students. It was hard for the older ones because they had to work to help out at home, even more so because the 1930s were very difficult. There was severe unemployment. We didn't always have enough food to satisfy our hunger.

Finally the situation improved in 1937 with the arrival of the Popular Front. I remember it very well. People talked about paid vacations. The Popular Front represented hope. For the first time, we took a vacation. At the time some Jews were going to Viry-Châtillon, a small country village only twenty kilometers from Paris. Two or three big families like ours had ordered a taxi. We took pans; we loaded up mattresses and everything we needed. I remember this vacation in 1937 very well. It was a memorable experience. In fact, it is the only family photo that I still have. We were very happy. My father, who was filled with ideas about liberty and everything Central European Jews believed about the France of the Rights of Man, had decided to establish himself permanently there, but like many others he would soon become disillusioned. I remember a cousin, Sima, who stopped over with us. She had to leave France. I also remember seeing other people at our place who were arriving from Poland when Laval was prime minister. Denied the right of asylum, they were sent away. The police accompanied them to the Gare du Nord for their return to Poland. This was already happening in 1934–1935, when people were saying, "Oh, yes, the foreigners are eating our bread." These are things I remember from age four, five, and six years old. They were speaking about foreigners, but since there weren't any others at the time, it was understood to mean Jews. No one was talking about Italians or Yugoslavs. There weren't any in France; they were going to America. The Jews were coming to France in sizeable numbers, even though some also expatriated to America. A part of my father's family immigrated to America. In fact, all our generation arriving in France in the 1930s had neither cousins, nor grandfathers, nor grandmothers living near where we settled. We have never known what a real family is. My father had a twin brother but he wasn't on good terms with him.

During the years 1936–1937 daily life was improving. My three sisters worked, and I happily went to school. The writer Roger Ikor describes this time very well in *Les Eaux mêlées*.[1] The men worked and the women stayed home. The men were automatically better integrated into everyday French life, even if they were working among Jews. The experience of going out and exchanging ideas was already very important; that didn't exist for the women. I want to emphasize that I learned to read at the age of four, thanks to my brothers. My father, who was a very intelligent man, read regularly and he wrote a little in French. At home there was always a newspaper, and even now not a day goes by that I don't read one. We were very close with our neighbors, whom we visited because they liked to discuss things with my father. That's why there was always a lot going on in our little two-room apartment.

We were not religious, even though my maternal grandfather had been a rabbi. Mama didn't eat ham, but she would buy it for us children, and contrary to the French who ate cheese at the end of a meal, we savored it as an hors d'œuvre before the meat. We respected some religious holidays. I remember Passover, the matzo balls and the open door for the prophet Elijah. Yom Kippur is more confused—I remember less about it. I also remember my two brothers' bar mitzvah. I remember throwing candy in the synagogue after the ceremony. But it stopped there. We did not observe the Shabbat. We really didn't observe anything at all. In our apartment building, some older people more or less held on to religion, but I didn't know anything more about it.

As the situation improved, we were able to rent an adjacent room, so my three sisters slept over in that room. In our two rooms there were folding beds. We did our homework on the end of the table, but we were still the first in the class. At that time, parents would continually repeat, "Study, study, never stop studying." I remember my mama's pride when she came to get me at school and I was on the honor roll. I also remember the first radio we bought in 1937. Everything came at once—the first vacation, the first radio. Things were improving a little.

Then came 1938 and the "phony peace." I remember it, too. I remember my father's pessimism. Then came 1939: the war. Then my father, like a good papa of children born in France, reported to the military authorities to be mobilized. He insisted on enlisting for France. They told him, "Monsieur, you have six children; go home." My parents and my three sisters were foreigners but the last three children had been born in France. I could read on our documents that I had been naturalized at the same time as my brothers by declaration in 1935—that is to say, only five years after my birth. However, the other five members of the family—my three sisters born in Poland and my parents—were still Polish and therefore considered foreigners by the French administration. At the time, it was very difficult to get naturalized. My parents didn't speak Polish; they usually spoke Yiddish, and they didn't speak French very well, especially Mama. We answered automatically in French because we went to school and our "native" language was French. In fact, the older children had arrived in France at very young ages. They went to school in France. They learned to count in French. Automatically for us, our mother tongue was French. However, even today, I adore Yiddish.

The "Phony War" began. At that time my older sister Suzanne was engaged to a Jew born in France and naturalized as a French citizen. The religious marriage took place in February 1940. The banns had been published for two weeks (twenty-one days were required at the time). The civil marriage was to take place in May 1940, but my sister's fiancé was killed in the war, in the well-known offensive on the Meuse River in May 1940. The banns had been published, but she wasn't officially married. I tell this because it reveals something very important that was to follow. Religiously she was married but for France it wasn't valid. She remained Mademoiselle Diament, a name that could sound French. Perhaps some member of the family had been a diamond cutter or something like that. In the past, names were often taken from occupations, places of origin, or characteristics. For example "Langer" was someone tall or "Mahler" was a painter.

The exodus began. We decided to leave Paris. A horse-drawn carriage was already reserved, but suddenly the Germans arrived. For some reason, the person who was supposed to pick us up never came. I remember Mama going out to run errands in the Faubourg du Temple. She came back and told us, "This is it; I saw them, they are here!" The Germans had arrived. Leaving was no longer an option. It was over. True, at the time no one knew all that was happening. We hadn't had contact with the Jews who had fled Germany. Of course, we were aware of their difficulties, but we were more concerned about the Jews from Poland or Russia. I remember my father being very interested in Palestine. He talked about Jabotinski. A friend who came to the house also spoke about him. But nothing more. We never thought about going to Palestine. I don't think it was really possible at the time for a family with six children. The people who were leaving didn't have big families. They were young, very enthusiastic, and idealistic. A family of six children had to either have the means or be very passionate. This was not our situation.

So the Germans arrived. The daily material difficulties intensified. Getting food became painstaking. Then came 1941. My second sister Simone (at whose home I stay when I come to Paris) knew a boy, a *goy*. At the end of 1941 she decided to marry him. I remember very well the mutterings and tears of my parents. But what could they do? She married him. He was a nice boy.

In 1942 the French government sold us our yellow stars, which counted against our clothing points. I don't remember the exact details. And then one day we had to go to the police station to declare ourselves as Jews. After that we had a food card with the imprint "Jew" on it. And we wore that star, with all that it implied: the last car in the subway, specific times to run errands, and, of course, all public places, such as concerts and theaters, were forbidden. My brother Georges and I would often forget the key when leaving the apartment—especially at the beginning. A locksmith, an old Frenchman on rue Saint-Maur, would see us coming and say, "Ah! The little Diaments went out again without the key!" I remember all that clearly. They also forbade radios. We weren't allowed to have one at home. We had to give ours up. Everyone was disciplined; we thought if we weren't they would punish us. Who knew what would happen? In our apartment building there was a couple. The wife was German and was absolutely adorable to us. When the Germans arrived in Paris, her family and some soldiers came to see her. She found a job at the Kommandantur. She offered to keep our radio for us and we accepted. That was rather curious.

Still 1942. Still in Paris. Still in the same place. I was still going to school, rue Parmentier. I had succeeded in the competition for scholarships. We began to hear rumors. By 1941 they had already arrested Jews and taken them to the French internment camps like Beaune-la-Rolande or Pithiviers. Given that these Jews were still in the internment camps, there wasn't a lot of anxiety about them. Only men were arrested; people said they were simply taken to work and that their families would be protected, but still we were hearing rumors. We decided that it would be better if Papa and my older brother Isidore, age eighteen, didn't sleep at home. I think they spent the night in the adjoining room—I don't recall exactly—but they were never in the apartment itself.

On July 16, 1942, at six o'clock in the morning, the French police suddenly appeared in the apartment building with their list. There weren't any Germans. Buses had been requisitioned. The police officers entered our apartment. They asked for "Monsieur Diament, Madame Diament, Suzanne Diament, Simone Diament, Fernande Diament." Papa wasn't there. Mama was there and they took her. My sister Suzanne, who hadn't had the time to be married, was taken, as well as my sister Fernande. My other sister, Simone, wasn't there. We told them she was married to a Catholic. I was there. I was watching. My brother Isidore was not at home at the time of the arrest. He was outside with my father. My two other brothers and I were French so for the time being they didn't bother us. I was then left alone at home with my youngest brother Georges.

The arrest took place at six o'clock in the morning with the operation coordinated all over Paris. I think they must have arrested fifteen thousand people. Our building was practically emptied. All at once, at six o'clock in the morning, that damned brigade of French cops invaded the building. I don't remember if there were one or two in our place. So I saw Mama taken away . . . I saw my sisters taken away . . . I was left alone with my brother. I was the baby of the family, really spoiled by everyone; I didn't even know how to light the stove. My brother Georges was four and one-half years older than I. So he was sixteen and I scarcely twelve years old. The two of us stayed there. We didn't know where they had taken our mother and sisters. We didn't know anything at all. During the course of the day we heard rumors.

Some people were detained at the Parisian Sports Center and others on rue de l'Aqueduc. They had picked them up in different parts of Paris to gather them at the Sports Center and then took them from there to Drancy. I had heard about arrests before, but not like this one. There had been arrests earlier, but only men. In 1941 there had been what was called the "roundup of the intellectuals"—in which the medical doctors, lawyers, and other professionals were arrested and held at Drancy. We knew that Drancy existed, but only for men; we thought it was a "work camp"—nothing more. In fact, I didn't know anything.

It seems to me that my childhood ended there. It seems that all at once I stopped being a child. I never again played with a doll. It stopped there. The neighbors were helpful. The first night they told us, "Don't sleep in your place." They put us up at their place. But how long could they do that? The next day the police returned, looking for my father. Of course, he was no longer sleeping in the apartment, but in the room next door. At that time, the French police didn't look for him there, which saved him. We began to get organized. During the day my father would return. He was ill, suffering from a serious sciatica attack that had him completely bent in half. He could still work, but I still see his tears . . . The Jews who found a job with an employer working for the Germans obtained German identity cards and they could protect their families. My brother Isidore had found a company that worked for the Germans. He wasn't being hunted because he was French. But my father was hunted.

We lived on rue Saint-Maur. We had to cross rue Parmentier in order to get to the Goncourt metro station, very close to where we lived. On August 17, 1942, very early in the morning, Isidore stepped out to see if everything was alright. I don't know if you are acquainted with the Goncourt station. Isidore walked down the steps. Everything seemed calm. He went back up to get my father. Everything was calm outside as well. But the cops were waiting down below—in the metro—not on the platform but beside the ticket window. And yet, when my brother went down, there was nothing. In the time it took for him to go back up and get my father, the police were there. And then what my brother heard when they asked for my father's papers! My father was fifty-two years old and he could hardly walk because of his sciatica. A police-man said to his colleague, "Leave him alone; it's only up to age fifty." The other one replied, "No, it's up to fifty-five. We're taking him." And they were French . . . There were only French. They took my father to the police station in the City Hall of the Tenth Arrondissement where he stayed several hours. From there, he was interned at Drancy where he found my mother. We received a card in which she wrote to us, "Our surprise was devastating when we saw your Papa arrive."

My older sister, Suzanne, who hadn't had time to marry, was only at Drancy for two weeks because at the time they weren't picking up World War I widows or wives of Jewish prisoners of war. As I have already explained, there were intellectuals at Drancy. A lawyer took an interest in Suzanne's situation. He moved heaven and earth to help her. He went all the way to the Commander's Office and he really saved her life. He succeeded in having her recognized as the "wife of a soldier killed in action for France," which was practically the same status as that of a war widow. Thanks to this lawyer, after two weeks she left Drancy and returned home. I remember her return. We lived just above the concierge's apartment. The concierge came up and called out, "Look, Madame Diament is back! Madame Diament is back!" I immediately thought of my mother, I felt really conflicted (I talked to my sister Simone about this only a short while ago)—part joy and part disappointment. I remember going to Drancy with Suzanne to try to catch a glimpse of our parents, but we were unable to see them. Despite the arrests, we continued to live in the same apartment. Where could we go? We had no money. What else could we do? Isidore was working and Simone, who was married, helped us.

After Suzanne was freed, she took up her work again at the Coty perfume factory. Later I heard that the managers had been anti-Semitic but they were very fair to her. I should mention that at the time the Coty Company was at Surenes in the Paris suburbs. Suzanne had always had to get up at five o'clock in the morning to get to work on time because in the 1940s there was no metro to the suburbs. So she started work again and the four of us stayed in the apartment— Suzanne, Isidore, Georges, and I. Simone was pregnant when my parents were arrested; she suffered such a shock that she almost miscarried. She went to the clinic and gave birth to a little girl on September 13, 1942, the night before our parents were deported. The day they wrote the card announcing their departure from Drancy, she was giving birth in the Bleuets Clinic on rue Parmentier, if I remember correctly. Unfortunately, the baby was born with a physical deformity. At three days old they had to operate on her spinal column. It was horrible because this child, hydrocephalic, also became blind. My sister and

I went to see her every afternoon at the hospital. The little girl died eight months later.

After that, I had to quit school and I started to work for an attorney with Simone. I was a stenographer, I answered the telephone, I also ran errands. I earned my first salary at the age of thirteen years, five months.

It was 1943. We lived as best we could, but there was always talk of roundups. We knew what that meant. Some days we couldn't go out; we were trapped at home. The challenges of finding food were growing more severe. Life was becoming truly difficult.

Rumors persisted. A non-Jewish neighbor had put his name on the room where my sisters slept. For security we hid there. Simone was protected, but her husband had been drafted for the STO in Germany. He refused, of course, so he also had to hide. It was less dangerous than it was for Jews, but it was very complicated all the same. Those who were married to non-Jews were protected except in certain cases. There were denunciations. My brother-in-law was a very nice guy, as was his family. Sometimes we would sleep at their house. They had moved to the Fifteenth Arrondissement near to the Citroën factory and several small precision machinery factories. From time to time I spent the night there. My brother-in-law, who had to hide, would move from place to place. One night Simone, who sometimes slept at our place, decided to go back to her place to see what was happening. We said, "Okay, but let's wait until tomorrow." That night there was a bombing by the English. So if we had slept at her place that night, we would have been in bed and wouldn't be here anymore. The bedroom had been destroyed. The next day we found the kitchen and the dining room, but no bedroom. There were fatalities in the building. You read about such things, you see it in the movies, you think: "This is not possible!" As you can see, we got through it as best we could.

It was January 1944. We had no news of our parents after that post-card—not from my parents or my sister Fernande. Nothing. Never. It was over. It was then that we began to hear the word Pitchipoï. This word invented by the Jews came into use during the Occupation. How did it originate? We didn't know. In fact, Pitchipoï is a place where people were being sent. No one knew where it was; that's where the expression came from. When the deportation from Drancy to Auschwitz began, people would ask us, "Where is your brother? Where is your sister?" We would answer, "At Pitchipoï." To this day when someone says Pitchipoï it means "completely unknown." There is a book, *The Children of Pitchipoï.* No one at the time could imagine what was really happening. Perhaps some people knew, but not in our circle. We had never heard anything about what was happening at the extermination camps. The UGIF tried to assist, but it was a double-edged sword because the Germans had demanded lists. It was classic. That is what took place with the Judenrat in Poland. At first the Jews thought that it was for their benefit. Finally, it all was turned against them and the Germans had lists of all the Jews.

On January 31, 1944, at exactly seven p.m. a plainclothes policeman who lived in the building and whom we knew well came up to our place and warned us, "Don't stay here; this evening they are picking up everyone." We dropped everything and hid in the room next door—Suzanne, my two brothers, and I. At three a.m. the Germans arrived. We heard them talking. They forced open the door of our apartment and then sealed it. They did not search elsewhere. The next morning we broke the seals, took some things, and then we dispersed. Suzanne went to hide with some other people. Even as a war widow, she was no longer protected but, on the contrary, was hunted. I went to the home of some *goy* friends who offered to make me a false identity card that didn't say "Jew," which was also written on my school identification card—on everything. These friends were charming. They knew us because they had a business nearby. I stayed with them until the false papers were ready.

We're almost up to May 1944. It was starting to feel like the end of the war. People spoke of the possible Landings. We could still buy papers and read them; there wasn't a lot of news but people always listened to London radio. Then we knew. We knew what was happening in Stalingrad. We learned of the first Landing at Dieppe in 1942, which was in fact a false Landing. Then there were the Landings in Algeria. A ray of hope began to shine.

The friends of whom I just spoke had found work for me as a maid on a farm a hundred kilometers east of Paris, in Esternay, a small village that had a busy railroad crossing. This farm was located fifteen hundred meters from the village. I was there with a family consisting of a mother, her son, daughter-in-law, and children. I had to help the children with the work in the fields and take care of the cows. These people had been given a story: for them I was an orphan; my sister was married to a Jew and couldn't take care of me so I had to take care of myself and find work. Most important of all, no one must find out that I was Jewish. It could have all been true; it was not unusual at the time to find children of my age working on farms. The best part of the story is that when I arrived, the old lady looked at me and took my face in profile in her hands and said, "It's curious, she looks Semitic." I was worried sick. I couldn't say a thing. And they also liked the Germans a lot in this house. When the Germans came looking for eggs or something, they always had some for them. For the French neighbors they had nothing. We listened to London radio like good French. Every day I heard, "Ah! The war will soon end and the Kikes will be back!" I was fourteen years old. I kept silent. I was without news of anyone. I didn't have any idea where my family was. There was no telephone contact because we were constantly bombed. I tried once or twice to call at the post office to connect with my sister at her work, but it was impossible to get connected.

The Normandy Landings took place. The Americans began to advance by August 24 or 25, 1944. Paris had been liberated the day before. I will never forget because it was my birthday. On the road I began to see the Americans advance. One day they sent me to the little village to buy bread. I didn't return to the farm. I left my shopping bag and I went down the road. I traveled by truck, jeep, horseback, bicycle; I passed Fontainebleau, which wasn't the most direct route because I was coming from the East. I don't remember where I spent the night. I finally arrived in Paris after twenty-four hours. Nothing was working yet. There was no metro, nothing.

I returned to rue Saint-Maur, where I had lived. I looked for the family. I found my sister Suzanne and then my brother Georges, and then I learned that my oldest brother Isidore had been taken on July 31, 1944. He happened to be in Belleville in one of the two or three cafés reserved for the Jews. That same day, the Germans unobtrusively arrived and took everyone who was still there. My brother was deported to Auschwitz with the next to the last transport, in August 1944. We learned about this when the deportees began to return. One day someone knocked at the door and we saw a twenty-year-old young man. It was our cousin, the son of my father's twin brother. He asked us if Isidore had returned. "No." Our cousin told us what had happened. He too had been deported, and one day during roll call at Birkenau, they called out "Diament." Two young men came forward. They didn't know each other. It is unbelievable. They never separated.

Later there was the infamous retreat—the infamous "death march"—from Auschwitz. They got as far as Buchenwald before they were separated. My cousin returned. My brother didn't. I only know he was taken in August 1944 on one of the last convoys to Drancy. I know he arrived at Auschwitz and that's all. He never returned. Telling this only takes a few sentences, and yet it is something I think about every day. I talked about it with my brother Georges not long ago. There is not a single day that I don't think about my parents . . . I'll continue . . .

When we got back to Paris, we found our apartment occupied by the neighbors, good Catholics, who owned the grocery store on the ground floor of the building. It was convenient for them, so they had put in a door to enlarge their apartment. They didn't want to give our place back to us. We had to go to court, which took until November 1946 to be resolved. Meanwhile, we didn't know where to go. We managed to find a little room where there was no electricity or water. A neighbor, a *goy* married to a Jew, made a hole in the wall for an electrical wire to let us at least have electricity. We lived there from August 1944 until November 1946. We weren't smart; we should have done as other returning Jews did. They threw out the people who occupied their lodgings. They put them out the door and told them, "This was mine and it will stay mine." But we were young and my brother Georges, wanting to avenge his parents, soon enlisted in the army. I stayed with my sister Suzanne. We lived in this little room and we worked.

The camps weren't liberated until April 1945. We began to go to the Gare du Nord and the Hôtel Lutétia. We never found a single person who had seen a member of our family or heard anything about them. Nothing. The waiting was absolutely horrible. We all reacted in different ways. This is when I told myself, "They made me a Jew; I will stay one to the end. I will only marry a Jew."

Later, once communication was reestablished, I sent a letter to the aforementioned farmers who had taken me in to explain the situation and to tell them the truth. They never answered. Some years later, after I was married, I went to see them. I was thrilled to learn that they were completely broke. I must admit that this pleased me.

Then we had to get organized and continue to live. I remember being overwhelmed to see on the news that the Russian and American armies had joined forces. I was fourteen and one-half or fifteen years old. I still believed in a brighter future, in the "tomorrow" they sang about. I thought something was going to change. Like everyone at that age, I was a Communist, but I was quickly disenchanted. I soon learned that it's always the same old people and they do the same old things and then everything starts over again, so I gave up anything political. I read all of Maxim Gorky, Nicolas Ostrowski. Clearly there was a kind of euphoria; nevertheless, in 1946 there were also pogroms in Poland. Then I gave up all hope of seeing this world change. I had lost all contact with my Polish family; even before the war the ties had been broken. This was the case with numerous families that had left and had practically no contact. We were originally from the area around Warsaw. I knew none of my uncles, aunts, cousins, any family members, which explains why we four who remained stayed very connected.

In 1946 I was very interested in everything Jewish or about Palestine. We received a lot of publications on every subject from the Stern group. I felt very attracted. I was sixteen years old at the time and I warned my sister Suzanne that I would very much like to immigrate to Palestine. She answered, "I will never let my sister leave." Once again I had to temporarily bury my desire deep inside myself. Georges rejected all that and only went out with *goys*. At the end of 1946 sister Suzanne bore a love child. She was not married. We raised the little one.

I was a cheerful young girl and I would sing, but I felt like I was forty years old. For example, I very much enjoyed my brother's friends. They were the same age as he—twenty-two—but I treated them like kids. It never occurred to me to flirt with any of them. I would sometimes babysit the children of a friend whose husband had been a prisoner of war. That's where I met Léon, the nephew of my friend's husband. Léon had been imprisoned and was one of the young Poles who came to Paris in 1938 after their *matura*[2] because they couldn't continue their studies in Poland. His parents and his two brothers died in the Warsaw ghetto. He was all alone after the Liberation when he returned to Paris. He would often come to his uncle's house. I was fifteen years old at the time. I was still a kid and he was eleven years older than I, but I grew up a little. He would always see me with a book in my hand. He was a very intelligent man who was continuing to study and wanted to get a master's degree, but couldn't finish it because he had to work with his cousin. Finally we started to go out together and we married in July 1948. I really was very young.

My husband became the manager for his cousin who had a very large clothing company. He then left to test his own wings. He took an accounting exam where he was twenty-first out of two hundred, which was brilliant. He then opened an accounting office and hired two employees. I stopped my work to help him, especially with the secretarial work. Working together was very pleasant. We lived in the Nineteenth Arrondissement in Paris, near the Laumière metro station, but my dream was to wake up near the Archevêché gardens in the center of the city. It was still affordable at the time and we could have managed it because my husband had begun to build a clientele. As I unfortunately could not have children, a two-room apartment would have been big enough for us.

We now skip to November 1966. I needed an operation because cancer was suspected. Two days before, in the morning, Léon hadn't felt well. In short—heart attack, hospitalization. I spoke with my doctor who told me that I could wait three or four days to see how my husband was, but no longer. When the doctor thought all danger was past, I went to the hospital with my little suitcase to say goodbye to Léon. We didn't know if we would see each other again. I will never forget the image of the nurse who was taking care of him—a good woman whose name I still remember—looking at the two of us. She sat down on the bed and started to cry. My husband and I calmly said goodbye to each other. I had my operation; it was not cancer. We both were released the same day, he from the hospital, me from the clinic. Both of us were back at home in bed. Two days later my husband left for a rehabilitation center and I settled into a hotel room two or three kilometers away.

It was November 1966. I remember this because we were thinking about taking our first trip to Israel. It was still too soon for my husband to fly. I didn't think we would emigrate because Léon wasn't ready. As for me, I had buried this desire, but I remained always very close to what Israel and Judaism represented. Then the Six Day War came. It drove my husband and me crazy. We were frightened because all that was close to our hearts. Through the years, we had given a lot of money to Israel, feeling it was the least we could do. We registered at the embassy. We wanted to welcome children at our house. We wanted to give blood. We did all that Jews could do. It is always the same problem, a fact that the non-Jews never understand: one can be Jewish without being religious. People would ask me, "So what are you? Are you French or are you Jewish?" I would answer, "I am French and Jewish." At the time of the Six Day War, the non-Jewish French, very happy about the reaction of Israel and her victory, would say to me with a lot of pride, "Ah! You see, eh, the Jews, the Israelis, how they really pounded the Arabs!" Automatically, I would answer, "It's not that you like the Jews so much, but you hate the Arabs even more."

And then, just when things started to go well, it all came to an end. In October of 1967 my husband had a second heart attack and it was over; he died that same month, after the Six Day War that we followed so closely. It's a fate common to Jews, with life's ups and downs. Life goes on. Always! You know why? First of all, there is that unique Jewish humor—that self-mockery. I believe Jews are at their best only in adversity. That's what worries me today about Israel. On the one hand everything seems to be going well, even if it isn't. We are somewhat the Chosen People in that country, and at the same time Israel has become a normal country. We have the same difficulties as the others and we react as they do. In my humble opinion that's where the country's problems lie.

After my husband died, I sold his business and took up my work again. I was thirty-seven years old; I was young and this ordeal had been very painful. Despite it all, even after this loss and with all the pain I felt, at thirty-seven, I still felt as though it wasn't over yet. You realize that despite everything life continues, because after all is said and done, even after such a difficult childhood, after such a difficult adolescence, there was always a ray of hope somewhere. Life is stronger than all of that. Even when I finally understood that my parents would never come back, despite it all, life continued. Not necessarily with the greatest of joy, that's for sure, because I felt old very soon. I aged very fast. A childhood with immigrant parents is already a difficult childhood with its material conditions, and just when things began to improve slightly, the war broke out, with all its consequences, and that meant that I never had the opportunity to play with dolls like other children. In fact, that's it. I don't remember ever playing with dolls. I had to earn my living very fast, very soon. That builds character.

So it was 1967. I started work. Little by little, the urge grew in me to do what I couldn't do at age sixteen. Of course, I didn't talk about it at all with my family because I knew that it would raise a general hew and cry, but circumstances caused me always to be independent about how I led my life. In 1970 I decided to make a trip to Israel. I was going to discover the country a little, to see what was happening, so as not to emigrate unprepared. In May I left for a four-week vacation with the European Tourism Club. From there, I took part in organized tours.

I traveled around a lot. I went to Jerusalem where I met friends who had emigrated there after the Six Day War. I liked Jerusalem a great deal. I got information about taking the intensive course in Hebrew, the *ulpan*, and told them I was planning to return soon. It was June. The *ulpan* began in January and I told myself, "In January I will be back here." That was why I took the tour of Israel—I knew that I had to learn the language after my arrival and that it would not be easy. It was nearly certain that I would not be able to continue working as a secretary, but I had only myself to take care of and I decided to do what I had always dreamed of doing.

When I returned to Paris, I told my boss that I was leaving in January for Israel. He was very surprised. Surprised and not surprised, because he knew my feelings. We used to discuss politics and many other things. Then I began to prepare my family. "What do you mean, you are going to leave us?" They all had their own families around them and I was alone. I didn't sell my apartment at first; I wanted to leave a way to come back. As I have always said, I went to Israel with a lucid enthusiasm. I thought I knew my people and I decided to try it. My brother said to me, "With your lifestyle—you like comfort—you'll be back in a year." But my sister-in-law, who was not Jewish and who was very sensible, said, "She won't be back." She was right.

I arrived in Jerusalem as planned. I took my *ulpan* and I lived as a student in a room. In Jerusalem I had a friend, but our paths soon separated. She knew almost no one and she encountered many difficulties. Jerusalem was a provincial place, very closed. I suggested she attend the last part of the *ulpan* and then go to Tel-Aviv, but she became discouraged. She hoped to find a husband, but one doesn't go to Israel to solve one's problems; that was a mistake many people made. I had all I needed in Paris. I had my family, my apartment, my work, my car. I no longer had my husband, but at thirty-seven nothing is hopeless, and anyway, I didn't intend to marry again.

I took the course at the *ulpan* for five months. I was a good student. In the afternoons I would sit and recopy all my class work. After five months I was able to speak some faulty Hebrew. Through people I had met, I found a job in Tel-Aviv and a room nearby. I shared the bathroom with another tenant. It was 1971. In September I was lucky enough to get a single room in the center of town, thanks to the Jewish Agency. I got help because I wasn't one of those people who bang on the table and declare, "I need something." I felt very comfortable in that place. I didn't have furniture because I hadn't had mine sent from Paris, but I was fine.

At the beginning of 1971 after the Six Day War, euphoria reigned, but I didn't much like what I had seen at the *ulpan*. There were many Americans and I think their arrival was a catastrophe. In talking with these young people, I realized that some came after having tried everything else. After having tried psychiatry, after having tried drugs, they were sent by their parents to Israel with a lot of money. The euphoria, in my opinion, damaged Israel a lot. It opened the door to many volunteers who arrived in the kibbutz. Then Israel opened to the entire world, for better or for worse. The country needed to evolve, but the change did not always take the best direction. We became somewhat the master race. That's when it began: "Chosen people, self-assured and domineering." You can't say that de Gaulle was completely wrong; Israel was drunk with her victory. Many people arrived, some good, some not so good. Everything opened up—Jerusalem, the Great Jerusalem. They started to think about Great Israel. They began to think about settlements. It all started at that time.

In Tel-Aviv, I started to work, but I had no interest in my new job and felt I was getting nowhere. I then went back to the France-Israel Association where I got to know some people. Through several contacts, I met people who, to this day, remain my best friends. One of them was a lawyer whose wife worked with him. She, too, is of French origin and has lived in Israel since the 1950s. This was an important contact for me. We had things in common. She was a year younger than I, her father had also been deported, and she was the only child left with her mother. Our relationship was excellent. Her husband had a lot of business with France and I could work with him in French. My Hebrew was still faulty. I never liked writing in Hebrew.

So I worked until Kippur. From the religious perspective, I learned about Israel with my first Kippur. I got up, I ate, I smoked a cigarette and suddenly, during the afternoon, I noticed life was stopping little by little. There was no longer any traffic. No one left in the streets, no radio. The airport was closed. I heard nothing more. At the time I lived near the zoo; I started to hear the animals. I really felt something settle on my stomach. It was very impressive. Anyone who hasn't been in Israel for Kippur doesn't know what Kippur is. I began to think about it. I thought about fasting because I wasn't comfortable. I had never done it before (I took off work but I didn't fast).

I had maintained contact with the secretary of the firm where I had worked previously. It was through her that I met my second husband, Tzvy. In September 1972 I fasted with him and I entered into Israeli life. I had to speak Hebrew. I continued *ulpan*—that was imperative. My husband, true to the tradition of Polish Jews, said to me, "You know, where I'm from, wives don't work." That was a problem for me because I had worked all my life. He then proposed that I help him with his business. I actually helped him in his little weaving business. I did the accounts and called on clients.

My second husband was born in Poland, but his family had left in the early 1930s to go to Romania by way of Kichinev, Iassi, and then Bucharest, where his father set up business. The family had been in textiles for several generations. His father started all over and was responsible for the Jewish community in Romania. He was killed by the Germans. My husband arrived in Israel in 1948 after having stayed in a camp at Cyprus. He was six years older than I. He already spoke Hebrew, as did everyone in his family, because he belonged to a very religious family of Zionists. My husband's mother dreamed of seeing her son become a rabbi. He was conflicted. He believed deeply but was not about to become a rabbi. Still, he studied four years in a yeshiva. Then he decided to work as an engineer in the textile industry. He met a young girl in Cyprus who became his wife. They were married very soon after their arrival in Israel and had two children. When I met him, he had had his divorce papers in hand for six weeks. We immediately felt we had a lot in common, but given his recent divorce, I told him it was too soon for him to think about marriage. I wasn't ready to think about marriage either.

We began to see each other regularly. I worked and I continued to go to the *ulpan* in the evenings. I led a pleasant little life. Israel was exactly as I had expected. Everyone comes here with their own expectations. People are like this or like that; I can't expect them to change. I take them as they are. I knew one thing: I was Jewish; I had what I wanted. That's all. Finally, my husband and I decided to try it out; we lived together for one month. Meanwhile I met his children. I remember the day we ended this trial month. I had left a drawing of the wandering Jew with a pack on his back and I went back to my place. That same evening, he was there. He asked me, "What shall we do?" I answered, "What do you think we should do?" I left with him. We decided to marry and make our life together.

Meanwhile, his daughter had met an Israeli boy who lived in America and they decided to get married. She came to us to announce this in July of 1971, the day we had planned to go to the rabbinate. Obviously, the daughter took priority. She married the following October and left for America. We were married in December of that same year.

For the first time, I became acquainted with the rabbinate in Israel, which gave me a bit of a problem. In the Jewish religion there is what is called the *halitzah*. I was a widow, and the deceased husband's brother must marry the widow or give his permission for her remarriage. When I presented myself, the rabbi asked me if my first husband had brothers. I answered that they died in the ghetto in Warsaw. "Well then, prove it." I then had a problem. I knew I could lie, but I also know nothing can be built on a false base. So what was I to do? Indeed, there had been so many cases in Israel after the war that they had to take precautions. Some women had declared their husbands dead in the deportation and then suddenly the husband reappeared after the woman was remarried. So I searched for people who had known the family of my first husband. Luckily I was able to find two who testified that his brothers really had died in the Warsaw ghetto. But it is a long process. I must admit that when you find yourself in front of three rabbis, you don't feel like lying. You know that you have to tell the truth. It is very impressive. I will never forget one of them who wore a long black robe and reminded me of Shylock, whom I had seen in the theater portrayed by Daniel Sorano. It ended well and we were able to marry in December of 1972.

I then had to confront another problem: my husband was very religious. Some members of his family are *Hahedim* (the word "*hahed*" means in fact that you fear God). They are very religious and very God-fearing, especially those who have returned to religion and who become even more fanatical than the others. It is difficult to live with these people. Even my husband put on the *tefilin* every morning. I had warned him that I didn't see myself wearing long sleeves and a wig, but I was ready to make concessions. As he was an intelligent man who had known another life, he answered that we would find middle ground. He asked me to keep a kosher home and not to cook on Saturday. That didn't bother me at all. I would prepare the Shabbat plate and I found it very pleasant. When Friday came we hurried around. I really omitted nothing. I was Jewish. My husband knew that I did all these ceremonial things for him. In return, he told me, "For you, away from the house, I am ready to go to your friends and do what you want." Everything went very well. My house was kosher to the point that even some of his family came to my house for Pessah (and still ate). Going to someone's house for the Seder indicates that things are as they should be, with four kinds of dishes. At our house, Pessah was Pessah. To this day, I keep the house kosher out of respect for him. If someone had told me that I would light the candles on Friday evening, that I would have a kosher home and that I would eat kosher at home, I would have said, "You're kidding; not I!" After eating all I had eaten in France, I would have said it was unthinkable, but when you meet an open-minded person, each takes a step toward the other. It goes very well and I assure you that I found great pleasure on Friday evenings during the Kiddouch.

Three months after our marriage, Benny, my husband's son, came to live with us. He was seventeen years old and wanted to study law. We were ready to help him in all respects. He left for the army as a pilot for six years. Young people generally go to the Kotel (the Wailing Wall) before their military service, whether or not they are believers, and we went with him there.

Nineteen hundred and seventy-three brought the first shot of the Yom Kippur War. It was the first trauma for Israel. This war truly destroyed something. This deeply shocked me. I will never forget the face of Golda Meir when she spoke on television at the time of Souccoth, shortly after Yom Kippur. Today I still think that this should never have happened to us. Never. It resulted from being a little drunk with pride after the victory . . . You know, as the saying goes, when the cat is no longer hungry, he falls asleep and doesn't see what's happening around him. That's exactly what happened. There were economic problems.

But I had a nice life. Friends began to show up. At that time I had lived in Israel for a year and a half. It all happened very fast. Just when I expected nothing, I acquired a new family, with brothers-in-law, sisters-in-law . . . No doubt at the beginning I seemed a little strange; I was the little Parisian who arrived. Then we moved. That's when we suffered a hard blow in February 1977. My husband had an accident at work. Given that he was an engineer, he repaired his own machines. When he was lying on the ground, a huge roll of metal came loose and fell on his back. In March 1977 an operation was performed on his spine—not very successfully. In July 1977, a second operation. That same month, Benny received his pilot's wings. My husband was convalescing and his condition was degenerating little by little until 1979 when he had to give up his factory. He first walked with a cane, then with crutches. Later it was a wheelchair. That's when we decided to make a trip to the United States despite my husband's handicap. In fact, after the army, Benny wanted to try his luck there. He found his mother and his sister again; he stayed there.

One of the reasons I'm not crazy about America is that the Israelis swear by her. It was the fashion at the time for the young Israelis to leave for America, the country where everything was possible. They were ready to do there what they weren't ready to do in Israel. As a Zionist, it bothered me greatly to see the young people finish the army and go off to America, most of the time to stay! They found a strong Israeli community in America. Of course, everyone has the right to lead his life as he wishes. I spoke later about this with Benny. I explained to him that the Israelis always talk about the "Jews of the *Gola.*" I told him: "But you, in fact, you are the new Diaspora! Look at yourselves! You live together, you speak Hebrew, your children go to Jewish schools. You do exactly what you criticize us for. Get it into your head that you have nothing to reproach us for. You speak of America as the land of plenty, but until the 1930s America was nothing. There had to be the influx of immigrants from Europe for America to develop." I had many discussions with Benny on this subject. He asked my advice one evening before Yom Kippur. I responded: "If your mother and sister weren't there, you wouldn't be leaving here. You have everything you need here. You want to try your luck. I would have done so after having studied. Study first. You can go back then. You may make a little money, but that doesn't mean that you will have the culture."

After all was said and done, he left.

In 1984 my husband was operated on for stomach cancer. He either didn't know or didn't want to know the truth. He had sold the business, but he knew how to stay busy. He had always loved photography. He developed this hobby within his physical limitations and he succeeded in completing a beautiful exhibition of portraits. I couldn't leave him alone because he was very limited. He underwent a serious operation, things dragged on, they more or less hid the truth from him. He couldn't do the radiation. Nothing at all. Ten months later, it was over. On December 31, 1984, while the world was celebrating New Year's Eve, I closed his eyes. Then, of course, the children came. My first husband died on the evening of Yom Kippur and the other on New Year's Eve. I don't care for holidays.

After my husband's death, I had to start back at square one. I had to work, but I wasn't forty years old anymore; I was fifty-four and one-half. Less than two months after his death, I found work in the surgery unit of a hospital. I stayed there ten and a half years. At the beginning, I sterilized the instruments, which I didn't like at all; I needed some human contact. I then helped the nurse care for patients before going into the operating room and they gave me a lot of autonomy. The physical work was hard, but it gave me considerable satisfaction. When you've known situations as bad as mine, only work can help, I think. That's what I did both times. I threw myself completely into my work. I must admit that starting life again as I did at over fifty years old is not easy. I had very good warm friends. I had kept my friends from fifty years ago, and I now had some others for thirty years. Undeniably, many things have changed, but even so one finds warmth and the family remains close. On Friday evenings we are together. In France people say, "We have to get together, we have to call one another." Here it is different: "Moshe . . . if you go by, come up . . . If I'm not there, I'm not there."

When I add it all up, I feel completely satisfied in Israel. The idea of returning to France has never even crossed my mind. When my husband died, my family suggested I return to France. I answered, "You forget that I made my *alyah*; for me it's out of the question." Three years ago as my retirement gift, I went to France to see my family. I also went for the eightieth birthday of my oldest sister. I had intended to make the trip next year for the eightieth birthday of my second sister, but as I don't think she is well physically, I thought it was wiser to go to France this year. In fact, I go especially to keep contact with my immediate family. They have stopped visiting me now. The last trip my brother and his friend made was at least eight years ago. My relationships with my in-laws are still very warm. Benny still lives in the United States. He married an Israeli girl. They have two daughters. His sister, who has a son, also lives in America.

From a material point of view, life is hard in Israel. Everything has become very expensive. I have practically no retirement pension from France; I left there too early. I have always worked with my husbands without pay. I manage to live reasonably well, but it is clear that I can't do anything extravagant. When I come back from a trip, I always feel a strong tug at the thought of "coming home." The apartment where I live belongs to me; it is pleasant and well located. I live quite comfortably. I have friends. On balance, I think it's amazing what I was able to do with my life. Everything began again at age forty: starting a home with a son, starting another career . . . I scarcely have free time. I take courses at the university; I go once a week to volunteer at the hospital. A little job came to me by chance as a reader for a publishing house. I make the selection of books that arrive in French before they are trans-lated; it is a real joy and I earn some money doing it.

At age sixty-eight I am doing what I always dreamed of doing. In a certain sense, I think that yes, my life is a success. I never complain. That's how I keep my friends. Everyone has his own story. If you take on a tragic air, you won't have anyone left around you. Personally, I am alone within my four walls, but that's life. That's all. In rereading this narration of my life, I see what is missing, but I have neither the audac-ity nor, even less, the desire to bare my soul.

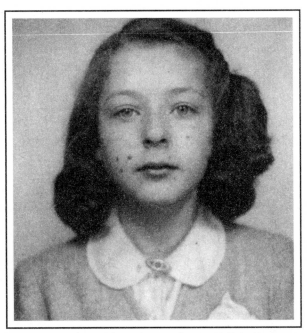

FIGURE 16.1. Gaby at age twelve in 1942 in Paris.

# 16

# Gaby Netchine-Grynberg

**May 21, 2003**

*Gaby Netchine-Grynberg is a psychologist. She works with children's cognitive and functional development and the study of psychological manifestations of dysfunctional disorder. She has done research at CNRS and has two children and four grandchildren.*

Dear Danielle,

You have invited me to hunt for a memory—to recall the memories of someone who has disappeared—the child, the adolescent that I was in another time, in another place. A familiar child whom I certainly knew, but from whom I have—or who herself has—progressively moved away. This is, of course, banal, but how can I re-create for you, for everyone, for myself, what really happened, what I really experienced? Since the last witnesses of my childhood have died—I was born in Paris in 1930 and it's now 2003—I have learned to accept the haziness of the past. Furthermore, I have a problem: what you ask of me is focused. But this fate was not our plan. What must I tell? The fate, itself a banality? The plan? Good grief! Must I go beyond the narrative itself?

Impossible. As for the authenticity of times long past, I can only guarantee my accounts of love and rebellion . . .

You asked about my "origins"; where did I come from? I will start there, even though as a child of political immigrants who came from Poland in 1922, happy to quickly become French, I never knew any family except my parents. Those faraway grandparents, those uncles and aunts, those dear friends, all those people to whom my parents were obviously close, for me belonged to the realm of letter-writing.

But I will try to retrace the memory of the past as told to me, the stories my parents told me about their lives as children at the beginning of the century, their century, the twentieth century in Czarist Poland in the industrial city of Lodz. Stories that evoked a family, certainly, but also the interwoven path of diverse individuals who, like people everywhere at that time in Europe, were struggling toward the modernity of their century, a formidable modernity then, as always, only dimly perceptible.

I believe my parents took shape somewhere in this uneven march that they shared with their friends, even more than within their family. I, in turn, was shaped not so much by being their child or by the forced lethargy of a hidden child, but in an equally uneven march, partly conducted with my parents, partly with my contemporaries who were also struggling. Except that *we* weren't cut down in the middle of our lives.

I'll start with my father's story of his childhood, which he told me on my twelfth birthday, March 20, 1942. He described his home in Lodz, the courtyard onto which the small lodgings opened, his own room at the top of a stairway. He told about the miracle of kerosene lamps, the dazzle of gas lamps. He spoke of the smell of bad breath in the little synagogue and the stench of bog toilets he endured because there, alone at last, he could read in peace. He described the faces of some of the ancestors—a drunk who went by horse-drawn carriage from inn to inn to drink, a fabric peddler who traveled far and wide to get merchandise, even a painter, because nothing was completely stratified. His father had told him about his own father who, having suffered the failure of a secular revolt that took place in Poland mid-nineteenth century, returned to traditional life and the love of the Talmud. Raised in poverty and religion following this decision, my grandfather developed a real hatred for those who driveled on, the eternal commentators on commentaries, who shut themselves off from the world of the living. To give a sense of the intensity of this rejection, I refer to the beginning of this grandfather's autobiography. He should have continued it and told in his own words about his flight to the United States at the end of the nineteenth century, his adventures as a peddler in the Far West and as a diver during the building of the Brooklyn Bridge (or was it the one in New Jersey?), his poverty and his solitude when he fell ill, his eventual return to Poland after having learned the English accounting system, which was highly esteemed in the textile industry in Lodz. Decidedly modern, he sent his first child, even though she was a girl, to the Russian gymnasium, and, of course, the two sons who followed, one of which was my father. All three fortunately breached the barrier of the *numerus clausus* imposed on Jewish children and became, respectively, a teacher, an engineer, and an entomologist. Except for my father, who didn't like the nationalists, this family—my grandparents, uncle, and aunt—left for Palestine in the 1920s. The one person absent from this story is my grandmother whom nonetheless my father said he loved dearly. The story of my father's childhood was long and detailed, so when lunch was served, he put aside the story of his teenage years for my next birthday. But less than six weeks later, he was arrested and disappeared into hell.

Looking at my mother's family, the generational path parallels the rapid shift from the traditional lifestyle, which was no doubt already deteriorating (but hasn't it always been that way?), to the industrial activity that created different kinds of work and new ways of life, and from that to make an escape—revolutionary or Zionist—into a world that people then were eager to take on, often to be taken down in the attempt. I know nothing about the background of my maternal grandfather, who wore mustaches like the Gauls, except that he came from the town of Kalisz, where his family intermixed rabbis with manufacturers of sheer fabrics that they sold in Russia. My grandmother's family descended from Sephardic Jews living in Strasbourg in the sixteenth century, according to a family tree that disappeared in the Holocaust. The family history made note of long lines of rabbis, of "miraculous rabbis" going back to the previous generation, that of my grandmother's uncles whom my mother knew. My mother's father was one of those men, technicians and businessmen at the same time who, with their German counterparts, at the turn of the century built the textile industry in Poland, more specifically in Lodz where my grandfather and his brothers-in-law established and owned a large part of that industry. (I inherited only four pillows and two tablecloths.) In this family, the women had leisure time and were not self-effacing. According to my mother, in her grandmother's generation and doubtless even further back, the women adhered to the Haskalah philosophy—a Judaism revisited by the Enlightenment, rational and open to civil society. They read the German Romantics in the original language, which gave them entry into the universal culture. My grandmother seems to have been a person of some prominence. Her generosity was widely known and her reputation spread to the Czar's military men, whose respect for her allowed her son to escape the draft that was so dreaded by the Jews.

How did these rich and completely secular people live? Based on what I know from the stories of my mother, from her cousins who were spread over the world during the 1920s and 1930s and whose numerous representatives I met after the war (mine), I strongly dispute Wajda's description in his 1975 film, *The Promised Land*, of the milieu of these great Jewish industrialists of Lodz, whom he characterizes as licentious and hedonistic capitalists in contrast to the poor and pure Polish proletariat. In the first place, the industrialists weren't all Jewish or German, nor the proletariat purely Polish. There were many proletarians who were Jews working in the factories of the Jewish industrialists. I met some of them whose lives were certainly hard and poor and whose rancor toward my family was tenacious. But the ethics of these industrialists were neither depraved nor dissolute. While religious faith rapidly faded, the family atmosphere remained austere, the morals strict, the family respected, the education rigorous. The children had to study. (What did they have to study? Everything! Knowledge was an end in itself.) In short, the categories of ethnicity and social status were far from being superimposed, and the record of the class war starting in Lodz concurrent with the development of the textile industry does not deserve such distortion.

I now must add that the children of these industrialists themselves participated sometimes in the class war; a good education opens one's eyes. So it was with my mother's oldest brother, he who had been saved from the draft. A brilliant young man, he abandoned his studies and position to organize with some friends a revolutionary working-class group inside the Bund. They chose the Bund because the Jews found an intractable anti-Semitism in the Polish workers' parties, and fighting against it seemed like a waste of time, since anti-Semitism would be resolved sooner or later by the Revolution or at least by social evolution (a point of view that I shared for a long time, but apparently anti-Semitism, like the phoenix, keeps rising from its own ashes). The Russian Revolution was starting; he helped spread it in the Czarist territories, and then was put in prison by either the Russians or Germans, who succeeded one another in Poland during World War I—

their war. He caught typhus and died before his thirtieth birthday. My mother was sure that her mother also died as a result and that, in a way, the entire family was broken and lost its spirit and cohesion by losing the two of them.

Doubtless such a trajectory is extreme in its contrasts, its brutality and its brevity. But it rather naturally introduces the story of the new generation—that of my uncle, of my parents, their cousins and friends who were ending their secondary studies at the end of their war—a generation born into secularization associated with industrialization, not to be confused with either political emancipation or the secularization of society, which was not yet accomplished under the reign of the Czar. This generation came of age mostly but not entirely in the Czarist gymnasia where these young Jews, relatively ignored by the Russians and totally ignored by the Polish, formed strong networks that they maintained all their lives, despite their geographical dispersion, their dangerous political involvements, and the new war, World War II, which was also theirs—only twenty years after the previous one ended—but was now my war, too. Young people formed groups that met regularly, sometimes at one person's home, sometimes at another's, then later, during the long excursions into the forests of birch and pine. Of course, there were a few romances, but there was a collective life within the group. If you were officially invited "for tea and discussion," there would be a debate about some literary movement or an evaluation according to the rules of the judiciary of some character from Pushkin. There was a prosecutor to describe the affair, a lawyer, and jury members. Nevertheless, their activities were not confined to the gymnasium. The period was aflame: pogroms of the Cossacks of the Czar; revolutionary movements, Zionist developments, the First World War, fall of the Czarist Empire, quickly followed by the war undertaken by Poland against the young Soviet Revolution. All these events accompanied this generation from elementary school to gymnasium and on to the university.

The choices and polemics were then between Zionism and socialism, socialism inside or outside the Bund, and between the numerous leanings the movement brought together—several paths to answers to the vital questions. My parents were educated in the juncture of these networks that brought together most of the Jewish youth. It was a juncture that was cultural as well as political, functioning as a sounding board for all the new knowledge, an initiation point for all the problems of the time, a center of motivation for all the commitments. If I could draw up the catalog of what my parents' library consisted of when they were in Poland, it would be a surprising library for the variety and topicality of the areas covered. I don't know of any study of those networks that helped an entire youth cohort, whose parents had already escaped the old way of life and the old social strata to form themselves into a group reflective of the culture and the commitments of their time. The movement was accomplished under the double aegis of the malaise and utopias of the time. Today it is too late and that is too bad. Decimated by the blows of history and the diversity of their choices, not labeled as a community because they were entering into the universal, their dual originality—where they came from and where they were going, or falling—placed them outside any specific annals.

During my entire childhood, before World War II (my war) and especially afterward, I saw these people visit us, one after another, expected or not, in good form or a little haggard. The doorbell would ring; I would open the door and these strangers, seeing me, would basically say that I was the living image of my father. I was used to it; I would make tea and call my mother. Others I met much later. What had they become after their post–World War I Poland (their war)? They were scattered throughout the universities in various European capitals, often chosen because of the discipline they studied. The majority had become Communist. Several couples, their engineering studies completed, returned to the USSR to help build the socialist society, and spent decades there and even survived (these are the only ones I heard about). Others engaged themselves in the party apparatus; others joined the International Brigades in Spain; one traveled from Greece on old boats to clandestinely transport weapons. Many were in various Resistance groups in France. One of them, very "Viennese" in appearance who was very close to my parents and always brought me chocolates, did economic spying on behalf of the USSR. I also knew a cousin of my mother, a historian, who had belonged to a group of Jewish partisans in the forests of Lithuania. He then left with his companions for Palestine where they founded northeast of Saint-Jean-d'Acre a kibbutz of former partisans specializing in the history of the Jews' fight against Nazism, but also specializing in Yiddish culture, novel then in that area. There was the wife of a minister of Gomulka, a sister to Golda Meir, a professor of mathematics at Yale, and quite a few middle-class "bourgeois bohemians" in Montparnasse—cousins from Lodz who had chosen French culture. We were very close to the latter ones, especially to the one I called Uncle Mark, a sweet eccentric, an esthete and a physicist, the last news of whom came from my father who wrote from the Compiègne internment camp, "I had the sad pleasure of finding Mark here," which he wrote shortly before the "departure." After the Liberation, my mother and I settled in Mark's apartment on rue d'Assas, where the atmosphere quieted me. I almost forgot cousin Edmund—a great specialist in lead soldiers and a friend of Romain Gary (*A European Education*) and adviser to Kissinger—who finished out his life listening to music on his Yankee wife's ranch. And there was a cousin who had a candy factory in Valence, another was an industrialist in Chicago, there was the professional Marxist of MAPAM with a big crown of hair—white when I knew him—and others as well.

"Gaby, you can't imagine," my mother would tell me, overwhelmed when one of them appeared after the war (our war). Actually I couldn't imagine, and furthermore I didn't want to. All these people spoke Polish, which I understood, but the exact meaning of their discourse escaped me, and if I asked for explanations, I, the intruder, was viewed with astonishment—who is interrupting us? My mother with whom I almost felt myself to be a partner would answer me, "My dear, it's untranslatable." Usually I didn't ask questions; we weren't of the same world. I was thus always surrounded, not by unspeakable secrets or taboos, but by the incommunicable. I was a foreigner to these cosmopolites. So don't talk to me about roots! In place of the horticultural metaphor, I prefer the cosmic model of the complexity of time/space, where it is necessary but difficult to anchor the observer's point of view, an observer who is always watching from elsewhere. (By the way, where the devil did Einstein's model come from?) The incommunicable was said and not said about a past always heavy with the coming catastrophes, but with refusal and hope interwoven many times over. I planned and carried out my hope and my revolt in a completely different way. All in all, my mother and her friends, and I and mine, have not so much faltered, as failed—but we did try.

What was the path of my parents themselves? Married at the end of World War I (their war) before leaving to study chemistry (always textile) in Warsaw, they didn't stay there very long. Their life in Poland came to an abrupt end in 1922, at the time of the Polish-Russian War, which served to obscure the military intervention of the European nations—including France—against the young Bolshevik Revolution. The students at Warsaw University were then ordered to join the war against the Soviets. My parents organized a movement against this war and against all such engagements. As a consequence, they were put in prison and then liberated, thanks to my maternal grandfather's money, but they promptly had to flee. They chose to go to France, land of liberty and the Rights of Man, where they completed their studies at the University of Strasbourg. They then decided to stay in that country where they thought they could become normal people, free from anti-Semitism, doing whatever they could for their universal objectives. They were promptly (but temporarily) rewarded for their choice with naturalization obtained in 1929 and went to settle in Paris in the Thirteenth Arrondissement.

My father was lucky. Despite the Depression, he found work. My birth was not what he would have wanted, because he thought that this world was no place to bring up a child. My mother insisted, and I was born on March 20, 1930. My mother then left professional life. Unfortunately for my parents—who were so attached to Paris and also to their numerous friends (always the network) who lived or passed through there—the company that hired my father was in full expansion, and he was charged with bringing up to speed the manufacture of products in the newly opened factories on the coast of Normandy at Villers-Cotterêts in 1933, and then at Honfleur in 1938. So we moved a lot. Another major event: at age seven, I had the great stroke of luck to suddenly get a big brother, my recently orphaned cousin Daniel, who returned from Palestine where he had been born twelve years earlier. Our life was pleasant—a nice house, garden, trips and a car, with no extra money, but never mind! Who worries about tomorrow when thinking only of today? Clearly my parents sometimes felt a little cheated. What happened to their great hopes? Instead of a better world, the dangers increased. The wonderful life in France? They suffocated in these little provincial towns, and with every new world event, at each turn of the Party's politics, they took the car and went to Paris to confer with friends, to understand and to criticize.

As for what happened to the Revolution in the USSR, they knew from some members of the network, but also as did everyone who was willing to know. As a matter of fact, it was hard for them to admit the truth and they constantly debated the problem. There was the rise of Nazism, certainly the joy of 1936, but also the rise of the Extreme Right in France, without mentioning the closing of the borders in Palestine and everywhere else in the world, the equivalent of a death sentence for Jews, all of which they knew about, too. From our beautiful garden of Villers-Cotterêts in which my father had planted birches, I could hear Hitler's speeches.

The war in Spain was closely followed as it went along, but I didn't understand what a civil war was. I understood a normal war, like the war of 1914–1918. At Villers-Cotterêts, where one of the first big tank battles had taken place, the forest was full of rusted helmets and bayonets, and in the wall at the back of the garden, just under the birds' nests, I enjoyed gathering, not eggs, but bullets stuck between stones. But a civil war? Was it one street against another street? No, I was told, but I never obtained a satisfactory answer. When the camps were opened in France to "shelter"—actually, to detain—the Spanish refugees, my parents loaded up the car with half my toys and lots of other things to take to the detainees. On the way, we saw a bus where hands were outstretched in a Nazi salute through the open windows. My parents responded with clenched fists. Daniel admired that and still talked about it decades later. I was unhappy; my toys were leaving, but then why start a quarrel? By the time we could open the car windows, wasn't the bus already too far away?

I remember very well also the debasing treaty of Munich. I was the one who went to buy the papers and I read them on the way home. On the one hand, I was sorry there would not be war because that would have been fun; on the other hand, I didn't want to see my father leave. It was I again who, during a nice vacation day in the mountains, first read the newspaper on the day of the Non-Aggression Pact between the USSR and Germany. When I told my parents about it, facing the depth of emotion I had unleashed, I tried to console them by saying that Stalin was only trying to gain some time, but they didn't listen to me. Soon, again in the car, on the way to pick up Daniel in his Scout camp, we spent a feverish night in Paris talking with the friends of the Comintern and, back at Honfleur, it was the war, mine and my parents', *our* war.

And that is where you are waiting for me, dear Danielle. You want me to return to the memory reserve, armed with my butterfly net, to catch some new memories. So be it, but I warn you: what this net will soon catch will be painful to remember and painful to relate, not because the memories are mine, but simply because such things happened. But a child is essentially too busy with growing up and discovering her own body, her own mind, the world. In the beginning, I was a little girl, but I soon went into puberty and that kept me very busy. And so forth. What I am going to tell is, in a certain way, only a normal love of life. That said, since we have to, let's do it.

At the beginning, the war was as amusing as I had hoped. My father, designated as being in a "special situation" at the factory, was not leaving and Honfleur at last came alive. At Honfleur I loved the lights, the sky, the mouth of the Seine that could be seen from my parents' room, the romanticism of the interconnecting waters of the estuary—today for the most part gone—that put the sea and its boats in the middle of the city, the presence in the streets of the past and of far off trips, about which our teacher detailed the landmarks for us with passion. But so what! It took a lot of dreams to overcome the cold and humid filth of this city, its moribund character continuously restated by the rhythmic sound of the dredgers fighting against the sands coming into the port, the narrow-mindedness of its petite bourgeoisie, who only appeared to have maintained middle class status while the evidence of poverty was real. With the war people were finally talking in the streets and in the shops, the walls were covered with posters read and commented upon, the town filled with Parisian refugees. At school, instead of vaunting a memorable past, the teachers talked about the maps of a war that was not yet really happening. In short, Honfleur was alive.

Our household also received its own share of refugees who filled the usually empty room on the third floor: a cousin from Montparnasse and an entire family—father, mother, and a child of my age—cousins from Lodz who that year were spending their vacation in France. There were three children at the house with new games usually played by young Polish peasants, introduced by the young cousin. From this family came the first bits of startling information: barely into Lodz, the Germans came to the home of the cousin, the president of the association of volunteers enlisted in the French army (with him it was just an affectation; he actually spent his vacations in France each summer after war was declared) and not finding him there, they shot his maid and his dog. No matter, we were going to win because we were the strongest. But soon the routine returned. Because there was no bombing in Paris, all the cousins left and the Calvados coast emptied of its late vacationers. I took up my reading again and my long solitary bicycle rides along the silt-filled basins and abandoned docks. (Children, even as protected as I was, were much freer than they are today.) Daniel improved his galena radio set.

All too soon came the merry month of May and inevitably the tenth of the month, May 1940. That morning like every other, I was late for school and I ran from basin to basin, when just in front of the Lieutenancy I stopped, petrified by the news coming over a loud radio. The

Germans had already deeply penetrated France, and how the devil could they be stopped now that they had surrounded the Maginot Line? Scarcely begun, the battle for France already seemed lost. More and more tardy, I started running again and amazingly, instead of teaching the class, the teacher was wringing her hands. Instead of scolding me, she asked me what the latest news was. Very often after that, I seemed to be saved from a reprimand for a bad grade or from the shame of some incident by an alert, a bombing, an invasion, an arrival of the police, or some other turn of events that worried me less than the revelation of my scholarly deficiencies in that period when I gradually stopped studying seriously. The personal life and career of children is school, isn't it?

A few days after this May 10, leaving in Honfleur my "special situation" father and my cousin Daniel—of an age who must finish the school year (ah, "studies or life")—my mother and I left Honfleur and took the train to the small village of Saint-Saturnin-des-Bois in west central France. There we were taken in by a charming old lady, a beekeeper who kept—in addition to her bees—cows, chickens, and rabbits. She was the mother-in-law of one of my father's colleagues and the grandmother of a girl my age who soon joined us along with her own mother. My new friend and I plunged into a rather cheerful, honeycomb-scented rural life. We would lead the cows to pasture, armed with canes and with our hair tied with tricolored pieces of yarn to show our convictions.

Unfortunately our pieces of yarn didn't save France, and soon the village's main street, which wasn't built for it, vibrated under the weight of a cohort of trucks from the Honfleur factory. My father was directing their flight toward Lacq, which already smelled of gas and where all the sectors of the company were converging. The emotion of finding one another, then the departure, thrilled Daniel and me as we crossed the open countryside standing atop one of the military trucks. Then we plunged anew into rural life, but this time it was a poor and bitter rural life—that of a little farm in the Landes in south central France where I learned to hoe potatoes, open and take out the kernels from pinecones warm from the cinders, and where Daniel practiced hypnotizing the chickens.

Then one morning Daniel wasn't there. After endless debates, my parents had decided to send him to the Unoccupied Zone because, born in Palestine, he was a British subject, thus an enemy alien in Honfleur in the Occupied Zone to which we were returning. The hope was that from Marseille, Daniel could take a boat to Beirut, and then get to

Palestine. Daniel, I was later told, had spent the night before his departure trying to convince my father to come with him to the Unoccupied
Zone. Why didn't he, then or later? I can only hypothesize. No doubt it
was Daniel's disappearance that made me feel vulnerable for the first
time.

In autumn, Honfleur again became a gray town, with squads of bil-
leted soldiers singing, "Heïli heïlo!" I raged against my parents because
they weren't taking advantage of the last merchandise in the stores, and
I decided to go alone to buy myself those shoes and that coat that
would last me for years, telling the merchants that my parents would
stop by to pay. Such was the power of a little ten-year-old bourgeois.

My parents had other concerns; should they declare themselves as
Jews? The statute about Jews had been issued and rigorously applied in
the "Forbidden Zone" of the Calvados coast. We were especially concerned since, as the only Jews in Honfleur, we were the target of all the
institutions. "Jew"—this term had no meaning for me. My mother's
cookbook was entitled *The Recipes of Aunt Marie*. The holidays observed at home were birthdays and Christmas, because the tree evoked
far-off forests (a mistaken sign of belonging; at that time a tree in Honfleur indicated we were outsiders; my classmates hung their stockings
from the mantle). To me, the Jews were doubtless a variety of Poles
with family members in Palestine and friends in the Comintern and a
Christmas tree. Hadn't my parents thought they would be able to forget
this annoying distinction in France? Certainly they had never hidden
their identity from those around them, even in Honfleur—so why did
they need to declare themselves? It simply didn't interest them. But they
didn't refuse either, especially not in adversity. So when by way of comment about this dirty business falling on our heads, I said, "What bad
luck to be Jewish!" I received one of the three slaps my father ever gave
me. It was an initiatory slap but not confirming, followed by an incomprehensible speech.

Okay. For a while life went on. I started junior high and I am still
grateful for my history textbook and the Latin texts that transported me
far from the daily blackness. During the winter we made a trip to Paris.
There I felt vulnerable again. For the most part, the cousins and friends
were still there and all appeared normal. But the anxious concern in
the looks they exchanged with one another made me understand that
we were in another universe. What was new about the war? The news
was grim, but it was mixed into a daily life that had lost none of its
dynamism at this point. My father's work was still absorbing and

interesting. He was very happy to have been able to save the workers of the factory from unemployment by putting in place products and practices to ease the loss of overseas connections. The war was simply, from time to time, a problem that in and of itself touched us little. We were no longer allowed to have a radio so we went to a neighbor's. Granted, we learned there had been some arrests, but not just Jews. The Nazis, both French and German, did their Nazi job. They killed the insane, the Communists, the Jews. That was normal; they were Nazis, weren't they? The war simply had to be won. To a world dichotomy, there was good and evil (I had the right to think this way; I was ten years old in a black universe); another dichotomy as a response: die or be saved. Are children really afraid of death? Of their own, I think not; but of their loved ones, it's another story. In any case, I was not afraid, but my pain and anger increased progressively, which didn't stop me from playing, reading, even from learning the third Latin declension. Neither did I ever feel that I was subjected to an exceptional fate for the simple reason that, as events unfolded around me and as I understood them, I wasn't. Ever since seventh grade, I had had classmates whose brothers or fathers—Resistance fighters—had been deported or shot, as was my junior high English teacher. The disaster was ongoing, and school continued.

Let's get straight to the point, or rather to the climax. On April 15 and May 1, 1942, two attacks were perpetrated at Moult-Argences against trains carrying German soldiers on leave, resulting in a total of some forty fatalities and numerous casualties. In Calvados, a number of hostages were arrested, Jews and Communists, including my father. He was sent to the Royallieu internment camp in Compiègne, then deported July 6 to Birkenau where the camp registers, still carefully kept on that date, show he died July 31, 1942. But this last part I learned only recently.

The days following this arrest were days of great confusion. My mother didn't know exactly where my father had been taken. She didn't say anything to me; she told me any old thing. I knew, but in fact I didn't know anything. Each of us in our own way, enclosed in our silence, pretended things were still normal, but in fact we knew nothing about what was happening. Many days later, a tiny note came from Royallieu: "Life is not in danger and that is the essential thing." Really? Who would believe this?

That's when, like others, we had to wear the star. My mother was humiliated for me. I didn't care. In Honfleur we were known, and the

French and German Nazis were doing their job. Normal. That day, it was the school principal who took me to class, to English class where I was welcomed by this teacher who would be shot a few weeks later. I sat as always beside my friend, she whose brothers, charming guys of twenty who engaged in a kind of folkloric Resistance, had just been taken back to their parents' home by the police, stripped and beaten in the presence of their parents and my friend before being deported and put to death. But neither she nor I spoke of anything other than what we usually spoke of. These two scenes—her nude, beaten brothers and my arrival in the English class wearing the star—she recounted to me two or three years ago. I didn't know the details about her brothers; my own story vaguely evoked something, but nothing striking. Once again, I didn't care. My memory of those days was of my mother's solitude and her haunted look in occupied Honfleur where we didn't have a lot left to do, except to wait for news of my father. Moreover, we no longer had money.

A few weeks passed. It was almost the end of the school year when an envelope came in the mail containing two small squares of paper. One was from a group of railway workers in Aisne in the center of France, giving the date my father was to be deported. The second contained the path the convoy would take with corresponding dates. Did they think we were going to attack the train? Very soon, the doorbell at home began to ring regularly. A young man, unknown to us, brought us his sleeping bag. "Take it, he will need it." Another left a camp cooking outfit that he said would be useful. How did the news spread? Briefly, with the help of these anonymous people, two large suitcases were stuffed and my mother, accompanied by a Swiss *goy*, husband of one of the cousins from Montparnasse, went from station to station to find this train. I was taken care of by my grade school teacher. Back home on the day prizes had been distributed, I found an express letter that my mother sent me from Paris, to where she returned unsuccessful. "Take the train tomorrow and join me." This I did, which was very difficult, but which I enjoyed. I thought playing cops and robbers was a nice way to end childhood.

The Vel' d'Hiv' Roundup at the Parisian Sports Center was announced; the police bigwigs (from where the information to leave Honfleur came) passed the information and it needed to be spread. We went to a boarding house at Montparnasse where Mama's cousin and her Swiss husband were. We took letters to friends and acquaintances, and the last day my mother and her cousin telephoned the Jewish names in the directory until they were exhausted. The days arrived (July 16–17, 1942). Let's move past this, save for a single episode: From our room in the boarding house, I saw coming out of the building across the street a thirty-year-old man, his raincoat on his arm, a suitcase in each hand, held by two cops. Twenty years later, his son committed suicide when he got his draft notice for the Algerian War.

We were taken in by my preschool teacher from Villers-Cotterêts. She had been widowed at age twenty during World War I. She had converted to socialism after seeing the poverty of the North during the 1920s and 1930s. She had just been removed from her position by the Vichy government and was settling into the Paris suburbs. There, as simply as we could, the three of us settled in. The years passed, more and more depressing. Our own group of friends had been decimated; some disappeared because they managed to escape, others because they didn't. We settled in with my teacher. My mother lost all her personality and I adjusted as best I could. The group around my teacher, neighbors and friends, understood and helped discretely, notorious collaborators included. Despite all that, I hated this nice little bourgeoisie—not explicitly evil, but deeply indifferent to anything that didn't affect their comfort. My anger was great and my disdain enormous; it extended to everyone who pretended not to know, who arranged things so they wouldn't know.

Now I have to tell about the Resistance fighters of the Red Poster, whose names and pictures were displayed on posters all over town. I stole one of these posters from a tunnel where I walked regularly. I would rub against the photos saying to myself that at least these clandestine fighters had made a commitment; they had done it for me and for others like me. They had wanted to know and had wanted to act accordingly. For the first time I noticed that quite a few names were Jewish. Through them, I existed—we existed.

Fortunately, there still was, on my solitary bicycle rides, the forest of Saint-Germain with its ponds where I could swim, the banks of the Seine, the islands, the view of bargemen. There were also irregular English verbs that baffled me, and the high school biology course that pleased me a great deal. When everyday life was too bad, I imagined myself to be a leaf on a tree that the wind rustled near the ballasts. In the summer of 1943, I learned to swim in the Seine. In the spring of 1944 there were the bombings. That I loved; *they* were afraid—the prudent ones, those concerned about themselves—but *we* weren't. To the bombs, we were all alike. *They* ran for shelter; my mother seemed absent, and I looked and laughed at the bomb fragments falling around me, twisting as they cooled. I heard a loud muffled rumble along the Seine; it was the bombing of Rouen! Then I was sad because I loved Rouen. At last there were the Normandy Landings, the arrival of the Allies, a few patriotic songs on the balcony of the City Hall, and I started pushing for us to leave for Paris. "Don't even think of it, Honey. Suppose the Germans return?" But we did take one of the first trains for Paris. We were given the key to the apartment of Uncle Mark, and in October I started eighth grade at the Lycée Victor Duruy.

After that? My mother found work in a Jewish organization that continued the work begun during the war: armed Resistance and the saving of children. First, she went to get them where they had been hidden and took them to the children's homes that opened one by one. I was astonished: Why a Jewish Resistance when there had been the FFI and the FTP? I was told that that FFI and the FTP limited themselves to armed resistance, but the resisters from the Jewish organizations had a suitcase full of weapons in one hand and a child in the other. That opened a fault line with regard to the FTP but didn't bring me any closer to the others. Slowly, my mother was becoming herself again; she took on responsibilities and soon was leading a major social service organization. She took care of the orphans of France as well as those who had to be evacuated quickly from Poland because of the new pogroms, and, directly from their migrations, the children of Maghreb and the babies born to them too soon.

I had a difficult adolescence; I was ill, rebellious, in revolt. After the Liberation, at fourteen, I began wanting to be a militant. My view of good and evil had already been disillusioned; where was the good? I tolerated neither Dresden nor Hiroshima. I didn't like it either that when the French population was asked to turn in their weapons, they simply rolled up their sleeves and started to rebuild a modern order. There were still supporters nostalgic for Vichy, visible by their graffiti on the walk to school. A short time with the Party institutions had rapidly convinced me that revolution was not their objective. The Stalinist trials went on. I quickly became radically left-wing and anarchist. I advocated for the witches, the countercultures, but not for any avant-garde who "marched forward," nor for any nationalists who "moved in the Historical direction." This position had support. There was Sartre, Sartre before *The Communists and Peace*, there was especially the complex Camus, and also "Merleau" (Maurice Merleau-Ponty). There were those who, as I, became passionate at every event and threw themselves into every political experiment. In short, I, in turn, had my own network, well consolidated later in 1968. Meanwhile, I failed at the study of chemistry and excelled in the study of psychology. The real me, the one at least with whom I have continuity, dates from when I met Serge. My mother found inner peace when her grandchildren were born.

What do I draw from all this; what remains, you ask me, dear Danielle? Certainly it has colored the implicit nature of the issues underlying my own quest and the militant choices I tried; but where did the impetus come from? Hadn't my parents and their friends, in their time, on their terms, reacted in the same way? Not that I was explicitly their disciple, except for having received culture and a vision of society from them, but like them, I had to weave together my own malaise and ideology. I failed more than they did. All that was bound to happen anyway. At age ten, at age twelve, I was already hooked into some time/space to (re)construct. What meaning has "Jewishness" taken on since the Holocaust? I couldn't remain ignorant, facing something so enormous. I tried to gather information. Then I admitted that my being Jewish was only valuable for me as one of the extremes of the human condition, one of the aspects of universal Otherness. Perhaps I see myself as the Jew Sartre describes as merely being someone seen as Jewish by other people, but as also drawing from that a well-informed, moral, critical, and distanced practice of human universality (such heroes have existed). Thus it has a meaning relevant for some particular moments of history, likely to undergo change, which couldn't fail to happen in time. What has been passed to me specifically from having been "made Jewish" makes me have great pity for those whose lives have been mutilated and, at the most intimate level, the inexpungible memory of J., my friend, my twin. What else stays with me? The radical shame I deserve today vis-à-vis the children of Bosnia and Rwanda— the same disdain I once had for those who continued to live quietly in the presence of the unspeakable. But, dear Danielle, I still also have my *joie de vivre*. Ah! I forgot: "What will my grandchildren make of all these stories?" you ask. That will depend on the kind of world they experience. What can we hope for?

There you are.

Affectionately,

Gaby Netchine-Grynberg

FIGURE 17.1. Philippe at age seventeen.

# 17

# Philippe Fouquey

*Philippe Fouquey, whose Jewish family has been French since 1789, is a son and brother of Resistance fighters. He is an architect, now retired. He also directed an international publication reflecting on the civic role of architecture and urbanism. He still shows, by his actions, a solidarity with the oppressed and those who fight against injustice.*

The transcribed interview with me conducted by Danielle Bailly on March 28, 2003, and which I rewrote, revealed to me certain things about my perception of my countrymen; it also brought to my attention that I was incapable of putting my family history together with the history of the Jews of Alsace and Lorraine, where the family originated. I then tried to juxtapose these two histories, which to be truthful, until this interview I didn't really differentiate from one another.

In the first part of this narrative—my family and personal history—I kept the form of the original interview common to all of us who gave testimony. The diversity of our responses is revealing and clearly shows that we were in different wars; our experiences were often dissimilar, but in certain cases analogous, as were the lessons each of us took from them. The second part—certainly a more general consideration about the "long-time French" Jews—treats successively history per se and the matter of assimilation, notably cultural assimilation, through generations.

## Part One: My Family Origins

I was born June 27, 1930, in Paris, so I am now seventy-three.

On my father's side of the family, I have an impressive family tree that shows descendants from a forefather in 1713. His name is Samuel Verte and he was a stableman for Louis XV! This tree, started by one of my uncles, a graduate of École Polytechnique, is complete up to our generation, with more and more details about my ancestors born at the end of the eighteenth century, and then throughout the centuries that follow. What I know best about the history of this branch of my family obviously begins about 1850 with the generation of my great-grandparents. My great-grandmother, born in 1848, was older sister to eight brothers. All first settled in Nancy, where they were already part of the haute bourgeoisie, then near the end of the nineteenth century they brilliantly made a fortune in Paris, associated—I should say "evidently associated"—in real estate. Perhaps it was the defeat of 1870–1871 that caused them to leave Lorraine. So mainly—aside from that part of the family in Lille and Le Mans I will get to shortly—it is in Paris that this branch of my family established themselves and where their lives unfolded. In Lille and Le Mans, one of the eight brothers in about 1880, like in a story by Zola (*Au Bonheur des Dames*), established two large department stores from two blocks of houses and shops that had been vacated by their inhabitants. He entrusted the stores to two nephews, cousins, who then became coproprietors. One of them was my grandfather. Born in 1872, he, like his own father, was from Bar-le-Duc. His wife, my grandmother, came, as did her own ancestors and their line, from Sarreguemine and Nancy. (Incidentally, she died at the Rothschild Hospital after her arrest in 1944 when she became very ill.)

At the time of my birth, my parents were in transit between Lille—where they lived before and where my paternal grandparents still lived—and Le Mans, where the family had sent my father to take charge of the big department store I mentioned earlier.

I have no written sources of information about my mother's family. Her own mother was from Lorraine (born at Raon l'Étape), but she was part of a large family named Lang from Alsace, in Altkirch. According to my mother, her paternal ancestors, prior to settling in Alsace, came from the Rhine region. One of my great-uncles was mayor of Belfort. My great-grandfather had a Spanish name, but I don't know why. This is all I know about the origin of the maternal branch of my family.

As you see, all my ancestors were from Lorraine or Alsace.

My mother's family left Alsace, perhaps for the same reasons—the defeat of 1870–1871—which may have led my father's family to leave Lorraine. The difference is that my maternal great-grandparents, along with some cousins, didn't go to Paris, but rather to Dijon. My great-grandfather and his oldest son established a real estate firm there, which flourished and became important in the entire Bourgogne region. This family certainly lived well and comfortably—I would even say with style—but none of its members ever really made a fortune.

In my grandparents' generation, besides those working in real estate, there was a lawyer and an industrialist (my grandfather, with a partner, had a factory in Colmar). All the members of this family from Dijon were musicians, from the great-grandfather, a colossus who knew everything about opera, to the grandmother, her brother, her sister, then their children (my mother and my uncle—who went to live in Marseille—and all the others). All were first prize winners at the Conservatory of Dijon, whether in piano, violin, or violoncello. This musical tradition is perpetuated in the family.

Arriving at the 1930s of which I have personal memories, I can describe my own childhood impressions.

The families from Paris and Dijon were very different from one another. In Paris there were often family reunions attended by many family members. My parents, my sister, and I would go from Le Mans where we were living at the time. The atmosphere there was a bit stilted—immense apartments, servants, beautiful automobiles.

In Dijon at that time—where my mother's family had expanded to twelve close-knit families, theirs was not a worldly life, but they shared chamber music at one another's homes. An excellent violoncellist with a sound I have never forgotten, Maurice Maréchal, often joined in with the musicians of the family. I remember experiencing in Dijon in this atmosphere every September, along with my sister and my cousins, a kind of happiness.

I also add that my mother, born in 1901, earned a master's degree in philosophy between 1918 and 1920, and would frequently go to Paris to hear the lectures of the philosopher Alain.

In brief, the Paris family was rich and influential, the Dijon family was affluent; the next generation—that of my mother—became the cultured elite.

The two families had in common several generations of atheism or agnosticism. I never heard them speak about Jews, their traditions, their holidays—the names of which I learned (but not the significance) only after the return of the Jews from Algeria in 1962.

Despite my characteristic birth name, it is only with Pétain that I learned, brutally and painfully, as you will see later, that I was "Jewish."

I've given a context for my family; now I will tell my personal story.

Before the war I arrived in Le Mans in 1932, at the age of two. My father, as I indicated earlier, managed a large department store there with four hundred fifty employees. It was a sizeable building, the second largest in the city, after the cathedral. At the top of the building, huge spaces had been left for the managers' apartments. We lived in one of them. It was perhaps economical and spacious, but we felt cut off from the city. Le Mans was a very Catholic city. Not to go to a parochial school, as in my case, was a little unusual for a young bourgeois. I went to the *lycée*. Not to join the Scouts of France, which was Catholic, was almost a sin. I joined the Éclaireurs Unionistes, which was Protestant, because there was no secular scout group in Le Mans. My father and a surgeon friend started the Rotary International Club in the city; perhaps he was unconsciously attempting a kind of institutional assimilation. My mother, unimpressed by the local "high society," had as her only friends the teachers of Greek and philosophy from her daughter's school. (My sister was six and one-half years older than I.)

When I was in fourth or fifth grade I found the classroom deserted one day. Yellow fever? No. My absent classmates finally came, dressed in what seemed to me to be a disguise—the little girls as underage brides and the little boys as pages or penguins—the first communion! I only knew it to be a sign of the Catholic religion and that I had no religion at all. I felt a little like a minority on that occasion. Then I never thought of it again. Anyway, at that time my sister also did a kind of communion, but not very Catholic; I learned later it was the bat mitzvah. But she got lots of nice presents, including a microscope. Where did this mystical spirit come from? I never found out. In short, we were Jews but no one thought it important enough to tell me about it. I was even ignorant of many other aspects of reality; for example, I only learned after the war that in 1936—during the Popular Front—my father had been shut in his office by his employees, and the other managers in theirs. At the time I knew nothing about it. This innocence would make even more overwhelming the successive extraordinary blows I would receive after the defeat of 1940 and under the Occupation.

### THE "PHONY WAR"

In September of 1939 my father, like everyone else, was mobilized. He was a lieutenant in the Thirtieth Battalion of assault tanks (old tanks manufactured in 1916). He was deployed east of the Maginot Line. He didn't believe in the efficacy of this Maginot Line. He read the pamphlets by de Gaulle about the war movement and talked to me about it later. The war—the real one, the dramatic one—began much later. For me, the "Phony War" (September 1939–May 1940) was a kind of rebirth. A large number of members of my family, both closely and distantly related, including about ten cousins, arrived in Le Mans from Paris, Lille, and Marseille. We lived, a little like camping out, in a large manor house ten kilometers from Le Mans, constituting a kind of marvelous phalanstery. We would go to school by bicycle and watch the bombardments of the city of Le Mans from afar. As a side benefit, I got acquainted with the most distant part of my family, notably the dynasty of descendants of the eight great-great-uncles. I discovered all sorts of things. Paradoxically, it was a happy, fruitful year.

### THE EXODUS

On May 10, 1940, the Germans attacked. The phalanstery broke up. Each nuclear family left in turn, by car or on the last trains in operation. My mother, my sister, two cousins, and I also left, heading toward the southwest. At Sables-d'Olonne we learned that Pétain "gave us the gift of his person" and I saw my usually upbeat mother crying. She explained but I understood little; I was nine years old. At Bordeaux we tried to take the last boat for the United States. There was a problem with the visa—failure. I would learn much later that even if we had succeeded, in no case would my father have followed us (patriotism—you stay to defend your country). I also learned later though, that in the eventuality of a defeat of France by the Nazis, my parents had no illusions; they had read *Mein Kampf.*

We then made our way toward Marseille where we could use the apartment of my two cousins and my maternal uncle, then mobilized in the French army of Weygand in Lebanon. En route we made a stop in the foothills of the Pyrenees. In one village we met a convoy of tank transporters. On the sides of the vehicles I saw the symbol of my father's battalion! My mother asked the driver, "What about the lieutenant?" The answer: "When we left him, he was with his tanks and a battle broke out against the German Panzers." We wouldn't have other news of my father for a long time. "And you?" my mother continued. Response: "We have orders to put the transporters in the sheds." Could this be called a "heroic" military success, since this village was one of the most remote of all the French villages? At the end of June 1940 after several twists and turns, we arrived in Marseille.

### MARSEILLE, RUE PARADIS

The trip from Le Mans to Marseille for me was completely fascinating and completing disorienting, but the first months, which coincided with the school vacation, went by very pleasantly because there was the sea. It was an easy life where no one talked about Pétain, already in power in Vichy, and where I began to discover the surroundings in which my two cousins lived. Their grandmother was there, as well as friends and other cousins. I also met an associate of my uncle, very nice, whose family lived in a big house on Avenue Frédéric Mistral belonging, I believe, to the grandmother of the little boy of whom I will speak in a minute. We lived on rue Paradis, not far from there. These two houses were situated in the wealthy neighborhoods of Marseille. In the house on Avenue Frédéric Mistral lived a group from Paris seeking refuge. In this group there was a little boy, exactly my age, who very quickly became my great friend and companion. (I'm referring to Pierre Vidal-Naquet.) Later he became a historian of Ancient Greece, and more importantly, he headed a crusade against torture during the Algerian War. After that, with a great deal of courage, he never ceased to defend causes that I consider essential. A paradox: I was Jewish and I didn't know it; he too was Jewish but he knew it. We didn't talk about this problem or about anti-Semitism. Not yet. He later wrote his memoirs and many other books, and I think I read that in 1942 he learned about the Dreyfus Affair from his father. We took the same classes in junior high.

Early in 1941, coming out of school, my friend and I were attacked by three or four pupils whom we didn't know who called us "dirty Jews." Back at home, I asked my mother, "Why did they call me 'dirty Jew'?" (See the film *Les violons du bal*.) I no longer remember her explanation, but that day for me was the beginning of my awareness. These attacks were renewed fairly often. They stopped after a friend of my classmate's family named Yvon Le Marc'Hadour, who was a remarkable classical vocalist, with great generosity came at the end of the school day and took the four boys in question aside and frightened them. The next day their habit of attacking us after school ended. My classmate stayed in Marseille while taking refuge here or there at times. But his father and mother were arrested and never returned from deportation.

Very soon, my mother contacted the Protestant Scout troops like those I had joined in Le Mans and I took up scouting again, this time in Marseille with my friend. It was pleasant; our den mothers and fathers acted appropriately and were kind. That said, I never understood why one day they took us on the Canabière to make up an honor guard, along with the rest of the population of Marseille, when Marshal Pétain was there. To tell the truth, it wasn't with enthusiasm—I'm speaking about our Protestant leaders who remained very guarded in their response—but the population of Marseille was in a state of enthusiasm, of delirium, completely hallucinatory. For me that was the second shock after these episodes of anti-Semitism at school, which had been calmed, and the very disagreeable daily salute of the colors and song to the Maréchal.

Knowing what to think of Marshal Pétain from discussions with my mother and other observations that I was able to make afterward—the first anti-Jew laws date from October 1940—I didn't understand why the population of Marseille had to show enthusiasm for Marshal Pétain. It was the same way elsewhere with the rest of the French population, the majority of whom followed him without hesitation after June 1940. At the time of which I am speaking, perhaps early in 1941, he had completely established his authority and that of his government. I didn't understand what these people were afraid of or what he would be able to protect them from, since they, being the majority, had nothing to fear from his Milice. It was the Jews, the Resistance fighters and certain others who had something to fear! This very strong, perhaps very instinctive awareness I had at the time was that of a ten-year-old child, and I remember very well my complete astonishment at seeing an entire population turn to this regime for some obscure reason. My natural tendency to assume people had the best of intentions that day was completely shaken.

I draw a connection between this position of the French people and the German situation. In fact, I recently read a book entitled *Defying Hitler: A Memoir,* written by a German, Sebastian Haffner,[1] about the German people's growing attraction to Nazism, between the end of World War I and 1933. This evolution in public opinion began very early, in stages shortly after 1926. The author of the book, clearly not Jewish, who lived during this time, describes his astonishment then; he felt all that was happening very painfully. At first he reacted like other Germans, but then successive crises of conscience made him distance himself and he ended up leaving Germany.

I was shocked the same way by the spinelessness of the French people, following after Pétain, a defeatist, even a traitor, I would say.

It's now 1941. My father, whom we learned had been taken prisoner, was repatriated, one of the last, very ill. He joined us in Marseille and quickly joined the Resistance network called Combat, in Marseille led by Defferre. My uncle, demobilized before my father's return, already grievously wounded in World War I, mobilized in 1940 to go to Lebanon, having also read *Mein Kampf,* and whose girlfriend—temporarily living in Marseille—was Argentinean, left France for Buenos Aires with my two cousins, also in 1941. (Once settled in Buenos Aires, he remained true to the family musical tradition and hosted there, after the war, several famous international quartets.)

### MARSEILLE, "L'ALGÉRIENNE"

A little later, we left this uncle's apartment to settle in a rural suburb of Marseille, not far from Château-Gombert, with a farm, a garden, vineyard, and a very nice house in the Algerian style. I traveled ten kilometers morning and evening in order not to leave my friends at school. My sister was already a medical student. We spent several pleasant months in this house, including a time when we hid a visitor, Jules Moch, who had been part of the Blum Cabinet during the Popular Front and who was a brother by marriage to my uncle, the aforementioned graduate of the prestigious École Polytechnique of the family tree. This visitor was also an alumnus of the same institution. He was a remarkably intelligent and straightforward man but somewhat naïve. He received mysterious visitors, political men on the run. After long weeks, he found a way to rejoin de Gaulle.

Shortly after his departure, the situation in Marseille began to deteriorate. The Germans invaded the Southern Zone on November 11, 1942. My parents found out they were being hunted and hardly ever returned to L'Algérienne. Were they hunted for being Jews or, in my father's case, as a Resistance fighter? I don't know. My sister also made herself scarce. I stayed alone at L'Algérienne with my maternal grandmother, who couldn't be moved. My mother explained to me how I was to act if they came to arrest my parents.

And one day at about eleven o'clock in the morning two guys came, about thirty-two to thirty-five years old, in cream-colored raincoats—French, Milice probably.

They asked for my parents; they searched the house from top to bottom. They found no one. They swore they would return. Then, before leaving, they discussed between themselves the usefulness of "taking the kid away." Then twelve years old, I joined in the discussion. The three of us argued over whether it was useful to arrest me so I could tell them where my parents were. It was so surreal that I was almost no longer afraid. Then they left, saying we'd get what was coming to us. Needless to say, this little episode looms large in my memory.

## MADAME BENOÎT

Just like in the theater, perhaps one or two days later my mother came back and a telegram arrived, signed with a name unknown to my mother: Madame Benoît. The text read: "I am Fanette's mother. Fanette and your daughter have a very good mutual friend, Antoinette. I think your children need some air. I am expecting them." Then she gave her address, at Poët-Laval, in the Drôme, near Dieulefit.

Two days later, my sister and I left to join this mysterious Madame Benoît, who was like I imagined Madame de Sévigné to have been. She was a pastor's daughter, married to an industrialist who was a pastor's son. We spent four happy months with her, safe at last. After the war, she became almost a second mother for my sister. I, too, often saw Monsieur and Madame Benoît again.

I consider Madame Benoît as one of the "Righteous," the criterion of this being for me the risk taken, the courage to brave being denounced, or facing the German patrols on the trains or at the Swiss border, and all the other braveries.

When taking risk attains heroism and someone provokes bad fate so often, victorious or not, he or she may become one of the "Righteous," honored and officially recognized at Yad Vashem. This was the case, for example, of the father of one of my wife's oldest friends, Jean Rist, who spent the war, among many other things, saving a number of Jews. He directed the communications network for the Resistance unit in the Loire region. He died in the course of an armed action, an interception by the Resistance fighters of the German garrison at Puy-en-Velay, when they tried unsuccessfully to return to Germany. Jean Rist was an exceptional person, as was Madame Benoît.

A thought comes to me about this courage: do we ourselves have, at the present time, a completely clear conscience about what we are doing or not doing with regard to the "undocumented" or any other injustice? I think that during the war, our fellow citizens had neither good nor bad conscience; they simply had no conscience about the fate of the Jews. The Jews were only part of a very distant landscape in the perception of the ordinary citizen of Vichy France. I think that the rare citizen who was aware of their difficulties sometimes helped them, but most often people just tried not to add a very real danger to the concern they had about their own survival in a conquered and occupied country. And then the Church: the consequences of childhood catechism, the propaganda, and popular opinion made people prudent when it concerned a creature as poorly understood as was the Jew (the God-killer?).

But back to these four months with Madame Benoît at Poët-Laval. I was happy and secure. From time to time phone calls came from my mother whom we couldn't be with because my parents were hunted. In Marseille it was a period of frequent roundups.

## LE CHAMBON-SUR-LIGNON

It is now 1942. In agreement with Madame Benoît, my mother decided to send my sister to Lyon so she could resume her study of medicine, under security conditions still unknown to me. A solution to protect me was also found. Thanks to a contact provided by Raymond Moch, the son of our guest at L'Algérienne, my mother and I met a certain Madame Baldovini, faithful suffragette of the aforementioned guest, from when he was deputy of La Drôme, before the war. This lady of a respectable age, also Protestant, originally from La Drôme, during the school year managed a small boarding house for boys in a village of Haute-Loire, le Chambon-sur-Lignon. That's where I was sent.

Le Chambon-sur-Lignon, like Jean Rist but as a town, was recognized as "Righteous" and honored at Yad Vashem. Situated on a high plateau of the Haute-Loire at nine hundred meters, it is mostly Protestant. At that time the town's ministers, Pastor Trocmé and Pastor Theis codirected the Collège Cévenol, a secondary school created in 1939. All the students, both boys and girls, lived in the various boarding houses of the area; most were separated from their families, others hidden as a family. Many of these children were Jewish, others were Protestants, originally from Nîmes or elsewhere. I was lodged with Madame Baldovini under a borrowed name, which didn't bother me. We children called ourselves by our names or first names, but also by our Scout names from the Protestant Scouts, because the same children met in class, in the boarding house, and in the Scout troops. Soon we didn't really distinguish between these different fields of activity. Apart from the blue eyes and blond hair of our beautiful teacher of Greek, I have hardly any memories of school work. And yet, this school, with its mostly Protestant, but sometimes Jewish or foreign (English, Hungarian) teachers, was of a high level.

I lived in Chambon with a strong feeling of security, except at the very beginning when I heard that the Gestapo was coming up. In fact, I had scarcely been at Chambon for three weeks when this threat was rumored. The episode of the Milice at l'Algérienne had been only six months earlier for me. After alerting Madame Baldovini, I fled by bicycle far from Chambon. She gave me a little money and I went to take refuge in the village of Saint-Agrève, also on the plateau.

A little later, in fact, the Gestapo really did come up to Chambon and they arrested all the boys in the boarding house Les Roches along with their principal, Daniel Trocmé. All were deported; none returned.

As for me, at Saint-Agrève I met the sister of my friend from Avenue Frédéric Mistral whom I knew well. This made my stay of several weeks in this place much more agreeable and less solitary, even if, in the common room of the little hotel, Hôtel Porte, where I had the habit of coming to read, a middle-aged man was also often there, reading as was I. One day the owner of the hotel, slightly flattered, came to tell me that it was Xavier Vallat, Commissioner of Jewish Affairs!

The entire Protestant population protected us, some for humanitarian reasons and others to be in accord with the values of their faith. For certain country folk of the area on the "plateau," the Jews were the chosen people. It was a matter of literal biblical interpretation. Among the sect at the Temple where I went on Sundays, the pastors spoke clearly, the hymns were Bach, the solidarity was tangible. The faith of the people seemed sincere.

During a colloquium organized at Chambon in 1990 by the Institute of Contemporary History,[2] what we had assumed at the time was confirmed as we learned that for the Protestants in general and for those of the plateau in particular, the fact that they were from a cultural and religious minority with an automatic resistance response since the time of Louis XIV had played an absolutely fundamental role in their decision not to accept what was accepted by the Catholic majority then leading France who supported Pétain. Other themes we hadn't known were revealed as well: First, there was the tension between the two courageous but nonviolent pastors, upon whom our entire community depended, and the organized Resistance fighters of the surrounding area who were ready to fight. Then we also learned of the existence, alongside us in 1942, of a group of young Jewish foreigners living protected on the farms around us that we did not know about at the time. These young people received subsistence, moral support, and instruction until one day when many of them were moved to Switzerland, thanks to the courage of others. One of those responsible for these rescues, for example, was Madame André Philip.

Collège Cévenol exists stronger than ever today. The students receive a humanist education there. Today it consists of real buildings nestled among the pines. During the war, the school was conducted in some gray stone houses of the village; we moved from one to the other in wooden clogs.

The experience at Chambon-sur-Lignon during the war profoundly marked those who experienced it.[3] In a certain way, we identify with one another. Even today, the "good" in each of us is instantly understood by the others because it is common to all. This "good" is that which tends to be worthy of these generous adult examples who protected us at their own risk and peril. What a terrible harvest of Jews and Righteous the columns of German tanks and French militia could have reaped if only they had taken the plateau route from le Puy up to Chambon! I am told that Chambon was well organized to protect its refugees in this kind of situation; and the Resistance fighters were ready to fight, but against the tanks . . .

We all felt we were living a free life, but with a special, guarded liberty. Our territory was a tiny space surrounded by all the dangers of the Occupation. In fact, we were constantly aware of and enchanted by our paradoxical liberty, but we kept our guard up. We still today have in common the memory of this fragile grace that coexisted with armed vigil.

## THE RHONE VALLEY

In the spring of 1943, after Saint-Agrève, I vainly tried to reestablish contact with my parents. In fact, it is they who contacted me after my return to Chambon. They invited me to come and spend the summer vacation in their new "residence," a little house with a small garden at Pierrelatte in the Rhone Valley between Valence and Avignon.

My father's Resistance activities were undertaken from then on with the Secret Army (AS), a unified military formed from three Resistance movements, of which Combat, his original network, was the main one. The mission of his group from then on was to transmit to London as much information as possible about German military traffic in a section of the Rhone Valley. Afterward, he was to receive his officer's pay by parachute drop from London. I also recently learned that the youngest son of our guests at L'Algérienne, Raymond Moch, who was reminiscing about this period of time with me, had been secretary to the leader of another branch of the AS, and it had been his job to assign occasional missions to my father.

At this time, my parents took a *nom de guerre*. Their name from that time is my name today.

I then took up the practice during the long vacations at Christmas and Easter of leaving the haven of Chambon to go down into this kind of cauldron full of Germans that was the Rhone Valley. The small local train that went down from Chambon to the Voulte on the right bank of the Rhone was no problem, but the trains that I had to take to get to Pierrelatte after that were often under German surveillance. My papers with my false name from Chambon, different from my name for the Rhone Valley, were a little too artificial and I was often scared.

I will skip over what I know of the extremely active life of my father, over the episodes that I know of the adventurous life of my sister—a medical student at Lyon and a Resister—over the rather worrisome and agitated, but sometimes happy vacations I spent with my mother, over the details of my life here and there. (For example, a Resister friend of my sister's, after three days and three nights of attacks in Vercors, hid with us.) I will also skip over my flight with my mother by bicycle, *in extremis*, after August 15, 1944. A secretary in the City Hall at Pierrelatte had telephoned to tell us the Gestapo was coming to arrest my father—who was on a mission we didn't know where—and we had to warn him at all costs not to return. I will also not describe my fascination when I, hidden in the dark by bushes, watched the German retreat.

I stayed at Chambon until April, 1945. I celebrated the victory in Paris.

I completed my secondary studies in Le Mans under my name from before the war, then I prepared myself for the School of Advanced Commercial Studies. I then changed course and decided to prepare to enter the School of Fine Arts in Paris. Meanwhile, my parents changed our name to protect us in the future from crimes of anti-Semitism. Their *nom de guerre* became official. It has become my name and that of my children and my grandchildren.

I prefer to move very quickly over the chain of events, major or minor, of my adult life, which have little to do with my life as a Jewish hidden child, first of all because I was no longer hidden except by my change of name, and then because my life was no longer implicitly different from the life of an ordinary citizen. The exterior appearances of my existence have been those of "Mr. Everyman" in peace time.

And yet . . . four years of the Occupation affected my entire life. Internally as an adult I am much less serene than I seem. This war, which I first experienced as a child, then as an adolescent, I experienced either as being close to arrest myself or as the risks of arrest my immediate family members were taking and what would then follow. Certainly there were long periods of a paradisiacal life—at Chambon in particular—but even so, I was vicariously anxious because I knew all about the perils that my immediate family ran daily and the difficult battles of the allied armies.

My fury against the Nazis, Pétain, and his band of assassins is intact today. And my wounds remain open. My experience of the war and all that I have learned about it since explain why I have always been concerned by all the injustices as absolute as the rejection of human creatures (because of being Jewish, for example). I am concerned by all racism, colonialism, and the colonial wars of today, the endless exterminations, as with the Tutsis-Hutus conflict. (See the book by Jean Hatzfeld, whose father was one of our teachers at Chambon.[4]) I am concerned by a minority's pitiless thirst for money that throws entire populations into poverty, by the clear consciences of the powerful, the injustice between North and South—in a word, by the law of the jungle. This concern doesn't go away. The awakening to injustice due to the war of 1939–1945 causes me to project and take unto myself the injustices done to others. And what I have sometimes tried with various groups to put an end to injustice and the unacceptable is certainly feeble, but I have made efforts. After the war, my involvement, induced by the horror of Nazism, could take the form of admiration for the sacrifice of the allied armies, including the Soviet army, or for commitments made voluntarily and lucidly.

In this regard, for example, I understood from 1946–1947—and I am not the only one—that the war issues were transformed into political ones. More precisely, I started considering that, in order for the world to finally move toward the construction of acceptable societies where I would perhaps be accepted, the battle against the Nazis had to be replaced with a battle for the Left. That is why for some years I became Communist, as did the aforementioned friend from Vercors and Lyon, Claude Alphandéry, the former head of the United Resistance Movements in Drôme-Ardèche and a Resistance companion of my sister. At the Liberation he was named president of the Committee of Liberation for the Drôme, and was the first Communist graduate of the School of National Administration. The medical doctor who lived in the Glass House (Maison de Verre), Jean Dalsace (a second cousin of my father's) who had performed admirably in the Resistance also became Communist. These several years of activism as a young bourgeois in the Communist Party weren't always comfortable or without contradictions, and were sometimes difficult to engage. But the examples of courage in the face of moral challenges experienced by my immediate family during the war just ended, allowed me to maintain perspective and keep these discomforts in their proper place when possible.

Among these models of courage, I would like to specifically describe two exploits: one violent and exemplary; the other illustrating the extraordinary courage of ordinary Resisters. Here is the first one. The oldest son of our guests at L'Algérienne, André Moch, graduated from Saint-Cyr, the French military academy, in 1939. Mobilized, he went to war. Demobilized, he joined the AS, after which he led an adventuresome life. It must be noted that this Resistance fighter and military officer had earlier decided with all his will that if the day came when he was going to be arrested, not knowing if he would be able to withstand torture, he would take down as many of the Gestapo as possible before being taken down himself, so as to not risk talking. One day this Resistance fighter went to visit cousins in Grenoble. He knew my paternal uncle so the two of them decided to meet at his cousins' home. My uncle had just left when the scenario foreseen by the Resistance officer unfolded just as he had imagined in all respects and he was killed resisting arrest. The Germans then caught up with my uncle at the tram stop where he was waiting and arrested him. It was 1944, and my uncle left with the last convoy and never returned. The example of this Resistance fighter had, and still has, a very strong impact on me. I feel capable, placed in a similar context to that confronted by the exemplary Resister, of accomplishing a similarly extreme action.

The second exploit concerns my sister, who survived a badly planned Resistance action, thanks to the intervention of my father's Resistance network, which got her out of a bad spot. She was sent by her group from Lyon to Paris to bring back a very large sum of money. The Germans learned about it and went to capture her on the return trip. My father's network had been warned about it and my father, learning it was his own daughter, succeeded in getting her off the Paris-Lyon train before it arrived in Lyon, where the Gestapo was waiting for her. A little family story, that's all.

In light of all that I have recounted, you see that I have built a crescendo during my account of the war, so that near the end it is about a boy become adolescent, at an age to understand, but who "endured" without yet being old enough to act—a kind of internal conflict that has never diminished. At the beginning, about 1940–1941, I was struck with completely unexpected and unforeseen blows; which then built in intensity, making me live the following several years with moments alternating between calm and torment, full of risks that I knew could be fatal for my immediate family and for myself. Why, after all that, would this reservoir of conflict be surprising?

In the later years of my life, I have put a damper on my anger—but it is a flame that doesn't go out. Without being "heroic," by adapting my capacity for action to my capacity for courage, I have put what courage I had to the service of my very active life as an architect. Then, as a parallel with my activities as initiator and constructor, I had for seventeen or eighteen years during the 1980s and 1990s, responsibility for a small international publication that I shared with its director. This publication, which played a role in the history of contemporary architecture, had, among other objectives, that of fighting to insure that architecture and urbanism would be at the service of people and society, and would not be exclusively a pretext to build large, splendid objects. It is a militant publication. For example, sharing our experience in various countries, we measure the weight and influence of money with its serious social ramifications, which is subscribed through the other actors in the "act of construction" in their relationships with us, the architects, who are generally economic dwarfs. It is a big problem. More generally, we try to detect and make known the anomalies and the injustices, but also the advances in the domain of architecture and urbanism.

Thus, after twenty years, the flame has again taken the place of the nightlight, and my anger, my discontent, still intact, have fairly often found a means of expression by reacting against certain states of affairs or tendencies, sometimes with insightful proposals.

As Danielle told me, "It is through your profession that you have tried to bring alive this sense of subversion and courage in relation to a certain established order that you are challenging." I would say, "If only." In fact, she is right, I try . . .

This is a good enough conclusion for this first part.


**Part Two: Historical and Cultural Considerations**

What is the meaning of this idea of "long-time French Jew"? There is no clear answer to this question, taking into account two series of considerations—one historical, one cultural, which includes the problem of integration into French society. I will look at the two successively, trying to understand how non-Jews think of me as different.

**HISTORICAL CONSIDERATIONS (BRIEF SUMMARY)**

I looked for answers to the following questions:

1. Where did the Jews from Alsace and Lorraine come from and how did they live?
2. Under what conditions were the French Jews emancipated by the Constitutional Assembly on September 17, 1791?
3. Were there periods of remission of anti-Semitism after that date?

On these points, the facts are known and featured in books, but for me these were discoveries.

*Some answers to question 1:*

> The presence of Jews on the current territory of France is very old, already attested to in Gaul under the Romans. Nevertheless it practically disappeared after their proscription by the Edict of Philippe le Bel in 1306, culminating in the infamous "anti-Jewish" campaign seen under his grandfather, King Saint Louis. [ . . . ] About one hundred thousand Jews had to leave the French kingdom, then a kingdom still limited by the Rhone, the Seine and the Meuse Rivers, to settle in the neighboring regions of Lorraine, Alsace, Rhine valley, Bourgogne, Dauphiné, Provence, Comtat Venaissin, Spain, and sometimes further, in Hungary or Poland. Actually, all through the fourteenth century, they continued to be recalled and expelled again.[5]

Note that Alsace and Lorraine were then part of the Holy Roman Empire.

The same authors then describe the reinstallation of Jews in Lorraine between the sixteenth and eighteenth centuries, and that of the Jews in Alsace after the seventeenth century. Excluded from the cities, they resided in the countryside, the less poor among them often providing horses to the royal cavalry, which in theory protected them because of their usefulness.

Concerning the life of the Jews from Alsace on the eve of the French Revolution, Badinter wrote:

At the mercy of a disrespectful and hostile Christian world, the "German" Jews led a miserable existence, brightened only by a lively faith with a demanding ritual and a warm family life.[6]

*Some answers to question 2:*
Concerning the history of the emancipation of the Jews, Badinter notes that the first indications for improvement of the Jews' status occurred before the French Revolution in the principalities of Germany. He details almost day by day the battle from 1789 to 1791 led by Abbot Grégoire, Clermont-Tonnerre, Duport, and others who favored this emancipation, adopted September 17, 1791, by an exhausted Constitutional Assembly, as Michelet writes, and against the will of the Alsatian deputies. Before this date, from 1789 to 1791, the majority of the deputies, when solicited on this matter, had regularly rejected the emancipation of the Jews of the East.[7]

*Some responses to question 3:*
Becker and Wieviorka write, citing F. Delpech:

> From the non-renewal of the Napoleonic decree against the Jews to the publication of the Jewish France of Drumont and to the revival of anti-Semitism, the Jewish communities of France knew a period of calm that was completely exceptional in their history [ . . . ].[8]

and continue by making this observation:

> In the shifting history of the Jews, the nineteenth century, three generations is a time to mark with a white stone, before entering another difficult time . . . In sum, the evolution in France of the Restoration is exactly the reverse of the one that took place in a number of European countries [ . . . ]. The reactionary period of Charles X provokes a number of anxieties but the monarchy of Louis-Philippe is welcomed by the Jews as well as the "revised Charter," which suppresses the status of Catholicism as State religion and recognizes it only as the religion of a majority of the French people, which opens the path to the disappearance of

discrimination [ . . . ]. The great mistrust that prevailed in the Napoleonic work was in a large part erased. King Louis-Philippe and his family showed (to the Jews) in daily life a respect equal to that which they had toward the other religions.[9]

What follows is known: the Dreyfus Affair at the beginning of the twentieth century; anti-Semitic organizations in the 1930s until the anti-Jewish laws of 1940; and the actions of the Vichy Milice. Since then, anti-Semitism has never disappeared. First as a larva, under cover, it dares to express itself more and more openly, no doubt because of geopolitical events.

## THOUGHTS ON ASSIMILATION AND CULTURE

It is clear that my family—both paternal and maternal—benefited from the favorable conditions described above, especially the respite in the nineteenth century. But it is difficult to know if this haute bourgeoisie was truly integrated into the French society. Did they adopt the culture and refinements of the French bourgeois society? On this point, I believe that to be assimilated into a group implies symmetry; the individual feels he belongs and is adopted by the group. There is the legal side (integration)—the acquisition of civil rights—and then there is the part that takes place in the mind (assimilation). One of my paternal great-grandfathers thus became an artillery colonel in the French army, having graduated, as did one of his cousins, from École Polytechnique. This indicates that at that time, French Jews already had unobstructed access to "knowledge." Polytechnique indicated to them, by means of economic and intellectual resources, access to a certificate of "Frenchness." That didn't prevent their being resented by their non-Jewish military colleagues as "cosmopolitans" or potential traitors (witness the Dreyfus Affair).

It is clear that my two families were well positioned socially and economically; it helped to be rich and nonobservant. The eight brothers—those active in real estate, as well as the industrialist of Colmar, the mayor of Belfort—could consider themselves assimilated. But was that really how their fellow citizens viewed them? Who is to say that the majority of their fellow citizens didn't consider them *first* as Jews and *secondly* as French? Assimilation and integration as seen by Jews and as seen by non-Jews doesn't really coincide. In my case, one could say I was "dis-integrated" by the Vichy regime.

As for the culture, one must define what that is! If one understands it as lifestyle, profession, leisure and entertainment, the level of knowledge, the three generations who preceded me differed little or not at all from the non-Jews of the same milieu. They were businessmen, industrialists, civil servants; they all believed in progress and science, were humanists, intellectuals, musicians. In contrast, between Jews and non-Jews, up until my generation, they did not mix and each married within their own group.

Concerning the progressive passage from money to culture in the course of generations, I would like to tell a story as an example. Annie, the only daughter of the youngest of the eight uncles, Uncle Edmond—whom I knew—was entrusted at the age of twelve to Dolly, a young English woman responsible to teach her language. Dolly transmitted to Annie many other things: love of literature, painting, music, and dance—and even English. Then each of these young women married a soldier returned from World War I. Annie married a young Jewish medical doctor, the aforementioned Jean Dalsace—son of the Treasurer-General of Epinal—who had been a war hero. Dolly married Pierre Chareau, who soon became known as an innovative designer of contemporary furnishings. The two couples were friends. Pierre designed interiors to serve as a setting for his furniture and living quarters for people who bought his furniture. The first such design was for Jean and Annie. Ten years later, about 1930, Pierre Chareau, associated with a young and talented Dutch architect, designed a mansion for them, astounding in its modernity and later studied and visited by architects from all over the world—the Glass House (Maison de Verre) rue Sainte Guillaume. In this setting, complemented with books, paintings, contemporary carpets, and furniture by Chareau, during friendly parties or private concerts, painters, musicians (Darius Milhaud, for example), and writers would gather. Some relatives of mine told me that Uncle Edmond, seeing this costly but magical and fantastic home, was surprised that his daughter preferred incomprehensible paintings by Picasso, Braque, and other artists of the time to fur or leather coats.

To conclude this theme of culture and assimilation, I have tried to disassociate culture acquired by study from that in which one bathes, transmitted by the family or caught by contagion, passion, proximity, or curiosity. The acquisition of the latter is inseparable from the culture of codes and language that give access to what is most profound in a given civilization. It is only when, because of education, the mastery of

memorized reflexes, the discrepancies in perception of the codes and
languages from one social group to another disappear, that one can
speak of cultural assimilation. This requires several generations and
much effort, because it is difficult. For any recent immigrant, this kind
of assimilation becomes a priority. This was possible a long time ago
for my family who came from elsewhere. Perhaps my family came originally from Poland or from Russia, chased, as were so many others, by
anti-Semitism, pogroms, poverty? I can't say why, but much of my reading, the painting of Chagall, certain films—like *Yentl*, which depicts re-
alistically a *shtetl* with its yeshiva and where the music almost reminds
me of half-forgotten tunes—today give me the impression that I was
born there. As for the "long-time French Jews" I am convinced there is
still within them the imponderable trace of codes, languages, and even
mixed reflexes, coming from that long ago time of intercultural crossing, and that they continue to distill, in the heart of the host country—
that is to say, their own country. Even totally atheist and secular, they
still also carry—but it is of their own doing—a kind of cultural heritage
to which, because of certain historical circumstances, they periodically
return with unfortunate consistency, and then they again become
"someone's Jew."

**In Conclusion**

As we've just seen, the "long-time French Jew" that I am—through my
ancestors—was somewhat disappointed during the war by the attitude
of the majority of his dear compatriots. This narration gives me an opportunity to confirm my awareness of the xenophobia and racism running through a portion of the French populace.

To put it more directly: I have been French since 1791, but during
the war it was French people "like me" who caused me to experience
episodes that were dramatic, iniquitous, traumatic—sometimes just by
their repetition, even if they seemed harmless. I know that the populace—the great mass of people—generally lean to one side or the other
according to the political, military, or other circumstances, and that it is
difficult for them to show solidarity and a sense of justice in their convictions. I note simply that those who were designated as Jews were
marginalized, dead or alive, during these four dark years.

All the same, I wonder, do I really want to share my "Frenchness" with those people? You may tell me perhaps that I am not making sense, because after September 1944, this same great mass of people suddenly claimed they were "Resisters" and returned in force to share their "Frenchness" with me . . . There would be much more to say . . .

FIGURE 18.1. Serge at age twelve in
October 1942 at the Lycée de Pau.

# 18

# Serge Netchine

**June 5, 2003**

*Serge Netchine is a psychologist working with children and child development, with interests in reading acquisition and epistemological research. He was a researcher at CNRS and later a professor at the University of Paris VIII. He has two children and four grandchildren.*

My family survived. During the time of hiding, I was not separated from my parents. Despite the difficulties, we were able to maintain a minimal level of emotional and material security. I appreciated the countryside in the Béarn region where we took refuge after the Vel' d'Hiv' Roundup. I followed a regular course of study at school. I was never depressed, thanks to the strong and confident political convictions transmitted by my parents, who provided me with an understandable interpretation of the unprecedented events that surrounded us. So even though I was touched by the flame, I wasn't burned. Yet the memory of that time weighs on me and has marked me throughout my life.

My parents were among the many militant workers coming out of the Jewish community in the Czarist empire after the end of the nineteenth century. Let's begin with my father, who early on declared himself a Bolshevik. He was born about 1880 at Kherson, in the south of the Ukraine, not far from the Crimea. His father owned a sawmill on the banks of the Dniepr. From a young age, he told me, he had shown a determination to evade and subvert a milieu that he judged to be stifling and backward. When nine or ten years old, he boarded the foreign ships that came up the Dniepr to meet the sailors arriving from far off lands. At the synagogue, hidden under the *talith* of his praying, teary-eyed father, he would fool around with the kid next to him. The children's discussions were about the nonexistence of God.

My father's choices became clearer in light of the tensions of a particular society at a particular time—that of Eastern European Jews at the turn of the nineteenth and twentieth centuries. Marginalized, despised, persecuted, they were also in the process of opening up to modernity. The new generations were seeking their own path and inaugurating totally new formulas to create refuge or deal with rejection, aimed at their own communities. For my father, the horizon didn't open upon Palestine or the port of New York, but upon the revolutionary adventure and the dream of a universal proletarian republic; hence his deliberate choice of a worker's life. He took this path with the vigor of his youth and the ardor of a faith retained throughout the vicissitudes of his life— a faith that, despite his conviction and statements of denial of Judaism, and perhaps paradoxically also because of them, portrays an indelible *Yiddishkeit*. Throughout his travels across Europe, as much as he wanted and felt himself to be Russian, and while living the fantasy of a country where Socialism would provide for the workers of the whole world, he was eager for his children to have access to culture, revealing his deeply inscribed Jewish origins. But as for any specific transmission of culture by him, there was none. He was convinced that Socialism and Communism would resolve all the problems of minorities and diversity. The reality, as we know, was completely different.

In Kherson he experienced the upheavals of the 1905 revolution in which he participated; imprisonment that was very hard; and upon leaving prison, the pogrom of Nikopol—similar to that spoken of by Babel in his *Odessa Stories*, the life of a clandestine agitator in Petrograd. This Russian part of his odyssey, hazardous but exciting, contrasts with his life in Germany where he took refuge after having deserted the Czar's army—a life of poverty, violence, xenophobia, and police terror. His first wife died of consumption some months after the birth of their son. He was expelled from Germany in about 1913. He then arrived in France, in fact just in time for World War I, in which he enlisted to defend the liberties he had at last found in France. He experienced the horror of the trenches and survived.

During the 1920s he met my mother. Her name was Kowalson, which meant "son of the blacksmith," a traditional trade of the Jews of Eastern and Central Europe. Her father was a blacksmith, shoeing horses, repairing the tools of the peasants, and sometimes reading the future in red-hot iron in a little village deep in the country, twenty miles from Kiev—Makéevka—where Jews and Russian peasants lived next to one another. My mother's life was no less exemplary than that of my father. At age sixteen she left home to begin an apprenticeship, first at Niejin, then in Kiev, in the fashion and fur workshops that were constantly permeated by political agitation and protests against the regime. Barely out of the apathetic rural area, she resolutely joined the movement, and as a result, found herself, too, in prison.

In short, my parents were made for each other. In a little maid's chamber in Paris they brought together their two children—his son, her daughter—their faith in universality (but with such an accent!); and the multiple planks of wood on which my mother fastened the pieces of fur for cutting, and, of course, the sewing machine. So their odyssey continued, but now in the context of a Parisian workers' novel. In 1928 an apartment with two rooms became available to them in a low-cost housing unit at Boulogne-Billancourt in the outskirts of Paris, and I was born (unplanned) in 1929.

During the following years, the family experienced two great joys. My brother earned First Prize in the Concours Général,[1] which really annoyed the right-wing press. "A Jew couldn't understand Racine," said Maurras. In the same vein, the journalist La Fouchardière railed against my brother in *L'Œuvre*, asking how "this Yid coming from Jerusalem by way of Moscow" could earn such a distinction. The other great joy was in 1936. My father, who during the previous years had relentlessly developed a political and unionist militancy that frequently got him fired, had been designated representative of the strike committee at his factory. He orchestrated and won everything—legalization of a union

group, canteen, medical visits and a nurse on site to care for work acci-
dents—except for the fact that after the movement subsided, the factory
closed and my father was fired.

So this was our situation in the autumn of 1940 in Occupied Paris.
My parents were nearly sixty years old, still holding on to the revolutionary vision of their youth. I was starting junior high at Lycée Janson
de Sailly, the flagship school of the haute bourgeoisie in the Sixteenth
Arrondissement. Well before wearing the yellow star, I had to fight hard
there. These xenophobic and racist attacks were aimed specifically at
me, because I was the child of a worker, and illustrated for me my parents' context for interpreting social conflict.

The exclusionary measures were quickly put into place, along with
the efforts to influence public opinion, and the inscriptions "Jüdisches
Geschäft" (Jewish Enterprise) in the shop windows. Then came the
roundups in the metro, the arrests, and the internments, which at first
seemed directed only at adult men. Were my parents afraid? No doubt
they were anxious, and they hid their anxiety poorly from me. As for
me, either I have transformed my memories or I wasn't afraid—at
least not until July 1942, until the Vel' d'Hiv' Roundup. Two episodes
stand out. During the night spent at my non-Jewish brother-in-law's
place, I heard the cries of the neighbor whose husband was being
taken away. The next morning, I came upon another terror-filled face,
that of another neighbor's husband wandering in the streets, who
begged me to go see if his wife and children, hidden elsewhere, had
escaped. That is when we understood completely that we had passed
from spectators to performers in a tragedy where, as prey, we must
flee as quickly as possible these hunters dressed in the uniforms of
French police.

This flight of my foreign parents, who had to get to Pau where my
father knew he could find work, was difficult for them with me, the
little French school boy, at their side. It barely avoided failing tragically
more than once for them and for me, especially the time I found myself
face to face with a German officer of the Kommandantur at Orthez, one
of the crossing points on the Demarcation Line between the Occupied
and Unoccupied Zones. I later learned from the trial of Papon, a high-
ranking civil servant, that this was one of the crossing points that filled
the Mérignac internment camp, an antechamber for deportation. Good
luck, the help of the people with us or other people who saw us wandering, and our own tenacity allowed the three of us to be together

again in Pau in October 1942. There we lived in an isolated shack in the country, about five kilometers from the center of town. It had no water or electricity but there was a hen that laid eggs, a big garden where we could grow vegetables, and it was surrounded by a forest of chestnut trees and meadows rich with mushrooms. Every morning we went for a long, invigorating walk, my father to his work, me to school. I went first because sometimes the bridge we had to take across the Gave River at Pau was barricaded by a police patrol. I would then return to warn my father, who would go back home that day. When the patrol was watching in the evening after his work, my father would wait in a nearby cafe until they left.

The apparent tranquility of this routine, which reinforced my father's absolute certainty that the Germans were lost from the time they declared war on Russia, contrasted sharply with the adventure of my brother (twenty years older than I) who was one of the leaders of the AS in Toulouse. Ambushed, he was jailed at Sisteron Fortress, and then liberated along with four companions by a false official telegram encrypted with the code used by the Vichy administration. One day we saw a strange person nearing the house—black glasses, fedora, thin brown mustache (he was blond), looking like a real gangster. It was my brother, in disguise after his escape, who was going to leave again for other dangerous adventures.

These events, which were both dramatic and farcical, inserted themselves rather strangely into the daily life of the good town of Pau. In Paris, things had been clear from what was seen in the streets—bilingual posters signed by von Stulpnagel listing the executed hostages and arrests in public places. Pau, at first glance, seemed cut off from all that. Even while keeping a healthy attitude of suspicion and dissimulation, I read the situation poorly. The terminology "Work, Family, Fatherland"— exalting the virtues of the return to the land, to artisan vocations, to sport—was spreading a falsely benevolent ideology in the same way the image of Marshal Pétain as an old tutelary in a decorated kepi, as a saint, was insistently presented in the store windows. But what did it really say about the culpability of these French people who had accepted the "lies that did us so much harm"? What threat did it hold for them? To whom was it directed? From August 1942, in Pau as throughout the Unoccupied Zone, arrests of Jews or French of foreign origin who had taken refuge there increased along with the hunt for Communists and Resistance fighters.

In this somewhat problematic context, I pursued normally my classical studies. I continued junior high from 1942 to 1944 at the Lycée Louis-Barthou, without excessive enthusiasm, need I say? The teachers knew I was Jewish, as my brother who had taught at this school had been dismissed a year earlier for this reason. It was a fragile situation that never got to a breaking point. I have to emphasize that no one was ever singled out by anyone in these classes, inflated by the arrival of numerous Jewish children, some of whom would from time to time disappear.

Arriving there with a black and white view, I didn't understand a lot of what was happening. Some teachers continued to espouse the teaching of the Third Republic, even the songs of the "ajistes"—members of the Auberges de Jeunesse (youth hostels) of the Popular Front of 1936. Others peppered their lectures with anti-Semitic remarks ("the good old-fashioned French anti-Semitism") that, to my knowledge, never went beyond traditional abuse. The case of the headmaster, however, was completely different. He was the spokesperson he was expected to be of the ingratiating ideology and, in fact, proved himself to be an "office assassin," according to the words used in the Papon trial. In the sports demonstrations to the glory of Pétain, we would all run together—he along with us—in little shorts. But that day he was dressed again in the customary attire of his job when at the ten o'clock recess we saw him turn over to the Gestapo agents waiting in his office a sixteen-year-old boy who was begging him to let him go. A Jew and Resistance fighter, this boy was not seen again after the deportation. (This headmaster faced no charges after the Liberation.)

Some time later, the older residential students who had just received their draft notices for the STO came to ask the headmaster (was it a provocation?) for permission to leave, by which they meant they were planning to disappear. Of course, he refused, and then an amazing insurrection occurred—perfectly orchestrated by the initiative of these residential students. They occupied the *lycée* right in the heart of the military occupation itself. One morning the entrance of the *lycée* was closed by a picket line, the classes cancelled, the disorder organized. The students sang "L'Internationale." After three days, the situation turned bad. The plainclothes police chased the scattering students through the streets of the town while a menacing group of people began to surround the *lycée*. One could sense that things were getting worse. There were negotiations with the headmaster. All the detentions were cancelled and the strike ended, while the older students went off to join underground Resistance units.

(Among these students was Georges Lapassade, who was to become a famous Leftist psychoanalyst. His distinctive Béarn mountaineer's accent was heard again years later in the 1968 student uprisings at the universities of Nanterre and Vincennes.)

So the dark moments, the disquieting clouds, the bath in an anesthetizing ideology while the diabolical surgeons went on operating, alternated with the bright moments, the fits of revolt such as I just described; but also the swimming in the torrent with buddies, the diving into the escapism of some films, and reading. True, the facade of benevolence faded. The hunts increased and the French police sent youth to Germany for the STO as efficiently as possible. The mountains above Pau filled with Resistance units, and on the access routes—the famous bridge over the Gave River at Pau in particular—control tightened. The Milice was omnipresent. If any ambiguity remained, the Germans cleared it up when, for several days on the central square at Pau, they left the body of a Resistance fighter hanging from a tree.

Attempting, sixty years later, to restore the atmosphere of that period as seen from the niche where we were no doubt risks creating many distortions. Also, so many years later, it is difficult to appreciate when, what, and how the experience of this period could affect the final phases of my intellectual and political trajectory. Nevertheless, certainly everything was deeply colored by it. The events of the war, as I understood them, found expression for a time—about fifteen or sixteen years—by what could be called a "blinding clarity." By this I mean blindness resulting from an excess of clarity, the context of bicolored reading mentioned earlier. Since then so many events have taken place to affect these retrospective readings, which at the same time accentuated my philosophical, historical, and political path. At no point in this passage could I, nor would I tomorrow, be able to consider the fact of being Jewish other than as one among the diverse, often perilous—and all the more precious—paths of access to the universal.

To close, there is one point upon which I must insist, which for me is the most striking characteristic: the actual, multiple help coming from people nearby while these events were taking place. Without Vichy's collaboration, the Nazis would not have been able to exterminate so many Jews living in France, but without the help—visible or invisible—of the people around us, few Jews could have survived. If I want to testify—and I do want to—it is first of all to give homage to the individuals who did what they did with full awareness of the risks they were taking. For example, to Jean Guibar, a Communist worker friend of my father's, who wanted to help me cross the Demarcation Line by having me pass as his son, and who was stopped with me at the Kommandantur at Orthez. Or to that young writer, whose name I don't know, who interrupted his work and put aside his manuscripts to organize a network for crossing the Demarcation Line near Montrichard. I was part of a group that he led by night across the countryside to ford the Cher River. Later he was arrested and deported and never returned. Likewise, I would like to give homage to the many anonymous people who complemented the actions of these exceptional individuals.

I think about the woman who, seeing a child in wet clothing sleeping in a railroad compartment on the train between Châteauroux and Toulouse (it was after the night I forded that stream), no doubt saved me from being picked up during the night at Toulouse by inviting me to dinner and to sleep at the hotel. The next morning she accompanied me to Pau without asking me a single question.

I also think of the countrywoman near Dax who one morning happened to find my parents—who had slept in a field after having failed in their first attempt at crossing the Demarcation Line. She helped them cross by paths she knew without asking for anything in return.

I also want to mention our old concierge of Boulogne, Madame Lagrange, who had the courage to confront the cops who came to arrest us, pretending not to know our address in Pau.

And the municipal employee at Pau who made new identity papers for my parents without stamping JEW on the documents. These are the people I know about, but what do I owe those who understood and kept quiet, or who helped without my knowing it? It is the same protective immersion that appears in the literature devoted to the saving of the children, by individuals or by networks, Jewish or not. The designation as "Righteous" that honors these singular and exceptional people should not obscure the "banality of good" in the social fabric that allowed the survival of about three-fourths of the adult Jews of France and six out of seven of their children.

# Chronology

(Events in France appear in regular type; world events in italics.[1])

**1939**

*September 3: Declaration of war by England and France against Germany.*

Internment in French camps of "enemy foreign nationals" (many were anti-Nazis).

**1940**

*May 10: German invasion of France.*

*June 10: Italian invasion of France.*

June 17: Pétain requests armistice from Germany.

June 18: Call to arms from London by General de Gaulle.

June 22: Armistice Agreement. Creation of the Demarcation Line between the Northern (Occupied) and Southern (Unoccupied) Zones.

July 10: Abolition of the French Republic, replaced by Vichy's État Français (French State).

Vote of the French Parliament of full powers to Pétain, dissolution of the Republic (replaced by État Français). Pétain made "Head of State."

*August: The Battle of England.*

August 27: Decree by Pétain abolishing the crime of racial abuse.

September 27: First German order defining and taking census of Jews in the Occupied Zone.

October: First internments of Jewish children in France.

October 3: First Statute Concerning Jews by the Vichy government. Jews were forbidden to participate in a wide range of occupations, hold political office, or serve in the military, judiciary, and civil service, with *numerus clausus* for the professions and performing arts.

October 4: Prefects can intern "foreigners of the Jewish race."

357

October 24: Meeting and handshake between Pétain and Hitler at Montoire, France.

November: The word "Jew" is stamped in capital letters, in red, on Jews' identity cards in the Occupied Zone.

## 1941

March 29: Creation of the General Commission on Jewish Affairs.

May 14: First mass arrests and internments of nearly 4,000 foreign Jews in Paris.

June: Census of Jews in the Unoccupied Zone.

June 2: Second Statute Concerning Jews by the Vichy government. The definition of who was considered to be Jewish was expanded. Jews were banned from most economic activities: banking, stock trading, advertising, university teaching, journalism, and publishing.

*June 22: German invasion of the USSR.*

July 18: Creation of the FVF (Legion of French Volunteer Soldiers). Fascist French engaged in the Wehrmacht to help Nazi troops.)

August 12: "Ill Wind" speech by Pétain, warning the population against the increasing influence of the French Resistance.

August 18: Drancy becomes an internment camp for Jews.

August 20: Roundup in the Eleventh Arrondissement of Paris of more than 4,000 French and foreign Jews.

August 21: Anti-Nazi assault led by Colonel Fabien in the Barbès metro station. Ninety-eight hostages shot in retaliation. Beginning of armed Resistance in France.

*September 8: Beginning of the Siege of Leningrad by the Germans.*

*November: Beginning of the Battle of Moscow.*

November 29: Creation of the Union of Israelites in France (UGIF) by Vichy.

*December 7: Japanese attack on Pearl Harbor.*

*December 11: United States enters the war.*

December 12: Arrest of 743 well-known Jews.

## 1942

January 20: Conference in Warsaw; specifics of the "Final Solution" (genocide of Jews) are determined.

February 12–14: Trial at Riom, especially against Léon Blum (former Prime Minister of the French Republic), of Jewish origin. The accused are turned over to the Germans and deported.

March 27: First convoy of deportees from France to Auschwitz.

May 6: Darquier de Pellepoix succeeds Xavier Vallat as head of the Commission of Jewish affairs.

May 29: Jews in the Occupied Zone are required to wear the yellow star.

*June 4: Battle of Midway (American victory against the Japanese in the Pacific).*

June 22: Laval, head of the government in Pétain's French State, is quoted as saying, "I hope for a German victory."

June 22–27: Roundups in Marseille; 800 arrested.

July 8: Statutes on Segregation in the Occupied Zone are enacted. Jews were forbidden access to live performances or public establishments such as movies, swimming pools, and parks. They were restricted to shopping between three and four p.m. when most stores were closed or, because of the shortages, had only empty shelves.

July 16–17: "Spring Wind Operation" (called Vel' d'Hiv Roundup) with more than 12,000 Jews arrested, including 4,051 children.

July 22: Statute on Economic Aryanization is enacted to take assets, real estate, businesses, and other belongings of value from Jews. Jews were subject to a curfew enforced between the hours of eight p.m. and six a.m., and were prohibited from owning radios, bicycles, or telephones, from entering a public place, and from changing their place of residence.

August: Transfer to Drancy of Jews interned in the Unoccupied Zone.

*August: The Germans penetrate the Caucasus to assure their access to oil.*

August 3: First ecclesiastical letter of protest against the persecution of the Jews by His Excellency Monsignor Saliège, Archbishop of Toulouse.

August 26–28: Roundups in the Unoccupied Zone with 6,000 arrests. During the course of the year and until the end of the war, many Jews tried to hide, often with the help of the French population, but there were also numerous denunciations and Vichy was zealous in its collaboration with the Nazis.

*September 6: Beginning of the Battle of Stalingrad.*

November: Formation of the Secret Army (AS), merging the non-Communist Resistance groups in the Unoccupied Zone.

*November: Battle of Alamein (British victory over the German Afrika Korps).*

*November 8: British and American landings in North Africa.*

November 11: Germans cross the Demarcation Line; total occupation of France.

During the year, 43,000 Jews, including 6,423 children were deported to the camps from France, with another 800 arrested in the north of France and deported by way of Belgium.

## 1943

Tracking and deportation of Jews is vigorously underway in all of France.

January 30: The Milice (pro-Nazi civil militia) is created.

*February 2: German defeat at Stalingrad.*

February 10: Jewish children are rounded up, even in the UGIF centers. Public opinion turns against the anti-Jewish measures, in varying degrees according the region of the country. People organized to help, and Jews adopted diverse survival strategies whenever possible. Engagement in the Resistance networks intensified, some of which were Jewish and included rescue of children with the help of non-Jews.

February 16: Most young working age men from all over occupied Europe are requisitioned by the Nazis to work in Germany's Obligatory Work Force (STO). Only in France is the requisitioning organized by the state (Vichy).

February–March: Coordination of the Resistance movements and extension of the Maquis (the networks of clandestine fighting cells).

*April 19: Uprising in the Warsaw ghetto.*

May 27: Creation of the CNR (National Council of French Resistance).

*July 10–September 4: Allied Landings in Italy.*

*July 25: Fall of Mussolini.*

September: Successive demonstration and sabotage attacks against the Germans.

September 9: After the Allied invasion of Italy, the Germans occupy the area formerly occupied by the Italians. Massive tracking and deportation in the region begins.

During the year, 17,041 Jews were deported, including 1,677 children.

## 1944

French police continue action against foreign Jews. The Gestapo, now free to act in the Southern Zone, multiply roundups of French Jews.

January–May: Battle of Montecassino in Italy.

January 10: Assassination of Victor Basch (well-known French philosopher) and his wife Hélène, both of Jewish origin.

March: Russian Army at the borders of Poland and Romania.

April 6: Nazi chief Klaus Barbie arrests forty-four children at Izieu (along with the adults caring for them).

April 13: The children and adults from Izieu are deported.

June 6: Allied Landings at Normandy.

June 10: Massacre by the Nazis at Oradour-sur-Glane; 642 civilians burnt alive, locked in the church.

June 20: Assassination by the Nazis of Jean Zay (Minister of Education and Fine Arts under the Popular Front, 1936–1939), of Jewish origin.

July 7: Assassination by the Nazis of Georges Mandel (former Minister of Mail, 1936–1938, and Minister of Colonies, 1938–1940), of Jewish origin.

August 15: Allied Landings in Provence.

August 20: Pétain forced to flee Vichy for Germany.

August 19: Departure of the last convoy of deportees. Opening of clandestine homes for children, Jewish and non-Jewish, to care for the orphans following the Liberation.

August 25: Liberation of Paris.

September 10: Abolition of the Vichy legislation.

## 1945

May 8: German surrender. End of the war in Europe.

August 6: American atomic bombing of Hiroshima.

August 15: Japanese surrender.

End of the Second World War.

Of the 75,721 Jews deported from France, including 11,000 children, only 2,500 returned, including an occasional adolescent. Another 3,000 died in the internment camps—from cachexia or illnesses—to which another 1,000 must be added, as those who were selected for summary execution or torture along with the Resisters, hostages, and other victims of police, Milice, and Nazi violence.

# Glossary

Abbreviations: Ar (Aramaic); Fr (French); Ger (German); Gr ( Greek); Heb (Hebrew);[1] Hun (Hungarian); Lat (Latin); Per (Persian); Pol (Polish); Rus (Russian); Yid (Yiddish).

*Agrégation* (Fr): Highly competitive examination that qualifies fourth- or fifth-year university students for teaching careers in lycées and/or universities (sometimes with a condition of completion of the Doctorat d'État in the case of university teaching).

*alyah* (Heb): Immigration of Jews to Israel.

Aryanization: Institutionalized suppression of Jewish involvement in commercial activity. In 1941 in Occupied France the Vichy government enacted laws dispossessing Jews of their businesses and assigning "Aryan" administrators.

*baccalauréat* (Fr): Also called *le bac* or *le bachot,* it is the diploma awarded upon successful completion of lycée in France and is generally required for university study.

*brevet* (Fr): Diploma of professional studies.

Bund (Yid): "Jewish Workers Union." Jewish Socialist Organization founded in 1897, bringing together Jewish workers from Eastern Europe to oppose Zionism and support the social, cultural, and linguistic status of the Jewish proletariat of Eastern Europe.

Comintern (Rus): Acronym designating the organization created by the Communists after the Russian Revolution of 1917 (Third International) and designed to lead the various national Communist Parties. It was founded by Lenin in 1919 and dissolved by Stalin—who replaced it with the Cominform in 1943.

*département* (Fr): Administrative division of France. Continental France is comprised of ninety-six *départements* with four additional overseas *départements* (Guadeloupe, Reunion, Martinique, and French Guiana).

363

**Diaspora** (Gr): Historical dispersion of Jews across the world, mainly as a result of expulsion or flight from persecution.

**Dreyfusard** (Fr): Supporter of Captain Alfred Dreyfus, a military officer of Jewish descent, falsely convicted and imprisoned for treason in 1894. The case divided French society until 1906 when Dreyfus was exonerated and reinstated as a major in the French army.

*frum* (Yid): Observant Jew with strong belief.

**gefilte fish** (Yid): Stuffed carp (one of the traditional dishes of the Ashkenazi Jews).

*Gola* (*Galut*) *(Heb)*: The collective of Jews dispersed in the world; theological equivalent of diaspora.

*goy* (Heb): Non-Jewish person.

**gymnasium** (Lat): Secondary school (the "lycée" in France) in the educational systems of Germany, Poland, Russia.

*Halitzah* (Heb): Renunciation by a brother-in-law of his religious duty that obliges him to marry the childless widow of his brother.

**Hashomer Hatzair** (Heb): Zionist Socialist Youth Movement.

*Haskalah* (Heb): Extension of the Enlightenment into Jewish society by introducing the secular disciplines into teaching and promoting rationalism and integration of Jews into modern societies.

*Heder* (Heb): Religious elementary school to teach Jewish children—boys and sometimes girls—the Talmud and the precepts of religious observance.

*Judenrat* (Ger): Organization of Jews in the ghettos—especially in the Polish ghettos—imposed by the Nazis in 1939, supposedly to solve various problems within the community; in reality to subject and control the Jewish population in the country.

*Kazatchok* (Rus): Rhythmic Russian folk dance.

*Kiddush* (Heb): Blessing over a cup of wine to begin the *Shabbat* and other occasions.

**klezmer** (Heb): Popular music of the Ashkenazi Jews, originally played by itinerant musicians who performed at festivals and weddings.

*Kommandantur* (Ger): German military central command, in Germany and in the territories occupied by the German Army.

*Kristalnacht* (Ger): "Night of Broken Glass": November 9 and 10, 1938, when Nazis in Germany and Austria initiated violence against Jews, followed by the internment of thirty thousand Jews at Buchenwald and Dachau.

*lycée* (Fr): French secondary school, both junior high (or *collège*) and senior high.

*mame loschen* (Yid): Affectionate term Yiddish-speaking Jews use for their language.

MAPAM (Heb): Israeli socialist workers party, created in 1948.

Maquis (Fr): Term for the rural Free French Resistance groups during the Occupation.

Milice (Fr): Parallel French police force, created in 1943 by Laval, led by Darnand to pursue Jews and Resisters.

*numerus clausus* (Lat): Use of a quota to restrict the number of individuals admitted to an institution. Implemented in Poland and in Russia at the beginning of the twentieth century to restrict the number of Jews admitted into secondary and higher education.

*oflag* (Ger): Detention camp for officers imprisoned in Germany during the Second World War.

Pessah (Heb): Passover: Commemoration of the flight of the Jews from Egypt led by Moses. See *Seder*.

"Phony War" (*drôle de guerre*): Time between the German invasion of Poland in September 1939 and the Battle of France in May 1940 when military response from continental Europe was inadequate.

*pilpul* (Heb): Intense Talmudic debates. By extension: oratorical jousts between erudite individuals who put forth contradictory arguments, a cultural activity in the traditional Ashkenazi community.

*pletzl* (Yid): A little square in a *schtetl*. By extension, Jewish quarter in the Fourth Arrondissement of Paris, near rue des Rosiers.

pogroms (Rus): Violence directed against the Jews and their neighborhoods during the Russian Empire 1881–1921, and all over Eastern Europe, often at the instigation of the government.

Purim (Per): Holiday that commemorates the deliverance of the Jews from persecution by Haman after Queen Esther intervened with King Ahasuerus.

*rabbanut* (Heb): Rabbinate; administrative authority judging the religious legality of certain situations in civil life such as marriage and divorce.

"Righteous Among the Nations": Recognition granted by Israel to non-Jews who risked their lives to save Jews during the Holocaust.

*sabra* (Heb): Jew born in Israel, said to be rough and prickly on the outside and tender inside, like the prickly fruit of the same name.

*schmates* (Yid): Fabric of poor quality; by extension, an object made of material of little value.

*schtetl* (Yid): Jewish village of Central and Eastern Europe.

Seder (Heb): Rite of Jewish Passover, recounting the flight from Egypt (Haggadah).

Shabbat (Heb): In the Bible, the seventh day of the week, a day of rest and meditation.

*shathen* (Yid): Matchmaker; hired to negotiate an arranged marriage between two families.

Shoah (Heb): The Holocaust.

*sider* (Yid): Book of prayers used to follow the synagogue service.

Succoth (Heb): Festival of the Tabernacles—harvest festival in which a cabin covered with greenery commemorates the fragile shelters where the Hebrews lived after the flight from Egypt.

*talith* (Heb): In the Jewish religion, shawl worn by the men for certain prayers.

*tefilin* (Heb): Phylacteries (small leather cases) holding slips inscribed with biblical passages worn by orthodox Jewish men during morning prayer.

*tsadik* (Heb): Hasidic guide, leader in religious observances of the community; by extension, pious and respected person that one consults for wisdom.

*ulpan* (Heb): Intensive course of Hebrew to aid rapid integration of immigrants in Israel.

*umentaschen* (Yid): Traditional Ashkenazi cakes for Purim, shaped to represent "Haman's ears" in reference to the story of Esther.

Vel' d'Hiv' (Fr): Rafle du Vélodrome d'Hiver. Massive roundup in Paris on July 16–17, 1942, of Jews for deportation.

*yad* (Heb): Representation (often in silver) of a hand with the forefinger pointed, used to follow when reading the biblical texts aloud at the synagogue without having to touch the sacred text directly with the finger.

Yad Vashem (Heb): The Holocaust Martyrs and Heroes Remembrance Authority in Jerusalem.

yeshiva (Heb): School for advanced Talmudic studies.

*Yiddishkeit* (Yid): Ensemble of the Yiddish language and culture of the Jewish community; global characteristic of its values.

**Yiddishland** (Yid): A "land" both mythic and real; real because during the nineteenth century across Eastern Europe from Poland to the Baltic States there were seven million Jews living and speaking Yiddish; mythic because it never existed as a political or geographic entity.

# French Acronyms

**AS**: Armée Secrète (Secret Army). Military organization of the United Resistance Movements (MUR) created by Jean Moulin and led by General Delestraint.

**CAP**: Certificat d'Aptitude professionel (Vocational Certificate). Qualification for direct access to certain careers or for further study leading to the *brévet d'études professionelles* (professional diploma).

**CAPES**: Certificat d'Aptitude au Professorat de l'Enseignment du Second Degré (Teaching Certificate). Qualification for secondary teaching.

**CCE**: Commission Centrale de l'Enfance (Central Committee for Children). Jewish Communist Organization. Branch of the Jewish Resistance Movement (UJRE) specifically concerned with the orphans of the Holocaust.

**CDJC**: Centre de Documentation Juive Contemporaine, Paris (Center for Contemporary Jewish Records).

**CNRS**: Centre National de la Recherche Scientifique (National Center for Scientific Research).

**CRIF**: Conseil Représentatif des Institutions juives de France (Council of Jewish Institutions).

**FFI**: Forces Françaises de l'Intérieur (Free French Forces). French fighting forces, both former military and Resistance fighters, organized inside France.

**FNDIRP**: Fédération Nationale des Déportés et Internés Résistants et Patriotes (National Federation of Deported and Imprisoned Resisters and Patriots).

**FTP**: Francs-Tireurs et Partisans (Partisan irregular riflemen). Resisters under direction of the Communist Party.

**MJC**: Maison des Jeunes et de la Culture (Center for Youth and Culture).

**MOI**: Main d'Œuvre Immigrée (Immigrant Workers Organization). Communist organization of immigrant workers in France, including numerous Jews during the years 1925–1947, that played an important

369

role during the Resistance.

**MRAP**: Mouvement contre le Racisme et pour l'Amitié entre les Peuples (Movement Against Racism and for Friendship Among Peoples). Formerly Movement Against Racism, Anti-Semitism, and Peace. Strongly connected to the UJRE.

**OSE**: Œuvre de Secours aux Enfants (Children's Aid Society). Jewish organization for children's welfare, credited with saving thousands of children during World War II. In France, the organization took responsibility for hiding Jewish children during the war and caring for orphans of the Holocaust in Children's Homes after the war.

**PCF** or **PC**: Parti Communiste Français (French Communist Party).

**STO**: Service du Travail Obligatoire (Obligatory Work Force). A Vichy government law of February 1, 1943, stipulated that workers from age sixteen through sixty and women without children from eighteen to forty years old could be sent to Germany to work.

**UGIF**: Union Générale des Israélites de France (Union of Jews in France). Controlled by the Vichy government.

**UJFF**: Union des Jeunes Filles de France (Union of Young Women of France). Communist organization.

**UJRE**: Union des Juifs pour la Résistance et l'Entraide (Union of Jews for Resistance and Mutual Aid). Communist clandestine organization, called Solidarité (Solidarity) until 1943.

**UJRF**: Union des Jeunesses Républicaines de France (Union of Young Republicans of France). Organization replacing Young Communists after the war.

# Notes

**FOREWORD BY PIERRE VIDAL-NAQUET**

1. Cohen, *Persécutions et sauvetages.*
2. Trans.: The *Cahiers* (statements to fellow Christians) were published under the direction of Jesuit Father Pierre Chaillet, urging opposition to Nazism in the name of Christian values.
3. Trans.: National Front (*Front national de l'indépendance de la France*) refers to the French Resistance movement group created in 1941 by members of the French Communist Party (PCF) and not to the 1972 French Far-Right political party (*Front national*).
4. Lafitte, *Un Engrenage fatal.*
5. Comte, *Sauvetages et baptêmes.*
6. Trans.: Pierre Vidal-Naquet died July 29, 2006.

**INTRODUCTION**

1. "Maréchal, nous voilà!"; first words of the national anthem under the Vichy government, which, having abolished the French Republic, established under the Occupation a collaborative regime, the "French State" (État Français) in place of France's parliamentary democracy.

**1. SIMON MARJENBERG**

1. Trans.: The Drancy internment camp northwest of Paris was the principal point of departure for the Nazi extermination camps from August 1941 to August 1944.
2. Steinberg, *L'Étoile et le fusil.*
3. The Nansen passport was created in 1922 by Fridtjof Nansen after World War I at the request of the League of Nations to restore identity to prisoners and refugees who had lost their papers and their permission to travel.

## 2. CHARLES ZELWER

1. Trans.: During the July 16–17, 1942, Vélodrome d'Hiver (Vel' d'Hiv')
   Roundup more than 12,000 Jews, including 4,051 children, were
   imprisoned in the Parisian Sports Center, then taken to Drancy internment camp and on to the concentration camps.
2. Trans.: An annual event sponsored by the French Communist newspaper *L'Humanité.*

## 3. NOËL KUPERMAN

1. See Søren Kierkegaard, *Either/Or,* translated from Danish by David
   F. Swenson and Lillian Marvin Swenson (Princeton: Princeton University Press, 1944), 30.
2. Léopold Trepper was the leader of the Red Orchestra, the principal
   intelligence network of the Red Army in Occupied Europe.
3. To learn more about the Weberei d'Auschwitz, consult the book by
   Françoise Maous, *Coma Auschwitz, numéro A5553* (Paris: Editions
   Le Comptoir, 1996).
4. The Hôtel Lutétia in Paris, after having served as headquarters of
   the Gestapo during the Occupation, became the reception area and
   temporary lodging for the rare French deportees returned from the
   concentration camps after the Liberation.
5. This episode is better known as the "Fiszbin Affair." Henri Fiszbin,
   secretary of the Paris Federation of the French Communist Party,
   was "relieved" of this position in 1979 because of his disagreement
   with the Party's policy at that time; he wanted to do away with
   "social classism."
6. Trans.: Jack Lang and Michel Guy each served much later as
   France's Minister of Culture. Jack Ralite was later Minister of Health
   and Minister of Labor.
7. Published in Paris: Éditions du Seuil, 1964. Performed at the Théa-
   tre National Populaire, 1966.
8. Hilberg, *Destruction.*
9. Trans.: The "Chant des Marais" ("Peat Bog Soldiers") is one of
   Europe's best-known protest songs, written by Johann Esser (a
   miner) and Wolfgang Langhoff (an actor), both imprisoned in the
   Börgermoor Nazi labor camp.
10. Trans.: Noël Kuperman died May 21, 2005.

### 4. FRANCIS BAILLY

1. Trans.: Francis Bailly died February 5, 2009.

### 5. ARNOLD ROCHFELD

1. Klarsfeld, *Memorial to the Jews.*
2. Poznanski, *Être Juif en France.*
3. Paxton, *Vichy France.*
4. Hilberg, *Destruction.*

### 6. DANIELLE BAILLY

1. In August 2000 I was interviewed by Betty Saville of Enfants Cachés (Association of Hidden Children) and some of my responses then are adapted here.
2. Freud tells of the same anti-Semitic occurrence with his own father (see Peter Gay, *Freud: A Life for Our Time* [New York: Norton & Co., 1988], 11–12]).
3. My brother, Gérard Schneck, obtained chronological information from family papers (rent and other receipts, pay slips, certificates), from audio tapes left by our parents, and from archive searches that allow me to tie my memories to verifiable facts.
4. This notice, entitled "Table of Jews Present in 1942 in Maine-en-Loire," is reproduced in *L'Eradication tranquille: Le Destin des Juifs en Anjou,* by Alain Jacobzone (Vauchrétien: Maine-et-Loire, 2002). My father, my mother, and I were mentioned on it by name with the dates and places of our births and the notation "left Angers as fugitives."
5. Trans.: "à la Papon" because Maurice Papon, who held positions of significant responsibility during World War II with police departments in Bordeaux and in Constantine (Algeria) and Paris after the war, was later convicted of having signed documents for the deportation of 1,690 Jews from Bordeaux to Drancy internment camp between 1942–1944.
6. See Marienstras, *Être un peuple en diaspora.*

### 7. DANIÈLE MENÈS

1. On May 11, 1926, Pilsudski marched on the capital. Despite the resistance of some military loyalists, every strategic point was

occupied. After a dramatic meeting between Pilsudski and the President of the Republic on a bridge over the Vistula on May 12, the loyalist troops were ordered to resist. The supporters of Pilsudski entered Warsaw only after street fighting that led to 379 deaths and 920 wounded. On May 25, the resistance ended (see Beauvois, *Histoire de la Pologne*, 307).

2. Hazan, *Orphelins*, 87. Rabbi Chneerson, who was conducting research about Jewish orphans, had sent a letter to all the mayors of France.

3. Trans.: Sup-Aero, or École nationale Supérieure de l'Aéronautique et de l'Espace (National School of Advanced Studies in Aeronautics and Space), is one of the most prestigious and selective graduate schools in France.

4. Finkielkraut, *Imaginary Jew*.

5. Trans.: The French spelling of "exile" as "exil" is kept in order to retain the play on words obtained by "Ex/il" ("ex-he," "he" referring to the father in the text).

### 8. NELLY SCHARAPAN

1. Short extracts of an earlier account by Nelly were published in *Vie et Mort des Juifs*, by Floss and Steinberg.

2. See the photo of this drawing at the beginning of this testimony.

3. Austerlitz was one of three camps where what the Nazis had looted was stored before it was taken to Germany. On this subject see Dreyfus and Gensburger, *Des camps dans Paris*.

4. It was Pierre Laval—and not the Nazis—who ordered the deportation of Jewish children from France.

5. Cyrulnik, *Un merveilleux Malheur*; *Les Villains*; *Le Murmure*.

### 10. RACHEL JEDINAK

1. Klarsfeld, *Memorial to the Jews*.

2. Ibid.

### 13. ÉDITH MOSKOVIC

1. See *Tsafon, Revue d'études juives du Nord* 41 (2001). Published here courtesy of the magazine's editor, Madame Danielle Delmaire.

2. Trans.: *Nylös*: Hungarian Fascist Political Party that governed Hungary from October 1944 to January 1945.

3. Trans.: Édith describes her large family as a "Thirteenth Tribe" in reference to the Twelve Tribes of ancient Israel descended from Jacob or one of his twelve sons or grandsons for whom the tribes are named.

4. Testimony given in a brochure offered to the residents of His when in 2002 a square in the village was designated Famille Moskovic.

5. The Saint-Cyprien camp was opened, along with others in the south of France, before the war to intern the Spanish Republicans who were fleeing the advance of Franco's troops, as well as undesirable foreigners. See Grynberg, *Les Camps de la honte: Les internés juifs des camps français, 1939–1944* (Paris: La Découverte, 1991).

6. Like Saint-Cyprien, the camp at Récébédou was first intended for Spanish Republicans. Ibid., 210.

7. The historian Maxime Steinberg provides a solid study of these roundups in *Les cent jours de la déportation*.

8. The so-called gathering camps were in fact internment camps. In *Les Miradors de Vichy*, Alexis-Monet describes the "un-life" in these camps, especially Récébédou. Malo also treats it in his book *Les Camps d'internement*. See also the very extensive work of Denis Peschanski, *La France des camps*.

## 14. NICOLE EIZNER

1. Trans.: Nicole Eizner died January 18, 2006.

## 15. ODETTE KOZUCH

1. Ikor, *Les Eaux mêlées*.

2. Trans.: The original reads *baccalauréat*; presumably *matura* is meant.

## 17. PHILIPPE FOUQUEY

1. Haffner, *Defying Hitler*.

2. Bolle (dir.), Colloque du Chambon-sur-Lignon.

3. The atmosphere of this time is well described in the book *Greater Than Angels*, by Carol Matas.

4. Hatzfeld, *Machete Season*.

5. Becker and Wieviorka, *Juifs de France*, 12.

6. Trans.: Badinter, *Libres et égaux*, 45.

7. Ibid.

8. Becker and Wieviorka, *Juifs de France*, 22.
9. Ibid., 35.

### 18. SERGE NETCHINE

1. Annual national competition that tests students who are between Première (11th) and Terminale (12th) grades over nearly every subject taught in French lycées. A ceremony is held in the main amphitheater of the Sorbonne and the prize awarded by the Minister of Education.

### CHRONOLOGY

1. Principal sources: Baruch, *Régime de Vichy* and *Servir l'État Français*; Durand, *La France dans la deuxième guerre*; Klarsfeld, especially *Memorial to the Jews*, *Le Calendrier*, and *Vichy-Auschwitz*; Becker and Wieviorka, *Les Juifs de France*.

### GLOSSARY

1. Precise definitions for certain religious terms of this glossary were provided by Monsieur Carol Iancu, Professor of History at Paul-Valéry-Montpellier III University and Director of the School of Advanced Judaic Studies.

# Selected Bibliography

*(Translations are from French unless otherwise noted)*

Alexis-Monet, Laurette. *Les Miradors de Vichy*. Preface by Pierre Vidal-Naquet. Paris: Éditions de Paris, 1994.

Association of Hidden Children of France. *Jewish Children of France during World War II*. Rockville, MD: Friends and Alumni of OSE-USA, 2003.

Association pour la recherche et la sauvegarde de la vérité historique sur la résistance en Creuse (Association for Research and Protection of Historical Truth about the Resistance in Creuse). *Le Sauvetage des enfants juifs en France*. Proceedings of the Colloquium at Guéret, May 29–30, 1996. Guéret: City Hall, 1996.

Azema, Jean-Pierre, François Bedarida, Denis Peschanski, and Henry Rousso. *Le régime de Vichy et les Français*. Paris: Fayard, 1992.

Badinter, Robert. *Libres et égaux*. Paris: Fayard, 1989.

Baruch, Marc-Olivier. *Le Régime de Vichy*. Paris: La Découverte, 1996.

———. *Servir l'État français: L'administration en France de 1940–1944*. Paris: Fayard, 1997.

Beauvois, Daniel. *Histoire de la Pologne*. Paris: Hatier, 1995.

Becker, Jean-Jacques, and Annette Wieviorka. *Juifs de France*. Paris: Liana Levi, 1998.

Bolle, Pierre. *Le Plateau Vivarais-Lignon, accueil et résistance: Actes du colloque du Chambon-sur-Lignon, octobre 1990*. Le Chambon-sur-Lignon: Société d'histoire de la montagne, 1992.

Centre de Documentation Juive Contemporaine (Center for Jewish Contemporary Documentation). *Activité des organisations juives en France sous l'Occupation*. Paris: CDJC (Série "Études et Monographies" numéro 4), 1993.

———. *Les Enfants de la Guette: Souvenirs et documents (1938–1945)*. Paris: CDJC, 1999.

City of Paris. *Le Temps de rafles, le sort des Juifs en France pendant la guerre*. Paris: Bureau d'Études Techniques, Hôtel de Ville, 1992.

Cohen, Asher. *Persécution et sauvetages: Juifs et Français sous l'Occupation et sous Vichy*. Paris: Cerf, 1993.

Collectif, numéro 85. *Organisation juive de combat Résistance/sauvetage—France, 1940–1945*. Paris: Éditions "Autrement" (Coll. Mémoires, numéro 85), 2002.

Comte, Madeleine. *Sauvetages et baptêmes: Les religieuses de Notre-Dame de Sion face à la persécution des Juifs en France (1940–1944)*. Paris: L'Harmattan, 2001.

Cyrulnik, Boris. *Un merveilleux Malheur*. Paris: Odile Jacob, 1999.

———. *Les Villains petits canards*. Paris: Odile Jacob, 2001.

———. *Le Murmure des fantômes*. Paris: Odile Jacob, 2003.

Dreyfus, Jean-Marc, and Sarah Gensburger. *Des Camps dans Paris: Austerlitz, Lévitan, Bassano*. Paris: Fayard, 2003.

Durand, Yves. *La France dans la deuxième guerre mondiale*. Paris: Armand Colin (coll. Cursus), 2001.

Enfants Cachés (Association of Hidden Children of France). *Enfants cachés 1940–1944*. Quarterly publication of the Association since 1993. Paris: Enfants Cachés.

———. *Mémoires d'enfants*. Statistical study of a survey by Jo Saville. Paris: Enfants Cachés, 1999.

Finkielkraut, Alain. *The Imaginary Jew*. Translated by David Suchoff and Kevin O'Neill. Lincoln, NE: University of Nebraska Press, 1997.

Floss, Myrian, and Lucien Steinberg. *Vie et Mort des Juifs sous l'Occupation*. Paris: Plon, 1996.

French Republic. *La Persécution des Juifs de France 1940–1944 et le rétablissement du la légalité républicaine*. Collection of official texts 1940–1999. Claire Andrieu (ed.) with Serge Klarsfeld and Annette Wieviorka. Paris: Documentation française, 2000.

Grumberg, Jean-Claude. *The Free Zone* and *The Workroom*. Translated by Catherine Temerson. New York: Ubu Repertory Theater Publications, 1993.

Grynberg, Anne. *Les Camps de la honte: Les internés juifs des camps français, 1939–1944*. Paris: La Découverte, 1991.

Haffner, Sebastian. *Defying Hitler: A Memoir*. Translated from German by Oliver Pretzel. New York: Farrar, Straus, and Giroux, 2002.

Hatzfeld, Jean. *Machete Season: The Killers in Rwanda Speak*. Translated by Linda Coverdate. Preface by Susan Sontag. New York: Picador, 2006.

Hazan, Kathy. *Les Orphelins de la Shoah*. Paris: Les Belles Lettres, 2000.

Hilberg, Raul. *The Holocaust Today*. Syracuse, NY: Syracuse University Press, 1988.

———. *Perpetrators, Victims, Bystanders: The Jewish Catastrophe, 1933–1945*. New York: Aaron Asher Books, 1992.

———. *The Destruction of European Jews*. 3 vols. New Haven: Yale University Press, 2003. Originally published in 1961.

Ikor, Roger. *Les Eaux mêlées*. Paris: Albin Michel, 1966.

Klarsfeld, Serge. *Memorial to the Jews Deported from France, 1942–1944: Documentation of the deportation of the victims of the Final Solution in France*. New York: Beate Klarsfeld Foundation, 1983.

———. *Vichy-Auschwitz: Le role de Vichy dans la solution finale de la question juive en France, Vol. 1 (1942), Vol. 2 (1943–1944)*. Paris: Fayard, 1983.

———. *The Children of Izieu: A Human Tragedy*. New York: Abrams, 1985.

———. *French Children of the Holocaust: A Memorial*. Translated by Glorianne Depondt and Howard M. Epstein, and edited by Serge Klarsfeld. New York: New York University Press, 1996.

———. *Le Calendrier de la persécution des Juifs de France: 1940–1945*. 2 vols. Paris: Fayard, 2001.

Lafitte, Michel. *Un Engrenage fatal: L'UGIF face aux réalités de la Shoah, 1941–1944*. Paris: Liana Levi, 2003.

Lazare, Lucien. *Rescue as Resistance: How Jewish Organizations Fought the Holocaust in France*. Translated by Jeffrey M. Green. New York: Columbia University Press, 1996.

Lévy, Claude, and Paul Tillard. *Betrayal at the Vel' d'Hiv'*. Translated by Inea Bushnaq. Preface by Joseph Kessel. New York: Farrar, Straus, and Giroux, 1969.

Malo, Eric. *Les camps d'internement du Midi de la France*. Toulouse: Bibliothèque Municipale, 1990.

Marienstras, Richard. *Être un peuple en diaspora*. Paris: Maspero, 1975.

Marrus, Michael R., and Robert O. Paxton. *Vichy France and the Jews*. New York: Basic Books, 1981.

Matas, Carol. *Greater Than Angels*. New York: Simon and Schuster, 1998.

Museum of the Resistance, the Deportation, and the Liberation of Lot. *La Persécution raciste et antisémite* (documents). Cahors, 1980.

Paxton, Robert O. *Vichy France*. Revised Edition. New York: Columbia University Press, 2001.

Peschanski, Denis. *Collaboration and Resistance: Images of Life in Vichy France, 1940–1944*. Translated by Lory Frankel. New York: Harry N. Abrams, 2000.

———. *La France des camps: L'Internement, 1938–1946*. Paris: Gallimard, 2002.

Poznanski, Renée. *Jews in France during World War II*. Translated by Nathan Bracher. Hanover, NH: University Press of New England for Brandeis University Press, in association with the Holocaust Memorial Museum, 2001.

Rayski, Adam. *The Choice of the Jews under Vichy: Between Submission and Resistance*. Translated by Will Sayers. Notre Dame, IN: University of Notre Dame Press, 2005.

Rousso, Henry. *The Vichy Syndrome: History and Memory in France since 1944*. Translated by Arthur Goldhammer. Cambridge, MA: Harvard University Press, 1991.

Steinberg, Maxime. *Les cents jours de la déportation des Juifs de Belgique*. Brussels: Éditions Vie Ouvrière, 1984.

———. *L'Étoile et le fusil*. 2 vols. Brussels: Éditions Vie Ouvrière, 1986.

*Tsafon, L'Année tragique des Juifs du Nord: 1942*. Northern Review of Jewish Studies 9, 10 (1992).

Vidal-Naquet, Pierre. *The Jews: History, Memory, and the Present*. Translated by David Ames Curtis. New York: Columbia University Press, 1996.

———. *Mémoires: La brisure et l'attente. 1930–1955*. Paris: Seuil, La Découverte, 1995.

Wieviorka, Annette. *The Era of the Witness*. Translated by Jared Stark. Ithaca, NY: Cornell University Press, 2006.

### FOR FURTHER READING IN ENGLISH

Federman, Raymond. *The Voice in the Closet*. Preface by Gérard Bucher. Buffalo, NY: Starcherone Books, 2001.

Friedlander, Saul. *When Memory Comes*. Translated by Helen R. Lane. New York: Avon Books, 1980.

Goldman, Pierre. *Dim Memories of a Polish Jew Born in France*. Translated by Joan Pinkham. New York: Viking Press, 1977.

Kofman, Sarah. *Rue Ordener, Rue Labat*. Translated by Ann Smock. Lincoln, NE: University of Nebraska Press, 1996.

Lévy, Claude, and Paul Tillard. *Betrayal at the Vel' d'Hiv'*. Translated by Inea Bushnaq. Preface by Joseph Kessel. New York: Farrar, Straus, and Giroux, 1969.

Lewendel, Isaac. *Not the Germans Alone: A Son's Search for the Truth of Vichy.* Preface by Robert O. Paxton. Evanston, IL: Northwestern University Press, 1999.

Perec, Georges. *W, or The Memory of Childhood.* Translated by David Bellos. Boston: Godine, 1988.

Samuel, Vivettte. *Rescuing the Children: A Holocaust Memoir (Sauver les enfants).* Translated by Charles B. Paul. Foreword by Elie Wiesel. Madison, WI: University of Wisconsin Press, 2002.

Semelin, Jacques. *Unarmed Against Hitler: Civilian Resistance in Europe, 1939–1943.* Translated by Suzan Husserl-Kapit. Preface by Stanley Hoffman. Westport, CT: Praeger, 1993.

Vegh, Claudine. *I Didn't Say Goodbye.* Translated by Ros Schwartz. Postface by Bruno Bettelheim. New York: E. P. Dutton, 1984.

# Translator's Note

The book *Traqués, Cachés, Vivants: Des Enfants juifs en France, 1940–1945* came to my attention as I conducted seminars on Jewish literature, funded by the American Library Association and Nextbook. Through mutual friend Judy Stein, Danielle Bailly and I began a collaborative effort, quickly turned friendship, to bring the book to the American reading public. I thank her, along with Larry Theye, Erica Hughes, Danièle Menès, Gaby and Serge Netchine, and Marilyn Gaddis-Rose, and the editors and staff at State University of New York Press, especially Kelli Williams-LeRoux and Zachary Moning.

And I thank the eighteen former "hidden children," ten of whom I have now met, for sharing their stories and thus reminding us of the fragility of our precious freedom and the importance of valuing and protecting one another.

—Betty Becker-Theye<br>
April 2009

# Biographical Notes

DANIELLE BAILLY, Docteur d'Etat in Linguistics, is professor emeritus and former head of Studies in Psycholinguistics and Didactics at the University of Paris VII-Denis Diderot.

PIERRE VIDAL-NAQUET (1930–2006) was one of the most important French contemporary historians and one of the founders of the new French scholarship on the Ancient Greek world. A political activist engaged in anticolonial struggles, he was also interested in Jewish history and one of the first to fight the revisionists and deniers of the Holocaust.

BETTY BECKER-THEYE, PhD in Comparative Literature and Translation, is professor emeritus and former dean of the College of Fine Arts and Humanities at the University of Nebraska at Kearney. She is an active life member of the American Translators Association.